OFF THE SHELF

The Healthfood Shopper's Brandname Cookbook

About the book

Written for those who are just discovering healthfoods (as well as the busy healthfood cook who is short of time and ideas) *Off the Shelf* is more than just a traditional cookery book. Not only a guide to the wide range of manufacturers' products now on the market, it is also a superb selection of recipes.

Because she understands and sympathizes with the cook who, faced with unfamiliar ingredients, may decide not to bother, Evelyn Findlater has arranged her book into alphabetical sections – soups, light vegetable dishes, pasta dishes, main meals, bread and pastries, cakes, biscuits, puddings, hot and cold, as well as dips, purées and pâtés. All the cook has to do is to look up the manufacturer's name and find a recipe from the huge choice she offers which suits his or her needs.

About the author

Evelyn Findlater started to incorporate more natural foods into her family's diet when she was a mother starting at Teacher Training College. She found there were few books giving information on how to cook these foods well and even fewer stimulating recipes.

She later started her own healthfood shop which she ran for four years – customers loved all the healthfood and asked if she would give wholefood cookery classes, which she did. The response was terrific and the classes stimulated her to write her first book *Wholefood Cookery Course* (Muller, 1983). She did a successful six-part series for Television South West in April 1983 and has just finished another live TV series on cooking for children.

Her books include *Making Your Own Home Proteins* (Century, 1985), *Natural Food Primer* (Thorsons, 1985) and *Vegetarian Food Processor* (Thorsons, 1985).

OFF THE SHELF

The Healthfood Shopper's Brandname Cookbook

EVELYN FINDLATER

CENTURY

London Melbourne Auckland Johannesburg

I dedicate this book to all the producers of natural food
and to my friend and typist Gill Bruton.

Copyright © Evelyn Findlater 1986
Designer Bob Vickers
Line illustrations Joy FitzSimmons
Colour photography Ian O'Leary
Home economist Judy Bugg
Back of jacket:
(Above left) Allinson: Pizza; Cheese and Mushroom Plait,
between pages 112 and 113
(Above right) Höfels: Rye Bread Rolls; Savoury Kibbled Wheat Scones;
Flaked Barley Bread, between pages 112 and 113
(Below left) Hugli: Carrot Cooler; Pumpkin Soup; Sprouted Soya Bean,
Lemon and Parsley Soup, between pages 32 and 33.

First published in 1986 by Century Hutchinson Ltd,
Brookmount House, 62–65 Chandos Place, Covent Garden,
London WC2N 4NW

Century Hutchinson Publishing Group (Australia) Pty Ltd,
16–22 Church Street, Hawthorn, Melborne, Victoria 3122

Century Hutchinson Group (NZ) Ltd,
32–34 View Road, PO Box 40–086, Glenfield, Auckland 10

Century Hutchinson Group (SA) Pty Ltd,
PO Box 337, Bergvlei 2012, South Africa

Set in Cheltenham Light

Printed and bound in Great Britain by
R.J. Acford, Chichester, Sussex

British Library Cataloguing in Publication Data
Findlater, Evelyn
Off the shelf: the healthfood shopper's brandname cookbook.
1. Cookery (Natural foods)
I. Title
641.5′637   TX741

ISBN 0 7126 1295 5
ISBN 0 7126 1496 6 (Pbk)

CONTENTS

LIST OF COLOUR PLATES

INTRODUCTION

The compilation of this book has been a challenging and rewarding task. When I first went into a health store a few years ago I was utterly bewildered and it took me years to find out what foods were available and how to prepare them.

This is an attempt to save you time and effort. The following pages, I hope, will help unravel the 'mystery' of the healthfood/wholefood produce so abundantly available today. Of course, these are not really mystery foods. Many of them have been in our culture and other cultures for thousands of years. They are, in fact, simple foods full of earth's bountiful goodness coupled with human inventiveness and they are our rightful heritage.

I am tempted in this introduction to preach a bit about findings in the vast field of nutrition which point out how badly we feed ourselves in the West, but I won't because not only do our health orientated magazines do this extremely well but also some of our national newspapers, television and radio programmes have at last begun to join in the battle for a healthier diet for all. I also want to write pages on the value of organically grown vegetables and 'free range' meat and dairy produce but again I will contain myself and let you delve gradually into the ancient world of 'real food'.

You will find in the book detailed descriptions of many products available, how to use the foods, and a fund of recipes (60 per cent of which have been created or adapted by me, the rest submitted by manufacturers), ranging from the traditional and simple to the exotic.

I would like to thank the manufacturers for information supplied, for their help with recipes, and above all for their enthusiastic commitment to feeding us while maintaining a deep and caring attitude towards the world we live in. Special thanks, too, to Mr Riley of the Health Food Store in Bideford for his kind assistance.

One word of advice before you start. Look at the labels and don't touch a packet or tin with additives or code numbers that you do not understand and you will help our producers to give you what you want.

Happy exploration!

Evelyn Findlater

1
SOUPS

CARRABAY

Carrageen Soup

Serves 8–10

25 g (1 oz) Carrabay Carrageen
2.3 litres (4 pints) cold water
1 head celery, with leaves, chopped
1 small can tomatoes (optional)
½ tbsp sea salt
1 tbsp Sunwheel Shoyu
½ tsp cracked black pepper
¼ tsp crushed red pepper
1 bay leaf
pinch each of sage and thyme
100 ml (4 fl oz) white wine (dry)

After washing the carrageen, cut it into small pieces. Put all the soup ingredients with the carrageen into a deep pot and simmer until tender, about 2 hours.

GELOZONE

Hearty Root Soup

Serves 4–6

1 medium onion, peeled and finely chopped
397 g (14 oz) can tomatoes
225 g (8 oz) swede, finely diced
100 g (4 oz) turnip, finely diced
175 g (6 oz) potatoes, finely diced
425 ml (15 fl oz) water
1 tsp Vecon
1 tsp Worcester Sauce (Holbrooks if you want a good vegetarian alternative)
2 tsp Gelozone
chives, sea salt and freshly ground black pepper to taste

Cook the onion gently with the tomatoes until soft. Cook the diced swede, turnip and potatoes in the water until very soft. Add the Vecon, Worcester Sauce, onions and tomatoes and simmer for 5 minutes. Mix 2 teaspoons Gelozone with a little of the soup and add to the saucepan. Remove the pan from the heat and liquidize in a blender. Add the chives and seasoning and cook for a further 5 minutes.

HÖFELS

Soya Flake Soup

Serves 4–5

It is preferable to soak the soya flakes overnight for this recipe.

2 cloves garlic, finely chopped
675 g (1½ lb) vegetables (e.g. carrots, swedes, parsnips, onions, leeks, celery), finely chopped
a little sunflower oil to fry
575 ml (1 pint) vegetable stock, made with hot water and 1 vegetable stock cube
225 g (8 oz) Höfels Soya Flakes, soaked overnight
single cream or yoghurt to serve (optional)

Fry the garlic and vegetables gently in the oil for 2–3 minutes; add to the vegetable stock and soya flakes and simmer for about 30 minutes or until tender. If a richer soup is desired, a few tablespoons of cream or yoghurt may be added after the cooking time, but cool the soup slightly first to prevent curdling.

HOLLAND & BARRETT

Chick Pea and Mint Soup

Serves 6

A refreshing and tasty Middle Eastern-style soup from my book *Vegetarian Food Processor* which is best served with Wholemeal Pocket Bread (see page 120 for the recipe).

225 g (8 oz), dry weight, Holland & Barrett Chick Peas
1 tsp sea salt
2 tbsp fresh mint
2 large cloves garlic, peeled
3 tbsp olive oil
1 tsp coriander seeds, crushed
juice of 1 lemon
freshly ground black pepper
fresh mint sprigs to serve

Wash the chick peas and pick over for stones. Soak in 1.2 litres/2 pints of cold water overnight, changing the water three times. Cook the peas in plenty of fresh water for 1 to 1½ hours until soft. Add the sea salt 10 minutes before end of the cooking time. Drain, reserving the cooking water, and add enough hot water to bring the level up to 1.2 litres/2 pints. Put the peas, water, mint, garlic and 2 tablespoons olive oil into a bowl. With steel blades in position on the food processor, purée the pea mixture, 3 ladles at a time, until quite smooth. Put the remaining tablespoon of oil into a clean, dry saucepan and lightly toast the crushed coriander seeds but take care not to burn. Now pour the chick pea mixture into the saucepan. Stir in the lemon juice and freshly ground black pepper to taste. Bring to the boil and let it simmer with the lid on for 10 minutes only.

To serve, garnish with a few young tops of mint, which look like small green roses, or just with a little chopped mint.

HUGLI

Here are two soups, one cold and one hot, taken from my books *Vegetarian Food Processor* and *Wholefood Cookery Course* respectively. They are a little different and very much enjoyed.

Carrot Cooler

Serves 6

Absolutely delicious and very simple to prepare using a food processor. Best with young new home-grown or new season carrots.

1 medium onion, peeled
2 tbsp safflower oil
1 large clove garlic, crushed
675 g (1½ lb) young carrots, scrubbed
½ tsp dried tarragon
850 ml (1½ pints) water
1½ Hugli Vegetable Stock Cubes
150 ml (5 fl oz) double cream
freshly ground black pepper and a little sea salt
50 g (2 oz) pistachio nuts, shelled ⎫
1 tbsp fresh parsley, very finely chopped ⎬ *to garnish*

Set the slicing plate of the food processor in position. Cut the onion in half and pack into the feed tube. Slice. Scoop out and leave the plate in position. Heat the oil in a heavy-bottomed saucepan and sauté the sliced onion and crushed garlic on low heat for 7 minutes with the lid on. Meanwhile slice the carrots, packing them well into the feed tube lengthwise. Sauté these with the onion for another 7 minutes with the lid on, then stir in the tarragon. Bring the water to the boil, stir in the stock cubes and pour the hot stock into the cooking vegetables. Leave to simmer on a low heat for 20 minutes. Set the steel blades in position on the processor and purée the soup, four ladles at a time, until quite smooth. Whisk the cream until it holds its shape but is still soft and stir this into the soup. Taste and add freshly ground black pepper and a little sea salt if needed. Place in a serving bowl and chill for 1 hour in the refrigerator.

To garnish, finely grind the pistachio nuts and mix them with the parsley and a little freshly ground black pepper. Sprinkle this over the chilled soup just before serving.

Pumpkin Soup

Serves 4–5

1 kg (2 lb) pumpkin, diced
3 large cloves garlic, crushed
2 tbsp safflower oil
1 level tsp aniseed or fennel seeds, crushed
2 tbsp fresh parsley, chopped
450 g (1 lb) fresh tomatoes, skinned and chopped
725 ml (1¼ pints) water
2 rounded tsps Hugli Instant Vegetable Broth Mix
freshly ground black pepper

Sauté the pumpkin and garlic in the oil for 3 minutes. Add the aniseed or fennel seeds and parsley and continue to fry for a further minute. Add the tomatoes and stir well in. Finally add the water, Hugli Vegetable Broth granules and black pepper to taste. Bring to the boil and simmer with the lid on for 20 minutes. Liquidize when slightly cooled and re-heat before serving.

Sprouted Soya Bean, Lemon and Parsley Soup

Serves 6

From my book *Vegetarian Food Processor*, this soup is jam-packed with goodness. The soya bean is a complete protein and when sprouted it is very digestible and has a pleasantly sweet and nutty flavour. You have to plan this soup a few days in advance because the beans take 3 to 4 days to sprout. You will need a blender or food processor.

175 g (6 oz), dry weight, soya beans, sprouted and cooked
1 bunch spring onions
100 g (4 oz) very small button mushrooms
1 rounded tbsp Hugli Instant Vegetable Broth Mix
6 tbsp fresh parsley, chopped
juice of 2 lemons
freshly ground black pepper

To sprout the soya beans. Wash them well and pick over for stones. Cover with 850 ml/1½ pints cold water and let them soak for 12 hours. Change the water three times. Drain the beans and place in a large jar. Cover the top with a piece of muslin secured with an elastic band and put in a warm place (an airing cupboard is perfect). Pour 575 ml/1 pint of cold water on to them three times a day and drain the water through the muslin. Repeat until the beans have 1.5 cm/½″ sprouts. This will take about 3 to 4 days. Once sprouted, cook the beans for 2 hours or more until soft, or pressure cook for 30 minutes. Do not add salt.

To make the soup. Measure out 1 litre/2 pints boiling water, including any cooking water from the beans. Put steel blades in position on the food processor. To one cup of sprouted beans add one cup of boiling water and purée all the beans. Now put the remaining hot water into a heavy-bottomed saucepan, bring to boil and pour the bean mixture into this. Chop the spring onions, using all the green and slice the mushrooms. Add these, with the Hugli Broth, parsley and lemon juice, to the soup. Stir well and add freshly ground black pepper to taste. Continue to simmer for 10 minutes more.

Serve with oven-toasted wholemeal bread: simply finger-slices of bread spread with polyunsaturated margarine and baked in the oven at 190°C/375°F Gas Mark 5, for 20 minutes until crisp. You can rub the bread with garlic before baking and sprinkle with shoyu* for really tasty toasted 'fingers'.

Yoghurt and Barley Soup (Turkish Style)

Serves 4–5

100 g (4 oz) pot barley (whole grain, not pearl barley)
725 ml (1¼ pints) hot water mixed with 1 Hugli Vegetable Stock Cube
2 large onions, peeled and chopped
2 tbsp sunflower oil
2 tbsp fresh parsley, chopped
1 tbsp fresh mint, chopped
575 ml (1 pint) natural yoghurt
a little sea salt and freshly ground black papper

Soak the barley overnight. Drain and boil in the vegetable stock water for 15 minutes. Sauté the onions in the oil, with a lid on the pan, until soft – about 10 minutes (take care not to burn them). Add them with the parsley and mint to the barley stock water and cook for 30 minutes with the lid on.

Just before serving whip the yoghurt and stir into the barley broth. Taste and season with freshly ground black pepper and sea salt (if needed).

LANE'S

Lane's herb salt is a mixture of sea salt and ground herbs.

Spring Vegetable Soup

Serves 6–8

This soup is from my book *Wholefood Cookery Course*.

850 ml (1½ pints) hot water plus 1½ tsps Lane's Herb Salt
6 small new potatoes, scrubbed and diced (leave skins on)
2 medium carrots, scrubbed and thinly sliced
1 small onion, peeled and finely chopped
100 g (4 oz) green peas, fresh or frozen
100 g (4 oz) young green beans, chopped into 2.5 cm (1") pieces
225 g (8 oz) frozen sweetcorn
½ small red pepper, de-seeded and chopped
½ small green pepper, de-seeded and chopped
1 tbsp fresh parsley, chopped
1 tsp lemon rind, grated
freshly ground black pepper

Put the hot water into a large saucepan, add the herb salt and bring to the boil. Add the potatoes, carrots, onions, peas (if fresh) and green beans. Cover, and simmer for 10–15 minutes. Add the sweetcorn and chopped peppers (if the peas are frozen add them now), then add the parsley, lemon rind and freshly ground black pepper and continue to simmer for another 10 minutes only.

Watercress Soup

Serves 6

4 medium potatoes, scrubbed and diced
1 large onion, chopped
1 litre (1¾ pints) boiling water
2 level tsps Lane's Herb Salt
1 good size bunch watercress, chopped, including stems as well as leaves
275 ml (10 fl oz) natural yoghurt
2 tbsps double cream (optional)
freshly ground black pepper
good pinch nutmeg

Put the potatoes and chopped onion into the boiling water with the herb salt and simmer for 15 minutes. Stir in the chopped watercress (save a few sprigs to garnish) and simmer for another 5 minutes only. Liquidize until quite smooth then heat through again. Mix the yoghurt, cream (if used), a few twists of freshly ground black pepper and the nutmeg together. Take soup off the heat, stir in the yoghurt mixture and serve immediately. (Do not re-heat after adding the yoghurt as the soup will then curdle.)

Garnish with tiny sprigs of watercress and a little more freshly ground nutmeg or black pepper.

LOSELEY

Beetroot and Fennel Soup

Serves 6

This recipe is taken from my book *Vegetarian Food Processor*. It is my version of Russian Borsch. It is traditionally served with sour cream but if this is not available I make my own by adding two tablespoons of double cream to 150 ml/5 fl oz natural yoghurt. Whisk the cream to a firm consistency, stir into the yoghurt and leave to chill in the refrigerator for 1 hour.

1 onion (175 g/6 oz weight after peeling and roughly chopping)
100 g (4 oz) fennel root, roughly chopped
3 cardamom seeds, podded
2 tbsp vegetable oil
2 medium potatoes, scrubbed (approx. 225 g/8 oz in weight)
450 g (1 lb) raw beetroot (weight after thinly peeling and chopping)
1 litre (1¾ pints) boiling water
1½ tsps herb salt or 1½ vegetable stock cubes
1 bay leaf
1 tbsp cider vinegar
¼ tsp freshly ground black pepper
150 g (5 fl oz) Loseley Natural Yoghurt plus 2 tbsp Loseley Double Cream, mixed together
a little freshly chopped parsley to garnish

Set the steel blades of the food processor in position. Put the roughly chopped onion, chopped fennel and the crushed cardamom seeds in the processor bowl and chop. Heat the oil in a heavy-bottomed saucepan. Sauté the onion, fennel and cardamoms for 6 minutes with a lid on. Cut scrubbed potatoes into approx. 2.5 cm/1" pieces. Set the steel blades in place and chop the beetroot and potatoes. Add the boiling water and herb salt or stock cubes to the sautéed onion and fennel mixture. Next add the potato, beetroot, bay leaf, cider vinegar and freshly ground black pepper, bring to the boil and then turn down to simmer. Put a lid on the saucepan and simmer for 25 minutes only. With steel blades in place blend the soup to a purée, adding 4 ladles of the mixture at a time to the processor bowl. Re-heat but do not boil. Pour into a serving bowl and drop the yoghurt and cream mixture into the centre. Sprinkle with a little chopped parsley and stir in just before serving.

Green Pea Soup with Croûtons

Serves 6

450 g (1 lb) peas, fresh or frozen (weight after podding)
850 ml (1½ pints) water with 1 vegetable stock cube dissolved in it
small bunch spring onions or 1 small onion, peeled and finely chopped
1 tbsp cold pressed sunflower oil or butter for frying
2 level tbsp 81% (wheatmeal) flour
2 tbsp Loseley Natural Yoghurt
2 tbsp Loseley Double Cream
sea salt and freshly ground black pepper
sprigs of mint and croûtons to garnish

Cook the peas with half the stock and the sprig of mint. If using fresh peas cook for 20–25 minutes, if frozen, 7 minutes only. In another pot sauté the spring onions or chopped onion until soft but not browned. Stir in the flour and continue stirring with a wooden spoon until the mixture bubbles slightly.

Remove from the heat and gradually add the remaining stock, stirring constantly. Cook gently, still stirring, until the sauce thickens. Cook for 2 minutes. Liquidize the cooked peas with their cooking water to a smooth purée. Sieve if not perfectly smooth. Blend the sauce with the pea purée and heat through, then add salt and pepper to taste.

Stir in the cream and yoghurt just before serving and garnish with sprigs of mint and croûtons.

Spiced Yoghurt Soup

Serves 4–6

This recipe is also in my book *Making Your Own Home Proteins*. It serves 6 as a starter, 4 as a main meal. In India and the Middle Eastern countries yoghurt is often used in soups and sauces. Mixing flour with the yoghurt before adding to a soup, stew or sauce will prevent it from curdling while cooking.

2 tbsp sunflower oil
1 large onion, peeled and chopped
2 cloves garlic, crushed
1 tsp cumin seed
½ tsp turmeric
¼ tsp clove powder
1 level tsp freshly ground coriander seeds
1 level tsp root ginger, freshly grated
1 cinnamon stick
1 fresh chilli, finely chopped
1 rounded tsp methi (fenugreek leaves)
225 g (8 oz) French beans or okra (ladies' fingers) cut into 1 cm/½" pieces
6 medium tomatoes, skinned and puréed in a blender
850 ml (1½ pints) water plus 1 vegetable stock cube or a little sea salt to your taste
2 tbsp gram (chick pea) flour
350 ml (12 fl oz) Loseley Natural Yoghurt

Heat the oil in a heavy-based frying pan and sauté the onion and garlic for 10 minutes with lid on. Add all the spices and herbs and continue to sauté for 2 minutes more on a low heat, stirring constantly. Take off the heat and stir in the beans and tomatoes. In a cup mix the gram flour with a little water to make a smooth, runny batter. Whisk the yoghurt with a balloon whisk and slowly add 275 ml/10 fl oz of the water until well blended together. Pour the gram flour mixture into this, whisking as you do so. Add the rest of the water. Bring this to the boil in a large heavy-based saucepan, stirring constantly, and stir in the sautéed vegetable and spice mixture.

NATURE'S WAY

The next two recipes have been devised by Chrissy Howell of Nature's Way.

Carrot and Cashew Nut Soup

Serves 6

2 large carrots
1 onion
1 medium potato
25 g (1 oz) butter or polyunsaturated margarine
75 g (3 oz) Nature's Way Broken Cashew Nuts
725 ml (1¼ pints) vegetable stock (make with hot water and 1¼ vegetable stock cubes)
275 ml (10 fl oz) milk
sea salt and freshly ground pepper to taste

Chop the vegetables. Melt the butter or margarine in a large saucepan and sauté the prepared vegetables until the onion is transparent. Add the cashews and cook for a further 5 minutes, stirring frequently. Add the stock, cover and simmer for 30 minutes. Add the milk and liquidize. Return the soup to the pan and re-heat to serving temperature. Season to taste.

Curried Split Pea Soup

Serves 4–5

225 g (8 oz) Nature's Way Yellow Split Peas
2 onions
50 g (2 oz) butter or polyunsaturated margarine
1 tbsp curry powder
1 tsp garam masala
1 tsp turmeric
1 tsp fresh ginger, grated
sea salt and freshly ground black pepper
little fresh chopped parsley to garnish

Soak the split peas overnight and cook in sufficient water to cover until the peas are tender. Peel and grate the onions and cook gently in the butter or margarine until transparent. Stir in the spices and cook for 1 minute more. Add this to the cooked peas, bring to the boil, simmer for 5 minutes more, season and then liquidize.

Sprinkle with chopped parsley to garnish.

PAUL'S TOFU

Pot Barley and Tofu Soup

Serves 4

This delicious, hearty and warming soup accompanied by wholemeal pitta bread stuffed with salad will provide a wholesome lunch or supper dish for four people. Instead of the savoury sautéed tofu you can simply chop up firm tofu and add as directed.

75 g (3 oz) pot barley (whole grain, not pearl barley)
850 ml (1½ pints) water
3 tbsps sunflower oil
1 large onion, peeled and finely chopped
2 cloves garlic, crushed
3 medium carrots, scraped and cut into 1 cm (½") sticks
2 medium potatoes, scrubbed and cut into small cubes
3 sticks celery, finely chopped
1 rounded tsp basil or mixed herbs
1 bay leaf
2 tbsps fresh parsley, chopped (when available)
450 g (1 lb) ripe tomatoes, skinned and finely chopped or canned tomatoes
1 level tbsp miso
350 g (12 oz) 2 cm (¾") cubes of Paul's Firm Tofu, prepared as Savoury Sautéed Tofu (see page 43)
1 tbsp shoyu
freshly ground black pepper

Wash the barley well and soak it in the water overnight, or for at least 4 hours. Drain and reserve the liquid, topping it up to 850 ml (1½ pints). Heat the oil in a large, heavy-based saucepan and sauté the onion and garlic for 5 minutes with the lid on. Add the carrots, potatoes, celery and drained barley, stir in the basil or mixed herbs, bay leaf and parsley and continue to fry for 3 minutes only. Add the chopped tomatoes and the tomato purée and barley soaking water. Bring to the boil and simmer gently for 20 minutes. Take off the heat, mix a few tablespoons of the hot soup with the miso to make a runny batter and stir this into the rest of the soup, blending well together. Finally, stir in the tofu cubes, shoyu and pepper and heat through just before serving.

For children who pick out vegetables or old

people who find it difficult to chew, this soup is even tastier when liquidized, but you might have to add a little more water as the soup will be quite thick.

Leek and Watercress Soup with Tofu

Serves 6–8 small portions

This is a very delicate-flavoured soup with thin rings of leek and chopped watercress cooked for just ten minutes. As in the previous recipe you can use the Savoury Sautéed Tofu or, as I prefer because of the light flavour, small cubes of plain unsautéed tofu.

1 litre (1³/₄ pints) water
1¹/₂ vegetable stock cubes or 2 level tsps herb salt
2 medium leeks, trimmed, washed and cut into thin rings
100 g (4 oz) small button mushrooms, sliced
1 bunch watercress, chopped (use stems too)
225 g (8 oz) Paul's Firm Tofu, cut into small cubes or as Savoury Sautéed Tofu (see page 00)
freshly ground black pepper to taste

Bring the water to the boil with the stock cubes or herb salt. Add the leek rings and simmer with the lid on for 5 minutes only. Add mushroom slices and continue to simmer for 3 more minutes. Add chopped watercress, tofu and black pepper and simmer for a few more minutes until the tofu is warmed through.
  Serve immediately, piping hot, in small bowls.

Spring Onion, Mushroom and Watercress Soup with Tofu

Serves 4–5

850 ml (1¹/₂ pints) hot water
1¹/₂ vegetable stock cubes or 1¹/₂ tsps herb salt
1 good size bunch of spring onions, chopped (use green stems as well as white parts)
1 large carrot, scraped and cut into oval slivers on a grater

100 g (4 oz) small button mushrooms, thinly sliced
1 bunch watercress, roughly chopped (use stems too)
225 g (8 oz) Paul's Firm Tofu, cut into 1 cm (¹/₂") cubes
freshly ground black pepper to taste

Bring the water to the boil with the stock cubes or herb salt. Add the spring onions, carrots and mushrooms and simmer with the lid on for 5 minutes only. Stir in the watercress and tofu cubes and simmer for only 3 minutes more.
  Serve immediately, piping hot, in small bowls.

PLAMIL

Tofu and Leek Soup

Serves 3–4

2 tbsp vegetable oil
75 g (3 oz) leeks, thinly sliced
1 small carrot, thinly sliced
1 good size tomato, skinned and chopped
1 tsp molasses sugar (optional)
575 ml (1 pint) diluted Plamil
275 g (10 oz) tofu
good pinch of dried herbs – oregano is good
¹/₂ tsp sea salt and a little freshly ground black pepper
fresh parsley, chopped, to garnish

Sauté the leeks and carrot in the oil until soft (5–7 minutes). Add the tomato and cook for a further few minutes. Stir in the sugar if using, the tofu, Plamil, herbs and seasoning. Blend in a liquidizer for a few seconds, adding more milk or stock if required. Return to the pan and heat through thoroughly but *do not allow to boil*. Check for seasoning and serve hot or cold with a generous sprinkling of chopped parsley.

PROTOVEG

The next five recipes come from *The Magic Bean* by Anna Roberts.

Apple and Celery Soup

Serves 4

2 large cooking apples
6 sticks celery
50 g (2 oz) Protoveg Natural Flavour TVP Mince
1 vegetable stock cube
1 tsp ground rosemary
1 tbsp sunflower oil
sea salt and freshly ground black pepper to taste
1 tbsp maize flour (cornmeal)
850 ml (1½ pints) water

Peel and roughly chop the apples and celery. Place all the ingredients in a large saucepan, mixing the maize flour with a little water first. Simmer for about 30 minutes. Blend the mixture or pass it through a sieve, re-heat and serve with squares of wholemeal toast spread with polyunsaturated margarine.

Broth

Serves 6–8

115 g (4¼ oz) Protoveg Ham Flavour TVP Chunks
2 carrots, sliced
1 turnip, chopped
1 onion, grated
50 g (2 oz) pot barley (whole grain barley, not pearl barley)
1 tbsp parsley, chopped
sea salt and freshly ground black pepper to taste
1.2 litres (2 pints) vegetable stock

Place the Protoveg TVP Chunks in a large saucepan and add all other ingredients. Bring to the boil, lower heat and simmer for about 1 hour, adding extra liquid if necessary.

Green Pea Soup

Serves 6

50 g (2 oz) Protoveg Ham Flavour TVP Chunks
225 g (8 oz), dry weight, green split peas, soaked overnight
1 large onion, chopped
1 tbsp corn oil
good pinch coriander
sea salt to taste
freshly ground black pepper to taste
850 ml (1½ pints) vegetable stock
single cream or top of the milk to serve (optional)

Reconstitute the Protoveg Chunks following the pack instructions. Sauté the chopped onion in the oil for 5 minutes. Drain the peas and put all the ingredients, including the liquid from the Soya Chunks, into a saucepan. Cook until the peas are soft (about 40 minutes). If desired, a small amount of single cream or top of the milk can be stirred in just before serving.

Lentil and 'Bacon' Soup

Serves 5

1 medium carrot, grated
1 medium onion, chopped
25 g (1 oz) polyunsaturated margarine
½ tsp celery seeds
850 ml (1½ pints) vegetable stock
1 vegetable stock cube
1 tbsp vegetarian Worcester Sauce
1 tbsp Protoveg Smokey Snaps Mince
100 g (4 oz) split red lentils

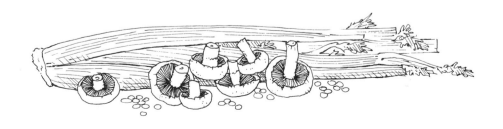

Sauté the carrot and onion in the margarine, using a large saucepan. After about 5 minutes add the remaining ingredients and simmer for 30–40 minutes, adding extra liquid during cooking if necessary.

Protoveg Vichyssoise

Serves 5

3 medium leeks, chopped
1 medium onion, chopped
1 tbsp sunflower oil
450 g (1 lb) potatoes, diced
1 tsp mint
seasoning to taste
575 ml (1 pint) vegetable stock
150 ml (5 fl oz) carton plain yoghurt
25 g (1 oz) Protoveg Smokey Snaps Mince

Sauté the leeks and onion in the oil until soft, but not brown. Transfer them to a large saucepan and add the potatoes, herbs and seasoning. Cover with the stock and cook for 30 minutes, adding a little extra water if necessary. Remove from the heat and put through a blender. Mix in the yoghurt and serve immediately, sprinkled with Protoveg Smokey Snaps.

Peel the onions, taking only the very outer brown skin off. Thinly slice and sauté in the oil until soft (about 15 minutes with the lid on). Take the lid off and continue to cook until the onions are golden brown (this adds a delicious flavour to the soup). Take 150 ml/5 fl oz of the measured water and stir in the kuzu, blending until smooth. Add the rest of the water to the browned onions, bring to the boil and simmer for 30 minutes. Add the kuzu mixture, stirring constantly, and simmer for 3 minutes more until the soup has thickened slightly. Stir in the tamari or shoyu. Take off heat. Heat through but do not boil.

Spread a little oil on the slices of French bread, sprinkle on half of the grated cheese, place on a baking sheet and bake at 180°C/350°F/Gas Mark 4 until the bread is crisp and the cheese is melted. Place a slice of bread in each soup bowl and pour over the hot onion soup. Sprinkle on the remaining cheese and serve immediately. If the soup bowls are heatproof you can place them under the grill for a minute to lightly brown the cheese if you wish.

SUNWHEEL

This is a delicious, authentic-tasting soup.

French Onion Soup

Serves 6

450 g (1 lb) onions
2 tbsp Sunwheel Cold Pressed Sunflower Oil
1.5 litres (2 pints) water
25 g (1 oz) Sunwheel Kuzu
3 tbsp Sunwheel Tamari or Shoyu
6 slices of French bread (see the recipe for a crispy
*   French loaf on page 125), cut 1.5 cm/1/2" thick*
a little more sunflower oil for spreading on bread
150 g (5 oz) Gruyère cheese, grated

Herby Miso Soup

Serves 4

4 medium potatoes, scrubbed and diced
3 carrots, cleaned and thinly sliced
2 onions, peeled and chopped
2 garlic cloves, chopped (optional)
3 tbsp Sunwheel Miso
1.4 litres (2½ pints) water
225 g (8 oz) beansprouts

Bring the potatoes, carrots, onions and garlic to the boil in the water and simmer for 20 minutes or until vegetables are soft. Blend the soup until smooth and thick. Dissolve the miso in some of the soup and add to the pan, stir well, add the beansprouts and serve immediately.

Kombu Aduki Bean Soup

Serves 4

150 g (6 oz) dry weight, aduki beans
1 onion, peeled and sliced
1 clove garlic
1 tbsp Sunwheel Cold Pressed Sesame Oil
½ tsp thyme
1 bay leaf
1 strip Westbrae Kombu, chopped into large pieces
850 ml (1½ pints) hot water
2 tbsp Sunwheel Shoyu
fresh parsley and wholemeal croutons to garnish

Soak the beans overnight, changing the water twice. Sauté the onion and garlic in the oil for 5 minutes, then add the thyme, bay leaf and chopped kombu. Rinse the soaked beans and add to onion mixture. Pour in the hot water, bring to the boil and cook until the beans are soft and mushy (about 40 minutes). Add the shoyu, taste and add more if necessary. Liquidize until smooth. Garnish with fresh chopped parsley and serve with wholemeal croutons.

Lentil and Miso Soup

Serves 4

The following recipe is taken from my book *Vegetarian Food Processor*. This wholesome and very nutritious soup is one of my favourites. It is a meal in itself. The combination of lentils with the miso makes a complete protein food. Miso has a salty flavour so no salt is needed in the recipe. It must be added at the end of cooking time or you destroy its valuable enzymes and nutrients.

2 medium onions, peeled
2 cloves garlic, peeled
3 sticks celery, washed
2 large carrots, scraped
145 g (5 oz) red split lentils
1.2 litres (2 pints) boiling water
2 tbsp tomato purée
few sprigs fresh parsley
1 bay leaf
2 slightly rounded tbsp Sunwheel Mugi Miso
freshly ground black pepper
1 tbsp lemon juice

Cut the onion roughly into 8 pieces, slice the garlic and chop the celery into approx. 3.5 cm/1½″ lengths, leaving on as much green as possible. With the steel blades in position on the food processor put the onion, garlic and celery into the processor bowl and chop. Scoop out and place in a medium-sized, heavy-bottomed saucepan. Slice the carrots lengthwise into approximately 2.5 cm/1″ sticks. Put in the processor bowl and with steel blades in position, chop. Transfer to the saucepan. (No need to wash the processor bowl as you will need it to liquidize the soup later.)

Wash the lentils, picking over for small stones. (A sieve is best – just let cold water flow over the lentils for half a minute.) Drain the lentils and add to the vegetables. Add the boiling water, tomato purée, parsley and bay leaf. Stir well and bring to the boil. Simmer for 20 minutes only. Put the miso in a small bowl, stir in some of the hot soup liquid and cream the mixture together, then pour into the soup, stirring well. With the steel blades in position, purée the soup, 4 ladles at a time, until smooth. Pour back into the saucepan, add freshly ground black pepper and lemon juice and heat through but do not boil.

VECON

Basic Vegetable Stock

Makes about 2 litres/3½ pints

This recipe is my own vegetable stock enhanced by Vecon. It is delicious for making gravies, brown sauces and in soups, wherever chicken stock is called for. At the end of each week, just before my weekly shopping trip, I make my stock with all the leftover vegetables such as odds and ends of peppers, softish carrots, outside tougher sticks of celery, outside leaves of lettuce, squashy tomatoes, in fact any vegetable you know will not go towards your main meals and would probably end up in the bin a few days later. Much better to use these in making this most delicious vegetable stock. The flavour will differ according to the vegetables you use. Summer is a good time for making stock, which freezes easily and is ever-ready to make your sauces, gravies and soups. Fresh herbs are always a wonderful addition but parsley and bay leaves, which are usually available, are sufficient and are in the basic recipe.

2 tbsps corn or sunflower oil
1 large onion, approx. 225 g (8 oz), peeled and
   roughly chopped
2 large cloves garlic, peeled and chopped
4 medium carrots, roughly chopped
4 outside sticks celery
green ends of leeks (even tough ends), roughly
   chopped (optional)
ends of green and red pepper, about 4 tbsps,
   roughly chopped
4 over-ripe tomatoes, skinned (optional)
4 rounded tbsps tomato purée
1 large bay leaf
3 tbsps parsley, roughly chopped (use stems as well)
2 rounded tsps Vecon
2 litres (3½ pints) hot water

Heat the oil in a large, heavy-based saucepan and sauté all the vegetables except the tomatoes for 2 minutes. Mash in the tomatoes and add the tomato purée, bay leaf and parsley. Stir the Vecon into the hot water and pour this into the vegetables. Bring to the boil, stirring constantly, then turn down to simmer, put on a lid and cook gently for 1 hour. Mash the vegetables roughly with a potato masher and strain through a sieve, pressing firmly with the masher to extract as much liquid as possible. Taste and add more Vecon if you require a more savoury flavour. (I don't think this will be necessary.) Your stock is now ready to use when required. It will be fine in the fridge for 3 days or it can be frozen in 575 ml/1 pint containers.

Leek and Potato Soup

Serves at least 12

3 large potatoes, scrubbed and coarsely chopped
2 tbsps cold pressed sunflower oil
4 sticks celery, chopped (tougher outer stalks are
   ideal)
4 large leeks, split, trimmed, washed and coarsely
   chopped (leave as much green on as possible)
1 heaped tsp dried dill
4 tbsps fresh parsley, chopped
3 tbsps lemon juice
2 litres (3½ pints) hot water
1 rounded dsrtsp Vecon
1 tsp cayenne pepper (optional)
freshly ground black pepper to taste
sea salt to taste
grated cheese to serve

Sauté the potatoes in the oil for 3 minutes. Add the celery and leeks and continue frying for 2 minutes. Stir in the dill, parsley and lemon juice, coating the vegetables well, then add the hot water. Add the Vecon, cayenne and black pepper and stir in over low heat. Taste and add more salt if needed, then cover tightly and simmer for 30 minutes. Liquidize, then re-heat slowly.

For an extra protein booster, instead of sprinkling grated cheese you could liquidize some tofu with the soup.

Vecon Nettle Soup

Serves 4–5

A thoroughly wholesome soup. Choose the tops of young nettles. No extra salt is needed because Vecon has a salty taste derived solely from concentrated vegetables.

1 litre (1¾ pints) (packed) young nettle tops
1 large leek, trimmed and cut in thin rings (use as
   much green as possible)
2 tbsp sunflower, corn or olive oil
2 medium size potatoes, washed and cut into very
   small pieces
1 litre (1¾ pints) hot water plus 1 rounded tsp
   Vecon
few twists of freshly ground black pepper
a little nutmeg
small carton natural yoghurt

Wash the nettles well in cold water. Heat the oil in a large, heavy-based saucepan. Sauté the leeks and potatoes for 3 minutes, stirring constantly. Pour in the hot water and Vecon, bring to the boil, then simmer with the lid on for 5 minutes. Add the washed nettle tops, and continue to simmer for 10 minutes more. Liquidize until smooth, return to the saucepan, add the black pepper and nutmeg and heat well. Remove from the heat, stir in the yoghurt and serve at once.

Vegetable Gravy

Serves 4–6

This is great with nut or bean roast, rissoles and croquettes.

575 ml (1 pint) hot Basic Vegetable Stock with
  Vecon (see page 20)
2 tbsps corn oil
1 rounded tbsp unbleached white flour
freshly ground black pepper to taste (optional)

Heat the oil in a heavy-based pan, stir in the flour and cook on moderate heat for 1 minute, stirring constantly. Gradually pour in the hot stock, again stirring constantly. Cook on low heat for 3 minutes, then add a few twists of freshly ground black pepper to taste.

WESTERN ISLES

Wakame and Miso Soup

Serves 4–5

1 litre (1¾ pints) water (including soaking water
  from wakame)
30 cm (12") strip Western Isles Wakame, washed
  and soaked for 10 minutes
1 large onion, chopped or sliced
175 g (6 oz) mixed vegetables, diced – carrots,
  potatoes, celery, etc.
1 rounded tbsp Western Isles Miso Purée
green garnish, for example, spring onion, chives,
  parsley

Boil the water and add the wakame, onions and vegetables. If using root vegetables, simmer for 10 to 15 minutes; if leafy, up to 10 minutes. Mix the miso with a little of the soup mixture until liquid, then add to the saucepan and simmer gently (do not boil) for a further 5–10 minutes. Garnish and serve.

WHOLE EARTH

Brown Rice and Corn Soup

Serves 4–5

1 leek, cleaned and chopped
1 medium onion, peeled and chopped
1 stick celery, chopped
1 red pepper, de-seeded and chopped
2 tbsp sunflower oil
1 can Whole Earth Brown Rice and Vegetables
2 tbsp Whole Earth Kensington Sauce
250 g (10 oz) sweetcorn
1 litre (1¾ pints) vegetable stock or water
shoyu or tamari to taste
sea salt and freshly ground black pepper

Sauté the chopped vegetables in oil for about 7–10 minutes, add the rest of the ingredients and bring to the boil. Taste and add a little more shoyu or tamari if necessary, then simmer for 20–30 minutes.

Brown Rice, Tofu and Miso Soup

Serves 4–5

1 stick celery, chopped
1 onion, peeled and chopped
4 mushrooms, thinly sliced
2 cloves garlic, chopped
2 tbsp vegetable oil
1 litre (1¾ pints) vegetable stock or water
1 can Whole Earth Brown Rice and Vegetables
1 tsp fresh ginger, chopped
150 g (6 oz) tofu, cut into cubes
2 tbsp miso

Sauté the celery, onion, mushrooms and garlic in the vegetable oil until tender. Mix the stock, Whole Earth Brown Rice and Vegetables and ginger together and bring to the boil. Add the vegetables and tofu and cook for 5 minutes. Add the miso and serve.

2
SALADS and SALAD DRESSINGS

APPLEFORD'S LTD

The following recipe is taken from my book *Vegetarian Food Processor*. I use fresh apricots, but you can use dried. Choose the full-flavoured apricot pieces. Wash well and soak in water with a heaped teaspoon of clear honey overnight. Cook for 10 minutes until most of the liquid is evaporated.

Black-Eye Beans with Apricot and Ginger Dressing

Serves 4

350 g (12 oz), dry weight, black-eye beans
6 fresh chillies, chopped
1 tsp sea salt

Dressing
175 g (6 oz) fresh apricots or 50 g (2 oz) dried
1 tsp Dietade *fruit sugar*
2 tbsp olive oil
1 tbsp Appleford's Cider Vinegar
1 tsp fresh ginger, grated
2 cloves garlic, chopped
1 tbsp shoyu

Wash the beans, removing any stones. Soak overnight, changing the water three times. Rinse. Set the steel blades in position on a food processor and blend the chopped chillies with 275 ml/10 fl oz water until you have a pulp. Put the beans, chilli pulp and 850 ml/1½ pints water into a saucepan, bring to the boil and cook, with lid on, for about 45 minutes or until soft, but not mushy. Add the sea salt 10 minutes before the end of the cooking time. Drain the beans and place in a serving bowl.

Wash, stone and cook the fresh apricots in a very little water with the fruit sugar, until soft and most of the water has evaporated. With the steel blades in position, blend together the apricots, olive oil, vinegar, grated ginger, garlic and shoyu until smooth. Stir into the warm beans and marinate for a few hours or overnight.

This is delicious with vegetable curry instead of dhal, or with a fresh green salad and pitta bread.

CARRABAY

In the following two salads dillisk or dulse is used in a delicious combination with vegetables, fruit and sprouted alfalfa seeds.

When I was very young it was possible to buy a handful of dillisk for one old penny. On the West Coast of Ireland, near Galway Bay, where I spent most of the summer holidays before the age of 10, a truly wholesome lunch of this delicious seaweed and periwinkles could be bought for just two old pennies – enough to generously fill two sandwiches. I can still smell those delicacies to this day, so my love of dillisk is perhaps tinged with romantic notions of those happy, freedom-filled holidays.

Dillisk Salad

25 g (1 oz) Carrabay Dillisk
1 sliced apple
2 large carrots
225 g (8 oz) alfalfa sprouts
½ ripe avocado, peeled, stoned and cubed
50 g (2 oz) currants or raisins

Dressing
100 ml (4 fl oz) Sunwheel Cold Pressed Sunflower or Olive Oil
2 tbsp lemon juice
2 tbsp Sunwheel Shoyu

Chop the dillisk finely. Mix all the salad ingredients together. Mix the dressing and pour it over the salad. Toss well and serve.

Shades of Green Salad and Dillisk

1 good size Cos or Webb lettuce
½ medium cucumber, cut into thin slices
1 bunch watercress, roughly chopped
2 handfuls sprouted alfalfa seeds
2 tbsp chopped chives or spring onions
25 g (1 oz) Carrabay Dillisk, washed and chopped

Dressing
3 tbsp Sunwheel Cold Pressed Safflower Oil
1 tbsp lemon juice
¼ tsp honey
¼ tsp sea salt
¼ tsp freshly ground black pepper
½ tsp Dijon mustard
1 clove garlic, crushed

Wash, towel dry and shred the lettuce. Mix all the salad ingredients together and place in a serving bowl. Shake all the dressing ingredients together and pour over the salad, tossing well to mix.

COUNTRY BASKET

Spaghetti Salad

1 packet (250 g) Country Basket Wholewheat Spaghetti
6 spring onions, chopped
few radishes, sliced
1 red pepper, de-seeded and chopped
50 g (2 oz) button mushrooms, sliced

Dressing
50 ml (2 fl oz) olive oil
2 tbsp wine vinegar or cider vinegar
¼ tsp mustard
1 tsp sugar
1 clove garlic
2 tsp parsley, chives or mint, chopped
sea salt and freshly ground black pepper

Put all the ingredients for the dressing in a screw-topped jar and shake well. Break the spaghetti into short lengths and cook as directed on the packet. Drain and toss in the dressing while hot. Add the prepared salad ingredients, cool and serve with cold meats or fish.

Variation

To vary this salad, replace the salad ingredients given with 4 sticks celery, chopped, 50 g/2 oz mixed nuts and raisins, and ½ can mandarin oranges, drained. This salad is especially good with cold chicken.

DIETADE

Egg Mayonnaise

2 eggs, hard-boiled cut in halves lengthwise
2 lettuce leaves
2 slices lemon
1 tomato, sliced

Mayonnaise
1 egg yolk
1 tsp Dietade Fruit Sugar
1 level tsp made mustard
¼ tsp sea salt
⅛ tsp ground white pepper
150 ml (5 fl oz) sunflower oil
1 tbsp cider vinegar
½ tsp lemon juice

First make the mayonnaise by putting the egg yolk into a small basin. Mix in all the seasonings except the vinegar and lemon juice. Place the basin on a cold, damp dishcloth. Add the oil to the mixture in the basin, drop by drop, and stir rapidly with a wooden spoon. When the egg and oil have formed a smooth ball, add the oil a little more quickly. When sufficient oil has been added, gradually add the cider vinegar and lemon juice.

Place the halved eggs on the lettuce leaves and pour the mayonnaise over them. Garnish with lemon and tomato slices.

GAYELORD HAUSER'S NATURAL SEASONINGS

Everybody's Favourite Salad

4 sticks celery, diced
1 medium eating apple, diced (do not peel)
100 g (4 oz) grapes, halved and de-seeded
2 tbsp plain yoghurt
¾ tsp Spike Seasoning
1 tsp fresh parsley, chopped
lettuce, hard-boiled egg and sliced tomato to serve

Mix all the ingredients together and serve on a bed of lettuce with hard-boiled egg and tomato slices to garnish. This salad can be varied by adding diced chicken, salmon or tuna.

HOLLAND & BARRETT

The following two recipes are taken from my book *Vegetarian Food Processor.*

Butter Bean and Cauliflower with Pepper and Tomato Vinaigrette

115 g (4 oz), dry weight, Holland & Barrett Butter Beans
1 small cauliflower, broken into small florets
sea salt

Dressing
3 tbsp cold pressed sunflower or olive oil
1 tbsp cider vinegar
pinch dry mustard powder
a little freshly ground black pepper and sea salt
1 tsp Holland & Barrett Clear Honey
1 clove garlic, crushed
½ small green pepper, de-seeded and chopped
1 tsp dried basil

Wash the beans and soak overnight, changing the water three times. Cook in fresh water, boiling vigorously for 10 minutes, then bubbling gently for about 40 minutes. Watch the beans as these break up very easily. Add a little sea salt 10 minutes before the end of the cooking time. Drain and leave to cool. Cook the cauliflower in a little salted boiling water for 3 minutes only. Drain and mix with the cooked beans.

To make the vinaigrette dressing, put all the dressing ingredients into a liquidizer or food processor and blend until smooth. Pour this mixture over the beans and cauliflower and toss well. Leave the mixture to marinate, turning with a fork a few times, for 1 hour or more before serving.

Chicory, Carrot and Sultana Salad

This recipe is taken from Joan Lay's *Book of Salads*.

4 heads chicory
3 large carrots
50 g (2 oz) Holland & Barrett Sultanas
mayonnaise to taste
lettuce to serve
25 g (1 oz) Holland & Barrett Walnut Pieces
4 eggs, hard-boiled
Fresh parsley, chopped

Slice the chicory and grate the carrots. Rinse the sultanas in hot water and drain. Mix all together in a bowl with the mayonnaise.

Serve on a bed of lettuce and garnish with walnut pieces. Halve the eggs, sprinkle with the chopped parsley and arrange around the salad.

Nutty Coleslaw with Yoghurt Mint Dressing

This recipe has been taken from Audrey Eyton's *F-Plan Diet*.

100 g (4 oz) firm, white cabbage, shredded
50 g (2 oz) carrots, grated
50 g (2 oz) fresh or frozen peas, cooked
50 g (2 oz) sweetcorn kernels, cooked
25 g (1 oz) Holland & Barrett Walnut Pieces, *roughly chopped*

Dressing
1 tbsp low-fat natural yoghurt
1 tbsp lemon juice
½ tsp chopped fresh mint or ¼ tsp concentrated mint sauce
sea salt and freshly ground black pepper

Blend all the dressing ingredients together. Mix all the prepared vegetables and nuts together in a bowl. Stir in the yoghurt mint dressing and serve.

Pineapple, Cheese and Raisin Salad

This recipe comes from Joan Lay's *Book of Salads*.

1 fresh, ripe pineapple
100 g (4 oz) cottage cheese
50 g (2 oz) Holland & Barrett Almonds or Cashews, *toasted*
1 heaped tsp Holland & Barrett Raisins
lettuce and watercress to serve

Peel the pineapple, cut in half lengthwise and remove the central core, leaving a furrow. Soak the raisins in hot water for 5 minutes, then drain. Combine the cheese, nuts and raisins and pack into the pineapple furrows. Put the pineapple halves back together (tie with string if necessary) and chill for 1½–2 hours. When thoroughly chilled, slice on to a dish of lettuce and watercress.

Potato Salad with Peach Chutney

1 kg (2 lb) potatoes, steamed, peeled and diced
4 sticks celery, finely chopped (use the inside stalks for salad, outside for soups)
1 teacup frozen peas, cooked for 2 minutes and drained
1 teacup frozen sweetcorn, cooked for 2 minutes and drained
1 small onion, peeled and finely chopped
4 tbsp mayonnaise
3 tbsp fresh parsley, chopped (leave some sprigs whole, for garnish)
3 tbsp Peach Chutney made with Holland & Barrett Dried Peaches and Raisins *(see recipe on page 215)*

Mix all the ingredients except the chutney and parsley together, taking care not to break up the potatoes. Carefully fork in the chutney, sprinkle on the chopped parsley and garnish with remaining parsley sprigs.

Red Cabbage and Pecan Salad

675 g (1½ lb) red cabbage, finely shredded
2 green eating apples, chopped in small pieces
 (leave skins on)
50 g (2 oz) raisins
1 small onion (about 75 g/3 oz when very finely
 chopped)
2 tbsp fresh parsley, chopped
50 g (2 oz) Holland & Barrett *Pecan Nuts, chopped*
 (leave a few unchopped for decoration)

Dressing
3 tbsp virgin olive oil
1 tbsp lemon juice
good pinch of freshly ground black pepper
1 small clove garlic, crushed
½ tsp Holland & Barrett *Clear Honey*
2 tsp grated horseradish or 1 tsp horseradish sauce

Place all the salad ingredients in a large serving bowl. Place all the dressing ingredients in a large screw-top jar and shake well together. Pour the dressing over the salad and mix well.

Rice, Mushroom and Green Pea Salad

Another recipe from Joan Lay's *Book of Salads.*

225 g (8 oz) Holland & Barrett *Long Grain Brown*
 Rice
175 g (6 oz) mushrooms
2 tbsp olive oil
4 tbsp lemon juice
100 g (4 oz) frozen peas
1 tbsp fresh parsley, chopped
sea salt and freshly ground black pepper
watercress and tomatoes to garnish
mayonnaise to serve

Simmer the rice in boiling, salted water for 20 minutes, strain and run cold water over. Drain well and put into a bowl. Clean and chop the mushrooms and mix with the oil and lemon juice. Cook the peas as directed, drain and cool. Add the mushrooms (and the oil and lemon mixture), the peas and chopped parsley to the rice, adding a little salt and pepper to taste. Mix well and pile into the middle of a platter. Surround with sprigs of watercress and slices of tomato. Serve with mayonnaise.

Russian Salad

This is a salad from an article by Janette Marshall called 'Slim Naturally' in *Here's Health.*

3 cold cooked potatoes
2 cold cooked carrots
3 small boiled beetroots
50 g (2 oz) Holland & Barrett *Cashew Nuts, toasted*
 and chopped
1 tbsp fresh parsley, chopped
1 tbsp chives or mint, chopped
½ tbsp tarragon, chopped
mayonnaise
green salad to serve

Cube the potatoes, carrots and beetroot, and mix with the mayonnaise and chopped herbs, taking care not to break the pieces of vegetable. Pile on a bed of green salad and sprinkle with toasted nuts.

Superb Salad

This recipe is another delicious salad from Janette Marshall's 'Slim Naturally' in *Here's Health.*

175 g (6 oz) beansprouts (try sprouting Holland & Barrett *Alfalfa, Mung or Aduki Beans)*
10 Holland & Barrett *Dried Dates*
1 cooked beetroot (about 100 g/4 oz)
3 small tomatoes
3 sticks celery
1 courgette (about 175 g/6 oz)
1 peach or nectarine
4 carrots (about 225 g/8 oz)
2 tbsp safflower or sunflower mayonnaise
175 g (6 oz) Wensleydale or Lancashire cheese,
 finely grated

Wash the beansprouts, shake dry and place in a large mixing bowl. Stone the dates and cut into slivers. Skin the beetroot and dice. Cut the tomatoes into eights. Finely slice the celery. Cut the courgettes in half lengthwise, then cut into three along the length while holding in shape. Turn the courgettes round and slice across the width to produce little fan-shaped pieces of courgette. Halve the peach or nectarine, remove the stone and dice the flesh. Finely grate the carrots. Place all the ingredients in a bowl with the beansprouts, add the mayonnaise and toss well, transfer to a serving bowl and serve.

Waldorf Salad

Serves 1

This recipe too comes from Janette Marshall's 'Slim Naturally' in *Here's Health*. It is a good salad to take in a lunchbox or for a picnic.

25 g (1 oz) Holland & Barrett Walnut Pieces
50 g (2 oz) fresh dates or 8 Holland & Barrett Dried Dates, chopped
2 sticks celery, chopped
1 tbsp quark or similar low-fat soft white cheese
freshly ground black pepper
1 eating apple, unpeeled, sliced and tossed in the juice of ½ lemon

Toss the walnuts, dates and celery with the quark and pepper, and pile in the centre of a serving dish. Arrange the apple slices around the edge.

For a picnic or lunchbox, just mix all the ingredients together.

Walnut and Celery Crunch

Serves 4

5 sticks celery, finely chopped
65 g (2½ oz) Holland & Barrett Walnut Pieces, roughly chopped
75 g (3 oz) Holland & Barrett Raisins
2 red-skinned eating apples, unpeeled
juice of 1 lemon
1 tbsp mayonnaise
1 tbsp natural yoghurt
freshly ground black pepper
lettuce leaves to garnish

Mix the celery and walnuts together in a bowl and add the raisins. Cut the apples into quarters and remove the cores. Dice the apples finely, toss in the lemon juice to prevent them from browning and add to the bowl. Stir in the mayonnaise and yoghurt and season generously with black pepper. Toss together thoroughly and serve garnished with lettuce.

LOSELEY

Beetroot and Mint Salad with Sour Cream or Yoghurt Dressing

675 g (1½ lb) raw beetroot, grated
225 g (8 oz) firm salad tomatoes, cut into wedges
½ large cucumber, cut into sticks 2.5 cm (1") long, soaked in cider vinegar for 30 minutes then drained
1 tbsp fresh mint, finely chopped
1 tsp fresh mint, finely chopped, to garnish

Dressing
150 g (5 oz) Loseley Soured Cream or yoghurt cheese (see below)
1 large clove garlic
1 tbsp lemon juice
½ tsp clear honey
¼ tsp freshly ground black pepper
good pinch sea salt to taste

To make yoghurt cheese, put 275 g/10 fl oz of Loseley natural yoghurt in a piece of muslin and leave to drip overnight or for at least 4 hours.

Make the salad by mixing all the vegetables together with a fork. Add the tablespoon of mint carefully to avoid squashing the tomatoes too much. Prepare the dressing by mixing all the ingredients together with a fork. Stir the dressing into the vegetables and garnish with the remaining mint.

Beetroot with Apple Mint Dressing

Very special, cooling and delicious.

675 g (1½ lb) raw beetroot
½ medium fennel root
1 tbsp olive oil
pinch sea salt
8 lettuce leaves

Dressing
425 ml (15 fl oz) Loseley Natural Yoghurt, dripped
    through muslin for 1–2 hours
2 eating apples
1 large clove garlic, crushed
2 tbsp lemon juice
1 tsp clear honey
1 tbsp fresh mint leaves, chopped
sea salt and freshly ground black pepper
1 tsp chopped mint to garnish

Peel the beetroot with a potato peeler, rinse and cut into quarters. Set the shredding plate in position on a food processor. Stack the beetroot horizontally into the feed tube and shred. Cut the fennel into chunks, pack into the feed tube and shred. Wash out the processor bowl. Mix the beetroot and fennel in a bowl with the olive oil and a good pinch of sea salt. Cover and set aside. Wash the lettuce and pat dry on absorbent kitchen paper. Put in a plastic bag and refrigerate until needed.

Scrape the yoghurt off the muslin through which it has been dripping and put in a bowl – it should be the consistency of mayonnaise. Set the steel blades in position on the food processor. Peel off a very thin skin from the apples, core and roughly chop. Place the apples in the processor bowl with the garlic, lemon juice, honey and mint and blend until smooth. Stir the apple purée into the yoghurt. **Important:** Do not add the yoghurt to the apples when blending in the machine or you will get a very runny sauce. Just stir the apple purée into the yoghurt as directed – this way it will remain reasonably thick. Taste and add sea salt and freshly ground black pepper to taste. Assemble the salad by spreading the lettuce leaves on a large platter and spoon on the beetroot and fennel mixture, piling high on each leaf. Make an indent in each pile and spoon the yoghurt dressing into the centre of each. Sprinkle a little fresh mint over the top to garnish.

Now for some Loseley salad recipes with an international flavour.

Cucumber and Loseley Yoghurt Salad

This is a recipe from Turkey.

1 cucumber, peeled and quartered lengthwise, cut
    into rough 2.5–3.5 cm (1–1½") pieces and
    drained
150 g (5 oz) Loseley Natural Yoghurt
1 clove garlic
mint leaves, chopped
sea salt and freshly ground black pepper

Pound the clove of garlic, add the chopped mint, seasoning and mix with the yoghurt. Stir into the cucumber, chill and serve.

The next two recipes are from India.

Potato Raita

Serves 4

2 large potatoes, peeled and sliced
150 g (5 oz) Loseley Natural Yoghurt
paprika pepper

Par-boil the potatoes in boiling, well-salted water for 7–10 minutes. Drain and cool. When cold, toss into the yoghurt and sprinkle with paprika. Serve chilled.

Tomato and Cucumber Raita

Serves 4

½ cucumber, peeled and diced
1 tbsp onion, finely chopped
2 firm tomatoes, diced
150 g (5 oz) Loseley Natural Yoghurt
1 tsp sea salt
pinch cumin (optional)

Place the cucumber and onion in a bowl and leave for an hour, then gently press any excess liquid from the cucumber. Add the diced tomato to the cucumber and stir in the yoghurt, salt and cumin (if used), turning with a spoon to coat evenly. Chill and serve.

Tzatziki

This is a Greek recipe.

1 cucumber
150 g (5 oz) Loseley Soured cream
150 g (5 oz) Loseley Lebnie
1 clove garlic, crushed
1 tsp fresh mint, chopped
1 tbsp fresh parsley, chopped
sea salt and freshly ground black pepper to taste

Coarsely grate the cucumber, leaving a few slices for decoration; drain and press out excess liquid. Beat the Loseley soured cream and lebnie together until smooth. Add the crushed garlic, herbs, salt, pepper and cucumber and mix well. Garnish with cucumber slices.

Serve with warm wholemeal bread.

MERRYDOWN

Strawberry and Cucumber Salad with Raspberry Wine Dressing

Very good served with cold fish or as a side salad.

1 cucumber (large and straight)
225 g (8 oz) strawberries (even sized)

Dressing
½ tsp dried mustard
sea salt
freshly ground pepper
½ tsp sugar
2 tbsp Merrydown Raspberry Vinegar
6 tbsp virgin or cold pressed olive oil

Thinly slice the cucumber, sprinkle with a very little sea salt and leave for 15 minutes. Rinse in cold water and pat dry with kitchen paper. Slice the strawberries.

Make the raspberry dressing by mixing all the dry ingredients, stirring in the raspberry vinegar and whisking well until mixed. Add the oil *very* slowly, so that it emulsifies.

Use a shallow white dish and arrange an overlapping flat circle of cucumber rings around the outer edge of the dish. Working towards the centre, arrange alternate overlapping rings of cucumber and strawberries, to give the effect of a large flower. Spoon over the raspberry dressing just before serving.

PAUL'S TOFU

Flageolet Beans with Tofu and Avocado Vinaigrette

350 g (12 oz), dry weight, flageolet beans

Dressing
50 g (2 oz) Paul's Firm Tofu
½ good size avocado
1 clove garlic, crushed
1 tbsp olive oil
2 tbsp lemon juice
1 tsp Dijon mustard
½ tsp clear honey
sea salt and freshly ground black pepper to taste

Wash the beans and remove any stones. Soak overnight, changing the water three times. Rinse. Bring to the boil, boil for 5 minutes and then simmer for 40 minutes or until soft. Add a little sea salt 10 minutes before the end of the cooking time. Drain and put in a serving bowl.

Set steel blades in position on a food processor. Blend all the dressing ingredients except the salt and pepper until smooth. Pour into a small bowl. Season with sea salt and freshly ground black pepper and stir into the warm beans. Marinate for a few hours before serving, stirring occasionally to coat the beans well.

Spiced Broccoli Salad with Tofu Mayonnaise

225 g (8 oz) fresh or frozen broad beans, lightly cooked
350 g (12 oz) broccoli florets, lightly steamed for 10 minutes
2 medium carrots cut into thin 3.5 cm (1½") sticks
2 tbsp sunflower oil
1 tsp ground coriander
1 tsp ground cumin seeds
1 dessertspoon lemon juice
1 dessertspoon shoyu
2 tbsp chopped chives or spring onions (use green ends also) to garnish
Basic Tofu Mayonnaise made with Paul's Firm Tofu *(see page 34 for recipe)*

Drain the broad beans and place in a serving bowl with the broccoli. Heat the oil in a frying pan and sauté the carrots over moderate heat until just beginning to soften – about 5–6 mins. Stir in the spices and cook gently for 1 minute. Add the lemon juice and shoyu, coating the carrots well. Stir carefully into the beans and broccoli and leave to cool. Sprinkle the chopped chives or spring onions over the salad and serve with Tofu Mayonnaise.

The salad can be served hot as an accompaniment to a main meal dish.

SUNWHEEL

Avocado, Orange and Onion Appetizer

6 medium oranges, peeled (take off as much pith as possible)
1 medium onion (approx. 150 g/5 oz when peeled)
1 medium avocado, peeled and stoned
3 tbsp Sunwheel Cold Pressed Safflower or Sunflower Oil
rind of 1 orange, very finely grated
2 tbsp lemon juice
¼ tsp freshly ground black pepper
¼ tsp mustard powder

½ level tsp clear honey
sea salt to taste (about ½ level tsp seems to be about right)
1 tbsp very finely chopped parsley and a bunch of watercress to garnish

Slice the oranges very thinly on a plate. Pour off the juice and save. Slice the onion very thinly in rings. Now place the avocado, oil, orange rind, lemon juice and saved orange juice, pepper, mustard, honey and salt in a liquidizer and blend together for 1 minute. Taste and add a little more seasoning or lemon juice if preferred.

Arrange the orange slices and onion rings on a serving dish, overlapping each other in circles. Place sprigs of watercress around the edge and in the centre. Pour on the avocado dressing, still allowing the orange and onion rings to be seen. Sprinkle a little parsley in a circle 2.5 cm/1" from the central watercress sprig.

Chinese Bean Sprout Salad with Sweet and Sour Dressing

350 g (12 oz) bean sprouts
100 g (4 oz) small button mushrooms
1 small green pepper, de-seeded and finely chopped
1 good size carrot, very thinly sliced in slanting ovals
1 bunch spring onions, cut in thin rings (use as much of the green stems as possible)
100 g (4 oz) fresh pineapple or peaches, chopped

Dressing
4 tbsp Sunwheel Cold Pressed Sesame or Sunflower Oil
1½ tbsp cider vinegar or lemon juice
1½ tbsp Sunwheel Shoyu
1 level tsp clear honey
¼ level tsp mustard powder
good pinch five spice or allspice
1 rounded tsp fresh ginger, grated
1 clove garlic, crushed

First mix all the ingredients for the dressing. Shake well in a screw-top jar and let the flavours merge for one hour before using. When ready, mix all the salad ingredients in a serving bowl and spoon over the dressing. You might not need all the dressing. Any left over will keep for a few weeks in the refrigerator.

Lettuce and Nasturtium Salad

1 good size Webb lettuce
large handful of nasturtium flowers

Dressing
2 egg yolks, hard-boiled
4 tbsp Sunwheel Cold Pressed Olive Oil
1½ tbsp lemon juice or *cider vinegar*
1 level tsp made mustard
sea salt and freshly ground black pepper
few chopped chives to garnish

Break off the lettuce leaves and leave whole unless very big. Wash and shake well. Place in a serving dish and arrange the nasturtium flowers on top. To make the dressing, mash the egg yolks and beat in 1 tablespoon of the olive oil. Then stir in the lemon juice or cider vinegar, mustard and the remaining oil. Stir well, season with sea salt and pepper and pour over the salad. Garnish with chopped chives.

Mediterranean Salad

2 medium potatoes, steamed, peeled and cubed
1 small green pepper, de-seeded and chopped
1 small red pepper, de-seeded and chopped
175 g (6 oz) piece bulb fennel, sliced
2 medium courgettes, washed, chopped into 2.5 cm
    (1″) sticks, soaked in cider vinegar for 10
    minutes, then drained
1 small onion, peeled and finely chopped
4 large tomatoes, chopped into segments
2 tbsp fresh parsley, chopped
1 tsp oregano
crisp lettuce leaves (Cos or *Webb) to serve*
3 large eggs, hard-boiled⎱
12 olives, halved⎰ *for garnish*
Real Mayonnaise, made with Sunwheel Cold
    Pressed Olive Oil *(see page 35)*

Mix all the ingredients together, except the lettuce, eggs and olives. When ready to serve, scoop large spoonfuls of the salad on to the crisp lettuce leaves, top with the olives, sliced eggs and spoonfuls of Real Mayonnaise. For this salad make the mayonnaise with Sunwheel cold pressed olive oil and blend in a large clove of garlic before spooning on to the salad.

Tabbouleh with Pine Kernels

This salad made with bulgur wheat is delicious served with thick natural yoghurt or cottage cheese. You can add many other vegetables to the bulgur if you wish.

225 g (8 oz) bulgur wheat
3 tbsp Sunwheel Shoyu
1 onion, small to medium, peeled
25 g (1 oz) parsley, finely chopped
15 g (½ oz) mint, finely chopped
6 firm tomatoes, cut in small wedges
3 tbsp Sunwheel Cold Pressed Olive or Sesame Oil
3 tbsp lemon juice
2 cloves garlic, peeled and chopped
1 very level tsp ground coriander
½ very level tsp ground cumin
½ tsp freshly ground black pepper
50 g (2 oz) pine kernels
1 bunch watercress to garnish

Soak the bulgur in enough boiling water to cover it by 2.5 cm (1″). Add 2 tablespoons of shoyu, cover and leave to stand for 20–30 minutes. (No cooking is required.) Roughly chop the onion and add the finely chopped parsley and mint. Fork into the chopped tomatoes. In a bowl blend the oil, lemon juice, garlic, coriander, cumin, pepper and the rest of the shoyu, until the dressing emulsifies. Pour this over the tomato mixture and then fork the dressing and vegetables into the prepared bulgur wheat. Fork in the pine kernels, leaving a few on top. Garnish with sprigs of watercress.

You can use buckwheat as a wholesome and very tasty alternative in this recipe.

Opposite: **Hugli** *(clockwise from top) Carrot Cooler, page 12, Pumpkin Soup, page 12, Sprouted Soya Bean, Lemon and Parsley Soup, page 13*

WESTERN ISLES

—Almond Rice Salad—

1 tbsp Western Isles Brown Rice Vinegar or *wine vinegar*
1 tbsp Western Isles Miso
2 tbsp water
340 g (12 oz), cooked weight, Western Isles Quick Rice *(175 g/6 oz dry weight rice)*
2 sticks celery, chopped (use centre parts)
½ cup toasted almonds, crushed
1 sprig mint, chopped

Mix the vinegar, miso and water together and combine with the rice, celery and almonds. Sprinkle with mint and serve.

To vary this salad, toss in Western Isles Mayonnaise, chill in the refrigerator for 1 hour, garnish and serve.

—Dulse Coleslaw—

170 g (6 oz) red or *white cabbage (or some of both), shredded*
handful of Western Isles Dulse, *washed and chopped*
2 medium carrots, sliced into matchsticks or *grated*
1 pepper (red or *green, or half of each), de-seeded and diced*
1 tbsp walnut pieces
1 tbsp raisins
Western Isles Mayonnaise *to taste*

Mix all the ingredients together and add the mayonnaise. Allow to marinate for half an hour before serving. Serve slightly chilled.

—Orange and Wakame Salad

A lovely salad in both appearance and taste.

Opposite: **Holland and Barrett** *Red Cabbage and Pecan Nut Salad (above) page 27, Butter Bean and Cauliflower with Pepper and Tomato Vinaigrette (below) page 25*

7.5 × 30 cm (3 × 12") strip Western Isles Wakame
1 Iceberg lettuce
1 bunch red radishes, cut into slices or petal shapes
3 oranges
2 tbsp Western Isles Miso

After soaking the wakame for 10 minutes, chop it finely and boil it in the soaking water for 10 minutes. Break up the lettuce into leaves and place in a bowl. Add the wakame and radishes. Peel two oranges, divide into half-segments and add to the salad. Dissolve the miso in the juice of the third orange and pour over the salad as a dressing.

WHOLE EARTH

—Brown Rice— and Baked Bean Salad

3 spring onions, chopped
2 stalks celery, chopped
1 red pepper, de-seeded and chopped
2 cans Whole Earth Brown Rice and Vegetables
1 can Whole Earth Campfire Style Baked Beans
25 g (1 oz) flaked almonds, toasted

Dressing
3 tbsp olive oil
1½ tbsp wine vinegar or *brown rice vinegar*
1 clove garlic, crushed
¼ tsp mustard powder
dash sea salt and freshly ground black pepper

Combine the vegetables with the Brown Rice and Baked Beans. Mix the dressing ingredients well. Pour the dressing over the salad, fold gently to mix, and top with the toasted almond flakes.

—Mixed Bean Salad—

1 can Whole Earth Baked Beans
1 small can butter beans, drained
2 stalks celery, finely chopped
1 onion, finely chopped
3 tbsp vinegar
2 tbsp olive oil

Combine all the ingredients. This salad is delicious served with wholewheat pitta bread and crisp, fresh lettuce leaves.

Dressings

GAYELORD HAUSER NATURAL SEASONINGS

Gayelord Hauser's Favourite Salad Dressing

4 tbsp olive oil
1 tsp spring onion, finely chopped
2–3 level tbsp wine vinegar or *cider vinegar*
2 level tsp Spike Seasoning
1 pinch of Santay Pure Garlic Seasoning
1 tsp Herbal Bouquet

Combine all ingredients. Keep refrigerated and shake well before each use.

Luscious French Dressing

1 clove garlic, crushed
4 tbsp wine vinegar or *2 tbsp cider vinegar mixed with 2 tbsp lemon juice*
1 tbsp Vege-Sal
½ tsp Spike Seasoning

1 tsp dry mustard
1 tsp honey
225 ml (8 fl oz) sunflower oil

Mix all ingredients in a covered jar and shake. Leave to stand in the refrigerator for 48 hours. This is sufficient for several salads. Keep refrigerated.

Yoghurt and Dill Dressing

175 g (6 oz) plain yoghurt
1 tbsp fresh dill
½ tsp Onion Magic
½ tsp lemon juice or *vinegar*

Combine all ingredients and mix well. Serve chilled with mixed salad.

LOSELEY

Soured Cream Dressing

1 clove garlic, crushed
1 tbsp wine vinegar
1 tsp French mustard
sea salt and freshly ground black pepper
150 g (5 oz) Loseley Soured Cream

Combine all the ingredients in a small bowl and the dressing is ready to serve.

PAUL'S TOFU

Basic Tofu Mayonnaise

A blender or food processor is ideal for making mayonnaise but you can use a hand whisk.

225 g (8 oz) Paul's Firm Tofu
3 tbsp soya milk or goat's milk
3 tbsp lemon juice
1 scant tsp sea salt
½ tsp dry mustard
freshly ground black pepper
4 tbsp sunflower oil

Blend all the ingredients except the oil until smooth. With the motor on high speed trickle in the oil until well mixed.

Variation

To make a pink mayonnaise, halve the quantities given for the Basic Mayonnaise and add:

1 clove garlic, peeled and crushed
1 small red pepper, de-seeded and finely chopped
1 level tbsp capers

Blend all ingredients together until smooth and pink. Great for potato salad.

Paul's Tofu and Avocado Dressing

100 g (4 oz) Paul's Firm Tofu, broken into pieces
1 medium avocado, peeled, stoned and roughly chopped
3 tbsp olive or sunflower oil
2 tbsp lemon juice
¼ tsp mustard powder
¼ tsp freshly ground black pepper
½ scant tsp sea salt
½ tsp clear honey
1 small clove garlic, crushed

Blend all the ingredients in a liquidizer or food processor until smooth and pale green in colour. This looks and tastes beautiful on a mixed green salad: crisp lettuce, watercress, cucumber, parsley, etc. Just trickle the dressing over the arranged salad and fork in when ready to serve.

SUNWHEEL

Umeboshi salt pickled plums are one of the most special of Japanese foods. They are highly prized for their health-giving properties, being rich in enzymes and lactic acid. They are an essential ingredient in a well-balanced Japanese meal as an aid to digestion.

Umeboshi Mayonnaise Sauce

Here is a recipe using the plums which goes particularly well with any fish dish or fresh green salad. Best made in a cool atmosphere.

2 umeboshi plums
150 ml (5 fl oz) water
1 egg yolk
¾ tsp ground coriander
approx 3 tbsp Sunwheel Cold Pressed Olive or Sesame Oil
1 tbsp parsley, finely chopped
1 tbsp spring onions, finely chopped

Boil the plums in the water for 5 minutes. Drain and discard the water. Squash the plums with a potato masher, then press with a spoon through a sieve to extract as much fruit purée as possible – you will need 1 tablespoon. Leave until completely cold. Put the egg yolk and the coriander in a small bowl with the umeboshi juice and, using a liquidizer or food processor, blend together. While blending add the oil drop by drop until the mixture thickens. (To do this well use a dropper for the oil.) Scoop out, and stir in the parsley and spring onions. Taste, and add a little sea salt if necessary.

Real Mayonnaise

225 ml (8 fl oz) Sunwheel Cold Pressed Sunflower, Safflower or Olive Oil
1 egg and 1 egg yolk
½ tsp mustard powder
scant ½ tsp freshly ground black pepper
½ tsp sea salt
1 tbsp fresh lemon juice
1 tbsp cider vinegar or wine vinegar

Place the egg and egg yolk, mustard, pepper, salt, and 2 tablespoons of the oil in a blender. Switch to low speed and blend together, then very slowly trickle in the oil, still on low speed. When thick pour in the lemon juice and vinegar. If it should curdle just scoop the mixture out, put another egg in the blender and gradually pour in the curdled mixture, keeping the blender speed low.

WHOLE EARTH

The next two recipes use Whole Earth Tomato Ketchup. Ketchups originated in Malaya, where early Dutch and English settlers soon discovered the flavour-enhancing properties of the native soya-based sauces. The Malay word *kechap* means 'taste'.

Russian Dressing

175 g (6 oz) mayonnaise
1 tbsp grated horseradish
2 tbsps Whole Earth Tomato Ketchup
1 tsp grated onion

Mix all ingredients well together. Delicious as a dip with raw or cold cooked vegetables.

Thousand Island Dressing

To the Russian Dressing ingredients above, add:

2 tbsp green olives, minced
1 tbsp green pepper, de-seeded and chopped
1 egg, hard-boiled and chopped
2 tbsp fresh parsley, chopped

Mix all the dressing ingredients together and serve with tossed salads.

3
LIGHT VEGETABLE DISHES

ALLINSON

Vegetable Fritters

Makes about 16

If you are making these for children you could leave out the onion and red pepper, but it is best to try them with these vegetables the first time as I feel children should get used to different flavours.

75 g (3 oz) Allinson Original 100% Wholewheat Flour, *plain*
25 g (1 oz) Allinson's Soya Flour
1 level tbsp baking powder
½ tsp sea salt
1 large egg
225 ml (8 fl oz) milk
1 small onion, peeled and finely chopped
1 small red pepper, de-seeded and finely chopped (optional)
175 g (6 oz) frozen sweetcorn, lightly cooked and drained
75 g (3 oz) Cheddar cheese, grated
sunflower oil for frying

Mix together the flours, baking powder, egg, salt and milk until smooth batter consistency. Pour this over the chopped onion and red pepper (if used), stir in the cooled, cooked sweetcorn and the cheese. Leave to stand for 30 minutes. Stir again. Heat 3 tablespoons of oil in a frying pan. Use 1 tablespoon of the mixture for each fritter, spreading them gently with the back of a spoon. Cook three at a time. Let them get crisp and golden on one side using moderate heat for 2 minutes, then turn over with a palette knife and cook for another 2 minutes. Serve with a salad for a very substantial and well balanced lunch or light supper dish.

BROADLAND

Stuffed Peppers

Serves 3–4

4 peppers (red, green or yellow)
100 g (4 oz) onion, peeled and shredded
1 small cucumber, peeled and chopped
a little vegetable oil
215 g (7½ oz) can sweetcorn
100 g (4 oz) Broadland Vegetable Suet
225 g (8 oz) tomatoes, skinned and diced
sea salt
freshly ground black pepper and celery salt to season
100 g (4 oz) Cheddar cheese, grated

Cut a slice from stalk end of each pepper and remove the seeds and pith. Bring the peppers to boil in plenty of water, then plunge them into cold water. Gently fry the onion and cucumber in the oil. Mix all the remaining ingredients together, except the cheese, and spoon the mixture into the peppers. Stand the stuffed peppers in an oven-proof dish, sprinkle with the cheese and bake at 180°C/350°F/Gas Mark 4 for 15 minutes.

CARRABAY

Carrageen Seafood Chowder

Serves 8

175 g (6 oz) each shredded onion, celery, mixed green and red peppers, potato and carrots
275 g (10 oz) can tomatoes
450 g (1 lb) smoked fish, diced
450 g (1 lb) white fish, diced
50 g (2 oz) polyunsaturated margarine
50 g (2 oz) Carrabay Carrageen
1.2 litres (2 pints) fish stock
sea salt and freshly ground black pepper

Melt the margarine and sauté all the vegetables, stirring to prevent sticking. Add the fish and continue cooking. Add the stock and bring to the boil, then add the carrageen and simmer until the vegetables are tender. Remove the carrageen, season and serve with brown bread or hot rolls.

DOVES FARM

Tempura or Pakora

Serves 3–4

Tempura is the Japanese name for this delightful method of cooking vegetables; Pakora is its Indian equivalent. The batter can be made more spicy by adding curry powder or chilli powder if you wish. I have only spiced it moderately in the recipe to suit most tastes. It is not strictly a main meal but it would be quite sufficient for a light lunch as the batter is protein-packed.

100 g (4 oz) Doves Farm Gram Flour (chick pea flour)
50 g (2 oz) Doves Farm Soya Flour
50 g (2 oz) Doves Farm Brown Rice Flour
1 level tsp coriander powder
1 level tsp sea salt
1 level tsp baking powder
425 ml (15 fl oz) milk
soya oil for deep frying
460 g (1 lb) raw vegetables (see note at end of recipe)
shoyu to serve

Blend the flours, sea salt, coriander, baking powder and milk together until smooth. Leave to stand for 1 hour and stir before using. Heat the oil to very hot as for cooking chips. Dip the vegetables in the batter and deep fry until golden brown. (Watch the oil does not burn, turn it down a little as you fry but still keep it quite hot.) Drain the Tempura on absorbent kitchen paper. To serve, sprinkle on a little shoyu. Just a few vegetables will make a huge plate of Tempura.

Note The raw vegetables are a matter of choice. I suggest thin onion rings, thinly sliced potato with skins on, small cauliflower florets, whole small mushrooms, sliced courgettes and aubergines. It is best to salt aubergine slices first and leave them to stand for 30 minutes, rinse and wipe before dipping them into the batter.

GAYELORD HAUSER NATURAL SEASONINGS

Mushroom Supreme

Serves 4

450 g (1 lb) large mushrooms
2 tbsp unsalted butter
2 tbsp shoyu
1 tsp Vege-Sal
2 tsp Hauser Broth

Wash the mushrooms and remove the stems. In a large, heavy, frying pan, melt the butter and add the mushrooms, cut side down. Cook for about 5 minutes on a medium heat. Turn the mushrooms and cook for about 5 minutes more. The mushrooms should be lightly browned. Sprinkle the Vege-Sal and shoyu over the mushrooms, making sure each mushroom is sprinkled. Mix the Hauser Broth with ¼ cup of water and pour into the pan and heat for a few minutes. Serve the mushrooms and sauce on triangles of wholewheat toast.

Oven Baked Beans

Serves 6

225 g (8 oz) haricot beans, dry weight
5 tbsp vegetable oil
4 tbsp molasses
1 onion, peeled and cut into wedges
1 tsp Vege-Sal
juice of ¼ lemon (about 2 dessertspoons)
1 tbsp tahini

Soak the beans overnight, changing the water three times. Rinse and boil vigorously in fresh water for 20 minutes. Drain the beans and place them in a casserole. Add the vegetable oil, molasses, onion, Vege-Sal and enough hot water almost to cover. Bake in the oven, covered, at 130°C/250°F/Gas Mark ½ for about 1½ hours until the beans are soft, stirring occasionally. Add hot water as needed to keep the beans almost covered. When the beans are tender, stir in the lemon juice and tahini. Remove the lid from the casserole and return to the oven until the top is browned. Serve garnished with parsley.

GRANOSE

Moh-Moh Dumplings with Minced Savoury Cuts

Makes 10

This recipe is adapted from a traditional Tibetan delicacy which I first found in the *Odiyan Country Cook Book* by Bill Farthing. Usually the dumplings are stuffed with minced meat and served in a meat-based soup, but I have experimented with various fillings such as soya mince, beans and vegetables; and, for a sweet delight, apple, raisin and cinnamon. All have been greatly enjoyed. It's well worth learning to make these dumplings.

275 g (10 oz) wheatmeal flour, plain
½ tsp sea salt
250 ml (about 9 fl oz) water

Filling
213 g (17½ oz) can Granose Savoury Cuts
2 tbsp sunflower oil
2 cloves garlic
½ tsp fresh ginger, grated (optional)
1 heaped tsp tomato purée
1 tbsp fresh parsley, chopped or coriander leaves, chopped
50 g (2 oz) each of minced onion, celery, mushrooms and red pepper
1 tbsp shoyu
few drops Tabasco sauce, to your own taste
50 g (2 oz) almonds, roughly ground

First make the filling. Mince the Savoury Cuts (reserve the sauce). Heat the oil in a pan and over low heat sauté the minced Savoury Cuts with the garlic for just 1 minute. One by one, stir in the ginger, tomato purée, parsley or coriander and minced vegetables. Cook for 2 minutes only. Add the shoyu, Tabasco and almonds and mix well. Cool the mixture by placing a piece of muslin in a colander and spooning the mixture into this. Leave to get completely cold. You will get a little juice dripping through. Save this for your sauce or soup.

Put the flour and salt into a mixing bowl and stir in the water. Form into a dough and knead in the bowl for 1 minute, then knead the dough on a floured worktop for 2 minutes more with lightly floured hands. Roll the dough with your hands into a sausage shape and cut into 10 equal portions. Place these in a polythene bag so that the dough does not dry out as you roll each piece out. Form each piece into a ball with your hands, then roll out into a small circle about 6 cm/2½" in diameter. Flatten the edges so that the centre is thicker to hold the filling. Hold the circle of dough cupped in one hand and fill the centre with about 1 tablespoon of the cold filling mixture. Pinch the edges of the dough into thin pleats and stretch the pleated edges up over the filling, twisting them into a knob at the top. Flatten the knob, which will then make the dumpling look like a little flattened doughnut. Grease a steamer, place the stuffed dumplings into this and steam for 20 minutes.

These are delicious served with most sauces and great in soups. I can't resist eating them all on their own. Try them in a Vegetable Soup. Simply add to the soup 7 minutes before the end of the cooking time.

HOLLAND & BARRETT

Stuffed Peppers with Rice and Pine Kernels

Serves 4 as an appetizer or 2 as a main meal with a fresh green salad.

100 g (4 oz) Holland & Barrett Long Grain Brown
  Rice
4 good size peppers (red and green mixed – choose squat, not pointed, ones)
1 medium onion, peeled
3 tbsp sunflower or *olive oil*
2 cloves garlic, crushed
100 g (4 oz) mushrooms
1 tbsp fresh parsley, chopped
1 large sprig mint, chopped
1 level tsp coriander seeds, crushed
4 large ripe tomatoes
1 tbsp tomato purée
1 tbsp lemon juice
75 g (3 oz) Holland & Barrett Pine Kernels
sea salt and freshly ground black pepper
50 g (2 oz) grated Cheddar or *Parmesan cheese*

Wash the rice well by placing it in a sieve and running cold water over it for 1 minute. Bring to the boil in double its volume of cold salted water, turn down to simmer and cook, tightly lidded, for 35 minutes. Drain if necessary and leave in a colander until needed.

Cut a circle round the top of each pepper to remove the stem and seeds. Place the peppers in a saucepan, cover with boiling water and leave to stand for 5 minutes. Drain well and set aside. Set the slicing plate in position on a food processor. Cut the onion in half, pack each half into the feed tube and slice. Scoop out and replace the slicing plate. Heat the oil in a heavy-based pan and sauté the onion and garlic for 7 minutes. Wash and wipe the mushrooms, pack into the feed tube of the food processor, caps to the outside, and slice. Sauté the mushrooms with the onion and garlic for a further 3 minutes. Add the parsley, mint and crushed coriander and continue cooking for 1 minute. Stir the cooked rice into the vegetables and, continuing to stir to coat the rice, cook for 1 minute more. Set the steel blades in position. Skin the tomatoes by cutting a small circle round the stem area, blanch in boiling water for 1 to 2 minutes, peel and roughly chop. Put in the processor bowl and blend until thoroughly mashed. Add the mashed tomatoes, tomato purée, lemon juice, pine kernels, sea salt and freshly ground black pepper to the rice mixture and cook for another minute.

Arrange the prepared peppers, open end up, in an oiled ovenproof dish. Spoon the rice mixture into the peppers and sprinkle on the grated cheese. Add 2 tablespoons of water to the dish and bake just above the centre of the oven at 180°C/350°F/Gas Mark 4, for 35–40 minutes.

LONDON HERB & SPICE CO.

French Beans in Sour Cream

Serves 4

450 g (1 lb) young French beans, topped and tailed
2 London Herb & Spice Co. Cook Bags for
  Vegetables
a little sea salt
1 150 g (5 oz) carton sour cream
1 small clove garlic, skinned and crushed
¼ tsp mustard powder
½ level tsp honey
¼ level tsp sea salt and a few twists of freshly ground black pepper
2 tsp lemon juice
1 tbsp olive oil

Bring approximately 275 ml/10 fl oz water to the boil, put in the cook bags, add about ½ level teaspoon of sea salt, add the trimmed beans and simmer with the lid on for about 5–7 minutes. Drain and place the beans in a serving dish. Mix the sour cream with the rest of the ingredients and stir into the still-warm cooked beans. Keep warm in the bottom of the oven, if serving hot, or chill for 30 minutes if serving cold.

LOSELEY

Brussels Sprouts with Almonds

Serves 4

675 g (1½ lb) brussels sprouts, prepared or frozen
150 g (5 oz) Loseley Soured Cream
15 g (½ oz) flaked almonds, toasted
freshly ground black pepper

Boil the sprouts lightly in salted water until just cooked. Drain, and return to the saucepan. Sprinkle with black pepper. Add Loseley soured cream and gently turn the sprouts in the cream over a low heat. Transfer to a serving dish and sprinkle with the toasted almonds.

Evelyn's Samosas

Makes 8–10

Samosas are deep-fried curry-stuffed pasties which melt in your mouth. When having a curry evening I serve these as an appetiser with drinks before the main meal, to stave off the hunger pangs of my guests which are caused by the delicious aromatic smells created when cooking these foods. Try to obtain chapati flour. It is wheat flour but much lighter than the wheat flour generally used in baking in Britain. The variety of fillings which can be used is endless but I have given below a quick, cheap, tasty and delicious filling for you to try.

350 g (6 oz) wholemeal chapati flour
pinch sea salt
100 ml (4 fl oz) Loseley Natural Yoghurt
3 tbsp sunflower oil or ghee (clarified butter)
soya oil for deep frying
little milk or milk and egg mixed, for brushing

Filling
2 tbsp corn or sunflower oil
1 large onion, peeled and finely chopped
1 rounded tsp garam masala
1 tsp fresh ginger, grated
1 tsp fenugreek leaf (methi)
1 level tsp coriander seeds, freshly ground
1 scant tsp cayenne pepper or chilli powder
2 good size potatoes, scrubbed, cut up in small chunks and steamed for 10 minutes, until soft but not mushy
1 cup (approx. 106 g/4 oz) frozen peas, cooked for 4 minutes in boiling water. (You can use leftover cooked lentils or any other pulses instead.)

Blend the flour, salt, yoghurt, oil or ghee together to form a soft dough. Knead gently together for a few minutes, shape into a ball, place in a bowl and cover with a plate. Leave to stand for 1 hour.

Sauté the onion in the oil until soft (about 7 minutes). Stir in all the spices and fry gently for 1 minute. Add the potatoes and continue to fry for another 2 minutes. Finally stir in the peas or leftover pulses. Leave the mixture to get cold.

When you are ready to make the Samosas, roll out the dough as thinly as possible on a floured surface and cut into 7.5 cm/3" squares. Place 1 tablespoon of the curried vegetable mixture in the centre of each square, brush the edges with the milk or milk and egg mixture, then fold over corner-to corner to make an envelope shape. Press the edges well together. Deep fry in hot oil until golden brown on both sides. Drain on absorbent kitchen paper and serve as soon as possible.

Leeks with Yoghurt and Tarragon Sauce

Serves 4

6 leeks
425 ml (15 fl oz) water
1 scant tsp sea salt
½ tsp freshly ground black pepper
½ tsp fennel seeds
a few sprigs parsley
1 bay leaf
chopped parsley or tarragon to garnish

Sauce
275 ml (10 fl oz) Loseley Natural Yoghurt
3 egg yolks
1 dessertspoon lemon juice
½ tsp mustard powder
½ tsp dried tarragon
sea salt and freshly ground black pepper

Trim off the coarse leaves from the leeks. Slit them to within 5 cm/2″ of the root end and wash thoroughly. Put the water, salt, black pepper, fennel seeds, parsley and bay leaf in a saucepan, bring to the boil and lower the heat to simmer for 15 minutes. Strain off the liquid and reserve. Cook leeks in the strained liquid for 10 minutes or until tender. Leave to marinate in the liquid while you make the sauce.

Set the steel blades in position on a food processor. Put the yoghurt, egg yolks, lemon juice, mustard powder and tarragon into the processor bowl and blend for ½ minute. Pour into a heatproof bowl and season with salt and freshly ground black pepper. Place the bowl over a pan of gently simmering water and cook, stirring constantly, until it thickens – about 15 minutes. Drain the leeks and either leave whole or cut into 5 cm/2″ chunks. Arrange them in a serving dish and pour over the sauce. Garnish with a little more tarragon or parsley.

Middle Eastern Fried Carrots

Serves 4
as an accompanying vegetable

This vegetable dish goes well with either vegetarian roast or meat roast dishes.

450 g (1 lb) carrots, scrubbed and cut into 5 mm
   (¼″) slanting ovals
a little sea salt
freshly ground black pepper
1 level tbsp unbleached white flour
2 tbsp olive oil
275 ml (10 fl oz) Loseley Natural Yoghurt
1 level tbsp fresh mint, chopped
½ tsp freshly ground cumin seeds

Bring 425 ml/15 fl oz water (slightly salted) to the boil, drop in the carrots and cook for 7 minutes only. Drain (reserve the liquid for soups) and pat dry with absorbent kitchen paper. Toss the carrots in the flour to which you have added a very little sea salt and freshly ground black pepper. Heat the olive oil in a heavy-based pan and over a moderate heat sauté the carrots until golden brown. Warm the yoghurt (do not let it boil or it will curdle). Place the carrots in a warm serving dish, spoon on the yoghurt and sprinkle with the chopped mint and ground cumin seeds.

Stuffed Courgettes with Mushroom and Lemon Cream Sauce

Serves 4
as a light meal

This recipe is from my book *Vegetarian Food Processor*.

4 medium courgettes
3 tbsp cold pressed sunflower oil or *butter*
sea salt and freshly ground black pepper to taste
2 tbsp lemon juice
450 g (1 lb) button mushrooms
1 slightly rounded tbsp wheatmeal flour
1 small carton Loseley Soured Cream
1 tbsp fresh parsley, chopped
pinch cayenne pepper
2 tbsp Parmesan cheese, freshly grated (optional)

Wash the courgettes, trim off the stalks and blanch in boiling water for 2 minutes only. Drain and cut in half lengthwise. Scoop out a shallow groove in each half (reserving the pulp). Arrange the courgettes, hollow side up, in a lightly oiled ovenproof dish and brush with 1 tablespoon of the oil. Sprinkle on a little sea salt, freshly ground black pepper and 1 tablespoon of lemon juice. Cover the dish tightly and bake in the centre of the oven at 180°C/350°F/Gas Mark 4 for 25 minutes. Wash and wipe the mushrooms. Set the slicing plate of the food processor in position, pack the mushrooms into the feed tube, caps to the outside, and slice. Heat the remaining oil in a heavy-based pan and sauté the mushrooms for 1 minute, tossing them as you fry. Sprinkle with a little sea salt and black pepper and cook for a further 2 minutes. Sprinkle the flour over the mushrooms and stir briskly with a wooden spoon to blend in well. Gradually stir in the sour cream, stirring continuously until it thickens. Take off the heat. Set the steel blades in position on the food processor. Put the parsley, cayenne and courgette pulp into the processor bowl and blend to a purée. Stir the purée into the mushroom mixture and cook very gently for 1–2 minutes more. Take off the heat and stir in the remaining tablespoon of lemon juice. Spoon this mixture into the baked courgette cases. These are delicious without the cheese but, if you like it, sprinkle the Parmesan cheese on top and grill until very light golden brown.

PAUL'S TOFU

The following two recipes using Paul's delicious Firm Tofu are taken from my book *Making Your Own Home Proteins*. I like to sauté the cubed tofu in a savoury mixture before adding to soups.

Savoury Sautéed Tofu

Serves 4

350 g (12 oz) Paul's Firm Tofu
3 tbsp shoyu
75 g (3 oz) wholemeal flour, plain
1 large clove garlic, crushed with a pestle and
*   mortar with ½ tsp sea salt or ½ tsp garlic salt*
freshly ground black pepper
1 rounded tsp mixed herbs
sunflower, corn or sesame seed oil for frying

Cut the tofu into 2 cm/¾″ cubes. Sprinkle half the shoyu in a large shallow bowl, place the tofu cubes on to this and pour the rest of the shoyu on top. Leave to marinate for a few minutes while you prepare the other ingredients. Mix the flour with the garlic and salt, or garlic salt, the pepper and mixed herbs in a shallow bowl. Shake off the excess shoyu from the tofu pieces and dip each one, coating well, in the flour mixture. Heat 6 mm/¼″ of oil in a frying pan and fry the tofu, turning it until it is golden brown on all sides. Drain on absorbent kitchen paper and keep warm in a low oven until needed, or cool if intending to use in a salad.

SLYMBRED

Slymbred Bacon-Stuffed Onions

Serves 1

1 large onion, peeled (leave whole)
2 slices Slymbred, crumbled
2 rashers lean bacon, chopped (cut all fat off)
1 tbsp sour cream
sea salt and freshly ground black pepper to taste
knob of butter or vegetable margarine

Cook the onion in boiling, slightly salted, water for 30 minutes. Drain and reserve 5 tablespoons of the onion water. Cut a slice off the top of the onion and carefully remove the centre, leaving about 1 cm/½″ thick onion shell. Chop the onion centre finely and mix with crumbled Slymbred and the bacon. Bind with the cream and season with salt and pepper. Return the mixture to the onion shell. Stand the filled onion in a shallow, heat-proof dish and pour in the onion water. Top with the knob of butter or margarine and bake, uncovered, in the centre of a moderate oven (190°C/375°F/Gas Mark 5) for 40–45 minutes, basting at intervals.

SUNWHEEL

Mushroom and Almond Stuffed Popovers

Makes 12–16

Light and delicious, these popovers can be served as an hors d'oeuvre or as a special Sunday breakfast treat. Toast the whole almonds in the bottom of the oven while the popovers are cooking.

150 g (5 oz) brown wheatmeal flour, plain
1/2 tsp sea salt
3 eggs, beaten
225 ml (8 fl oz) milk
2 tbsp Sunwheel Cold Pressed Sunflower Oil
Filling
225 g (8 oz) small button mushrooms, thinly sliced
2 tbsp Sunwheel Cold Pressed Sunflower or Sesame oil
50 g (2 oz) almonds (toasted while the popovers are cooking)
2 tbsp fresh parsley, very finely chopped
2 tsp lemon juice
1 tsp Sunwheel Shoyu
freshly ground black pepper

Pre-heat the oven to 220°C/425°F/Gas Mark 7. Grease the popover tins (or bun tins) and heat them in the pre-heated oven. Mix all the ingredients together with a hand whisk, blender or food processor. When the tins are smoking hot, fill them to just under halfway up the sides with batter and bake for 20 minutes. Reduce the heat to 180°C/350°F/Gas Mark 4 and continue to bake for 15 minutes more. You will obviously have two trays, so place one just above the centre and one just below the centre of the oven and change them over after 30 minutes of the cooking time – not before or they will go flat. When cooked the popovers will automatically sink in the centre ready to be stuffed. Stuff them while they are still hot, so make the stuffing while the popovers are cooking.

To make the stuffing, sauté the mushrooms in the oil for 3 minutes only. Chop the toasted almonds to a rough breadcrumb consistency and stir into the mushrooms. Add the other ingredients and cook for just 1 minute to evaporate some of the juices. Spoon into the hot popovers and serve immediately.

Wholewheat Breakfast Pancakes

Makes 12 good size pancakes

These pancakes are slightly richer than usual but as they form a main part of the meal if eaten at breakfast the 3 eggs in this delicious batter can be thrown in without guilt. I love these spread with Sunwheel no sugar Pear and Apple spread and a dollop of yoghurt cheese. To make the cheese just drip a carton of natural yoghurt through muslin overnight and scrape off the thick, creamy cheese in the morning. Roll them up with this filling while the pancakes are still hot. Make these thicker than the usual crêpe – you will need a pancake pan or griddle for best results. Separating the eggs gives you a light, fluffy pancake.

225 g (8 oz) 100% wholewheat flour, plain
2 tsp baking powder
1 level tsp sea salt (optional)
1 level tbsp clear honey (optional)
425 ml (15 fl oz) milk
4 tbsp Sunwheel Cold Pressed Sunflower or Safflower Oil
3 eggs, separated
a little oil to brush pan

Sift the flour, baking powder and salt (if used) together. Whisk the honey (if used), milk, oil and egg yolks together. Whisk the egg whites until stiff and fold in without beating. Brush the pan or griddle with a little oil and heat until very hot. Turn down to a moderate heat and spoon 2 tablespoons of the mixture in at a time. Spread out and cook briskly on one side until the edges are golden brown and bubbles appear. Shake the pancakes loose and flick over with a palette knife. Cook other side until a light golden brown.

These are also delicious made with a mixture of wholewheat and buckwheat flour. I use say 150 g/ 5 oz wholewheat and 75 g/3 oz buckwheat. You can also add ground sesame or sunflower seeds to the batter – 2 tablespoons of either is sufficient, giving variety of flavour and extra goodness.

Japanese Seaweed Pancakes

Follow the recipe for Wholewheat Breakfast Pancakes but use 150 g (5 oz) 100% wholewheat and 75 g (3 oz) buckwheat flour, omit the honey and add the following ingredients to the batter mixture:

2 rounded tbsp Sunwheel Hiziki soaked in cold
  water for 10 minutes, then well drained (reserve
  the soaking water for stock or soup)
1 medium onion (about 6 oz/175 g in weight),
  peeled and very finely chopped

Stir the hiziki and onion into the batter mixture just
before making the pancakes. Fry as directed in the
recipe, but spread them out thinly so that the onion
and seaweed get cooked more quickly.

Delicious spread with butter or with a nutritious
mixture of Sunwheel tahini, shoyu and water. To
make the spread, simply combine 2 tablespoons of
tahini with 2 teaspoons shoyu. The mixture will
stiffen, so *slowly* incorporate enough cold water to
form a creamy consistency (about 2 tablespoons of
water will be sufficient).

WESTERN ISLES

Pepper Stew Starter

Serves 6

3 tbsp olive or sunflower oil
1 large Spanish onion, peeled and chopped
2 cloves garlic, crushed
2 large green peppers, de-seeded and chopped
2 large red peppers, de-seeded and chopped
1 level tsp marjoram
1 bay leaf
450 g (1 lb) ripe, fresh tomatoes, skinned or 425 g
  (15 oz) can tomatoes, chopped
2 tbsp Western Isles Shoyu
1 level tsp clear honey
2 tbsp lemon juice
pinch cayenne pepper (optional)
1 tbsp tomato ketchup (Whole Earth's is free from
  additives)

Heat the oil in a large, heavy-based saucepan and
sauté the onion and garlic for 10 minutes. Add the
chopped peppers to the onion and garlic and
continue to cook for 5 minutes. Add all the other
ingredients and leave to simmer gently for about 20
minutes until the juice from the tomatoes has
evaporated.

Serve hot or cold as a starter. It is also delicious
on oven-toasted wholemeal bread. Simply slice the
bread, spread with polyunsaturated margarine or
butter and bake in the oven for 15 minutes at 190°C/
375°F/Gas Mark 5 until crisp. (Whole Earth
wholemeal bread is delicious if you have no time to
bake your own.)

Vegetables in Aspic

Serves 4

This makes a delicious, appetizing summer meal.

100 g (4 oz) fresh tofu
725 ml (1¼ pints) water
Western Isles Shoyu *to taste*
25 g (1 oz) agar-agar
340 g (12 oz) carrots (or other firm vegetables), cut
  into chunks and blanched
8 broccoli spears, blanched

Boil the tofu for 5–10 minutes and cut into cubes.
Heat the water and shoyu until warm, add the agar-
agar and simmer until dissolved. Add the vegetables
and tofu and leave to set.

For variety, add cold cooked Western Isles Buckwheat Spaghetti which has been marinated in
Western Isles Brown Rice Vinegar.

WHOLE EARTH

Stuffed Tomatoes

Serves 2

1 can Whole Earth Brown Rice and Vegetables
4 large tomatoes
1 leek, chopped and sautéed
4 mushrooms, sliced and sautéed
100 g (4 oz) pine kernels or cashews (optional)
25 g (1 oz) fresh parsley, finely chopped
75 g (3 oz) Cheddar cheese, grated (optional)

Cut the tomatoes in half through the centres and
scoop out the seeds. Mix together all the remaining
ingredients except the cheese. Fill the tomato shells
with the rice mixture, sprinkle with cheese, if used,
place in an oven-proof dish, cover loosely with
greaseproof paper or aluminium foil and bake at
200°C/400°F/Gas Mark 6 for 30 minutes.

To vary this recipe try courgettes, marrow or
peppers instead of tomatoes.

4
PASTA DISHES

COUNTRY BASKET

Creamy Tuna and Spaghetti

225 g (8 oz) Country Basket Wholewheat Spaghetti
  (broken into small pieces)
25 g (1 oz) polyunsaturated margarine
25 g (1 oz) wholemeal flour
275 ml (10 fl oz) milk
Worcester Sauce
sea salt and freshly ground black pepper
juice of ½ lemon
1 green pepper, de-seeded and diced
100 g (4 oz) canned sweetcorn
75 g (3 oz) Cheddar cheese, grated
1 tbsp fresh parsley, chopped
200 g (7 oz) tuna fish

Boil the spaghetti in salted water until just tender.
Drain. Make a sauce with the margarine, flour and
milk by putting them in a saucepan over a gentle
heat and whisking into a smooth, creamy sauce.
Cook for a few minutes, then remove from the heat
and add the seasoning, lemon juice, diced peppers,
sweetcorn, 50 g/2 oz of the cheese and the chopped
parsley.

Drain the oil from the tuna and flake the fish. Add
to the sauce. Stir in the cut spaghetti, pour into a
greased oven-proof dish and sprinkle the remaining
cheese on top.

Brown under a hot grill for few minutes until
bubbling and golden brown. Serve immediately.

Spaghetti and Cauliflower Soufflé

100 g (4 oz) Country Basket Wholewheat Spaghetti
1 cauliflower, broken into florets
25 g (1 oz) wholemeal flour
25 g (1 oz) margarine
275 ml (10 fl oz) milk
sea salt and freshly ground black pepper
1 tsp mustard powder
3 eggs, separated
75 g (3 oz) frozen peas, defrosted
100 g (4 oz) cheese

Pre-heat the oven to 190°C/375°F/Gas Mark 5.

Cook the spaghetti as directed on the packet in
boiling, salted water until tender. Drain well. Cook
the florets of cauliflower in another saucepan until
just cooked, then break up even more.

Make the sauce by whisking the flour, margarine
and milk together in a saucepan over a low heat
until it thickens. Allow to boil for a few minutes,
then add the seasonings and mustard. Cool slightly
before adding the 3 egg yolks. Mix in the
cauliflower, peas, spaghetti and 75 g/3 oz of the
grated cheese. Whisk the egg whites until stiff and
gently fold into the mixture. Pour into a greased
oven-proof dish and sprinkle with the rest of the
cheese. Bake in the pre-heated oven for 35–40 mins
and serve immediately.

Broccoli makes an interesting variation for this
recipe, but if it is used omit the peas.

Spaghetti Loaf

225 g (8 oz) Country Basket Wholewheat Spaghetti
3 eggs
150 g (5 fl oz) milk or natural yoghurt
100 g (4 oz) cheese, grated
50 g (2 oz) butter or margarine
1 small onion, peeled and chopped
1 small green pepper, de-seeded and chopped
1 small red pepper, de-seeded and chopped
1 tsp sea salt and a pinch freshly ground black
    pepper

Pre-heat the oven to 180°C/350°F/Gas Mark 4.

Cook the spaghetti as directed on the packet. Rinse and drain. Lightly beat the eggs in a bowl and mix in all the other ingredients, stirring well together. Pour into a greased 450 g/1 lb loaf tin and bake in the pre-heated oven for about 40 minutes.

To serve, turn out on to a dish and serve with tomato or mushroom sauce.

Spaghetti Stir-fry

Serves 4–6

225 g (8 oz) Country Basket Wholewheat Spaghetti
2 tbsp vegetable oil
3 chicken breasts, finely sliced
1 large onion or 6 spring onions, peeled and
    chopped
1 clove garlic, crushed
2 tsp root ginger, chopped or 1 tsp ground ginger
1 red pepper, de-seeded and sliced
2 sticks celery, sliced
50 g (2 oz) mushrooms, sliced
75 g (3 oz) French beans
225 g (8 oz) bean sprouts

Sauce
1 tbsp arrowroot
275 ml (10 fl oz) chicken stock
2 tbsp shoyu
2 tbsp dry sherry
sea salt and freshly ground black pepper

Cook the spaghetti as directed on the packet and drain. Heat the oil in a large frying pan or wok. Add the pieces of chicken and stir-fry until cooked. Remove and drain on kitchen paper. Stir-fry the onion, garlic and ginger and then add the red pepper, celery, mushrooms, French beans and bean sprouts in turn.

Blend the cornflour with some of the stock and then add the remaining sauce ingredients. Return the chicken to the pan, pour on the sauce and stir-fry over a high heat, until the vegetables are tender but still crisp. Serve immediately.

Spaghetti Ring

225 g (8 oz) Country Basket Wholewheat Spaghetti
2 tbsp oil
1 onion, peeled and chopped
1 clove garlic, crushed
2 tbsp tomato purée
2 tbsp wholemeal flour
150 ml (5 fl oz) water
1 can sweetcorn with peppers, drained
1 egg, beaten
1 can meatballs in tomato sauce

Pre-heat the oven to 180°C/350°F/Gas Mark 4.

Break up the spaghetti and cook as directed on the packet. Drain. Heat the oil in a pan and add the onion and garlic. Fry for a few minutes until soft. Add the tomato purée and work in the flour and water, stirring all the time to make a thick, smooth sauce. Remove from the heat and add the tinned corn and beaten egg. Mix well and finally add the cooked spaghetti. Pour into a greased 20 cm/8″ ring mould and cover with foil. Bake in the pre-heated oven for about 30 minutes. When cooked turn out on to a warm serving dish and fill the centre with meatballs in tomato sauce, or a sauce of your choice. Alternatively, allow to cool and serve cold as a pasta salad ring filled with watercress.

Tomato Spaghetti Bake

Serves 4–6

225 g (8 oz) Country Basket Wholewheat Spaghetti
1 tbsp vegetable oil
2 tbsp margarine
1 Spanish onion, peeled and chopped
100 g (4 oz) button mushrooms (sliced)
395 g (14 oz) can tomatoes
75 g (3 oz) soya beans (soaked overnight)
2 tbsp tomato purée
sea salt and freshly ground black pepper to taste
1 bay leaf

Topping
2 cartons (total 275 g/10 fl oz) natural yoghurt
2 tsp wholemeal flour
sea salt and freshly ground black pepper
¼ tsp dried oregano

Cook the spaghetti in salted water as directed on the packet. Drain and rinse in cold water. Toss in the oil and place into a greased, oven-proof 1.5 litre/2½ pint dish. Cook the soya beans in boiling water for about 20 minutes, then drain.

Melt 1 tablespoon of the margarine, add the chopped onion and fry until transparent. Add the mushrooms and sauté a few minutes. Add the tomatoes with their juice, tomato purée, bay leaf, salt and pepper. Allow to simmer for about 10 minutes, then add the cooked beans. Cover the spaghetti with the tomato sauce mixture and then with the yoghurt topping, made by whisking all the ingredients together.

Bake in the oven at 190°C/375°F/Gas Mark 5 for about 30 minutes. Serve with a green salad.

EUVITA

Cheese Tagliatelle

Serves 4

275 g (10 oz) Euvita Wholewheat Tagliatelle
sea salt and freshly ground black pepper
75 g (3 oz) polyunsaturated margarine
75 g (3 oz) cheese, grated

Cook the tagliatelle in a large saucepan of boiling, salted water for 8 minutes, or until tender. Drain and pile into a large, warmed serving dish. Season well with pepper and salt. Cut the margarine into pieces and mix into the tagliatelle with the cheese. Serve hot.

Lasagne Rolls

Serves 4

½ packet Euvita Wholewheat Lasagne or Lasagne Verdi (green)
225 g (8 oz) minced chicken and ham in equal proportions
25 g (1 oz) polyunsaturated margarine
50 g (2 oz) mushrooms, to garnish
25 g (1 oz) brown wheatmeal flour, plain
275 ml (10 fl oz) milk
1 egg
sea salt and freshly ground black pepper
a few tomatoes, cut into quarters
a few sprigs parsley

Cook the lasagne in boiling, salted water for 5 minutes. Drain and place flat on a clean tea towel. Spread minced chicken and ham on each piece of lasagne and roll up loosely. Place in an ovenproof dish and keep warm in the oven. Melt the margarine and fry the mushrooms for 2–3 minutes. Drain and keep hot. Add the flour to the remaining margarine, stir and cook for 3 minutes, then remove from the heat and gradually add the milk. Bring to the boil, stirring constantly until thickened. Beat the egg and add to the sauce, season with salt and pepper and continue to heat gently, but do not boil. Pour the sauce over the lasagne rolls and garnish with the mushrooms, tomatoes and parsley sprigs.

sauce, cover with the remaining grated cheese and finally sprinkle the flaked almonds on top. Bake for 20–25 minutes in the pre-heated oven. Before serving, garnish with parsley. Serve with salad.

Macaroni Cheese Special

Serves 4

275 ml (10 fl oz) water
6 large tomatoes, finely chopped
pinch sea salt and freshly ground black pepper
2 bay leaves
225 g (8 oz) Euvita Wholewheat Macaroni
1–2 cloves garlic, chopped finely (optional)
1 large onion, peeled and chopped
100 g (4 oz) mushrooms, sliced
1 small green pepper, de-seeded and chopped
50 g (2 oz) polyunsaturated margarine
1 small can sweetcorn, drained
175 g (6 oz) Cheddar cheese, grated
25 g (1 oz) flaked almonds
1 tbsp fresh parsley, chopped, to garnish

Pre-heat the oven to 180°C/350°F/Gas Mark 4.
   Place the water in a saucepan and add the tomatoes, salt, pepper and bay leaves. Stir well, then gently simmer over a low heat. Bring a large saucepan of salted water to the boil, add the macaroni and cook for 10–12 minutes, covering with a lid. When cooked, drain in a colander, cover and put to one side. Fry the garlic (if used), onion, mushrooms and chopped green pepper gently in the margarine. Oil a large, deep, oven-proof dish, and put into it half the macaroni. Remove the bay leaves from the tomato sauce and spoon half the sauce over the macaroni. Spoon on the sweetcorn and half the cheese. Tip the remaining macaroni into the fried vegetables, mix well and add to the ovenproof dish. Pour on the rest of the tomato

Spaghetti Milanese

Serves 4

275 g (10 oz) Euvita Wholewheat Spaghetti
25 g (1 oz) polyunsaturated margarine
1 onion, peeled and finely chopped
25 g (1 oz) plain wheatmeal flour
275 ml (10 fl oz) water
57 g (2¼ oz) can tomato purée
¾ tsp dried mixed herbs
175 g (6 oz) lean cooked ham
100 g (4 oz) mushrooms, sliced
sea salt and freshly ground black pepper

Cook the spaghetti in a large saucepan of salted, boiling water for 10 minutes or until soft. Drain and keep hot. Melt the margarine in a large pan and fry the onion until transparent, add the flour, mix well and cook for 2–3 minutes. Remove the pan from the heat and gradually add the water. Add the tomato purée and herbs and return to the heat. Stir continuously, bring to the boil and cook until the sauce has thickened. Dice the ham and add to the sauce with the mushrooms. Season and cook for 5–10 minutes over a gentle heat. Place the spaghetti in a large serving dish, add the sauce, mix together and serve immediately.

LOSELEY

Spaghetti and Mushrooms

Serves 6

450 g (1 lb) wholewheat spaghetti
2 tbsp olive oil
sea salt and freshly ground black pepper
225 g (8 oz) button mushrooms
100 g (4 oz) butter or polyunsaturated margarine
1 tbsp unbleached white flour
150 ml (5 fl oz) dry white wine
275 g (10 oz) Loseley Natural Yoghurt
3 egg yolks
3 tbsp fresh chives, chopped

Boil the spaghetti fast in a large pan of salted water for about 15 minutes. Drain and toss in the olive oil, seasoning to taste. Meanwhile, chop and sauté the mushrooms in the butter or margarine. Sprinkle on the flour, stir in the wine and cook for a few minutes. Blend the yoghurt with the egg yolks, chives and seasoning and add to the mushrooms. Heat thoroughly, stirring with wooden spoon – don't allow the mixture to boil. Toss into or pour over the spaghetti and serve at once.

PREWETT'S

On the packets of Prewett's Main Course it states 'Serves 2' but that is only if you are using the contents to make burgers. Each packet will serve 3–4 as part of a recipe.

Pasta Medley

Serves 3–4

1 packet Prewett's Main Course, Bacon Flavour
175 ml (6 fl oz) warm water
1 tbsp Prewett's 100% Wholemeal Flour
2 tbsp vegetable oil
50 g (2 oz) onion, peeled and chopped
2 sticks celery, chopped
1 green pepper, de-seeded and chopped
1 red pepper, de-seeded and chopped

275 ml (10 fl oz) vegetable stock made with hot water and ½ vegetable stock cube
freshly ground black pepper
225 g (8 oz) wholewheat noodles
75 g (3 oz) Cheddar cheese, grated

Add the water to the bacon flavour mix and stir. Divide into 12 pieces; roll each piece into a small ball and coat with flour. Chill for 15 minutes until firm. Heat the oil in a frying pan and fry the savoury balls until an even golden brown. Add the chopped onion, celery, chopped peppers and stock, cover and simmer gently for 15 minutes. Meanwhile, cook the noodles in a separate pan of boiling salted water for 12–15 minutes, or as directed on the packet, until tender. Stir the noodles into the vegetable mixture with the cheese, season with pepper and serve.

RECORD

The following two recipes using Record pasta are firm favourites in our household, with adults and children alike.

Lasagne

Serves 6

575 ml (1 pint) skimmed milk
½ level tsp ground mace
40 g (1½ oz) unbleached white flour
1 small carton sour cream
150 g (5 oz) Parmesan or Cheddar cheese, freshly grated
sea salt and freshly ground black pepper
225 g (8 oz) Record Wholewheat Lasagne
1 tbsp olive oil
Bolognese sauce (see Spaghetti Bolognese recipe on page 68)
a little basil or marjoram

Heat the milk with the mace in a medium-sized saucepan. With a fork blend the flour with the sour cream until smooth. Stir in a little hot milk and blend well. Stir this into the hot milk, beating vigorously. Bring to the boil, still stirring, and cook for 30 seconds. Take off the heat and mix in 75 g/ 3 oz of the grated cheese and seasoning. Turn on the oven to 180°C/350°F/Gas Mark 4.

Bring a large pot of water to the boil, add a little sea salt and 1 tablespoon of oil. Slide in the sheets of lasagne one at a time. Cook for 12–15 minutes following packet directions. Drain the sheets of lasagne by draping them over the edge of a colander. Oil a large, rectangular oven-proof dish. Place a layer of lasagne in the base, spoon on half the Bolognese sauce and add another layer of lasagne. Spoon on the rest of the Bolognese sauce and top with the remaining lasagne. Pour the warm white sauce over the lasagne, sprinkle with the remaining cheese and a little basil or marjoram and bake in the preheated oven for 1 hour. If not brown enough then put under a hot grill for 2 minutes until golden brown on top.

Spaghetti or Tagliatelle Bolognese

Serves 6

100 g (4 oz) soya (TVP) mince, beef flavour
2 medium onions or 1 large Spanish onion, peeled and finely chopped
1 clove garlic, crushed
3 tbsp olive oil for frying
4 sticks celery, finely chopped
1 green pepper, de-seeded and chopped
100 g (4 oz) small button mushrooms, sliced (optional)
2 tbsp fresh parsley, chopped
1 heaped tsp basil
1/2 tsp marjoram
2 bay leaves
50 g (2 oz) hazel, almond or cashew nuts, roughly ground (optional)
794 g (1 lb 12 oz) can tomatoes, chopped
2 tbsp tomato purée
freshly ground black pepper to taste (approx. 1/2 tsp)
sea salt or 1 vegetable stock cube
1 tbsp lemon juice (optional but enhances the flavour)
350 g (12 oz) Record Wholewheat Spaghetti or Wholewheat Tagliatelle
Parmesan or Cheddar cheese, freshly grated
1 tbsp olive oil

Reconstitute the soya mince by just covering it with hot water and leave to swell for 10 minutes. Sauté the onion and garlic in 3 tablespoons of oil for 5 minutes, add the celery and sauté for another 5 minutes. Add the green pepper and mushrooms and continue frying for another 3 minutes. Stir in the parsley, basil, marjoram and bay leaves. At this stage add the reconstituted soya mince. Stir into the vegetables for 2 minutes so that it absorbs the flavours. This is important. Add the nuts and finally the tomatoes, tomato purée, pepper and sea salt or stock cube. Mix all the ingredients together well and simmer for 35 minutes. Taste and add the lemon juice if you wish.

To cook the pasta bring a large pot of water to the boil, add a little sea salt and 1 tablespoon olive oil. Slide in the pasta and cook for 15 minutes or as directed on the packet. Drain in a colander, stir in a little more oil and serve with the sauce, topped with a generous amount of grated cheese.

SUNWHEEL

Buckwheat Spaghetti Savoury with Arame and Cashew Nuts

Serves 4

Buckwheat spaghetti is a very light, thin, delicately-flavoured pasta and well worth experimenting with. Use it with Bolognese sauce as you would ordinary spaghetti, or as in this recipe with a crunchy vegetable sauce and arame.

³/₄ packet Sunwheel Buckwheat Spaghetti, *cooked as directed on the packet*
15 g (¹/₂ oz) arame, soaked in cold water for 15 mins

Sauce
2 tbsp Sunwheel Cold Pressed Sunflower Oil
1 large onion, peeled and chopped
2 cloves garlic, crushed
2 medium carrots, cut in thin, slanting ovals
2 sticks celery cut in 1.5 cm (¹/₂ in) slanting pieces (use as much of the green ends as possible)
1 good size courgette, cut in slanting ovals
1 tsp sweet mixed herbs
75–100 g (3–4 oz) small button mushrooms, sliced
100 g (4 oz) broken cashew nuts, lightly toasted in the oven
4 good size ripe tomatoes simmered for 5 minutes, then strained and mashed
1 tbsp tomato purée
1 dessertspoon lemon juice
1 tbsp Sunwheel Shoyu
freshly ground black pepper
chopped parsley or watercress to garnish

While the spaghetti is cooking, the arame soaking and the nuts toasting (15 minutes at 180°C/350°F/Gas Mark 4), sauté the onion, garlic, carrots and celery in the oil for 5 minutes. Add the courgettes and herbs and continue to sauté for 2 minutes more. Add the mushrooms and cashews. Cook and stir for 1 minute. Add the drained arame and cook and stir for 1 minute. Stir in the mashed tomatoes and tomato purée. Cook and stir for 2 minutes more. Finally stir in the lemon juice, shoyu and a few twists of freshly ground black pepper. Heat through (do not cook any more), then stir the mixture into the cooked buckwheat spaghetti and garnish with either chopped watercress or parsley. Serve with a fresh green salad.

VECON

Veconetti

Serves 3 (or 4 as a starter to a meal)

Any pasta shapes may be used for this dish.

225 g (8 oz) wholewheat pasta shapes
2 tbsp sunflower oil
1 clove garlic, chopped or *crushed*
1 onion, peeled and chopped
2 sticks celery, sliced
50 g (2 oz) shelled mixed nuts, chopped
2 large tomatoes, chopped
1 tsp dried oregano
2 tsp Vecon
freshly ground black pepper
1 cup cooked beans or *100 g (4 oz) cooked meat*
1 tbsp fresh parsley, chopped
150 ml (5 fl oz) natural yoghurt
Parmesan cheese, grated, to serve

Cook the pasta in boiling, salted water as directed on the packet. Drain, rinse and toss in 1 tablespoon of the oil. Keep the pasta warm. Heat the remaining oil in a pan, add the garlic, onion and celery and cook for 5 minutes. Stir in the nuts and cook for a further 2 minutes. Add the tomatoes, oregano and Vecon and cook for 5 minutes more. Season with pepper, stir in the cooked beans or meat and heat through. Remove the pan from the heat and stir in the parsley. Add the pasta to the pan with the yoghurt and mix gently, to coat. Pour into a warmed serving dish and sprinkle with Parmesan cheese (or hand the cheese separately).

5
MAIN MEALS

DOVES FARM

Gram Flour Curry

50 g (2 oz) Doves Farm Gram Flour *(chick pea flour)*
575 ml (1 pint) water
50 g (2 oz) butter or *polyunsaturated margarine*
1 large onion, peeled and chopped
2 cloves garlic, sliced
2 green chillies, sliced
1 tsp ground paprika
1 tsp ground fenugreek (methi)
1 tsp ground cumin
1 tsp ground turmeric
1 large tomato, chopped
1 large potato, scrubbed and diced
1 large carrot, scrubbed and diced
1 small aubergine, peeled and cubed
juice of 1 lemon
1 tsp brown sugar

Mix together the gram flour and water and set aside. Melt the butter or margarine in a large skillet and lightly fry the onion, garlic and chillies. Add the spices and stir. Add the chopped tomato to the pan, followed by the potato, carrot and aubergine. Turn down the heat and cook for about 10 minutes. Stir in the gram flour and water mixture and leave the pan gently simmering until all the vegetables are cooked. Stir occasionally to prevent sticking. Before serving stir in the lemon juice and brown sugar.

Italian Polenta
Serves 6

The following recipe is made with maize meal (known as polenta in Italy) which has a delicious, nutty flavour. It is also gluten free. The recipe is an authentic Italian dish with a slight variation.

175 g (6 oz) Doves Farm Corn *(maize)* Meal
2 tsp herb salt or sea salt
275 ml (10 fl oz) cold water
575 ml (1 pint) boiling water
vegetable oil for frying
1 large onion, peeled and finely chopped
2 cloves garlic, crushed
1 medium green pepper, de-seeded and chopped
1 small aubergine, chopped (optional)
1 medium courgette, sliced (optional)
100 g (4 oz) button mushrooms, washed and sliced
1 tsp dried mint
1 tsp celery seeds
freshly ground black pepper
396 g (14 oz) can tomatoes
2 tbsp tomato purée
50 g (2 oz) sunflower seeds
100 g (4 oz) Cheddar cheese, grated

Pre-heat the oven to 190°C/375°F/Gas Mark 5.

Mix the corn meal, 1 teaspoon of herb salt or sea salt and cold water together and add this to the boiling water, stirring well. Bring to the boil, stirring continuously, and simmer for 5 minutes. Stir once or twice while simmering. Place in a large, square, greased oven-proof dish. Sauté the onion and garlic for 7 minutes, then add the green pepper, aubergine, courgette and mushrooms. Sauté for a further 5 minutes, then add the mint, celery seeds, herb salt and pepper. Stir well and add the tomatoes, tomato purée and sunflower seeds. Simmer for 20 minutes with the lid on, then spread over the corn meal. Sprinkle with the cheese and bake for 30 minutes.

GAYELORD HAUSER NATURAL SEASONINGS

This collection of delicious recipes using Gayelord Hauser Natural Seasonings has been devised by Gayelord Hauser himself.

Chicken Espagnol

Serves 4–6

As chicken breasts are expensive in a recipe for 4–6 people, a 2.3 kg/4 lb roasting chicken may be substituted, roasted in the usual way.

4–6 chicken breasts
1 large can whole tomatoes
425 ml (15 fl oz) chicken broth or *2 stock cubes dissolved in 425 ml (15 fl oz) water*
1/8 tsp cumin powder
1/8 tsp cayenne or *chilli powder*
1 tsp Herbal Bouquet
Santay Pure Garlic Magic *and* Onion Magic *to taste (1/2 to 1 tsp each)*
3 onions, peeled and cut into julienne strips
3 green peppers, de-seeded and cut into julienne strips
3 carrots, scraped and cut into julienne strips
1 tbsp Vegit or *1 tsp Spike Seasoning or Vege-Sal*

Cook the chicken breasts in the oven at 170°C/325°F/Gas Mark 3, for 35–45 minutes. While the chicken is cooking prepare the sauce: cut the tomatoes into very small pieces, or purée them in a blender. Place the tomatoes in a saucepan and add the chicken broth or stock and bring to the boil. Add the onions, peppers and carrots and cook for 10–15 minutes. Add all the seasonings and cook for another 5 minutes.

Place the cooked chicken breasts in a large casserole dish and spoon the sauce over them. If using whole chicken, slice and place in the casserole dish and cover with sauce. Place in a warm oven (turned off after baking the chicken), ready to serve with fluffy rice.

Delicious Nut Loaf

Serves 4

175 g (6 oz) onion, peeled and minced
3 tbsp celery, leaves and all, minced
100 g (4 oz) mixed nuts, finely chopped
2 medium tomatoes, cooked for 5 mins in their skins, then skinned and mashed
2 tbsp raw beetroot, grated
3/4 tsp Vege-Sal
pinch crushed thyme
1 egg, lightly beaten
75 g (3 oz) wholewheat breadcrumbs, toasted (weight after toasting)

Combine the ingredients in the order listed. Mix well after adding the egg, then add the toasted breadcrumbs and mix in lightly. Pack into a buttered 450 g/1 lb loaf tin and bake in a moderate oven (180°C/350°F/Gas Mark 4) until firm enough to be turned out – about 45 minutes. This loaf takes only 20 minutes to make, and is nutritious and inexpensive.

You can use chopped seeds – sunflower, pumpkin or pine kernels – instead of nuts, all are delicious; or a mixture of nuts and seeds.

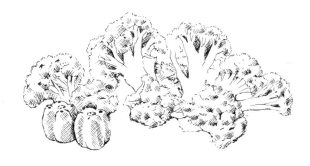

Fish Dee-lish

Serves 4

1 large tomato, sliced
1 leek, white part only, chopped
4 fillets sole
2 tbsp plain yoghurt
Vegit *to taste*
1 tbsp fresh parsley, chopped
1 tbsp wheatgerm

Pre-heat the oven to 180°C/350°F/Gas Mark 4.

Line the bottom of an oven-proof baking dish with the tomato and sprinkle with the chopped leek. Place the fillets of sole on top of the leek and spread with the yoghurt. Sprinkle very generously with Vegit and top with the chopped parsley and wheatgerm. Cover and bake for 15 minutes. Uncover and bake for 5 minutes more, or until the fish flakes easily.

Gayelord Hauser's Easy Chicken Casserole

Serves 4

1 medium onion, peeled and chopped
4 medium potatoes, scrubbed and thinly sliced
¹/₂ tsp Lemon Pepper
¹/₂ tsp thyme
100 g (4 oz) mushrooms, sliced
2 tsp Vegit
450 g (1 lb) boneless chicken meat, sliced
¹/₂ cup water or stock or white wine
a little more Vegit
Santay Pure Garlic Magic (optional)

Layer the onion and potatoes in a heavy saucepan. Sprinkle with Lemon Pepper and thyme. Add a layer of mushrooms and sprinkle with the Vegit. Top with the chicken slices and moisten with the water, stock or wine. Sprinkle with a little more Vegit for colour, and add a little Santay Pure Garlic Magic if desired. Bring to the boil, cover, reduce heat and simmer for about 25 minutes, or until the chicken and potatoes are tender.

Gayelord Hauser's Moussaka

Serves 4

450 g (1 lb) lean lamb, minced
5 tbsp cold pressed sunflower oil
1 large aubergine, unpeeled, sliced 5 mm (¹/₄") thick
1 large onion, peeled and thinly sliced
1 large green pepper, de-seeded and sliced
450 g (1 lb) fresh ripe tomatoes cooked in their
*   skins for 5 minutes, then skinned and mashed*
oregano
Spike Seasoning
4 eggs, lightly beaten

Pre-heat the oven to 180°C/350°F/Gas Mark 4.

Sauté the meat in 1 tablespoon of the oil until no longer pink. Beginning with the aubergine, arrange all the ingredients, except the beaten eggs, in alternate layers in a 2.3 litre/4 pint casserole dish. Sprinkle each layer with a little oregano and Spike and drizzle with oil. Bake in the oven for 1 hour. Remove, pour beaten eggs over the centre of the moussaka, cover and return to the oven for not more than 15 minutes. Serve at once with brown rice.

High Protein Spaghetti

Serves 4

3 medium tomatoes, peeled and cut into chunks
4 courgettes, cubed
450 g (1 lb) wholewheat or buckwheat high protein
*   spaghetti, cooked*
2 tbsp olive oil
Spike Seasoning
Vege-Sal to taste
¹/₂ cup fresh parsley, chopped
grated cheese, preferably Parmesan, to serve

Combine the tomatoes and courgettes in a lightly oiled, shallow roasting pan and place in a pre-heated oven at 150°C/300°F/Gas Mark 2 for 5–7 minutes, or until the vegetables are heated through but barely cooked. Meanwhile cook the spaghetti following packet directions and toss with the olive oil and Spike seasoning. Mix the heated vegetables and spaghetti, add Vege-Sal to taste, sprinkle with chopped parsley and serve with grated cheese.

Protein-rich, Especially Tasty Lentil Burgers

Serves 4–5

275 g (10 oz), dry weight, red split lentils
725 ml (1¼ pints) cold water
225 g (8 oz) mushrooms, finely diced
1 green pepper, de-seeded and finely diced
1 stalk celery, finely diced
1 carrot, finely diced
½ tsp Santay Pure Garlic Magic
1 small onion, peeled and finely diced
150 g (5 oz) shelled walnuts, chopped
olive oil to fry
1 tsp Lemon Pepper
1 tsp Spike Seasoning
1 tsp chilli powder
½ tsp dry mustard
25 g (1 oz) raw rolled oats
5 tbsp tomato paste
2 eggs, beaten
dash vegetarian Worcester Sauce

Soak the lentils in the cold water for 2 hours. Drain and cook lentils in fresh water until soft and all the water is absorbed. Sauté the mushrooms, green pepper, celery, carrot, Santay Pure Garlic Magic, onion and chopped walnuts in the olive oil with the Lemon Pepper, Spike, chilli powder and dry mustard. Combine the sautéed vegetables with the lentils and rolled oats and mash gently so that the vegetable chunks are not broken up. Add the tomato paste, beaten eggs and Worcester Sauce. Mix well and form into flat patties. Chill 1 hour, then grill on both sides until crisp and golden brown.

Sesame Halibut Steaks

Serves 3

Toast sesame seeds in a thick, dry pan over medium heat, stirring constantly, until they turn golden and begin to 'pop'.

3 halibut steaks, about 2.5 cm (1 in) thick
1 tsp Spike Seasoning
3 tsp vegetable oil
100 g (4 oz) soft wholewheat breadcrumbs
3 tbsp sesame seeds, toasted
½ tsp thyme
3 tbsp melted margarine

Pre-heat the oven to 180°C/350°F/Gas Mark 4.

Place the halibut steaks in an oiled baking tin, sprinkle with the Spike and vegetable oil. Combine the breadcrumbs, sesame seeds, thyme and melted margarine. Spread this mixture on top of the fish steaks and bake uncovered for about 30 minutes in the pre-heated oven until the fish flakes easily.

Tasty Open-face Omelette

Serves 1

1 medium courgette
1 egg
1 tbsp milk
1 pinch Onion Magic
1 pinch Spike Seasoning
1 pinch Herbal Bouquet
unsalted butter to fry

Steam the courgette for 5–10 minutes until just cooked. Chop into small cubes. Beat together the egg, milk, Onion Magic, Spike, and Herbal Bouquet for a few seconds. Heat an omelette pan, add a little unsalted butter and allow it to melt. Add the mixture and cook for a few seconds until the omelette is cooked underneath. Sprinkle the diced courgette on top of the omelette, then place under a heated grill to brown the top. Serve immediately.

This delicious appetizing omelette can be made in a dozen different ways with any of your favourite vegetables: for example, sliced onion, sliced tomato, sliced potato, cheese or olives. Served with a crisp salad, these omelettes are tops.

Vegetarian 'Meat' Loaf

Serves 3

*175 g (6 oz) cooked red beans (use canned if you
   wish, but drain and rinse well)*
½ green pepper, finely chopped
65 g (2½ oz) walnut halves, finely chopped
100 g (4 oz) wholewheat breadcrumbs, toasted
2 tbsp vegetable oil
2 tbsp milk
¼ tsp celery seed
1 tsp Vege-Sal
1 egg, lightly beaten

Pre-heat the oven to 180°C/350°F/Gas Mark 4.

Combine all the ingredients and mix thoroughly.
Spoon the mixture into a lightly oiled shallow
baking pan and pat into a loaf shape. Bake in the
pre-heated oven for 30 minutes. Serve with tomato
sauce.

Vegetarian Nut Steak

Serves 4

100 g (4 oz) shredded carrots
100 g (4 oz) pine nuts (kernels) finely chopped
2 eggs, beaten well
¼ tsp powdered sage
½ tsp celery seed
½ tsp Vege-Sal
2 tbsp margarine, melted
*75 g (3 oz) wholewheat breadcrumbs, toasted
   (weight after toasting)*

Pre-heat the oven to 180°C/350°F/Gas Mark 4.

Add the carrots and pine nuts to the eggs and mix
thoroughly. Add the sage, celery seed, Vege-Sal and
margarine and mix in the breadcrumbs. Drop in
heaped teaspoonsful on to a lightly oiled baking
sheet and bake in the pre-heated oven for 15–20
minutes, or until the mixture is nearly firm, then
place under a pre-heated grill to brown the top.

GRANOSE

Beefy Potato Ring

Serves 4

170 g (6 oz) Granose Beef Flavour TVP Mince
100 g (4 oz) button mushrooms, sliced
25 g (1 oz) butter or polyunsaturated margarine
225 g (8 oz) onion, peeled and chopped
1 large egg
1 tbsp fresh parsley, chopped
1 tsp mixed herbs
salt to taste
900 g (2 lb) potatoes, cooked and mashed

Fry the mushrooms gently in the butter or margarine
and arrange them in the base of a 1.8 litre/3 pint
ring mould. Reconstitute the TVP according to the
instructions and fry with the onion. Add the herbs
and salt, then the potato, mixing all well together.
Beat the egg and add to the mixture. Spoon the
mixture into the mould, pressing down lightly to
level the top. Stand the mould on a baking sheet
and bake in a fairly hot oven, 200°C/400°F/Gas Mark
6, for about 30 minutes. Turn out on to a serving
dish and serve with peas and tomatoes.

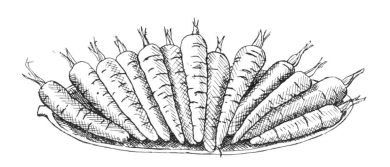

Country Casserole with Savoury Cuts

Serves 4

The following recipes are taken from my book *Making Your Own Home Proteins.*

275 g (10 oz) Granose Savoury Cuts
1 large onion, peeled and chopped
1 clove garlic, crushed
2 medium to large carrots
3 sticks celery, chopped (using green leaves also)
1 good size green pepper
1 bay leaf
2 tbsp fresh parsley, chopped
1 tsp sweet mixed herbs
1 tbsp wholemeal flour
1 tbsp tomato purée
725 ml (1¼ pints) hot stock or hot water with 1¼ vegetable or beef stock cubes added
175 g (6 oz) broad beans (frozen peas will do)
shoyu to taste

Drain and chop the Savoury Cuts into bite-size pieces. In a medium-sized saucepan sauté the onion, garlic and carrots for 6 minutes. Add the Savoury Cuts and fry for 2 minutes. Add the celery and green pepper and continue to sauté for 4 more minutes. Stir in the bay leaf, parsley and herbs and cook for 1 minute. Add the flour and, stirring constantly, cook for 1 minute. Mix the tomato purée with the stock and gradually add this to the vegetables and Savoury Cuts stirring constantly as you do so. Now add the broad beans or peas. Bring to the boil, then transfer to a casserole dish, cover and bake in the oven at 190°C/375°F/Gas Mark 5, for 30–40 minutes. Finally, stir in the shoyu, but taste before you do so as you might find the flavour sufficiently delicious without it.

This casserole makes a delicious filling for a pie. Simply top with a savoury shortcrust pastry (use a little cheese in the mixture) before baking. Prick the top, brush with egg and bake as above.

Curried Granose Tender Bits

Serves 4

You will find Tender Bits a good alternative to beef and equally delicious. This recipe has quite a list of ingredients, because I prefer not to use a bought curry powder, but you will find the flavour of this curry well worth the effort. Buy small amounts of herbs and spices, as they lose their flavour if not used up within a few weeks, and always store them away from direct sunlight. I have listed the spices separately from the vegetables so that you can have them measured out on a plate before starting the cooking.

Spices
50 g (2 oz) tamarind
1 very slightly rounded tsp turmeric
1 slightly rounded tsp ground cumin
1 slightly rounded tsp ground coriander
1 rounded tsp methi (fenugreek leaf)
1 level tsp chilli powder or cayenne pepper
3 cardamoms, podded and the seeds ground
cinnamon stick
¼ tsp clove powder
1 rounded tsp fresh ginger root, grated
1 level tsp black mustard seeds

Vegetables
350 g (12 oz) Granose Tender Bits
3 tbsp sunflower oil
1 large onion, peeled and chopped
2 large cloves garlic, crushed
2 medium potatoes, scrubbed and cut into cubes (leave skins on)
2 sticks celery, chopped
½ medium cauliflower, broken into florets
1 large green pepper, de-seeded and chopped
1 small cooking apple, cut into small chunks
4 good size tomatoes, skinned and chopped
1 tbsp tomato purée
100 g (4 oz) French beans, fresh or frozen (leave whole)
sea salt to taste

Drain and cut the Tender Bits into 1.25 cm/½″ cubes and steam for 10 minutes. Soak the tamarind in 1 teacup of boiling water for 20 minutes, then strain through a sieve. You will have a tangy, thickish liquid. Set this aside. In a large saucepan heat the oil and sauté the onion, garlic and cubed potatoes for 10 minutes with the lid on. Add the Tender Bits, celery, cauliflower florets, green pepper and apple and continue to cook for 5 more minutes. Now add all the spices and sauté for 2 minutes. Take care not to burn the mixture. Stir constantly. Add the chopped tomatoes, tomato purée, tamarind liquid and beans. Stir gently, add salt to taste, bring to the boil over medium heat, turn down to simmer and cook with the lid on for 30–40 minutes.

Serve with Surinam rice. Yoghurt mixed with cucumber, a little chopped mint and a dash of honey is a perfect accompaniment to this or any other curry dish.

Granose Nuttolene Croquettes

Makes about 20

Nuttolene Meatless Savoury Loaf is made from peanuts and salt. It is gluten free and high in protein.

225 g (8 oz) Granose Nuttolene
250 g (9 oz) potato, cooked and mashed
100 g (4 oz) soft wholemeal breadcrumbs
50 ml (1¾ fl oz) lemon juice
50 g (2 oz) tartare sauce
1 tbsp fresh parsley, chopped
1 tsp basil
sea salt to taste
1 egg, beaten
wholemeal flour or crisp breadcrumbs for coating
vegetable oil for deep frying

Mash the Nuttolene with a fork. Mix together all the ingredients (except the egg and flour or crisp crumbs). Form into croquettes, coat with beaten egg and the flour or breadcrumbs, and deep fry.

Granose Nuttolene Loaf

Serves 4–6

25 g (1 oz), dry weight, brown rice
50 g (2 oz) grated carrot
5 eggs
425 g (15 oz) can Granose Nuttolene
283 g (10 oz) can tomato soup
75 ml (3 fl oz) milk
25 g (1 oz) onion, peeled and grated
1 tsp fresh parsley, chopped
1 tsp sea salt

Boil the rice and carrot together until the rice is tender. Beat the eggs together. Mash the Nuttolene with a fork and mix well with the rice, carrot, tomato soup, milk, onion, parsley and salt. Blend in the eggs, place in a well-greased 900 g/2 lb loaf tin and bake for 1½ hours in a moderate oven, 180°C/350°F/ Gas Mark 4. Serve cold, sliced, with salad.

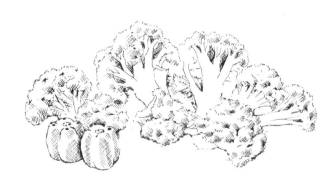

Granose Quick Cottage Pie

Serves 4–6

225 g (8 oz) Granose Beef Flavour TVP Mince
850 ml (1½ pints) vegetable stock (make with 1½
*   vegetable stock cubes and hot water)*
450 g (1 lb) diced vegetables (onions, carrots,
*   celery, turnips, etc.)*
1 tbsp vegetable oil
1 tbsp unbleached white flour
1 tsp mixed parsley, basil, thyme or herbs to taste
sea salt and freshly ground black pepper
450 g (1 lb) potatoes, peeled, boiled and mashed
25 g (1 oz) butter or polyunsaturated margarine
4 tbsp milk

Reconstitute the mince as directed, with the vegetable stock. Heat the oil in a large frying pan and stir in the vegetables. Add the reconstituted mince and stock, sprinkle in the flour and stir the mixture over a low heat until it boils. Add the herbs and seasoning and simmer until the vegetables are tender. Boil and mash the potatoes, using the butter or margarine and milk. Place the mince mixture in a shallow pie dish and arrange the mashed potato in a lattice pattern across the top. A large plain nozzle on a piping bag is ideal. Bake in a moderate oven, 180°C/350°F/Gas Mark 4, until the potato is lightly browned, or heat gently under the grill until crisp and lightly browned on top.

Moussaka with Savoury Cuts

Serves 4

*275 g (10 oz) Granose Savoury Cuts, drained and cut
    into bite-sized pieces*
1 large aubergine (about 225 g/8 oz in weight)
4 tbsp vegetable oil
2 medium onions (about 275 g/10 oz in weight)
1 large clove garlic, crushed
*1 level tsp dried marjoram or 1 tbsp fresh
    marjoram, chopped*
6 medium tomatoes, skinned
1 generous tbsp tomato purée
*150 ml (5 fl oz) stock or hot water plus ½ vegetable
    stock cube*
freshly ground black pepper
3 large courgettes (about 450 g/1 lb in weight)

Batter Topping
2 tbsp gram flour (chick pea flour)
2 eggs
275 ml (10 fl oz) natural yoghurt
1 tbsp fresh parsley, chopped
sea salt
freshly ground black pepper to taste

Drain the Savoury Cuts. Slice the aubergine thinly,
place in a colander, put a plate with a weight on top
and leave to stand for 30 minutes to get rid of bitter
juices. Heat 2 tablespoons of the oil in a pan and
sauté the onion and garlic for 7 minutes until soft.
Stir in the Savoury Cuts and marjoram and sauté for
2 minutes. Blend the skinned tomatoes, tomato
purée and stock until smooth and pour this over the
onions and Savoury Cuts. Season with a little black
pepper. Cover and simmer on low heat for 7
minutes more. Rinse the pressed aubergines and
pat dry. Heat the remaining oil in another pan and
sauté the aubergines and courgettes until golden.
Oil a large oven-proof dish and arrange a layer of
aubergines and courgettes in the base. Spoon a
layer of the tomato mixture over these, then another
layer of aubergines and courgettes, and so on,
finishing with aubergines and courgettes on top.

To make the topping, beat the eggs lightly, add
the yoghurt and beat together again lightly. Gradually mix in the flour, sea salt and black pepper and
very finely chopped parsley. If you have a liquidizer
or food processor just blend the whole lot until
smooth. Pour over the moussaka and bake in a pre-
heated oven, 180°C/350°F/Gas Mark 4, for 35 to 40
minutes or until golden brown.

Soya Chunk Goulash

Serves 4

100 g (4 oz) Granose Beef Flavour TVP Chunks
1 large onion, peeled and finely chopped
1 large clove garlic, crushed
3 tbsp sunflower oil
1 large green pepper, de-seeded and chopped
1 bay leaf
1 vegetable stock cube, crumbled
1 slightly rounded tbsp paprika
1 level tbsp unbleached white or wholemeal flour
1 rounded tbsp tomato purée
*794 g (1 lb 12 oz) can tomatoes, chopped and
    puréed in a liquidizer*
*1 small carton soured cream or thick natural
    yoghurt*

Soak the soya chunks according to the packet
instructions. Sauté the onion and garlic in the oil for
10 minutes until soft and transparent, add the green
pepper and continue to sauté for 3 more minutes.
Stir in the bay leaf, stock cube, soya chunks
(drained), paprika and flour and cook very gently
for just 1 minute more. Add the tomato purée and
tomatoes and cook with the lid on for 25–30
minutes. Remove from the heat and stir in the sour
cream or natural yoghurt just before serving. Serve
with brown rice or a simple fresh salad.

Soyapro 'Chicken' Croquettes

Serves 4

This recipe is great for using up left-over cooked
rice.

25 g (1 oz) unbleached white flour
275 ml (10 fl oz) milk (cow's, goat's or soya)
¼ tsp ground mace
1 small bay leaf
a little sea salt and freshly ground black pepper
1 medium onion, peeled and finely chopped
1 clove garlic, crushed (optional)
1 tbsp sunflower oil
1 can Granose Soyapro Chicken-like Flavour (TVP)
*4 sticks celery (tender centre sticks), very finely
    chopped*
2 tbsp fresh parsley, very finely chopped

1 level tsp marjoram or *1 tbsp fresh, chopped*
2 eggs
225 g (8 oz) cooked rice (weight when cooked)
1 tbsp wholemeal flour, beaten egg and wholemeal
  breadcrumbs to coat

Make a sauce with the flour and milk by mixing the flour with a little of the cold milk to form a smooth creamy paste. Heat the rest of the milk and stir gradually into the flour paste. Pour back into the saucepan and bring to the boil over moderate heat, stirring constantly. When slightly thickened add the mace, bay leaf, a little sea salt and freshly ground black pepper and simmer for 5 minutes. Take off the heat and leave to cool. Sauté the onion and garlic in the oil until soft. Mash the Soyapro and stir it with the sautéd onion and garlic, celery, parsley and marjoram into the sauce. Take out the bay leaf. Whisk the eggs lightly and stir with the cooked rice into the sauce mixture. Line a baking sheet with greaseproof paper. Oil it, spread the mixture thinly on the oiled paper and chill in the refrigerator overnight. When ready to fry, cut the chilled mixture into 5 cm/2 in squares, dip them in wholemeal flour, egg and breadcrumbs, then deep fry in hot oil until golden brown. (This will take about 4 minutes only.)

—Soyapro Stroganoff—

Serves 4

350 g (12 oz) Granose Soyapro Beef-like Flavour
  (TVP)
50 g (2 oz) Granose Margarine
1 medium onion, peeled and finely chopped
100 g (4 oz) button mushrooms, sliced
1 tbsp tomato purée
1 tsp Dijon mustard
1 tbsp unbleached white flour
1 small carton sour cream
sea salt and freshly ground black pepper
a little lemon juice to taste

Cut the Soyapro into small cubes. Heat 25 g/1 oz of the margarine in a pan and sauté the onion for 4 minutes. Stir in the mushrooms and continue to fry until the vegetables are soft and beginning to colour. Stir in the tomato purée, mustard and flour and continue to cook over low heat for 2 minutes, then carefully blend in the sour cream. Heat the remaining margarine in another pan and fry the sliced Soyapro over medium heat until lightly browned. Stir into the sauce mixture and season with a little salt and pepper and lemon juice to your taste.

—Spiced Lentil and— Peanut Butter Fritters

Serves 4

225 g (8 oz) red split lentils
425 ml (15 fl oz) water
3 level tsps curry powder
1 cinnamon stick
50 g (8 oz) Granose Peanut Butter (smooth)
2 medium onions, peeled and finely chopped
3 medium tomatoes, skinned and finely chopped
1 tbsp lemon juice
a little sea salt
25 g (1 oz) wholemeal breadcrumbs
a little sunflower oil for frying

Wash the lentils well and cook in the water with the curry powder, cinnamon stick and a little sea salt for 15 minutes. (Take care that the mixture does not burn – cook on low heat with the lid on.)

Heat the peanut butter in a non-stick frying pan and cook the onions and tomatoes in this until smooth. When the lentils are cooked take out the cinnamon stick and stir in the lemon juice. Mix all the ingredients together in a bowl.

To fry, heat a little oil in a non-stick frying pan and drop spoonsful of the mixture into this. Fry over moderate heat for 2 minutes on each side. Serve with a fresh salad.

HÖFELS

Barley with Mushrooms and Peas

Serves 4

225 g (8 oz) pot barley (not pearl barley)
725 ml (1¼ pints) vegetable stock which can be made with hot water and 1 vegetable stock cube
2 tbsp vegetable oil
1 large onion, peeled and chopped
½ teacup green peas, fresh or frozen
450 g (1 lb) mushrooms
pinch of Höfels Sea Salt

Heat the pot barley in a dry, heavy-based pan until golden. Add the vegetable stock, oil, onion and peas and simmer very gently until the barley is soft and the liquid is absorbed (this will take about 1 hour). Fry the mushrooms and add to the barley grains. Season with sea salt to taste.

Boston Baked Beans

Serves 2

To cook soya beans, see instructions in the recipe for Soya Bean Croquettes below.

1 onion, finely chopped
25 g (1 oz) Höfels 100% Wholemeal Norfolk Flour
50 g (2 oz) butter or polyunsaturated margarine
225 g (8 oz), cooked weight, Höfels Soya Beans
½ tsp made mustard
1 tbsp cider vinegar
1 tbsp molasses
1 level tsp sugar
pinch of Höfels Sea Salt

Fry the chopped onion very gently in the butter or margarine; stir in the flour and enough water to make a smooth sauce, then add all the other ingredients and mix well. Cook very gently for about 20 minutes.

Soya Bean Croquettes

Serves 4

600 g (12 oz), cooked weight, Höfels Soya Beans *(it is best to cook plenty, drain and freeze what you do not need)*
2 onions, peeled and finely chopped
2 cloves garlic, chopped (optional)
1 tsp dried herbs or 1 tbsp fresh herbs (oregano, basil, dill)
1 egg, beaten
pinch Höfels Sea Salt
sufficient wholemeal breadcrumbs to form a stiffish mixture
vegetable oil for frying

Soak the soya beans overnight, changing the water three times. Pressure cook for 30 minutes or cook in fresh unsalted water until soft (about 2½ hours). Drain and mash the cooked soya beans and mix with all the other ingredients. The mixture should be stiff enough to form into balls – flatten these slightly and fry very gently in the oil for about 5 minutes each side. These can be served hot or cold, with vegetables or salads.

Soya Flake Rissoles

Serves 4

115 g (4 oz) Höfels Soya Flakes
1 large onion, peeled and chopped
50 g (2 oz) brown breadcrumbs
2 tsp chopped herbs
1 clove garlic, chopped
½ tsp Höfels Sea Salt
1 egg, beaten
vegetable oil to fry

Soak the soya flakes for 2–3 hours, then cook gently in the liquid with the chopped onion for 20 minutes. Drain off the surplus liquid before adding the breadcrumbs, chopped herbs, chopped garlic, salt and beaten egg. The mixture should be fairly stiff. Shape the mixture into rissoles and fry gently in hot oil for a few minutes on each side. They are delicious hot or cold.

Soya Beans in Tomato Sauce

Serves 3–4

To cook soya beans, see List of Ingredients

1 onion, peeled and chopped
15 g (½ oz) butter or *polyunsaturated margarine*
450 g (1 lb) tomatoes (if fresh ones are not
*   available a 375 g/15 oz can is ideal)*
225 g (8 oz), cooked weight, Höfels Soya Beans
1 rounded tbsp tomato purée
1 rounded tsp sugar
pinch Höfels Sea Salt
1 bay leaf (oregano, dill or *basil could be used)*
1 clove garlic, chopped (optional)
2 tsp tamari or *Worcester Sauce*
½ vegetable stock cube dissolved in 150 ml (5 fl oz)
*   hot water*
soya flour or Höfels Norfolk Flour *to thicken*

Fry the onion very gently in the butter or margarine for 3–4 minutes. Chop the tomatoes, add them to the onions with all the other ingredients except the flour, and cook very gently for 45 minutes. At the end of the cooking time thicken with a little soya flour or Höfels Norfolk flour.

Wheat and Nut Savoury

Serves 4

225 g (8 oz) mixed nuts, ground finely
50 g (2 oz) Höfels Flaked Wheat
50 g (2 oz) brown breadcrumbs
1 large onion, peeled and finely chopped
1 carrot, peeled and grated
mixed herbs
575 ml (1 pint) vegetable stock
Höfels Sea Salt

Mix all the ingredients well and put into a greased 450 g/1 lb loaf tin and bake for 30 minutes at 180°C/350°F/Gas Mark 4.

HOLLAND & BARRETT

Arabian Couscous

Serves 6

You will need to steam the couscous or bulgur wheat for this dish. Couscous is a grain produced from semolina which is a variety of wheat. Bulgur is very similar but superior nutritionally and is produced from wholewheat. You can use either for this wonderful tasty meal. In North Africa a special pot called a couscousier is traditionally used, but a muslin-lined steamer or snug fitting muslin-lined colander placed on top of a deep saucepan will be just as good. The saucepan has to be deep because there is quite a large volume of vegetables to cook.

Sauce
3 tbsp olive oil
2 medium onions, peeled and coarsely chopped
2 large cloves garlic, crushed
3 medium carrots, scraped and cut in 1 cm (½")
*   slanting ovals*
225 g (8 oz) potatoes, thinly peeled and coarsely
*   chopped*
1 turnip, peeled and coarsely chopped
1 large green pepper, cut into 4 cm (1½") thickish
*   strips*
3 medium courgettes, quartered lengthwise then cut
*   into 2.5 cm (1") sticks*
150 g (5 oz), dry weight, Holland & Barrett Chick
*   Peas, soaked overnight and cooked in fresh*
*   water for 1 hour*
1 generous tsp ground coriander
1 generous tsp ground cumin
1 generous tsp turmeric
½ tsp ground mustard seeds
1 scant tsp chilli powder or *cayenne pepper*
350 g (12 oz) ripe tomatoes, skinned and puréed
1 tbsp tomato purée
100 g (4 oz) Holland & Barrett Sultanas
425 ml (5 fl oz) water and 1 tbsp lemon juice
sea salt to taste
sprig of mint, parsley or *coriander to garnish*

Couscous or Bulgur

350 g (12 oz) Holland & Barrett Couscous or Bulgur Wheat
425 ml (15 fl oz) cold water and a little sea salt (about ¾ tsp)
2 tbsp olive oil

First prepare the couscous: pour the couscous or bulgur wheat into a bowl and pour over the cold water to which you have added sea salt. Soak for 10 minutes. Drain and rub 2 tablespoons of olive oil lightly into the grains to keep them separate. Rub them lightly with your fingertips several times during the next 10 minutes.

To prepare the sauce, heat the olive oil in a large, thick saucepan and sauté the onion, garlic, carrot, potato and turnip for 10 minutes, tossing gently to cook all evenly. Add the green pepper and courgettes and continue frying for 3 more minutes. Stir in the cooked chick peas, coriander, cumin, turmeric, mustard seeds and chilli powder. Cook, taking care not to burn it, for 1 minute. Add the tomatoes and tomato purée, sultanas, water and lemon juice. Stir well, and add sea salt to taste. Bring to the boil and turn down to simmer.

Place the soaked couscous into a muslin-lined colander, steamer or couscousier if you have one. Put a lid (or foil) on top and simmer for 30 minutes until the vegetables are soft. When cooked, pour the couscous into a large serving dish and fork in a little oil or butter to keep grains separate. The sauce goes in the centre of the couscous. Decorate with sprigs of mint or parsley or, even better, coriander leaves. Serve with yoghurt and cucumber salad.

Almond and Mushroom Bake

Serves 4

175 g (6 oz) Holland & Barrett Split Almonds
175 g (6 oz) wholemeal breadcrumbs
175 g (6 oz) button mushrooms, wiped and finely chopped
175 g (6 oz) carrots, scrubbed and finely grated
1 onion, peeled and finely chopped
1 clove garlic, crushed
1 stick celery, finely chopped
1 tsp olive oil
2 tbsp fresh parsley, chopped
¾ tsp dried thyme
freshly ground black pepper
2 free range eggs
2 tbsp vegetable stock

Pre-heat the oven to 190°C/375°F/Gas Mark 5.

Place the almonds in the goblet of a liquidizer and grind until almost smooth. Place in a large mixing bowl and stir in the breadcrumbs. Mix the mushrooms and carrots into the breadcrumb mixture. Cook the onion, garlic and celery in the olive oil over a low heat for 3 minutes without browning. Add to the bowl with the parsley, thyme and pepper. Beat the eggs and pour on to the mixture. Add the stock and mix in thoroughly to bind the mixture. Lightly oil a 900 g/2 lb loaf tin and place the mixture inside, pressing down firmly. Cover with foil and bake in the centre of the pre-heated oven for 25 minutes. Remove the foil and cook for a further 10 minutes uncovered. Serve hot or cold.

Cashew Nut Risotto

Serves 4

1 tbsp sunflower oil
100 g (4 oz) onion, peeled and finely chopped
1 clove garlic, crushed
100 g (4 oz) carrot, scrubbed and finely diced
1 small cauliflower divided into florets
½ tsp ground cumin seeds
¼ tsp ground coriander
¼ tsp ground turmeric
225 g (8 oz), dry weight, Holland & Barrett Long Grain Brown Rice
475 ml (17 fl oz) vegetable stock
1 bay leaf
1 green pepper, de-seeded and chopped
3 tbsp sweetcorn kernels
100 g (4 oz) Holland & Barrett Cashew Nuts
50 g (2 oz) Holland & Barrett Sunflower Seeds
freshly ground black pepper

Place the oil in a large saucepan, add the onion, garlic and carrot, and cook gently for 2 minutes. Add the spices and cook for a further minute. Now add the cauliflower florets and cook for one minute. Stir in the rice thoroughly until the grains become transparent. Now add the stock and bay leaf, bring to the boil, cover and simmer for 20 minutes over a low heat. Add the chopped green pepper and the sweetcorn and turn off the heat. While the mixture completes cooking, toast the cashew nuts and seeds lightly in a pan and then stir into the rice. Season with freshly ground black pepper and serve.

Opposite: **Sunwheel** *(clockwise from top) Chinese Bean Sprout Salad, page 31, Mediterranean Salad, page 32, Tabbouleh Salad with Pine Kernels, page 32*

Lentil and Mushroom Bake

Serves 4

Really delicious served with a rich gravy.

175 g (6 oz) Holland & Barrett Red Split Lentils
400 ml (14 fl oz) hot stock (made with hot water and ¾ of a vegetable stock cube)
1 bay leaf
curl of lemon rind (no pith)
1 medium onion, peeled and chopped
2 tbsp sunflower oil
50 g (2 oz) button mushrooms, sliced
½ tsp ground cumin
½ tsp ground coriander
1 rounded tbsp parsley, chopped
1 level tsp dried marjoram or 1 dsrtsp fresh, chopped
1 tbsp fresh lemon juice
50 g (2 oz) Holland & Barrett Mixed Sunflower, Sesame and Pumpkin seeds, *lightly toasted in oven for 15 minutes at 160°C/325°F/Gas Mark 3*
40 g (1½ oz) Holland & Barrett Breakfast Porridge Oats
50 g (2 oz) Cheddar cheese, grated
1 tbsp sunflower oil (optional)

Pre-heat the oven to 180°C/350°F/Gas Mark 4.

Wash the lentils well in a sieve and remove any stones. Place in a medium sized, heavy-based saucepan and add the hot stock, bay leaf and lemon rind. Bring to the boil and leave to bubble for 4 minutes with the lid off. Turn down to simmer and cook for 12 minutes more. Take off the heat, and remove the bay leaf and lemon rind. Leave the pan covered while you prepare the other ingredients.

Sauté the onion in 2 tablespoons of oil until soft (about 5 minutes). Add the mushrooms and sauté for another 3 minutes only. Stir in the cumin, coriander, parsley, marjoram and lemon juice and remove from the heat.

In a food processor or blender grind the toasted seeds and porridge oats until powdery. Take out 2 level tablepoons of this mixture. Stir the sautéed vegetable mixture and ground seeds and oats into the lentils. Mix the grated cheese with the 2 tablespoons of ground seed and oat mixture. Oil a small baking tray well and form the lentil mixture into a loaf shape on it. Press on the cheese, seeds and oat mixture. Prick with a fork and sprinkle over

Opposite: **Vecon** *Veconetti (above) page 52, Vegetable Casserole (below) page 97*

the remaining tablespoon of sunflower oil (optional). Cap loosely with baking foil and bake in the pre heated oven for 40 minutes. Remove the foil 10 minutes before the end of the cooking time to brown the loaf.

Serve with Vecon Vegetable Gravy (see page 22) new potatoes boiled in their skins and lightly cooked spring greens for a tasty, delicious, wholesome and balanced meal.

Millet and Cheese Croquettes

Makes 10

This recipe is from my book *Wholefood Cookery Course*. The croquettes are very tasty and nutritious served with chutney and salad. You will need enough oil to semi-deep fry. A large, thick frying pan is best – don't use a chip pan.

225 g (8 oz), dry weight, Holland & Barrett Wholegrain Millet
1 tbsp sunflower oil
a little sea salt
100 g (4 oz) Cheddar cheese, grated
1 dessertspoon dried sage
1 medium onion, peeled, chopped and sautéed
1 level tsp cayenne pepper
1 egg yolk
beaten egg to coat
vegetable oil to fry

After weighing the millet, measure the amount using a cup. Heat the oil in a heavy-based saucepan and add the millet, toasting it on moderate heat and stirring with a wooden spoon for a few minutes until lightly browned. Measure out 3 times the volume of millet in boiling water and add, plus a little sea salt. Simmer, tightly lidded, for 20–25 minutes, by which time all the water will be absorbed and the grains soft. While the millet is still hot add the cheese, sage, sautéed onion and cayenne pepper. Stir in well, add the egg yolk and press the mixture firmly together like a dough. Form into 10 balls, press them into croquette shapes by flattening to 2.5 cm (1 in) thick, and brush with a little beaten egg. Heat enough oil in the pan to come to just over halfway up the croquettes. The oil must be very hot, as for chips, before putting the croquettes in. When they are a deep golden brown, turn them over and cook the other side.

If making these for children omit the cayenne pepper.

Rice and Pine Kernel Risotto or Bake

Serves 4–6

225 g (8 oz) Holland & Barrett Long or Short Grain
  Italian Brown Rice
*double the volume of rice (measure when dry) in
  hot water*
1 rounded tsp Vecon
2 tbsp sunflower oil
1 good size onion, peeled and finely chopped
1 large clove garlic, crushed
*2 medium carrots, cut into 2 cm (¾ in) long thin
  sticks*
3 sticks celery, chopped
*1 medium courgette, sliced in 2 cm (¾ in) long thin
  sticks*
*small green pepper or red and green pepper mixed,
  de-seeded and chopped*
75 g (3 oz) small button mushrooms, sliced
2 tbsp fresh parsley, chopped
1 tsp basil
½ tsp dried tarragon
396 g (14 oz) can tomatoes, mashed
75 g (3 oz) pine kernels
1 tbsp shoyu
freshly ground black pepper (optional)
150 g (5 oz) Cheddar cheese, grated (if baking)

Wash the rice well by placing in a sieve and letting
cold water run through the grains for ½ minute.
Place in a medium sized, heavy-based saucepan.
Add the hot water and Vecon, bring to the boil, turn
down to simmer and cook with a tight lid on for 30
minutes if baking, 40 minutes if making a risotto.
Drain the rice in a colander. Heat the oil in a frying
pan and sauté the onion, garlic and carrots for 5
minutes with the lid on. Add the celery, courgettes,
peppers, mushrooms, basil and tarragon and cook
for 5 minutes more. Stir in the parsley and mashed
tomatoes, bring to the boil, turn down to simmer
and cook for 1 minute more. Fork this mixture with
the pine kernels into the cooked rice. Season to
taste with shoyu and black pepper. (Your risotto is
now ready. If baking, simply transfer the mixture
into a well-oiled oven-proof dish. Sprinkle on the
grated cheese and bake at 190°C/375°F/Gas Mark 5
for 30 minutes (without a lid).
Serve with either steamed broccoli or a fresh
green salad.

Spiced Rice and Chick Pea Balls

Makes 10

225 g (8 oz), dry weight, Holland & Barrett Short
  Grain Italian Brown Rice
*double the volume of rice (measure when rice is
  dry) in water*
1 scant tsp sea salt
1 medium onion, peeled and very finely chopped
1 large clove garlic
1 tbsp sunflower oil
2 rounded tsp either medium or hot curry powder
*1 rounded tsp methi (fenugreek leaf – optional but
  great)*
*1 rounded tsp dried sage or 1 rounded dsrtsp fresh,
  chopped*
100 g (4 oz) canned chick peas, drained
50 g (2 oz) Holland & Barrett Cashew Nuts, *finely
  ground*
2 tsp fresh lemon juice
2 tsp shoyu
1 egg, lightly beaten
soya, corn or sunflower oil for semi-deep frying

Wash the rice well in a sieve by running cold water
through the grains for ½ minute. Place in a medium
sized, heavy-based saucepan, add the water and sea
salt and bring to boil. Turn down to simmer, cover
with a tight lid and cook for 35–40 minutes. (All the
water should by then be absorbed.) Leave the lid on
while you prepare other ingredients.

Sauté the onion and garlic in the oil for 5 minutes,
stir in the curry powder, sage and methi and cook
for 1 minute more, stirring frequently. Mix together
the rice, onion mixture, ground cashews, chick
peas, lemon juice and shoyu, and finally add the
lightly beaten egg. Mould the mixture, pressing
together firmly with the hands. Form into golf-size
balls. Heat enough oil in a frying pan (not a chip
pan) so that it reaches halfway up the rice balls.
Cook on one side in hot oil until golden brown.
Turn over carefully with a fork and cook the other
side until golden. Drain on absorbent kitchen paper
and serve hot with a fresh salad or cold as a
wholesome munchie.

HUGLI

Butter Bean (or Lima Bean) Casserole

Serves 4

This recipe is from my book *Wholefood Cookery Course*.

225 g (8 oz) butter beans, soaked overnight (change the water 3 times)
2 medium onions, peeled and finely chopped
3 sticks celery, finely chopped
2 tbsp sunflower oil
1 tbsp fresh parsley, chopped
1 level tsp oregano
1 clove garlic, crushed
5 tomatoes, skinned and chopped
1 rounded tsp Hugli Instant Vegetable Broth Mix
freshly ground black pepper
4 largish potatoes, steamed or baked with jackets on (cook extra potatoes the day before and save them)
100 g (4 oz) Cheddar cheese, grated

Cook the beans in fresh water for 45 minutes and reserve 200 ml/7 fl oz of the cooking liquid. Put the cooked beans in a casserole dish with the cooking liquid. Sauté the onion and celery in the oil for 5 minutes and add the parsley, oregano and garlic. Stir well in, then add the tomatoes, Instant Vegetable Broth Mix and pepper. Heat through and taste, adding a little more Instant Vegetable Broth if necessary, then fork into the bean mixture. Slice the potatoes, leaving the skins on, and place, overlapping each other, over the bean mixture. Sprinkle with grated cheese and bake for 30–35 minutes at 190°C/375°F/Gas Mark 5 until golden brown.

Millet and Mushroom Bake

Serves 4

Another recipe from my *Wholefood Cookery Course*.

3 tbsp oil for frying
225 g (8 oz) whole grain millet
2 medium carrots, scrubbed and cut into 2.5 cm (1") thick sticks
1 large onion or 2 medium, peeled and chopped
1 clove garlic, crushed
175 g (6 oz) button mushrooms, sliced
1 tbsp fresh parsley, chopped
1 tsp lemon thyme or thyme
850 ml (1½ pints) boiling water and 1½ Hugli Vegetable Stock Cubes to make stock
1 small aubergine, thinly sliced in rings (optional)
100 g (4 oz) Cheddar cheese, grated
2 medium tomatoes, thinly sliced in rings

Put 1 tablespoon of the oil in a large, thick saucepan and heat it well. Add the millet, and toast it for 5 minutes until lightly browned. Transfer to a large, greased casserole dish. Sauté the carrot, onion and garlic in the remaining oil for 3 minutes. Add the mushrooms and sauté for 2 minutes only. Stir in the parsley and lemon thyme or thyme. Fork this vegetable mixture into the toasted millet, pour on the stock and stir gently. Pop the slices of aubergine and tomato on top of the liquid. They will sink a bit at first but will settle on top later. Sprinkle the cheese over the sliced vegetables, cover with a tight lid and bake for 1 hour at 180°C/350°F/Gas Mark 4.

ITONA

Bolognese Sauce

Serves 4

2 tbsp corn or sunflower oil
1 large onion, 225 g (8 oz) in weight, very finely chopped
1 large clove garlic, crushed
2 sticks celery, very finely chopped
175 ml (6 fl oz) hot water
75 g (3 oz) Itona Beef Flavour TVP Mince
1 small green pepper, de-seeded and finely chopped
1 small bay leaf
1 level tsp basil
400 g (14 oz) can tomatoes, chopped
1 tbsp tomato purée
1 tbsp lemon juice (optional)
sea salt and freshly ground black pepper to taste

Heat the oil and fry the onion, garlic and celery for 10 minutes on low heat with the lid on. Pour the hot water over the soya mince and leave to stand for 10 minutes. Squeeze the mince gently to remove excess water and add to the pan, stirring it in well with the cooking vegetables. Add the green pepper, bay leaf and basil. Stir well together and fry for 2 minutes on medium heat. Add the tomatoes and tomato purée and lemon juice if used. Stir well and taste, adding a little sea salt and pepper if necessary.

Serve with wholemeal or buckwheat spaghetti.

Cottage Pie

Serves 4

2 onions, peeled and chopped
2 large carrots, scrubbed and finely chopped
2 tbsp sunflower oil
100 g (4 oz) Itona TVP Beef Flavoured Mince, *reconstituted following packet directions*
3 tbsp unbleached white flour
1 tbsp tomato purée
425 ml (12 fl oz) water
1 vegetable stock cube
freshly ground black pepper to taste
675 g (1½ lb) potatoes, peeled, cooked and mashed
25 g (1 oz) cheese, grated

Gently fry the onions and carrots in oil until transparent. Add the reconstituted TVP mixed with the flour and tomato purée, and gently mix in the water and stock cube. Season, stir gently, bring slowly to the boil and allow to simmer for 3 minutes. Pour the mixture into a heated oven-proof dish. Cover with prepared mashed potatoes, sprinkle with grated cheese and bake at 190°C/375°F/Gas Mark 5, for 25 minutes, or grill until crisp and golden brown.

To vary this recipe, add a little Marmite or Worcester Sauce to the TVP mixture.

Pork with Lemon

Serves 4

225 g (8 oz) pork fillet
225 g (8 oz) Itona Natural Unflavoured TVP Chunks, *reconstituted as directed on packet*
25 g (1 oz) vegetable oil
150 ml (5 fl oz) dry white wine
4 level teaspoons ground cumin
2 cloves garlic
sea salt and freshly ground black pepper
6 slices lemon
2 level tsps ground coriander

Cut the meat into 2.5 cm/1 in cubes and brown in the fat, turning continuously to prevent sticking. Stir in just over 150 ml/5 fl oz of the wine and add the cumin. Peel the garlic and crush it over the meat, then season to taste with salt and pepper. Bring the mixture to the boil, lower the heat and simmer for about 25 minutes or until tender. Add the TVP, the remaining wine and the lemon slices cut into quarters. Continue cooking, stirring, until the sauce thickens slightly. Stir in the coriander and serve with plain boiled rice and a lightly steamed green vegetable.

Pot Barley Bake

Serves 4

This recipe is from my book *Vegetarian Food Processor*.

350 g (12 oz) pot barley
850 ml (1½ pints) water for soaking
1 level tsp sea salt
2 medium onions, peeled
3 tbsp sunflower oil
1 clove garlic, crushed
75 g (3 oz) Itona Beef Flavoured TVP Mince

4 sticks celery
100 g (4 oz) mushrooms
2 tbsp fresh parsley, chopped
1 level tsp basil
freshly ground black pepper
6 medium tomatoes
1 tbsp tomato purée
1 tbsp shoyu

Topping
2 eggs
225 ml (8 fl oz) natural yoghurt and milk mixed, half
    and half
sea salt and freshly ground black pepper
50 g (2 oz) farmhouse Cheddar cheese, grated

Wash the barley and soak for 6 hours or overnight. Bring to the boil in the soaking water and sea salt. Simmer with the lid on for 20–25 minutes. Drain and save 200 ml/7 fl oz of the cooking water, if any is left. Pre-heat the oven to 190°C/375°F/Gas Mark 5. Set the slicing plate in position on the food processor. Cut the onions in half lengthwise, pack each half into the feed tube and slice. Heat the oil in a heavy-based saucepan and sauté the onion and garlic for 10 minutes with the lid on. Soak the Itona Mince in the retained barley water, or just hot water, for 10 minutes until it has swollen and absorbed the liquid, then sauté with the onion for 5 minutes, stirring and coating the TVP well with the onion and garlic. Set the steel blades in position. Cut the celery in smallish chunks, wash and wipe the mushrooms. Place the celery and the whole mushrooms into the processor bowl and chop finely. Scoop out and add to the onions and mince. Stir in the parsley, basil and freshly ground black pepper and fry over gentle heat for 3 minutes. Skin the tomatoes by cutting a circle around the stalk end and immersing in boiling water for 5 minutes. With the steel blades still in position, blend the tomatoes with the tomato purée and shoyu until smooth. Pour this into the mince and vegetable mixture and cook gently for a few minutes only. Pour this into a greased baking dish and spoon the barley over the top.

To make the topping, set steel blades in position and blend the eggs, yoghurt, milk, sea salt and black pepper for a few seconds. Pour this mixture over the barley and sprinkle on the cheese. Bake in the pre-heated oven for 25 minutes. If liked, place under a hot grill for a few minutes to crisp the top. Absolutely delicious served with lightly cooked spring greens or broccoli tops.

Rogan Josh Soya Chunk Curry

Serves 4

This is my favourite curry. Traditionally lamb is used in the recipe, but TVP beef flavoured chunks absorb the delicious flavour of the sauce and cost only a quarter of the price. Well worth your efforts, as the resulting curry is superb.

150 g (5 oz) Itona Beef Flavoured TVP Chunks
1 small carton natural yoghurt
100 ml (4 fl oz) water
good pinch sea salt
225 g (8 oz) onions, peeled and finely chopped
7 g (¼ oz) fresh ginger, grated
2 cloves garlic, crushed
1 tbsp fresh parsley, chopped
400 g (14 oz) can tomatoes
3 tbsp sunflower oil or ghee

Spices I
3 cardamoms, podded and crushed
good pinch clove powder or 3 cloves
1 bay leaf
½ cinnamon stick
½ tsp turmeric
½ tsp cayenne pepper or chilli powder
1 tsp ground coriander seeds
1 tsp ground cumin

Spices II
1 dessertspoon methi (fenugreek leaves)
1 dessertspoon garam masala

Soak the TVP chunks in hot water for 2 hours to reconstitute. Drain and squeeze out any excess water. Allow the chunks, spices I, yoghurt, water and a good pinch of sea salt to marinate for at least one hour. Then cook on a low heat for 30 minutes. Blend the onions, ginger, garlic, parsley and tomatoes in a blender and process for just a few seconds. (Do not make a purée. The mixture should have the texture of bolognese sauce.) Heat the oil in a pan and fry spices II for 1 minute over gentle heat. Stir in the blended mixture and cook on a low heat with the lid on for 15 minutes. Combine all ingredients in a large saucepan and cook gently together for 30 minutes more. Serve on a bed of Saffron Rice, accompanied by lightly cooked french beans sprinkled with toasted sesame seeds.

Itona Beef Stew

Serves 4

50 g (2 oz) sunflower oil
2 carrots, scraped and sliced
2 medium onions, peeled and thickly sliced
1 stick celery, sliced
½ green pepper, de-seeded and sliced
50 g (2 oz) mushrooms
1 clove garlic, crushed
100 g (4 oz) Itona Beef Flavour TVP Chunks
    reconstituted following directions on packet
1 rounded dessertspoon wholemeal flour
285 ml (10 fl oz) hot stock made with ½ vegetable
    stock cube and water
sea salt to taste
freshly ground black pepper
1 bay leaf

Heat the sunflower oil in a frying pan and sauté all the vegetables for 5 minutes. Add the reconstituted TVP. Stir in the flour and cook for ½ minute; blend in the stock and bring to the boil, stirring constantly. Taste and add sea salt and freshly ground black pepper if necessary. Transfer to a casserole, add the bay leaf, cover and cook in a slow oven, 160°C/325°F/Gas Mark 3, for 1 hour.

Soya Chunk Steak Casserole

Serves 6

125 g (4½ oz) packet Itona Beef Flavoured TVP
    Chunks, *soaked in 575 ml (1 pint) hot water for at*
    least 2 hours
2 tbsp sunflower oil
1 large onion, peeled and chopped
1 large clove garlic, crushed
2 good size carrots, scrubbed and chopped
3 sticks celery, chopped
1 small green pepper, de-seeded and chopped
1 tbsp fresh parsley, chopped
1 tsp dried or 1 tbsp fresh marjoram, chopped
1 bay leaf
½ vegetable stock cube
1 rounded tbsp wholewheat or unbleached white
    flour
1 rounded tbsp tomato purée
575 ml (1 pint) hot water
100 g (4 oz) frozen peas (optional)
1 tbsp shoyu

Drain the soya chunks well and discard the soaking water. Heat the oil in a large, heavy-based saucepan and sauté the onion, garlic, carrots and celery for 7 minutes with lid on. Add the soya chunks, green pepper, parsley, marjoram, bay leaf and ½ stock cube. Continue to fry for 3 minutes more, coating the chunks with the oil and vegetable mixture by stirring constantly. Blend the flour with the tomato purée and stir into the vegetable mixture. Stirring constantly, pour in the hot water. Blend well and cook for 2 minutes. Transfer to a casserole dish, stir in the frozen peas, cover and bake at 180°C/350°F/Gas Mark 4 for 45 minutes to 1 hour. When cooked, stir in shoyu to your taste.

The casserole can be simmered on top of the cooker, closely lidded, when it will only take about 30 minutes to cook. Serve with steamed jacket potatoes, or a grain such as brown rice, buckwheat or millet. It also makes a delicious filling for a pie, topped with wholemeal pastry.

LONDON HERB & SPICE CO.

Coq au Vin

Serves 6

25 g (1 oz) polyunsaturated margarine
2 tsp sunflower oil
4 medium chicken joints
225 g (8 oz) onion (weight after peeling and
    chopping)
425 ml (15 fl oz) dry red wine
1 London Herb & Spice Co. Cook Bag for Chicken
2 cloves garlic, crushed
2 level tsp sea salt
2 rounded tbsp tomato purée
175 g (6 oz) whole button mushrooms
1½ level tbsp arrowroot
2 heaped tbsp fresh parsley, chopped

Heat the margarine and oil in a heavy pan and fry the chicken joints, skin sides down first, until golden brown on both sides. Remove from the pan and keep hot. Fry the chopped onions until turning a light gold then pour in 275 ml (10 fl oz) of the wine, add the Cook Bag, garlic, salt and tomato purée and bring to the boil. Replace the chicken in the pan, cover and simmer for 45 minutes–1 hour, or until the chicken is tender. Add the mushrooms and simmer for a further 10 minutes. Thicken by blending the arrowroot into a smooth cream with the remaining wine and adding the mixture to the pan. Cook gently until the sauce thickens. Remove the Cook Bag, stir in the parsley and serve.

Golden Fish Bake with Pasta

Serves 4

Use a Cook Bag for Fish, Rice and Pasta dishes, which is a mixture of dill, tarragon, fennel seed and white pepper.

150 g (5 oz) wholemeal pasta shells or *other small shapes*
425 ml (15 fl oz) boiling water
1 level tsp sea salt
1 London Herb & Spice Co. Cook Bag
4 plaice fillets
1 oz butter, melted
1/2 level tsp paprika
50 g (2 oz) Cheddar cheese, grated

Arrange the pasta in the base of a fairly large oven-proof dish. Add the boiling water, salt and Cook Bag and mix well. Arrange the plaice fillets on top and coat with the melted butter. Sprinkle with the paprika and grated cheese and bake for 30 minutes at 220°C/425°F/Gas Mark 7. Serve with a green vegetable.

Lamb Casserole

Serves 6

The Cook Bag used in this recipe is a mixture of juniper berries, bay leaf, cloves and thyme, and is recommended for darker meat or red bean dishes.

2 tbsp sunflower oil
1.5 kg (3 lb) middle neck of lamb
1 tbsp fruit sugar
sea salt and freshly ground black pepper
4 slightly rounded tsp unbleached white flour
2 leeks, weight 275 g (10 oz) when roughly chopped (use as much green as possible)
6 medium to large ripe tomatoes, skinned and finely chopped
4 medium carrots, scrubbed and cut in large chunks
1 large juicy clove garlic, crushed
425 ml (15 fl oz) hot water plus 3/4 (Hugli) vegetable stock cube
2 London Herb & Spice Co. Cook Bags
225 g (8 oz) French beans, topped and tailed and cut into 3.5 cm (11/2") pieces.

Pre-heat the oven to 160°C/325°F/Gas Mark 3.
 Heat the oil in a large, heavy-based saucepan or flame-proof casserole dish and brown the lamb pieces on all sides. Sprinkle on the fruit sugar and stir until it caramelizes (not too brown). Add a little sea salt and a few twists of black pepper. Stir in the flour and on a very low heat cook for a few minutes (without burning). Add the leeks, tomatoes, carrots and garlic, stir well together and, still on a low heat, cook for 1 minute to coat the vegetables with the meat juices. Add the vegetable stock, stirring constantly. Pop in the Cook Bags. Bring to the boil (if the stock does not almost cover the other ingredients, then top up with hot water). Transfer to a casserole dish, cover and bake in the oven for approximately 11/2 hours. Steam the cut French beans for 10 minutes or until tender and add these to the casserole 5 minutes before the end of the cooking time.
 Delicious with either plain boiled brown rice or jacket potatoes and lightly steamed broccoli or spring greens cooked in the minimum amount of water, a little sea salt and 1 tablespoon vegetable margarine.

Red Bean Hot Pot

Serves 4

The Cook Bags used here are recommended for dark meat dishes, but I think they go equally well with red kidney beans. The mixture is juniper, bay leaf, clove and thyme.

*175 g (6 oz) dry weight, red kidney beans or 1 can
    red kidney beans, drained and rinsed
3 tbsp olive oil
1 large onion, peeled and chopped
2 cloves garlic, skinned and crushed
3 sticks celery, chopped (use green leaf ends also)
2 medium carrots, scraped and cut in slanting ovals
2 medium courgettes, cut in slanting ovals
1 small green pepper, de-seeded and chopped
100 g (4 oz) small button mushrooms (leave whole)
2 London Herb & Spice Co. Cook Bags, opened
350 g (12 oz) ripe tomatoes, skinned and chopped
    (to skin, blanch in hot water for 5 minutes)
1 level tbsp tomato purée (optional)
a little sea salt and freshly ground black pepper
3 good size potatoes, scrubbed and steamed for 15
    minutes and cut into thin rings (leave skins on)
a little melted butter or polyunsaturated margarine
    to brush top of potato rings*

If using dry beans, wash them and soak overnight, changing the soaking water three times. Rinse and cook in fresh water. Bring the water to the boil with beans in and boil vigorously for 10 minutes with the lid off. Top up with more water if necessary, turn down the heat, cover and simmer for 35 minutes more. (If the beans are still hard at the end of this time then they were probably old stock and will need more cooking time.) Only add salt 10 minutes before the end of the cooking time or the beans will stay hard. Heat the oil in a heavy-based saucepan or flame-proof oven casserole dish and sauté the onion and garlic with the lid on for 5 minutes, then add the celery, carrots, courgettes and green pepper and continue to fry for 2 minutes more. Add the mushrooms and fry for 1 minute. Add the contents of the Cook Bags, reserving a good sprinkling for the top of the Hot Pot. Stir in the tomatoes, drained beans and tomato purée. Sprinkle on a little sea salt and black pepper to taste, If not already in a casserole dish, now transfer to one and arrange the potato rings slightly overlapping on top of the bean mixture. Brush with either melted butter or polyunsaturated margarine, sprinkle on the reserved Cook Bag mixture and bake at 190°C/375°F/Gas Mark 5 for 30 minutes or until lightly browned.

LOSELEY

Baked Tuna-stuffed Potatoes

Serves 4

*4 large potatoes
198 g (7 oz) can tuna, flaked
150 ml (5 oz) Loseley Soured Cream
100 g (4 oz) streaky bacon, chopped
25 g (1 oz) butter or polyunsaturated margarine*

Bake the potatoes in the oven until tender. Slice off the potato tops and scoop out the flesh, leaving a thin shell. Mash the potato, stir in the tuna with its oil, add butter or margarine, soured cream and seasoning. Spoon the mixture back into the potato shells, place the chopped bacon on top of the potatoes, return the potatoes to the oven in a shallow, oven-proof dish for 25 minutes at 220°C/ 425°F/Gas Mark 7.

The tuna fish could be replaced by any other savoury filling – diced cooked chicken, mushrooms and ham or cheese and onion, for example.

Cauliflower Cheese with Walnuts or Almonds

Serves 4

*1 large cauliflower
2 tbsp butter or polyunsaturated margarine
1 tbsp arrowroot
150 g (5 oz) Loseley Natural Yoghurt
50 g (2 oz) hard cheese, preferably Parmesan
25 g (1 oz) blue cheese, preferably Stilton
sea salt and freshly ground black pepper
1 tbsp walnuts or almonds, chopped
whole walnuts or almonds, to garnish*

Lightly steam the whole cauliflower, place in a serving dish and keep warm. Make a sauce by melting the butter or margarine and gradually blending in the cornflour and seasoning. Add the yoghurt and cheese and heat thoroughly, stirring well until the sauce thickens – but don't let it boil. Mix in the chopped nuts and pour the sauce over the cauliflower. Garnish with whole nuts and serve.

Liver Casserole

Serves 3

175 g (6 oz) lamb's liver, cleaned and trimmed,
  chopped into small pieces
vegetable oil, butter or lard for frying
4 rashers streaky bacon, chopped
1 large onion, peeled and finely sliced
225 g (8 oz) mushrooms, sliced
1 green pepper, de-seeded and chopped
275 ml (10 fl oz) stock made with ½ to ¾ vegetable
  stock cube
2 tbsp sherry
150 ml (5 oz) Loseley Soured Cream

Lightly fry the liver to seal in the juices, transfer to a casserole dish and keep warm. Fry the chopped bacon and finely sliced onion until golden brown and transfer to the warm casserole. Lightly fry the sliced mushrooms and chopped green pepper and add to the casserole, pour over the stock and sherry, and cook for 45 minutes in the oven at 170°C/325°F/Gas Mark 3. Stir in the soured cream just before serving. Serve with rice or creamed potatoes.

Smoked Trout or Mackerel with Apple and Horseradish Sauce

Serves 6

175 g (6 oz) apple sauce
150 ml (5 oz) Loseley Soured Cream
1 tsp tarragon vinegar
4 level tsp horseradish sauce
sea salt and freshly ground black pepper
6 portions smoked trout or mackerel
lettuce leaves to serve
paprika and lemon slices to garnish

Mix together the apple sauce, soured cream, vinegar and horseradish sauce. Season with salt and pepper to taste. Arrange the portions of fish on a bed of lettuce on a serving dish and pour sauce over each fillet. Dust with paprika and garnish with lemon slices.

LOTUS

Blanquette of Chiplets with Mushrooms

Serves 2–3

65 g (2½ oz) Lotus Unflavoured TVP Chiplets
  soaked in 275 ml (10 fl oz) water in which has
  been dissolved 1 tsp Lotus White Stock Powder
275 ml (10 fl oz) milk
1 bay leaf
225 g (8 oz) mushrooms, sliced
50 g (2 oz) butter or polyunsaturated margarine
1 tbsp vegetable oil
1 clove garlic, crushed
25 g (1 oz) brown wheatmeal flour
juice of ½ lemon
chopped fresh parsley to garnish

While the chiplets are soaking, warm the milk with the bay leaf and allow to infuse. Gently cook the mushroom in 25 g/1 oz of the butter with the vegetable oil for a few minutes. Do not overcook. Add the garlic. Melt the remaining butter in another pan, add the flour and cook gently for 5 minutes to make a roux. Remove the bay leaf from the milk, gradually mix the milk into the roux and cook to thicken. Gently heat the chiplets in their stock and cook to absorb the remaining liquid. Add the chiplets to the white sauce together with the lemon juice. Season to taste. Garnish with chopped parsley and serve with creamed potatoes and grilled tomatoes or salad.

Caper Hot Pot

Serves 4

75 g (3 oz) Lotus Unflavoured TVP Chunks, *soaked*
in 575 ml (1 pint) water in which has been
dissolved 2 tsps Lotus Brown Stock Paste
225 g (8 oz) tomatoes, *chopped*
50 g (2 oz) onion, *peeled and chopped*
40 g (1½ oz) capers, *chopped*
40 g (1½ oz) gherkins, *chopped*
dash of *vegetarian Worcester Sauce*
1 tbsp French mustard
100 g (4 oz) mushrooms, *chopped*
450 g (1 lb) potatoes, *sliced*
a little *vegetable oil*

Soak the chunks in the cooled stock for 30 minutes.
Add the other ingredients except the potatoes and
transfer to a greased casserole. Top with the sliced
potatoes, sprinkle with a little cooking oil and bake
in the oven at 180°C/350°F/Gas Mark 4 , for 30
minutes or until brown on top.

This can be simmered on top of the stove, when it
will only take about 20 minutes to cook. Then top
with cooked mashed or sliced potatoes, sprinkle on
a little oil, and brown under the grill.

Chilli con Lotus

Serves 4

350 g (12 oz) can red kidney beans
75 g (3 oz) Lotus TVP Brown Mince, *soaked in*
275 ml (10 fl oz) water in which has been
dissolved 1 stock cube or 1 tsp Lotus Brown
Stock Paste
1 tbsp *vegetable oil*
1 large onion, *peeled and chopped*
1 green pepper, *de-seeded and chopped*
425 g (15 oz) can tomatoes
1–2 level tsp chilli powder, *to taste*
1 tbsp cider vinegar or *wine vinegar*
1 level tsp brown sugar

Cook the onion gently in the oil until transparent.
Add the green pepper and cook for 4–5 minutes.
Add to the mince in a saucepan with the beans,
tomatoes and other ingredients. Simmer for 15
minutes to blend the flavours then season to taste
and serve. Suitable accompaniments are brown rice
and green salad.

Chiplets à La King

Serves 2–3

40–50 g (1½–2 oz) Lotus Unflavoured TVP Chiplets
soaked in 275 ml (10 fl oz) cool water in which
has been dissolved 1 tsp stock paste or cube
25 g (1 oz) butter or *polyunsaturated margarine*
50 g (2 oz) dry sherry
50 g (2 oz) button mushrooms, *sliced*
50 g (2 oz) red and green peppers, *diced*
1 small can vegetable soup (e.g. mushroom)
1 egg yolk mixed with 150 ml (5 fl oz) cream
cayenne pepper

Soak the chiplets for 20 minutes until soft, then
bring to boiling point. Strain. Melt the butter or
margarine and cook the chiplets in it for a few
minutes. Add the sherry and reduce the heat. Add
the mushrooms and diced peppers and cook for a
few minutes, taking care not to overcook. Add the
soup and bring to boiling point. Add the egg and
cream mixture, then immediately remove from the
heat. Check the seasoning and serve with a little
cayenne sprinkled on top. Good with brown rice.

Chiplets Paella

Serves 4

50 g (2 oz) Lotus Brown Unflavoured TVP Chiplets
soaked in 275 ml (10 fl oz) water in which has
been dissolved 1 tsp Lotus Brown Stock Paste
225 g (8 oz) long grain brown rice
good pinch saffron or *1 level teaspoon turmeric*
2 tbsp vegetable oil
1 onion, *peeled and chopped*
1 green pepper, *de-seeded and chopped*
225 g (8 oz) tomatoes, *chopped*
25 g (1 oz) seedless raisins or *sultanas*
sea salt and freshly ground black pepper to taste

Soak the chiplets in the stock for 20 minutes until
soft. Bring to the boil and simmer gently until all the
liquid is absorbed. Cook the rice with the saffron or
turmeric in 2 cups of water until the water is
absorbed. Heat the oil and cook the onion until
transparent. Add the green pepper and cook for 5
minutes. Add the tomatoes and cook for a few
minutes more. Mix all ingredients together, season
to taste and serve.

Chunks in Mustard Cream Sauce

Serves 4

50 g (2 oz) Lotus Unflavoured TVP Chunks soaked
in 425 ml (15 fl oz) water in which has been
dissolved 2 tsp Lotus Stock Paste
225 g (8 oz) mushrooms, sliced
50 g (2 oz) butter or polyunsaturated margarine
25 g (1 oz) wholewheat flour, seasoned
1 tbsp vegetable oil
2 small shallots or 1 small onion
1 tbsp Dijon mustard
1 dsrtsp redcurrant jelly
2 tbsp double cream
1 tbsp port or dry sherry
sea salt and freshly ground black pepper

Soak the chunks in cool or cold stock for 30 minutes or until soft, then bring slowly to boiling point and drain. Keep the stock. Lightly cook the mushrooms in half the butter. Toss the chunks in the flour and brown in the hot oil in another pan, using only sufficient to cover the bottom of the pan. Chop the shallots and cook in the pan with the remaining butter. Add any flour left over. Gradually blend in the stock and simmer to make a smooth sauce. Season to taste. Stir in the mustard, redcurrant jelly and cream. Add the chunks and mushrooms, lastly add the port or sherry and bring to boiling point. Serve with brown rice topped with grated nutmeg and dotted with butter.

Stuffed Marrow

Serves 4

1 medium vegetable marrow
50 g (2 oz) Lotus Unflavoured TVP Mince soaked in
275 ml (10 fl oz) water in which has been
dissolved 1 tsp Lotus Brown Stock Paste
100 g (4 oz) wholewheat breadcrumbs
2 tbsp fresh parsley, chopped
1/2 tsp mixed herbs
1 small onion, grated
4 tomatoes, chopped
1 tbsp tomato purée
1 egg (optional)
225 g (8 oz) long grain brown rice
sea salt and freshly ground black pepper to taste

Parboil the marrow for 5 minutes. Cut in half lengthwise and scoop out the seeds. Soak the mince in the stock for 15 minutes, or until it is soft. Add the breadcrumbs and other ingredients to the mince, adding a little more liquid if necessary. Pile the mixture into the marrow, cover with greased paper and bake in the oven at 200°C/400°F/Gas Mark 6, for 45 minutes until tender. Serve with a rich brown sauce and baked potatoes. (A sauce could be made in the pan in which the marrow has been cooked, using the tasty juices.)

This stuffing can be used with other vegetables such as green peppers, onions, etc.

Lotus Dinner Party Chunks

Serves 4

2 medium onions, chopped
vegetable oil to fry
50 g (2 oz) mushrooms, chopped
50 g (2 oz) tomatoes, chopped
1 dessertspoon brown flour
1 tsp Lotus Brown Stock Paste
275 ml (10 fl oz) water
1 heaped tsp tomato purée
sea salt and freshly ground black pepper
1 tbsp wine (optional)
50–75 g (2–3 oz) Lotus Brown TVP Chunks soaked
in water or stock made with Lotus Brown Stock
Paste (directions for soaking are on the packet)
Lotus Brown Savoury Coater

Make a sauce by gently cooking the onion in approximately 1 tablespoon of vegetable oil till transparent. Add the mushrooms and a further tablespoon of oil. Cook for about 5 minutes, then add the chopped tomato and cook for a further 3–5 minutes. Add the flour, mix well and cook another 3–5 minutes. Gradually mix in 275 ml/10 fl oz water and cook to thicken. Add 1 teaspoon Brown Stock Paste and the tomato purée. Mix well and simmer gently till all ingredients are well blended together. Season to taste. A spoonful of wine may be added, if liked, to enrich the flavour. Meanwhile, drain the chunks, toss in Brown Savoury Coater and brown on all sides in a very little oil. Pile on to a dish and serve with the sauce either poured over, or served separately.

The chunks, after browning, make excellent 'finger pieces' to serve with cocktails as appetizers.

Spring Casserole

Serves 4

75 g (3 oz) Lotus Unflavoured Brown TVP Chunks
1.2 litres (2 pints) water in which has been
*   dissolved 4 tsps Lotus Brown Stock Paste*
1 medium turnip, diced
1 medium carrot, diced
1 medium onion, peeled and sliced
1 tsp dried mint or 1 dessertspoon fresh mint
100 g (4 oz) shelled peas
100 (4 oz) green beans, sliced
shredded cabbage or lettuce
1 tsp wholewheat flour (optional)
sea salt and freshly ground black pepper
shredded spinach (optional)

Soak the chunks in the cold stock for 30 minutes. Add the turnip, carrot, onion and mint. Bring to the boil and simmer gently for 10–15 minutes. Add the peas, beans and cabbage and simmer for 5–10 minutes. If lettuce is used and/or spinach they should not be added until just before serving. Care should be taken that none of the green vegetables is overcooked. A teaspoon of wholewheat flour mixed with a little cold water can be added 5 minutes before serving and heated to thicken. Check the seasoning and serve with new potatoes.

Soya Athenium

225 g (8 oz), cooked weight, Lotus Soya Grits
2 cups mixed celery, carrots and marrow or
*   courgettes, chopped*
sliced tomatoes
50 g (2 oz) black olives, minced or chopped
100 ml (5 fl oz) stock (can be made with Lotus
*   Brown Stock Paste – follow directions on packet)*

Mix the vegetables, olives, stock and grits all together. Season to taste. Put into a heat-proof casserole. Bake in hot oven till brown.

Soya Grits Savoury Loaf

175 g (6 oz) Lotus Soya Grits, soaked
1 large onion, peeled and chopped
2 cloves garlic, crushed
4 sticks celery, chopped
50 g (2 oz) polyunsaturated margarine or butter
2 tomatoes, chopped
2 tbsp tomato purée
100 g (4 oz) wholewheat breadcrumbs
4 tbsp fresh parsley, chopped
1 tbsp dried thyme
1 egg, beaten
dried breadcrumbs to coat
sea salt and freshly ground black pepper

Pre-heat the oven to 190°C/375°F/Gas Mark 5.

Cook the grits until soft, then drain off any excess moisture and mash. Fry the onion and celery until tender in butter or margarine. Add the garlic, tomatoes and tomato purée and cook for a further 5 minutes. Mix in the grits, breadcrumbs, parsley, thyme, egg and seasoning (according to taste). Well grease a 450 g/1 lb bread tin and sprinkle with dried crumbs, which should stick to the greased tin. Put the soya mixture into the tin, smooth the top, cover with a piece of greased paper or foil and cook in the pre-heated oven for 1 hour. Leave to stand for a few minutes after removing from the oven, then slide a knife around the edge and turn out on to a warmed serving dish. Serve with a tasty gravy, roast potatoes and green vegetables.

Tomato grits

150 g (5 oz) Lotus Soya Grits
*   1–2 tsp Lotus Flavour-Mix dissolved in 450 ml*
(16 fl oz) water to make stock
1 onion, peeled and chopped
1 tbsp vegetable oil
1 clove garlic, crushed
1 tsp dried sage
½ tsp celery salt
1 can concentrated tomato soup (do not dilute)
sea salt and frehsly ground black pepper

Soak the grits in the stock, then simmer until most of the stock is absorbed. Gently cook the onion in the oil until soft. Add the garlic, sage, herbs and celery salt and cook for a further 2 minutes. Add the concentrated soup and the grits, season to taste and cook for 5 minutes. Serve with a vegetable of your choice and brown rice.

NATURE'S BURGER

Hearty Open Omelette

Serves 3

3 free range eggs
2 tbsp milk plus 1 tbsp water
¼ tsp sea salt
twist of black pepper
1 dstsp sunflower margarine
pinch of oregano or mixed herbs (optional)

Filling
75 g (3 oz) Nature's Burger Mix
100 ml (4 fl oz) water
1 small courgette, cut in thin rings
50 g (2 oz) button mushrooms
50 g (2 oz) grated cheese to top

Mix the 100 ml/4 fl oz water with the Burger Mix, form into burgers and cook as directed on the packet. Drain on absorbent kitchen paper. Sauté the courgettes and mushrooms lightly in a very little sunflower oil. Crumble up the burgers and place in a small oven-proof dish with the sautéed vegetables and keep them warm while you make the omelette.

Separate the eggs and whisk the whites until stiff Beat in the salt and a little black pepper. Beat egg yolks with the milk and water until thickish, then fold them into the whites. Melt the margarine in a frying pan and spoon in the omelette mixture. Cook on moderate heat until the underside is golden brown. Still in the pan, place the omelette under a hot grill for 20 seconds. Spoon on the burger and vegetable filling, sprinkle the cheese on top, with a pinch of oregano or mixed herbs if you wish. Return to the grill, cook until the cheese is just tinged with a light golden brown, and serve immediately with a fresh green salad.

Nature Burger Soufflé

Serves 4

75 g (3 oz), dry weight, Nature's Burger Mix
100 ml (4 fl oz) water
25 g (1 oz) unbleached white flour
275 ml (10 fl oz) milk
25 g (1 oz) sunflower margarine
little sea salt and freshly ground black pepper
3 free range eggs, separated

Pre-heat the oven to 180°C/350°F/Gas Mark 4.

Make up the Nature Burger Mix with the water as directed on the packet and cook as directed. Drain on absorbent kitchen paper. When cooled slightly, chop into small pieces. Put the flour in a medium mixing bowl, stir in 2 tablespoons of the milk and blend to a smooth paste. Bring the rest of the milk to the boil in a heavy-based saucepan and gradually pour this into the paste, stirring constantly. Return to the pan and bring to boil, stirring constantly with a wooden spoon. Simmer for a few minutes until thick. Remove from the heat, stir in the margarine and season to taste (not too much as the burger mix is savoury enough). Return to a low heat and cook for 3 minutes more. Remove from the heat, cool slightly, then stir in the chopped burgers. Beat the egg yolks one at a time into the sauce. Whisk whites until stiff. Fold the whites carefully into the soufflé mixture, using a metal spoon. Pour this mixture into a well-greased 1.2 litre/2 pint soufflé dish. Place the dish in a pan of hot water and bake in the centre of the pre-heated oven for 40 minutes until well risen and golden brown.

NATURE'S WAY

Barley and Bean Casserole with Herby Dumplings

Serves 4–5

1 large carrot, peeled and diced
1 large onion, peeled and chopped
1 tbsp vegetable oil
1 tbsp wholemeal flour
1.2 litres (2 pints) vegetable stock or 1½ vegetable
   stock cubes dissolved in 1.2 litres (2 pints) water
1 tsp yeast extract
1 tsp dry mustard
225 g (8 oz) mushrooms, sliced
100 g (4 oz) Nature's Way Pot Barley, soaked for 4
   hours overnight (not pearl barley)
100 g (4 oz) Nature's Way Butter Beans, soaked
   overnight
50 g (2 oz) Nature's Way Haricot Beans, soaked
   overnight

Dumplings
100 g (4 oz) brown wheatmeal flour, self-raising
1 tsp baking powder
40 g (1½ oz) soft vegetable margarine
1 tbsp mixed herbs
cold water to mix

Cook the carrots and onions in a large saucepan with the vegetable oil for 5 minutes over a moderate heat. Stir in the flour, then gradually add the stock, stirring all the time and slowly bringing back to the boil. Add the yeast extract, mustard, mushrooms, barley and beans. Stir well and cover. Cook over a low heat for 1 hour or transfer to a casserole dish and bake at 190°C/375°F/Gas Mark 5.

Make the dumplings by sieving the flour and baking powder into a mixing bowl. Rub in the margarine until the mixture resembles bread-crumbs, stir in the herbs and pepper and mix to a soft dough with cold water. Form into balls or roll out and cut into six scone shapes with cutters. Add to the casserole for the last 20 minutes of the cooking time.

Nutty Mushroom Roast

Serves 3–4

50 g (2 oz) polyunsaturated margarine
100 g (4 oz) button mushrooms, chopped
1 medium onion, peeled and chopped
50 g (2 oz) Nature's Way Mixed Nuts, chopped
100 g (4 oz) cheese, grated
75 g (3 oz) wholemeal breadcrumbs
1 tsp yeast extract
sea salt and freshly ground black pepper to taste
1 egg, beaten

Melt the margarine over a low heat, add the mushrooms, onion and nuts and cook for 15 minutes. Add the grated cheese, breadcrumbs, yeast extract and seasoning. Finally add the beaten egg. Mix thoroughly, place in a greased baking dish and bake in the oven at 190°C/375°F/Gas Mark 5 for 30 minutes until nicely browned.

Spiced Black-eye Beans

Serves 4

225 g (8 oz) Nature's Way Black-eye Beans, *soaked overnight*
2 onions, peeled and finely chopped
50 g (2 oz) polyunsaturated margarine
50 g (2 oz) Nature's Way Cashew Nuts
4 cloves garlic, crushed
1 green chilli, finely chopped
½ tsp paprika
1 tsp turmeric
½ tsp ground cumin
2 tsp ground coriander
1 tsp fresh ginger, grated
50 g (2 oz) Nature's Way Brown Lentils
500 ml (1 pint) vegetable stock
1 tbsp desiccated coconut
1 tsp freshly ground black pepper
2.5 cm (1") cinnamon stick
1 tsp garam masala

Place the beans in a saucepan with half the chopped onion and cover well with cold water. Bring to the boil and then simmer until tender – about 45 minutes. Drain.

Melt the margarine and gently sauté the rest of the onion with the cashew nuts, garlic, chilli, paprika, turmeric, cumin, coriander and ginger. Stir together, add the beans, lentils and vegetable stock and stir again. Add the remaining ingredients and simmer gently for 30 minutes. Serve with brown rice.

Pine Kernel and Olive Stuffed Tomatoes

Serves 4

8 large, firm tomatoes
6 tbsp olive oil
1 large onion, peeled and finely chopped
1 clove garlic, crushed
75 g (3 oz) Nature's Way Pine Kernels
12 black olives, stoned and chopped
100 g (4 oz) wholemeal breadcrumbs
2 tbsp fresh parsley, chopped
1 tbsp chives, chopped
1 tbsp Parmesan cheese, grated
25 g (1 oz) butter or *polyunsaturated margarine*

Place the tomatoes on a board and cut off the tops with a sharp knife. Discard the tops. With a teaspoon scoop out and discard the seeds, taking care not to pierce the skin. Set the tomatoes aside. In a frying pan heat the oil over a moderate heat, and sauté the onion and garlic for 10 minutes. Remove from the heat and stir in the pine kernels, olives, breadcrumbs and herbs. Using a teaspoon, fill the tomatoes with the breadcrumb mixture. Place the tomatoes in an oven-proof dish large enough to take them in one layer, sprinkle with the Parmesan cheese and top each one with a little butter or polyunsaturated margarine. Bake at 190°C/375°F/Gas Mark 5, for 20–25 minutes.

PAUL'S TOFU

Tofu Burgers

100 g (4 oz) bulgur wheat
2 tbsp shoyu
1 onion (approx. 150 g/5 oz), very finely chopped
225 g (8 oz) Paul's Firm Tofu
2 tbsp fresh parsley, chopped
1 tbsp sunflower oil
2 tbsp green pepper, de-seeded and very finely chopped
freshly ground black pepper
1 level tbsp arrowroot or *1 medium egg*
soya oil for frying

Put the bulgur in a small mixing bowl and stir in the shoyu. Add enough water just to cover by 5 cm/2", put a lid on the bowl and leave to stand for 20 minutes. Sauté the onion in the oil for 5 minutes with lid on until soft. Stir the onion into the bulgur mixture with all the other ingredients, taste and add more shoyu if necessary. Divide into portions, mould the burgers well with the hands and shallow fry in hot oil for 3 minutes on each side until golden. Drain well on kitchen paper and serve hot with a tomato sauce and steamed green vegetables, or cold with salad.

Children like these served in baps and spread with tomato sauce (try Whole Earth Ketchup) for a light lunch. Give them an apple afterwards and they will have had a pretty wholesome midday meal.

Tofu Risotto

Serves 5

This rich Italian sauce with tofu, stirred into brown rice, makes a truly nourishing and delightful meal.

350 g (12 oz), dry weight, Italian short or *long grain brown rice*
1 level tsp sea salt
3 tbsp olive or *sunflower oil*
1 large onion, peeled and finely chopped
2 large cloves garlic, crushed
2 sticks celery, finely chopped (use tender stalks)
2 medium courgettes, cut into thin rings
½ red and ½ green pepper, cut into small pieces
100 g (4 oz) button mushrooms, thinly sliced
1 large bay leaf
1 rounded tsp dried basil or *1 tbsp fresh basil*
½ tsp tarragon
450 g (1 lb) fresh ripe tomatoes, skinned and chopped or *canned tomatoes*
1 tbsp tomato purée
1 tbsp lemon juice
1–2 tbsp shoyu
freshly ground black pepper to taste
350 g (12 oz) Paul's Firm Tofu, sautéed (see recipe on page 43)

Measure out the rice in cupfuls while dry. Wash well by placing in a sieve and letting cold water run through the grains for 1 minute. Place in a medium sized, heavy-based saucepan with a tight lid. For the Italian rice which is in this recipe, add twice the volume of water to the rice, sprinkle in the salt, bring to the boil, turn down to simmer, and cover and simmer for 35 minutes. The water should all be absorbed and the grains separate. (Do not stir or take off the lid during cooking time or the rice will become 'sticky'.)

While the rice is cooking, prepare the sauce. Heat the oil in a large, heavy-based saucepan and sauté the onion and garlic for 6 minutes with the lid on. Add the celery and continue to cook for 4 minutes more with the lid on. Add the courgettes, chopped peppers and mushrooms, this time stirring the vegetables for 2 minutes. Add the bay leaf, basil, tarragon and pepper and simmer for 1 minute. Add the skinned tomatoes, tomato purée, shoyu (taste after 1 tablespoon is added – you may not need more) and lemon juice. Mix well and heat through, stirring constantly. Place the savoury sautéed tofu on top of the sauce, cover and keep on a low heat until the tofu is warmed through. Finally, fork in the cooked rice. Serve with either a fresh green salad or steamed green vegetable such as broccoli, French beans or runner beans.

Tofu Tempura with Sweet and Sour Sauce

Serves 5

Tempura is the Japanese name for deep-fried battered vegetables, meat or fish. (In India these are called pakora.) The batter can be made with wholemeal flour or unbleached white, but I prefer the delicate taste and crisp texture achieved by using a mixture of gram flour (chick pea flour), brown rice flour and soya flour. By using a polyunsaturated oil with a high 'smoke' point and heating it up well, you make sure the tempura absorbs the minimum amount of fat.

When making this recipe with vegetables, choose a selection from thin slices of carrot, broccoli florets, whole button mushrooms, French beans, onion rings, and thinly sliced aubergine and peppers. Dip these in the batter, deep fry in hot oil, drain on kitchen paper and serve hot sprinkled with shoyu or sweet and sour sauce. See how quickly they disappear!

450 g (1 lb) Paul's Firm Tofu, cut into 2.5 cm (1") cubes
shoyu

Batter
75 g (3 oz) chick pea flour
40 g (1½ oz) soya flour
40 g (1½ oz) brown rice flour
just under 1 level tsp baking powder
just under 1 level tsp sea salt
about 250 ml (9 fl oz) cold water

Opposite: **Granose** *Soya Chunk Goulash (above) page 60, Moussaka with Savoury Cuts (below) page 60*

Overleaf: **Itona** *Rogan Josh Soya Chunk Curry, page 69*

Sauce

3 tbsp sesame or sunflower oil
1 medium onion, peeled and finely chopped
2 cloves garlic, crushed
1 medium carrot, scraped and thinly sliced in
*   slanting ovals*
1 small can bamboo shoots, well drained and
*   sliced or 1 small turnip, peeled and very thinly*
*   sliced*
1 small green pepper, cut in thinnish rings, then
*   quartered*
1 level tsp fresh ginger root, grated
1/2 level tsp five spice or allspice
100 g (4 oz) fresh pineapple, finely chopped or use
*   canned*
1 1/2 tbsp clear honey
3 tbsp cider vinegar
2 tbsp shoyu
2 tbsp tomato purée
1 tbsp arrowroot
275 ml (10 fl oz) water

Soya oil for deep frying
wholemeal flour for coating tofu

Sprinkle shoyu over the cubes of tofu in a shallow bowl and leave to marinate while you prepare the batter and sauce.

To make the batter, sieve the flours into a mixing bowl with the baking powder and sea salt and gradually add the water to form a smooth, light and creamy batter. Cover, and leave to stand for 30 minutes, while you prepare the sauce.

To make the sauce stir-fry the onions, garlic, carrots and bamboo shoots or turnip in the hot oil for 3 minutes only. Add the peppers and continue to stir-fry for 2 more minutes. Stir in the grated ginger, five spice or allspice and chopped pineapple. Set aside while you mix all the other ingredients in a medium-sized bowl, gradually adding the water as you would to make a batter. Pour this over the vegetables, return to a gentle heat and cook until the mixture thickens slightly, stirring all the time. Set aside, to be re-heated when the tofu tempura is ready.

Heat soya oil for deep frying. Pick up pieces of tofu with a fork, letting the excess shoyu drip back into the dish. Roll each in wholemeal flour and dip

Previous Page: **London Herb and Spice Co** *Red Bean Hotpot (above) page 72, Golden Fish Bake with Pasta (below) page 71*
Opposite: **Prewett's** *Gougère with Asparagus, Mushroom and White Wine Sauce (above) page 143, Broccoli Pancakes with Spiced Kidney Bean Filling (below) page 82*

into the batter by placing each piece again on a fork and letting the excess batter drip back into the bowl. Deep fry until golden brown. Drain on absorbent kitchen paper and place in a serving dish, pouring the re-heated sweet and sour sauce over the top.

Serve with plain boiled brown rice. I use Surinam long grain rice for Eastern-type dishes as it is lighter in texture and takes only 25 minutes to cook.

Vegetable Casserole with Tofu

Serves 4

This very simple, tasty casserole can also be used as a filling for a pie. Just place the mixture in a pie dish and top with wholemeal pastry (see my basic Wholemeal Pastry recipe on page 129 and bake for 30 minutes at 190°C/375°F/Gas Mark 5.

1 large onion, peeled and chopped
1 large clove garlic, crushed
2 medium carrots, scraped and cut into thin 2.5 cm
*   (1") sticks*
3 tbsp sunflower oil
3 sticks celery, chopped
1 medium green pepper, de-seeded and cut into
*   small pieces*
1 tbsp fresh parsley, chopped
1 tsp mixed herbs
1 tbsp wholemeal flour or unbleached white flour
1/2 vegetable stock cube dissolved in 575 ml (1 pint)
*   hot water*
1 generous tbsp tomato purée
1 teacup frozen peas
1 tbsp shoyu
350 g (12 oz) Paul's Firm Tofu, sautéed (see page 43
*   for recipe)*

Sauté the onion, garlic and carrot in the oil for 5 minutes only. Add the celery and continue to sauté for 3 more minutes. Stir in the green pepper, parsley and mixed herbs and fry for 2 more minutes. Stir in the flour and cook, stirring constantly, for 1/2 minute. Add the water in which you have dissolved the 1/2 stock cube, plus the tomato purée and stir with the peas for 1 minute more. Stir in the shoyu. Place this mixture into a casserole dish, cover and bake at 190°C/375°F/Gas Mark 5 for 25 minutes. Fork in the tofu and bake for a further 5 minutes until the tofu is warmed through. Serve with either a whole grain or potatoes steamed in their jackets.

PREWETT'S

Basic Pancake Batter

Makes 12 pancakes

100 g (4 oz) Prewett's 100% Wholemeal Flour
2 large eggs
275 ml (10 fl oz) milk
½ tsp sea salt
2 tbsp olive or *sunflower oil*
extra oil for frying

Using a blender, food processor or by hand, mix in the flour, eggs, half the milk and the sea salt until smooth. Gradually add the remaining milk, followed by the oil. Leave to stand for 2 hours. By leaving the batter to stand, starch cells in the flour will swell, the batter will thicken slightly and your pancakes will be much lighter. When you are ready to make the pancakes, beat the batter vigorously. Have a small bowl of oil plus a piece of kitchen paper, screwed into a ball, at the ready. Dip the paper into the oil and wipe it over the base of the pan, leaving a thin coat of oil on the surface. Heat the pan well, then drop 2 tablespoons of the batter into the pan. Tilt it so that the batter covers the base. It will cook in about half a minute (watch the heat – adjust it to avoid burning). Toss the pancake over with a palette knife and cook the other side for just under half a minute. The first one might stick but as you regulate the heat so that the pan stays evenly hot this will not happen. The pancakes can be stacked one on top of the other until you are ready to fill them. They can also be frozen successfully. De-frost completely before use and peel off each one carefully.

Broccoli Pancakes with spiced Kidney Bean Filling

Makes 10

225 g (8 oz) broccoli or *sprouting broccoli tops*
100 g (4 oz) Prewett's 100% Wholemeal Flour
½ tsp bicarbonate of soda
225 ml (8 fl oz) milk
1 level tsp sea salt
2 eggs
2 tbsp sunflower oil
4 tbsp cold water
little soya oil for frying

Filling
175 g (6 oz) dry weight, red kidney beans, soaked overnight
1 dessertspoon clear honey
1 tsp sea salt
1 large onion, peeled and finely chopped
2 tbsp olive oil
1 recipe quantity Spiced Tomato Sauce (see page 221)
75 g (3 oz) farmhouse Cheddar cheese, grated

Cook the broccoli in a little salted water for 10 minutes. Drain well and chop. Allow to cool. Mix together the flour, bicarbonate of soda, milk, salt, eggs and oil until smooth. Add the cold chopped broccoli and stir until a green-speckled batter is achieved. Cover and leave to stand for 2 hours. Stir in the cold water. The mixture should be a runny batter consistency. Test by taking out 1 tablespoon of the batter: if it pours off the spoon easily and spreads with a little help from the back of the spoon it is just right. If too thick then add a little more cold water. Brush a small, heavy-based frying pan with oil. Heat well, then turn the heat down to medium high, spoon in 2 tablespoons of the mixture and spread thinly into a circle with the back of a spoon. Cook for half a minute, turn over with a palette knife and cook for another half minute. When cooked, pile the pancakes on top of each other on a plate. They will not stick. Put to one side.

Rinse the soaked beans and bring to the boil in 850 ml/1½ pints of water. Boil for 10 minutes, then add the honey and simmer for 45 minutes–1 hour, until the beans are soft but not mushy. Add the teaspoon of sea salt just before the end of the cooking time. Drain the beans, discarding the cooking water. Sauté the onion in the oil until soft, about 5 minutes, then stir in the cooked and drained beans, plus half the cold Spiced Tomato Sauce, and cook gently for 10 minutes. Grease a large square or rectangular oven-proof dish. Fill and roll up each pancake in the dish, placing them side by side (2 tablespoons of the mixture will be ample for each). Heat the remaining tomato sauce and trickle this over the pancakes. Finally, sprinkle on the grated cheese. Bake at 180°C/350°F/Gas Mark 4 for 25 minutes.

Serve with a fresh green salad of Webb lettuce, cucumber, watercress and parsley, and a lemon and olive oil dressing.

Chicken and Mushroom Bake

Serves 3–4

1 packet Prewett's Main Course, Chicken Flavour
200 ml (7 fl oz) warm water
100 g (4 oz) button mushrooms, finely chopped
25 g (1 oz) Prewett's Soft Vegetable Margarine
25 g (1 oz) Prewett's 100% Wholemeal Flour
275 ml (10 fl oz) skimmed milk
freshly ground black pepper
25 g (1 oz) cheese, finely grated

Pre-heat the oven to 200°C/400°F/Gas Mark 6.

Lightly grease a 575 ml/1 pint, deep pie dish. Add the warm water to the Main Course Mix and stir well. Place in the greased dish and smooth the top. Bake for 15 minutes. Meanwhile make a mushroom sauce. Melt the margarine in a pan over a low heat and stir in the flour. Cook for 1 minute, then gradually add the milk, beating well to make a smooth sauce. Bring to the boil to thicken, then reduce the heat to simmer and stir in the chopped mushrooms. Season with black pepper and keep hot until the baked mixture is ready. Pour the sauce over the chicken mixture and sprinkle the grated cheese on top. Turn down the oven to 180°C/350°F/Gas Mark 4, and bake for 15 minutes until golden brown. Serve at once.

Mushroom and Almond Pilaf

Serves 4

A pilaf is an Eastern dish which is basically rice with added spices. It is served with cooked meat and vegetables or nuts and vegetables. Try it with Main Course, as in this recipe, and see how delicious it is. I have added a few blanched, toasted almonds to garnish.

1 packet Prewett's Main Course, Chicken Flavour
4 level tbsp Prewett's Sunflower Margarine
2 medium onions, peeled and chopped
1 large clove garlic, crushed
225 g (8 oz) Italian long grain brown rice, soaked for 2 hours and drained
225 g (8 oz) small button mushrooms
725 ml (1¼ pints) hot water plus 1 vegetable stock cube
good pinch saffron
1 tsp methi (fenugreek leaf) – optional but great

½ tsp chilli powder or cayenne pepper
1 teacup frozen or fresh peas, cooked
40 g (1½ oz) blanched and toasted almonds (to toast simply place the dry nuts on a baking tray and put in the oven at 150°C/300°F/Gas Mark 3, for 15–20 mins)
1 tbsp fresh parsley or coriander leaves, chopped

Reconstitute the Main Course Mix as directed and form into four large burgers. Grill for 5 minutes, turning once. Place on a plate and leave to cool. Heat the margarine in a heavy-based saucepan and sauté the onion and garlic until soft. Add the well drained rice and button mushrooms and continue to fry for 3 minutes more. Stir in the hot stock, saffron, methi and chilli or cayenne. Bring to the boil, stirring constantly. Turn down to simmer, cover and cook gently for 30–35 minutes until all the water is absorbed. Stir the cooked peas into the rice. Crumble the now cool burgers and fork gently into the rice mixture. Place in a serving dish and garnish with the toasted almonds and chopped parsley or coriander leaves.

Savoury Leek Plait

Serves 4

175 g (6 oz) Prewett's 100% Wholemeal Flour
75 g (3 oz) Prewett's Soft Vegetable Margarine
cold water to mix
1 packet Prewett's Main Course, Sausage Flavour
200 ml (7 fl oz) warm water
100 g (4 oz) leeks
skimmed milk to glaze

Sieve the flour into a mixing bowl and add the bran from the sieve. Divide the margarine into small knobs and add to the flour. Rub in finely, using the fingertips, until the mixture resembles fine breadcrumbs. Place in the refrigerator while preparing the filling. Heat the oven to 200°C/400°F/Gas Mark 6. Stir the sausage mix into the warm water. Trim away the coarse green leaves and roots from the leeks and roughly chop. Place in a bowl and stir in the sausage mix. Make a soft dough by adding cold water to the pastry mix, and roll out on a lightly floured surface to a rectangle 25 cm × 20 cm/10″ × 8″. Trim the edges. Arrange the filling along the central third. Slash the pastry on either side at 1 cm/½″ intervals into strips, fold over the top and bottom to enclose the filling, then arrange the strips alternately across the filling. Place the plait on a baking tray and glaze with milk. Bake in the centre of the oven for 15–30 minutes until golden brown.

Parsley Pancakes with Leeks, Mushrooms and White Wine

Serves 4

The white wine is a luxury and not essential. Add it if you are making this recipe for a dinner party. You will probably have to buy 900 g/2 lb of leeks to get 450 g/1 lb when trimmed.

1 recipe quantity of Basic Pancake Batter (see page 82)
50 g (2 oz) fresh parsley sprigs, stems included
450 g (1 lb) leeks, weight when trimmed
3 tbsp sunflower oil
225 g (8 oz) small button mushrooms, sliced
725 ml (1¼ pints) milk
50 g (2 oz) Prewett's Brown Wheatmeal Flour
½ level tsp ground mace
½ top mustard powder
25 g (1 oz) polyunsaturated margarine
Sea salt and freshly ground black pepper
100 g (4 oz) farmhouse Cheddar cheese, finely grated
150 ml (5 fl oz) dry white wine

Blend the parsley sprigs with the batter ingredients. Make pancakes as directed and stack one on top of the other until ready to fill. Trim the leeks by cutting a slight indent around the area where the coarse leaves begin and pull off the dark, coarse leaves to reveal the lighter green leaves underneath, still attached to the white ends. Wash the leeks well. Cut into 1.5 cm/¾″ rings. Heat the oil in a pan and sauté the leeks for 7 minutes with the lid on. Add the mushrooms to the leeks and sauté for 3 minutes, coating the mushrooms well with the leek juices. Remove from the heat and leave to one side. In a bowl blend half the milk, flour, mace and mustard until smooth. Gradually add the remaining milk and continue to stir until well blended. Heat the margarine in a heavy-based saucepan, pour in the milk mixture and bring to the boil, stirring constantly. Turn down to a very low heat and cook for 2 minutes, then take off the heat, season with sea salt and freshly ground black pepper and stir in half the grated cheese.

Halve the sauce and stir one half into the leeks and mushrooms. Fill 8 pancakes with the leek mixture (about 2 tablespoons to each pancake), roll each one up and place in a well-greased baking dish. (Any remaining pancakes may be frozen for later use.) Add the wine to the remaining sauce and trickle this over the pancakes in the dish, leaving the ends free of sauce. Sprinkle on the remaining cheese and bake at 200°C/400°F/Gas Mark 6 for 20 minutes, until golden brown on top.

PROTOVEG

Burger Cheese Salad Baps

Makes 4

My children and their friends love this very quick and familiar, tasty tummy filler.

100 g (4 oz) Protoveg Burgamix (TVP)
½ tsp basil
1 small onion (about 75 g/3 oz when peeled and very finely chopped)
4 wholemeal baps (see page 124 for recipe)
1 thin slice of Cheddar cheese per bap
1 small onion cut into very thin rings
tomato ketchup
2 thin slices of tomato per bap
few crisp lettuce leaves (Cos, Webb or Chinese leaf)

Place the Burgamix in a bowl, add the basil and the very finely chopped onion and hydrate as directed on the packet. When hydrated squash well together for 1 minute, then form the mixture into burgers and fry as directed.

Heat the baps in the oven, split and place a burger on one half of each, then put a slice of cheese and three thin rings of onion on top of each burger. Grill the halves for 1 minute until the cheese is soft. Remove from the heat and put a little ketchup, two tomato slices and some crisp lettuce leaves on each half, top with the other (warm) half of the bap and see how much these are enjoyed.

The following recipes using Protoveg products are taken from two excellent books by Anna Roberts: *The Magic Bean* and *The Protoveg Cook Book*.

Hamburger Rissoles

Serves 5

115 g (4½ oz) Protoveg Pork Flavour Mince (TVP)
2 tsp yeast extract
1 tbsp tomato ketchup
1 tbsp vegetarian Worcester Sauce
1 tsp mixed herbs
salt and pepper
1 onion, peeled and finely chopped
vegetable oil to fry
1 egg, beaten

Hydrate the Protoveg with yeast extract, tomato ketchup, Worcester Sauce, herbs and seasoning. Meanwhile, cook the onion in a small quantity of oil. Drain any liquid from the Protoveg and keep for stock. Add the mince to the onion and cook until the mixture is firm. Allow to cool, then bind with the beaten egg, form into rissoles and grill or fry.

Homely Potato Layer Pie

Serves 5–6

175 g (6 oz) Protoveg Sosmix (TVP)
handful of cashew nuts
2 leeks
3 carrots
4 medium potatoes
1 tbsp chives
sunflower oil
polyunsaturated margarine

Hydrate the Sosmix as directed and add the cashews. Prepare the vegetables. Cut the leeks into rings, grate the carrots and slice the potatoes thinly. Soften the vegetables and chives in a little oil. Put half the potatoes in the bottom of a greased oven-proof dish and layer the rest of the vegetables on top. Cover with a layer of Protoveg, top with the remaining potatoes, dot with margarine and bake for 35 minutes at 180°C/350°F/Gas Mark 4. Serve with wholemeal rolls and homemade chutney.

Jumbo Grills with Vegetables

Serves 6

225 g (8 oz) Protoveg Jumbo Grills or Soya Slices (TVP)
1 tbsp vegetarian Worcester Sauce
2 tbsp fresh or 1 tbsp dried chives
450 g (1 lb) raw potatoes, diced
100 g (4 oz) whole button mushrooms
100 g (4 oz) fresh or frozen peas
3 sticks celery, chopped
vegetable stock (use water in which you have cooked vegetables) or water

Hydrate the grills or soya slices by the method given on packet. Put them and the liquid into a very large saucepan with the Worcester Sauce and chives. Simmer for 30 minutes. Add the vegetables, with a further quantity of vegetable stock or water to cover. Simmer until the vegetables are cooked.

Leprechaun's Crock

Serves 4–5

50 g (2 oz) Protoveg Menu (TVP)
1 tbsp tomato purée
1 tsp mixed herbs
1 small wholemeal loaf
150 ml (5 fl oz) milk
sea salt and freshly ground black pepper to taste
75 g (3 oz) vegetable rennet cheese, grated

Hydrate the Protoveg Menu according to the packet instructions, adding the tomato purée and herbs. Simmer until the liquid is absorbed. Cut the top from the loaf to a depth of 5 cm/2". Scoop the bread from the inside of the lower portion. Crumble this and mix with the milk. Season to taste. When the Protoveg is ready, mix this into the crumbs. Pack the mixture into the crust of the loaf, sprinkle with cheese and replace the 'lid'. Wrap in foil and bake for 25–30 minutes at 190°C/375°F/Gas Mark 5.

This is delicious hot or cold, cut into thick slices for a substantial meal with mixed vegetables or salad. Also excellent for lunch boxes.

Nut Roast

Serves 6

50 g (2 oz) polyunsaturated margarine
1 large onion, peeled and chopped
2 large carrots, scrubbed and grated
75 g (3 oz) Protoveg Natural Flavour Mince (TVP)
225 g (8 oz) mixed nuts, ground (do not use
  peanuts)
1 tsp mixed herbs
2 free range eggs
2 tsp yeast extract

Melt the margarine and sauté the chopped onion and grated carrots in a saucepan with the lid on for 10 minutes. Soak the Protoveg. Add the nuts, drained mince and mixed herbs and mix well. Beat the eggs, mix in the yeast extract and add to the Protoveg mixture. Place in a greased loaf tin and cook in a moderate oven, 180°C/350°F/Gas Mark 4, for 45 minutes. Serve with cooked vegetables or a mixed salad.

Leftover cooked vegetables can be used in the nut roast. Add when the nuts are mixed in. This produces a roast better served with salad.

Paprika Jumbo Grills

Serves 4

8 Protoveg Jumbo Grills or Soya Slices (TVP)
2 large onions
50 g (2 oz) polyunsaturated margarine
1 tbsp paprika
1 green pepper, cut into strips
3 large tomatoes, skinned and chopped
sea salt
150 ml (5 fl oz) sour cream
a little water or stock
1 tbsp wheatmeal flour
150 ml (5 fl oz) single cream

Hydrate the grills or slices according to packet instructions. Chop and fry the onions in the margarine until transparent. Sprinkle the paprika into the onions and cook for a few minutes, add the grills and pepper strips and simmer for another 5 minutes. Mix in the skinned and chopped tomatoes, the sea salt and sour cream, adding a little extra water or stock if the mixture is too thick. Allow 30–45 minutes' cooking time. Blend the flour with the single cream and add this to the mixture. Stir thoroughly. Simmer for another 2–3 minutes. Serve with green pasta and a colourful side salad.

Pork-style Curry

Serves 3

50 g (2 oz) Protoveg Pork Flavour Chunks (TVP)
285 g (10 fl oz) natural yoghurt
725 ml (1¼ pints) water
1 tbsp chick pea flour (gram flour)
4 tbsp ghee or sunflower oil
½ tsp mustard seed
½ tsp cumin seed
1 tsp fenugreek leaf (methi)
3 or 4 whole cloves
25 cm (1") cinnamon stick
1 tsp turmeric
1 tsp coriander
1 tsp cayenne pepper
½–1 tsp sea salt
1–2 tbsp sugar

Hydrate the Protoveg by the simmering method described on the packet, until the liquid is just absorbed. Beat the yoghurt, water and chick pea flour together. In a separate pan, heat the ghee or sunflower oil and add to it the mustard seed, cumin seed, fenugreek, cloves and cinnamon stick. Stir rapidly until the spices are heated. When the mustard seeds dance, add the yoghurt liquid and continue to mix well. Lower the heat and add the turmeric, coriander, cayenne, salt and sugar. Simmer for 15–20 minutes, then add the Protoveg and simmer for a further 10 minutes. Remove the cloves and cinnamon stick just before serving.

Serve with long grain rice. Side dishes of banana, coconut, raisins, mango chutney or lime pickle complete this meal.

Note Cayenne controls the pungency of the curry. If a milder or hotter curry is required, reduce or increase the cayenne to personal taste.

Protoveg Casserole

Serves 4

55 g (2 oz) Protoveg Ham Flavour or Natural Flavour
  Chunks (TVP)
25 g (1 oz) Protoveg Smokey Snaps Mince (TVP)
1 medium onion, peeled and chopped
450 g (1 lb) potatoes, peeled and sliced
450 g (1 lb) carrots, scraped and sliced
100 g (4 oz), dry weight, red lentils, washed
sea salt and freshly ground black pepper to taste
vegetable stock or water

Hydrate the chunks in hot water, as directed on the packet, while the vegetables are being prepared. Put all the ingredients in a large casserole. Cover with stock or water and a lid and place in the oven at 220°C/425°F/Gas Mark 7 for 15 minutes. Reduce the heat to 180°C/350°F/Gas Mark 4 and cook for about 1½ hours or until the lentils are soft. This casserole can be cooked in a large covered saucepan on the cooker top if preferred. Stir occasionally to prevent sticking. The cooking time for this method is about 45 minutes.

Protoveg Croquettes

Serves 4–5

3 large potatoes
50 g (2 oz) Protoveg Pork Flavour Mince (TVP)
1 tsp marjoram
1 tsp oregano
3–4 tbsp wholemeal breadcrumbs
2 tbsp corn oil

Scrub the potatoes (do not peel) and grate finely. Hydrate the Protoveg mince (see page 227) with the herbs until the liquid is absorbed. Mix the potatoes, mince and breadcrumbs together to a consistency that can be moulded into small balls. Heat the oil. Place the balls of Protoveg in the oil, flattening with the back of a spoon and fry until brown on both sides. Serve hot or cold with a salad.

Protoveg Fritters

Serves 6

115 g (4½ oz) Protoveg Natural Flavour Mince (TVP)
200 ml (7 fl oz) water
2 small bay leaves
1 tbsp yeast extract
1 large onion, peeled and finely chopped
vegetable oil to fry
100 g (4 oz) wheatmeal flour
2 free range eggs, beaten
200 ml (7 fl oz) milk
1 tsp mixed herbs
freshly ground black pepper

Simmer the Protoveg in water with bay leaves and yeast extract until the liquid is absorbed. Meanwhile, lightly fry the onion in a little oil. Place the flour in a bowl, mix in the beaten eggs, milk, herbs and seasoning, add the Protoveg and mix thoroughly. Heat oil for shallow frying in large frying pan.

Drop spoonfuls of the Protoveg mixture into the pan and fry, turning frequently, until golden brown. Serve hot with vegetables and gravy or cold with a salad.

Protoveg Pork Mince can be used as an alternative to vary this recipe.

Protoveg Ravioli

Serves 5

Pasta
225 g (8 oz) brown wheatmeal flour
½ tsp sea salt
25 g (1 oz) polyunsaturated margarine

Filling
115 g (4½ oz) Protoveg Menu (TVP)
2 tomatoes, skinned
2 sticks celery
½ tsp oregano
freshly ground black pepper

Sieve the flour and salt together, rub in the margarine and mix with a little water to make a stiff dough. Knead until smooth, divide into two portions and roll out thinly. Hydrate the Protoveg Menu, until all the liquid is absorbed. Chop the tomatoes and celery, mix in the oregano and pepper to taste and add these to the Protoveg. Place teaspoonsful of mixture on one layer of pastry, leaving 2.5 cm/1" between each mound of filling. Brush the second layer of pastry with milk and place this on top of the pastry and filling, pressing firmly between each mound. Cut into squares. Leave on a well floured tray for 2 hours. Heat a saucepan of well-seasoned stock or water and boil the ravioli parcels for 15–20 minutes. Drain and serve with a tomato sauce and grated cheese.

Risotto Vegetal

Serves 6

50 g (2 oz) Protoveg Beef Flavour Mince (TVP)
1 medium onion, peeled and chopped
vegetable oil to fry
575 ml (1 pint) vegetable stock
sea salt and freshly ground black pepper
225 g (8 oz) brown rice, cooked
100 g (4 oz) sweetcorn
2 carrots, scraped and grated
1/2 red pepper, de-seeded and diced
1/2 green pepper, de-seeded and diced
6 large cabbage leaves

Hydrate the Protoveg following the packet instructions, keeping any excess liquid to use with the stock. Cook the chopped onion in a little oil until transparent, then add the stock, seasoning, rice and Protoveg and cook for 5 minutes. Add the sweetcorn, grated carrot and finely diced peppers. Stir, and cover the saucepan. Simmer for about 15 minutes or until all the liquid has been absorbed. Meanwhile, drop the cabbage leaves in boiling salted water for about 5 minutes. To serve, arrange the leaves on a suitable dish and pour the Protoveg mixture on to the centre of them. Serve immediately.

Shepherd's Surprise Pie

Serves 4–6

1 small onion, peeled and chopped
2 tbsp vegetable oil
1 small green pepper, de-seeded and chopped
1 tbsp ground cumin
1 tbsp coriander
1 tsp ground ginger
425 g (15 oz) can red kidney beans
575 g (20 oz) can tomatoes
225 g (8 oz) pineapple pieces
75 g (3 oz) Protoveg Natural Flavour Mince (TVP)
2 tsp mixed mustard
sea salt and freshly ground black pepper to taste
4 large potatoes, cooked and mashed
2 tbsp sunflower seeds
1/2 tsp ground nutmeg
polyunsaturated margarine

Fry the onion in the oil until soft. Add the green pepper, cumin, coriander and ginger and cook gently for a further 2 minutes. Carefully add 75 ml/

3 fl oz water. Mix in the drained kidney beans, chopped tomatoes with juice, pineapple pieces and Protoveg. Cook for 15 minutes. Add the mustard and seasoning and simmer for 15 minutes to let the flavours mingle. Pour the mixture into a greased pie dish and cover with mashed potato, roughing the potato into peaks. Sprinkle sunflower seeds and nutmeg over the surface and dot with margarine. Brown under a medium grill for 10 minutes. Serve with a green vegetable.

Sosburg Loaf

Serves 5–6

100 g (4 oz) Protoveg Burgamix (TVP)
100 g (4 oz) Protoveg Sosmix (TVP)
3 slices wholemeal bread, crumbled
2 medium onions, peeled and finely grated
2 medium carrots, scrubbed and finely grated
2 tsp mixed dried herbs
2 tbsp tomato purée
2 tsp yeast extract
1 free range egg (optional)
water or vegetable stock

Mix all the ingredients together in a large bowl, beating the yeast extract with the egg, if used. Add more water or vegetable stock until the mixture is soft and pliable. Press firmly into a greased loaf tin, cover with a piece of greaseproof paper and bake for 30–40 minutes at 180°C/350°F/Gas Mark 4. Serve with roast potatoes, green vegetables and gravy.

This loaf is delicious cold with salad, or thinly sliced for sandwiches with mustard or pickles.

Stuffed Cabbage Leaves

Serves 4

4 large cabbage leaves
50 g (2 oz) Protoveg Beef Flavour Mince (TVP)
1 small onion, peeled and chopped
225 g (8 oz) can tomatoes, chopped
1 tsp yeast extract
150 ml (5 fl oz) hot water
1/2 tsp mixed herbs
1 tbsp tomato ketchup
4 drops tabasco sauce
1 tsp lemon juice
freshly ground black pepper
sea salt

Blanch the cabbage leaves in boiling water for 5 minutes, cutting out the stalks if they are tough. Hydrate the Protoveg Mince as directed on the packet and add the onion, and the tomatoes with their juice. Dissolve the yeast extract in the hot water and add this to the Protoveg Mince. Bring to the boil. Add the herbs, tomato ketchup, tabasco, lemon juice and seasoning to taste. Turn down the heat and simmer for 15 minutes or until the liquid has reduced and the mixture is fairly dry. Divide the mixture into four and place a quarter on each cabbage leaf. Roll the cabbage leaves into parcels, place in a covered oven-proof dish and bake for about 30 minutes at 180°C/350°F/Gas Mark 4. Serve with brown rice.

Protoveg Sweet and Sour

Serves 5

115 g (4½ oz) Protoveg Natural Chunks (TVP)
1 vegetable stock cube
1 tbsp shoyu
2 medium onions, peeled
25–35 g (1–2 oz) polyunsaturated margarine
50 g (2 oz) unbleached white flour
3 tbsp cider vinegar
2 tbsp honey
sea salt and freshly ground black pepper to taste
1 small can pineapple chunks or three 1.5 cm (1")
  slices of fresh pineapple

Hydrate the Protoveg chunks with water, stock cube and shoyu for 20–30 minutes. Meanwhile, slice the onions and fry gently in the margarine for 10 minutes or so, until soft, but not brown. Mix in the flour, blending well to disperse any lumps. Gradually add 575 ml/1 pint of stock, stirring thoroughly. The hydration liquid can be used as part of this quantity. When the sauce thickens, add the cider vinegar and honey and seasoning to taste. Mix in the Protoveg and the chopped pineapple and juice. Cover and cook very gently for 10–15 minutes. Serve with crispy noodles.

REAL EAT

Bobotie

Serves 4

This recipe was devised by Vicky Booth of Manchester.

1 packet Real Eat Vegeburger, Herb & Vegetable
  Style
20 g (¾ oz) polyunsaturated margarine or butter
1 onion, peeled and finely chopped
1 dessert apple, peeled, cored and finely chopped
275 ml (10 fl oz) milk
sea salt and freshly ground black pepper
2 dessertspoons medium hot curry powder
1–2 slices wholemeal bread
25 g (1 oz) sultanas or raisins
1 tsp lemon juice
2 tsp wine vinegar or cider vinegar
3 eggs
25 g (1 oz) almonds, flaked
2 bay leaves

Pre-heat the oven to 180°C/350°/Gas Mark 4.

Make up the Vegeburger Mix with 1 egg and 100 ml/4 fl oz of water and set aside. Melt the margarine in a frying pan, add the onion and apple and fry gently for 5 minutes until softened and lightly coloured. Crumble in the Vegeburger Mix and fry for a further 2–3 minutes. Stir in the curry powder and cook, stirring, for 2 minutes more. Remove from the heat.

Put the bread in a large bowl with 2–3 tablespoons of the milk. Break up with a fork and add the Vegeburger Mix, onion, apple, sultanas, vinegar and lemon juice. Stir well. Spread the mixture in a 1.5 litre/2½ pint shallow, oven-proof dish. Beat the remaining milk with 2 eggs and season to taste with salt and pepper. Pour this over the Vegeburger mixture and scatter the flaked almonds over the surface. Lay the bay leaves on top. Cover and cook in the centre of the oven for 30 minutes. Remove the lid and cook for 15 minutes more, until golden and set.

Serve hot with boiled rice and traditional curry accompaniments such as desiccated coconut, chutneys, sliced onion and poppadoms, or with a green salad.

Cheese Filled Burgers

Either grate, or slice thinly, some Cheddar cheese and work it into the centre of your Vegeburgers when you are shaping them. It will be beautifully melted and gooey inside when the burgers are cooked. Experiment with other cheeses and even other fillings. Sorry slimmers, but low fat cheeses won't melt so well!

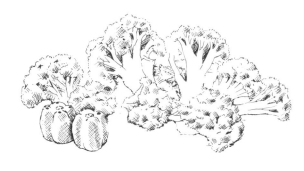

Italian Herb Sauce

Serves 2–4

This recipe has been devised by Jean Rowland of Litherland.

1 packet Real Eat Vegeburger, Herb & Vegetable Style
2 tsp vegetable oil, preferably olive
1 small onion, peeled and diced
2 small courgettes, sliced
1 pinch (about ½ tsp) oregano
1 tsp dried parsley
425 g (15 oz) can tomatoes

Cook 4 Vegeburgers following the instructions on the packet and crumble into small pieces. Heat the oil and sauté the onion and courgettes for about 10 minutes, then add the herbs and tomatoes, including the juice. Simmer for another 5 minutes and then add the cooked Vegeburger pieces. Stir well and cook for another 5 minutes until thoroughly heated.

Serve hot with your favourite pasta – it is especially good with tagliatelle (flat green noodles).

Kibbey

Serves 4

This is a version of a traditional Arabic dish.

1 packet Real Eat Vegeburger, Herb & Vegetable Style
175 g (6 oz) fine bulgur
1 large onion, peeled and diced
2 dessertspoons fresh parsley, chopped
25 g (1 oz) pine kernels
sunflower oil to fry
a little oil, butter or margarine

Rinse the bulgur and soak in enough water to cover for 30 minutes. Make up the Vegeburger mix following packet directions and set aside. Sauté the diced onion and parsley in a little oil until transparent. Set aside. Sauté the pine kernels until lightly browned and mix with the sautéed onion and parsley. Drain the bulgur and squeeze out all the water very thoroughly. Mix with the soaked Vegeburger Mix.

Oil the bottom and sides of a 25 cm × 18 cm/ 10″ × 7″ baking tin at least 3.5 cm/1½″ deep. Spread one half of the bulgur/Vegeburger mixture on the bottom of the tin and press smoothly. Now spread the onion mixture on top and cover evenly with the rest of the Vegeburger/bulgur. Brush the top with a little oil or melted butter or margarine and bake at 200°C/400°F/Gas Mark 5, for 30 minutes.

Mom's Lasagne

Serves 4–6

This recipe was devised by Margaret Sams of Ealing.

1 packet Real Eat Vegeburger
8 sheets lasagne
1 large onion, peeled and chopped
2 cloves garlic, chopped
2–3 tbsp vegetable oil
2 tbsp tomato purée
400 g (14 oz) can tomatoes, chopped
¼ tsp oregano
3 tbsp Cheddar cheese, grated

Bechamel Sauce
50 g (2 oz) butter or polyunsaturated margarine
40 g (1½ oz) wholemeal or wheatmeal flour
725 ml (1¼ pints) hot milk or ½ milk/½ water (or use soya milk)
pinch nutmeg
sea salt

Make up the Vegeburger Mix following packet instructions (omit the egg if desired), cook 4 Vegeburgers and set aside. Cook the lasagne following packet instructions, drain and lay out on a towel until needed. Sauté the chopped onion and garlic in the oil until slightly browned. Mix the tomato purée with ½ teacup of water and add, together with the tin of chopped tomatoes. Cook for 10 minutes more, stirring occasionally. Add the oregano, then crumble the cooked Vegeburgers into the mixture, stir well and cook for another 5–10 minutes.

Make the Bechamel sauce by melting the butter or margarine and adding the flour. Keep stirring and then slowly add the hot milk (or milk/water, or soya milk), stirring until slightly thickened. Add nutmeg and salt to taste.

Put a thin layer of the tomato mixture in the base of a large rectangular oven-proof dish. Put in a layer of lasagne, then another layer of tomato mix, repeating until all the ingredients are used up. Pour the Bechamel sauce on top and poke the lasagne with a sharp knife so that the sauce soaks in a little. Sprinkle the grated cheese on top and bake at 180°C/350°F/Gas Mark 4 for 40 minutes.

Nutty Scotch Eggs

Serves 4

This recipe was devised by Miss Jevon of Stourbridge.

4 eggs hard-boiled, cooled and shelled
1 packet Real Eat Vegeburger
1 tbsp 100% wholemeal flour
1 egg, beaten
75 g (3 oz) cashews or peanuts, chopped

Make up the Vegeburger Mix following packet instructions and divide into four parts. Dust the eggs with flour then coat evenly and thinly with the Vegeburger Mix. Brush the covered eggs with beaten egg and roll them in the chopped nuts, pressing the nuts well into the Vegeburger covering. Bake in the oven at 190°C/375°F/Gas Mark 5, for 30 minutes.

The traditional manner of cooking Scotch eggs is by deep-frying. The baking method is superior, however, but it does take a little longer. If serving halved, cool before cutting lengthwise. These are good served with a tomato sauce.

Vegherd's Pie

Serves 4

3 large potatoes, peeled and chopped into large
pieces
1 packet Real Eat Vegeburger, Herb & Vegetable
Style
1 egg
1–2 litres (2–3 pints) water
4 tbsp shoyu
6 tbsp 100% wholemeal flour
2 large onions
2 tbsp oil
2 large carrots
½ tsp mustard powder
2 tsp butter or polyunsaturated margarine
(optional)

Boil the potatoes until they are soft enough to mash. Mix the packet of Vegeburger Mix with the egg and 50 ml/2 fl oz of the water. Set aside. Mix the shoyu and wholemeal flour in a jar with half the remaining water, cover and shake vigorously, then pour into a large saucepan with the rest of the water. Heat gently and stir for a few minutes until you have a thick gravy.

Dice the onions and sauté in the oil. Slice the carrots and add to the onions. After 5 minutes quickly crumble in the soaked Vegeburger Mix, sauté for another minute, add the mustard and put the mixture into the bottom of an oven-proof dish. Pour the gravy over, ensuring that it soaks into the 'Vegherd's Pie' mixture. Mash the potatoes with ½ teacup of their cooking water and 2 teaspoons of butter or margarine (optional) and spread evenly on top of the vegetables. Score with a fork and cook in the oven at 200°C/400°F/Gas Mark 6 for 30 minutes, or until just starting to brown.

SLYMBRED

Slymbred Surprise Cheese Loaf

Serves 4

1 large onion, peeled and chopped
1 large green pepper, de-seeded and chopped
25 g (1 oz) polyunsaturated margarine
175 g (6 oz) mushrooms, sliced
12 Slymbreds, crumbled
3 eggs, beaten
salt and pepper to taste
110 g (4 oz) grated cheese
½ tsp mixed herbs
sliced tomatoes and watercress to serve

Sauce
400 g (14 oz) can tomatoes
½ onion, peeled and chopped
sea salt and freshly ground black pepper to taste
dash of Worcester Sauce

Gently fry the onion and green pepper in the margarine until soft but not browned. Add the mushrooms and cook for a further 2 minutes. Remove from the heat and add all the remaining ingredients except the cheese and herbs. Mix thoroughly. Grease a 900 g/2 lb loaf tin and press the mixture into it. Sprinkle with the cheese and herbs and bake in a moderate oven, 180°C/350°F/ Gas Mark 4, for 45 minutes.

Serve hot with sliced tomatoes and watercress and pour over the tomato sauce, made by blending all the sauce ingredients together in a liquidizer and heating in a pan for 5 minutes before serving.

SOUP BREAK

Barbecued Ribs

Serves 6

1 onion, peeled and diced
1 tbsp cooking oil
2 tbsp brown sugar
1 tbsp tomato purée
2 tbsp French mustard
1 sachet Soup Break, Tomato and Beef Flavour
1 kg (2 lb) spare ribs of pork

Lightly fry the onion in the oil, until browned. Add the sugar, tomato purée and mustard. Make up the Soup Break as directed on the packet and add to the pan, bring to the boil and cook for 5 minutes. Pour the sauce over the pork ribs and place in a moderately hot oven, 190°C/375°F/Gas Mark 5, for 1–1½ hours, basting frequently.

Chicken Hot Pot

Serves 4–6

2 tbsp vegetable oil
4 sticks celery, sliced
2 onions, peeled and sliced
4 rashers back bacon, diced
1.5 kg (3 lb) roasting chicken
675 g (1½ lb) potatoes, peeled and cut into quarters
4 carrots, peeled and cut into quarters
3 sachets Soup Break, Chicken Flavour
grated rind of 1 lemon

Heat the oil in a large, flame-proof casserole and add the celery, onions and bacon. Fry over a low heat for 10 minutes, then remove the vegetables and bacon with a slotted spoon and reserve. Add the chicken to the pan and brown on all sides, turning it over with a spoon. Return the bacon, celery and onion to the pan with the potatoes and carrots. Make up the Soup Break and add to the pan with the lemon rind. Bring to the boil, cover and cook in a moderate oven, 180°C/350°F/Gas Mark 4, for 1½ hours or until the chicken is tender. Serve with a green vegetable.

Fish Chowder

Serves 4

2 rashers lean bacon, diced
1 onion, peeled and diced
450 g (1 lb) haddock, skinned and cut into 2.5 cm (1″) pieces
396 g (14 oz) can tomatoes, chopped
2 potatoes, peeled and diced
1 sachet Soup Break, Minestrone Flavour
150 ml (5 fl oz) skimmed milk

Fry the bacon until transparent, add the onion and fry until soft. Add the fish, the tomatoes and the potatoes. Make up the Soup Break as directed on the packet, add to the pan and bring to the boil. Lower the heat and simmer for 15 minutes until the potatoes and fish are cooked. Stir in the milk and serve as a main meal with crusty bread or as a very filling but not too fattening lunch.

Hungarian Goulash

Serves 4

675 g (1½ lb) chuck steak, cut into cubes
1 tbsp cooking oil
25 g (1 oz) butter or polyunsaturated margarine
1 large onion, peeled and chopped
2 cloves garlic, crushed
3 sachets Soup Break, Oxtail Flavour
4 tbsp tomato purée
1 tbsp paprika
sea salt and freshly ground black pepper
150 ml (5 fl oz) natural yoghurt

Fry the steak in the mixed oil and butter (or margarine) over a high heat until well browned. Add the onion and garlic and continue frying until the onion is transparent. Make up the Soup Break as directed on the packet and add to the pan with the tomato purée, paprika, salt and pepper. Bring to the boil, then lower the heat and simmer, covered, for 2 hours (alternatively cook in a moderate oven, 180°C/350°F/Gas Mark 4), until the meat is tender. If liked, thicken the sauce with a little cornflour when cooked. Serve topped with a swirl of yoghurt.

Mediterranean Chicken

Serves 4

2 tbsp oil
4 chicken joints
2 large onions, peeled and diced
2 cloves garlic, sliced
2 red peppers, de-seeded and diced
2 sachets Soup Break, Chicken Flavour
396 g (14 oz) can tomatoes
1 tsp mixed herbs

Heat the oil in a large frying pan and fry the chicken on all sides until golden. Add the onion, garlic and peppers and cook for a further 2–3 minutes. Make up the Soup Break as directed on the packet and add to the pan with the tomatoes and herbs. Bring to the boil, cover, and simmer for 30–45 minutes until the chicken is tender. Remove the chicken from the pan, place on a serving dish and keep hot. Pour the sauce into a liquidizer or food processor and blend until smooth. Pour the sauce over the chicken and serve with a crisp green salad.

Rich Steak and Mushroom Stew

Serves 4

450 g (1 lb) lean stewing steak
25 g (1 oz) butter or polyunsaturated margarine
2 onions, peeled and diced
225 g (8 oz) mushrooms, sliced
2 sachets Soup Beak, Beef Flavour
1 tbsp Worcester Sauce
675 g (1½ lb) cold cooked potatoes
a little extra butter or polyunsaturated margarine

Melt the butter or margarine in a flame-proof casserole. Cut the steak into cubes and fry until browned. Add the onions and mushrooms and cook for a further 5 minutes until the onion and mushrooms have softened. Make up the Soup Break as directed on the packet and add to pan with the Worcester Sauce. Bring to the boil, cover and cook in a moderate oven, 180°C/350°F/Gas Mark 4, for 2 hours.

Thinly slice the potatoes, arrange in a layer over the beef, dot with a little extra butter and return to the oven, uncovered, for a further 30–40 minutes, until the potatoes are golden. Serve with a green vegetable.

Sweet and Sour Pork

Serves 4

675 g (1½ lb) lean pork, cubed
1 tbsp cooking oil
1 onion, peeled and diced
1 red pepper, de-seeded and sliced
4 carrots, peeled and thinly sliced
2 sachets Soup Break, Tomato and Beef Flavour
1 small can pineapple in natural juice
2–3 tbsp vinegar

Lightly fry the pork in the oil until browned. Add the onion, red pepper and carrots and fry for another 3–4 minutes. Make up the Soup Break as directed on the packet and add to the pan with the contents of the can of pineapple and the vinegar. Bring to the boil, cover, and simmer for 30–40 minutes until the pork is tender. Serve with boiled rice.

Sweetly Sauced Liver

Serves 4

450 g (1 lb) lamb's liver, sliced
25 g (1 oz) butter or polyunsaturated margarine
1 tbsp made English mustard
1 tbsp tomato purée
2 tbsp mango or other sweet chutney
1 sachet Soup Break, Oxtail Flavour

Lightly fry the liver in the butter or margarine until brown and add the mustard, tomato purée, chutney and Soup Break made up as directed on the packet. Bring to the boil, then simmer for 8–10 minutes until the liver is tender. Serve with noodles or boiled potatoes and carrots.

Vegetable Casserole

Serves 4

2 medium aubergines
1 large onion, peeled and thickly sliced
2 cloves garlic, chopped
1 green pepper, de-seeded and cut into strips
1 red pepper, de-seeded and cut into strips
4 courgettes, sliced
6 tomatoes, sliced
1 sachet Soup Break, Minestrone Flavour

Slice the aubergines thickly, sprinkle with a little salt and leave for 20 minutes, then rinse and drain. Dry on kitchen paper. Heat the oil in a large frying pan, add the vegetables and fry, turning frequently, for 10 minutes. Make up the Soup Break as directed on the packet and pour it over the vegetables. Bring to the boil, then cover and simmer gently for 30–40 minutes. Serve hot or cold.

SUNWHEEL

Buckwheat Savoury with Hiziki

Serves 4

Buckwheat has a very distinctive flavour and is quite delicious with a piquant vegetable sauce. It contains rutic acid which is known to have a good effect on the circulatory system, is rich in iron and the B vitamins. It is best to buy ready-toasted buckwheat which only takes 15 minutes to cook.

25 g (1 oz) Sunwheel Hiziki
3 tbsp Sunwheel Cold Pressed Sunflower Oil
225 g (8 oz) ready toasted buckwheat
850 ml (1½ pints) boiling water
1 scant tsp sea salt
2 medium onions, peeled and chopped
1 clove garlic, crushed
2 medium courgettes, sliced
1 green pepper, de-seeded and chopped
1 level tsp ground coriander
1 level tsp paprika
½ cinnamon stick
1 bay leaf
1 tsp fresh mint leaves, chopped
225 g (8 oz) fresh ripe tomatoes
2 tbsp lemon juice

Soak the hiziki for 10 minutes, then drain. In a heavy-based saucepan heat 1 tablespoon of the oil, add the buckwheat and stir over gentle heat for 2 minutes. Pour on the boiling water. Add the salt and simmer on a low heat with the lid on for 15 minutes. Heat the remaining oil in a pan and sauté the onion and garlic for 5 minutes with the lid on. Add the courgettes and continue to sauté for 3 minutes more. Add the green pepper and sauté with the other vegetables for 3 minutes. Stir in the coriander, paprika, cinnamon stick, bay leaf and mint. Skin the tomatoes by cutting a circle around the stalk end and immersing in boiling water for 5 minutes. Mash the tomatoes with the lemon juice and add to the sautéed vegetables with the drained hiziki. Stir well and simmer with the lid on for 15 minutes. Stir occasionally.

Serve the buckwheat and the sauce in separate bowls. The buckwheat is very soft when cooked and will become soggy if mixed with the sauce too soon before eating.

Curried Cabbage with Arame

Serves 4

½ packet Westbrae Arame
2 tbsp Sunwheel Cold Pressed Sunflower Oil
1 medium onion, peeled and sliced
1 tsp curry powder
225 g (8 oz) cabbage
1 tbsp Sunwheel Shoyu

Soak the arame in cool water for 15 minutes. Remove the arame and carefully reserve 50 ml/ 2 fl oz of the liquid; discard the rest. Sauté the onion in the oil until soft, stir in the curry powder and sauté for 3 more minutes. Add the cabbage and reserved soaking water. Cover and simmer for 2 minutes. Toss in the drained arame and the shoyu, then cover and simmer until tender but crisp, about 5–8 minutes.

Hiziki and Toasted Almond Risotto

Serves 4

I love hiziki. It is similar in appearance to arame but stronger in flavour. Here is a very tasty recipe and I think a good introduction to this delicious seaweed.

75 g (3 oz) almonds, blanched and split
225 g (8 oz) dry weight, Italian short grain organic brown rice
25 g (1 oz) Sunwheel Hiziki, soaked in cool water for 10 minutes
575 ml (1 pint) water
sea salt
2 tbsp Sunwheel Cold Pressed Sesame Oil
225 g (8 oz) leeks, trimmed (leaving as much soft green on as possible) and cut into thin rings
1 medium courgette cut into thin 2.5 cm (1") sticks
100 g (4 oz) small button mushrooms
100 g (4 oz) frozen peas
4 medium-sized ripe tomatoes, skinned and mashed
225 g (8 oz) bean sprouts, washed and towel-dried
1 tbsp Sunwheel Shoyu

Toast the almonds on a lightly oiled oven tray, at 180°C/350°F/Gas Mark 4 for 15 minutes, or until lightly browned. Meanwhile, wash the rice in a sieve by letting cold water run through the grains for ½ minute. Put in a medium sized, heavy-based saucepan, add the water and a very little sea salt. Bring to the boil, then turn down to simmer. Cover tightly. If the lid is not well-fitting, cover with foil overlapping the rim of the pan and then put on the lid. Simmer for 35 minutes. By then all the water will be absorbed and the grains separate and still firm but not too crunchy.

Heat the oil in a frying pan and sauté the leeks and courgettes for 6 minutes (3 minutes with the lid off, 3 minutes with the lid on). Add the mushrooms and drained hiziki and cook for 2 minutes only with

the lid off. Stir in the mashed tomatoes and the frozen peas and simmer, stirring constantly, for 1 minute. Add the bean sprouts, almonds (save a few for garnish) and shoyu and cook for 3 minutes more, stirring constantly.

Stir this mixture into the cooked rice and sprinkle on a few toasted almonds. Serve with a watercress, crisp lettuce and cucumber salad for a delightful meal. Adding 2 tablespoons of sesame seeds to the rice before cooking will add not only more nutrients but also a delicious nutty texture and flavour.

Luxury Nut Roast

Serves 6

See page 86 for a less expensive nut roast.

75 g (3 oz) pistachio nuts (weight when shelled)
75 g (3 oz) pine kernels
50 g (2 oz) pumpkin seeds
100 g (4 oz) almonds or hazel nuts
175 g (6 oz) wholemeal breadcrumbs
1 medium onion, peeled and finely chopped (approx 175 g/6 oz when chopped)
2 tbsp Sunwheel Shoyu
3 tbsp Sunwheel Cold Pressed Sunflower Oil
2 standard eggs
3 tbsp fresh parsley, chopped
few pumpkin seeds for top of roast
2 tbsp cold pressed sunflower oil for sprinkling over the loaf and potatoes

Pre-heat the oven to 190°C/375°F/Gas Mark 5.

Grind the nuts and seeds so that they look like medium to fine breadcrumbs (not too powdery). Mix all the Ingredients together, moulding well with your hands. Grease a roasting tin. Form the nut mixture into a loaf shape, flatten the top slightly and place on the tray. Pour a little oil over the top and sprinkle on a few pumpkin seeds. Cap the roast loosely so that the foil does not stick to the roast and bake for 45 minutes on the middle shelf of the pre-heated oven.

Potatoes that have been steamed for 10 minutes to soften slightly can be roasted with the nut roast. Serve with gravy (see page 22 for Vegetable Gravy) and Cranberry Sauce (see page 217 for recipe).

Nori-wrapped Savoury Rice Balls

Makes 10

225 g (8 oz) short grain brown rice
575 ml (1 pint) water
50 g (2 oz) sunflower seeds
50 g (2 oz) sesame seeds
50 g (2 oz) pumpkin seeds
2 tbsp Sunwheel Cold Pressed Sunflower Oil
1 onion, (175 g/6 oz in weight when peeled and
finely chopped)
1 tbsp fresh parsley, finely chopped
1 tbsp fresh marjoram, chopped or 1 level tsp dried
1 tbsp Sunwheel Shoyu
1 tbsp lemon juice
2 egg yolks if deep frying
few sheets of nori, lightly toasted in the oven

Wash the rice in a sieve by running cold water through the grains for ½ minute. Bring to the boil with the water. Turn down to simmer, cover tightly and simmer for 35 minutes. Remove from the heat but leave the lid on for 10 more minutes; then cool the rice in a colander while you prepare the other ingredients. (Leaving the lid on will make the rice softer and easier to mould into balls.)

While the rice is cooking toast the seeds on a dry baking sheet in the oven, at 180°C/350°F/Gas Mark 4, for 15 minutes, until lightly browned. Finely grind the seeds in a food processor or blender. Sauté the onion in the oil until soft and with just a tinge of golden brown. Stir in the parsley, marjoram, shoyu and lemon juice and stir this mixture into the slightly cooled rice. Mould well together, kneading the ingredients. Form into golf-ball sized balls and either wrap immediately in the lightly toasted nori sheets (cut them to size) or add the egg yolks, mould well together and deep fry the rice balls. Drain on absorbent kitchen paper and then wrap while still warm in the nori sheets.

Note It is important to add the egg yolks if deep frying, or the mixture may break up.

Red Bean and Aubergine Moussaka

Serves 4

The aubergine is a staple vegetable of the Middle East and the main ingredient in moussaka. Minced beef or lamb are often used but in this recipe red kidney beans, which go extremely well with aubergines, are substituted. It is a rich dish, just right for a special dinner party – add a glass of red wine to the liquid when entertaining, instead of the water.

175 g (6 oz) red kidney beans
sea salt
1 tsp honey
3 aubergines (each approx. 225 g/8 oz in weight)
4 large tomatoes
1 tbsp tomato purée
1 level tsp instant vegetable broth mix
150 ml (5 fl oz) hot water or red wine
6 tbsp Sunwheel Cold Pressed Sunflower or Olive
Oil
2 medium onions, peeled and cut in half lengthwise
freshly ground black pepper

Topping
1 rounded tbsp gram flour (chick pea flour)
1 rounded tbsp wheatmeal flour
1 egg
225 ml (8 fl oz) milk, goat's or cow's
3 tbsp natural yoghurt
sea salt and freshly ground black pepper
75 g (3 oz) Cheddar or Parmesan cheese, finely
grated (optional)

Wash the beans and soak overnight, changing the water three times. Bring to the boil in fresh water. Boil for 10 minutes, then simmer for 40 minutes more or until soft. Add a little sea salt (about 1 level teaspoon) and the honey 10 minutes before the end of the cooking time. Drain the beans, discarding the cooking liquid. Wash and thinly slice the aubergines. Arrange the slices in layers in a colander, sprinkle each layer with sea salt and leave to stand for 30 minutes (this process draws off bitter juices). Meanwhile, skin the tomatoes by cutting a circle around the stalk and blanching in boiling water for 5 minutes. Set the steel blades of a food processor in position. Put the tomatoes, tomato purée, instant vegetable broth and hot water or wine into the processor bowl and blend until smooth. Pour into a jug. Rinse out the processor bowl and wipe dry. Set the slicing plate in position and slice the onions, a half at a time (stand them upright in the feed tube).

Heat 2 tablespoons of the sunflower or olive oil and sauté the onion, covered, for 7 minutes until soft. Stir in the beans, the tomato/stock liquid and freshly ground black pepper and cook gently with a lid on for 10 minutes. Rinse the aubergine slices and pat them dry in absorbent kitchen paper. Sauté them in the remaining sunflower or olive oil until golden.

Oil a large oven-proof baking dish. Arrange a layer of aubergines and the oil you cooked them in, in the base of the dish, spoon a layer of the bean mixture over these, another layer of aubergines and so on, finishing up with a layer of aubergines. Now turn on the oven to pre-heat to 180°C/350°F/Gas Mark 4.

To make the topping, set the steel blades in position and place the gram flour, wheatmeal flour, egg and half the milk into the processor bowl and blend until smooth. Gradually add the remaining milk through the feed tube with the motor still on. Finally blend in the yoghurt. Season with freshly ground black pepper and sea salt. Pour the batter over the aubergine mixture, place in the centre of the pre-heated oven and bake for 35–40 minutes until golden brown and bubbling on the top. If liked, sprinkle finely grated Cheddar or Parmesan cheese over the top before baking.

VECON

Vegetable Casserole

Serves 4

100 g (4 oz), dry weight, whole green lentils, cooked
450 g (1 lb) potatoes, scrubbed and sliced
2 medium carrots, scrubbed and sliced
1 large parsnip, peeled and sliced
2 large onions, peeled and sliced
2 medium leeks, cleaned and sliced
100 g (4 oz) sweetcorn
100 g (4 oz) mushrooms, sliced

sea salt and freshly ground black pepper
2 tbsp fresh parsley, chopped
1 tbsp fresh mint, chopped
grated rind 1 orange
850 ml (1½ pints) hot Vecon stock
50 g (2 oz) Cheddar Cheese, grated

Pre-heat the oven to 325°F/170°C/Gas Mark 3.

Grease a 2 litre/3½ pint casserole, and arrange in it the lentils and vegetables in layers, seasoning each layer with salt, pepper and herbs and finishing with a layer of overlapping slices of potato and parsnip. Mix the orange rind into the hot stock and pour over the vegetables. Cover the casserole with foil, then with a lid, stand it on a baking tray and bake in the pre-heated oven for 2½ hours, or until the vegetables are tender. Remove the lid and foil, sprinkle the cheese on top and cook under a hot grill until the cheese bubbles and browns. Serve hot.

WESTERN ISLES

Curried Rice

Serves 4

1 good size onion, peeled and chopped
1 tbsp Western Isles Sesame Oil or butter
50 g (2 oz) cashew nuts
50 g (2 oz) raisins, washed
1 apple, sliced
2 tbsp Western Isles Shoyu
1–2 tbsp curry powder
680 g (1 lb 8 oz) Western Isles Quick Brown Rice, cooked (225 g/8 oz dry weight rice)

Sauté the onion in sesame oil or butter until soft. Add all the remaining ingredients except the rice. Cover and simmer for 1 minute. Mix in the rice and cover to warm through.

Delicious with hot pitta bread. Try it chilled in summer, too, as a salad.

Jambalaya

Serves 6

450 g (1 lb) mushrooms, sliced
1 tsp Western Isles Sesame Oil
2 medium green, red or *yellow peppers, de-seeded
   and chopped*
1 large Spanish onion, chopped
2 sticks celery, chopped
375 g (14 oz) can tomatoes
1 tbsp Western Isles Shoyu
1 tsp paprika
¹/₃ tsp cayenne pepper
¹/₂ tsp ground cumin
*680 g (1 lb 8 oz) cooked Western Isles Quick Brown
   Rice (350 g/12 oz dry weight)*
fried banana rings
desiccated coconut

Sauté the mushrooms lightly in the sesame oil. Add the peppers, onions, celery, tomatoes, shoyu and spices and continue to sauté until all the vegetables are soft. Mix in the cooked rice and pour the mixture into an oiled baking dish. Bake for 1 hour at 150°C/300°F/Gas Mark 2. Garnish with fried banana rings and desiccated coconut.

Hiziki Vegetable Patties

Serves 4

*1 rounded tbsp Western Isles Hiziki, soaked for 15
   minutes, drained and chopped*
¹/₂ tsp sea salt
1 onion, peeled and minced
2 tbsp french beans, blanched and chopped
1 medium carrot, grated
¹/₂ tsp fresh ginger, grated
1 clove garlic, crushed
120 ml (4 fl oz) water
50 g (2 oz) 100% wholemeal pastry flour
50 g (2 oz) oatmeal or *porridge oats*
1 rounded tbsp Western Isles Sunflower Oil
watercress to garnish

Mix the hiziki, salt, vegetables, ginger, garlic and water together. Stir in the flour and oatmeal, form into patties and fry in hot oil until they are golden brown on both sides. Serve with watercress as a garnish.

Hiziki with Rice and Almonds

Serves 4

This beautiful and simple dish is one of my favourites.

1 large onion, finely chopped
2 tbsp Western Isles Sesame Oil
*15 g (¹/₂ oz) Western Isles Hiziki, soaked for 15
   minutes, drained and chopped*
*450 g (1 lb), cooked weight, Western Isles Quick
   Brown Rice (225 g/8 oz dry weight rice)*
*75 g (3 oz) almonds, toasted for 15 minutes in a
   moderate oven*
100 g (4 oz) frozen peas, cooked for 3 minutes
a little Western Isles Shoyu
2 tsps lemon juice (optional)

Sauté the onion in the oil for 10 minutes until soft and just slightly browned. Stir in the chopped hiziki and cook for a further 3 minutes. Stir in the rice, almonds and peas and heat through. Now stir in the shoyu (about 1 level tablespoon should be enough) and lemon juice. Cook for just 1 minute more, then serve immediately if eating hot – but it tastes great cold too as a rice salad.

You can add prawns to this recipe, and it tastes delicious. Simple stir them in when you add the rice, and heat through.

Nori Tempura

Serves 4

Nori is the quickest sea vegetable to prepare. One can simply toast it lightly over an open flame until it turns green and crisp, then cut it into strips and eat it with a sprinkling of shoyu or tamari. The batter for this recipe needs to stand overnight in a cool place.

275 ml (10 fl oz) water or *sparkling bottled water*
100 g (4 oz) 100% wholemeal flour
pinch sea salt
Western Isles Sesame Oil for deep frying
350 g (12 oz) lightly cooked diced vegetables
*2 sheets untoasted nori cut into 5 cm (2 in) wide
   strips*

Mix the water, flour and salt together, beating rapidly to avoid lumps. Leave the batter in a cool place overnight. (Sparkling water lightens the batter, but still water gives a good result. The batter should lightly coat the back of a spoon.) Heat the oil until it begins to smoke. Dip dessertspoons of the vegetables into the batter, roll each in a strip of nori, secure with a toothpick and drop into the oil. Fry until golden brown, drain and serve hot. You can dip nori strips into the batter and deep fry on their own, too.

Western Isles Quick Brown Rice

Serves 4

Before cooking, wash the rice in a saucepan under a running tap until the water runs clear.

175 g (16 oz) Western Isles Quick Brown Rice
cold water in proportion 1 cup water to 1 cup rice
up to ½ tsp sea salt

Use a heavy, tight-lidded saucepan. Bring the rice and water to the boil uncovered and add the sea salt. Boil for 3 minutes, then cover and simmer without stirring until all the water is absorbed (about 20 minutes). Remove from the heat and leave to stand for 5 minutes, then turn out into a serving dish.

To pressure cook the rice, use 1½ times the volume of water to rice (i.e. 3 cups water to 2 cups rice) and cook for 15 minutes after reaching pressure. Pressure cooking ensures that the rice is more evenly cooked.

WHOLE EARTH

Baked Beans à la Provençale

Serves 2

1 medium onion, peeled and chopped
2 tbsp olive oil
3 cloves garlic, chopped
440 g (15½ oz) can Whole Earth Baked Beans
½ jar Whole Earth Italiano Sauce
100 ml (4 fl oz) water

Sauté the onion in the olive oil until it becomes translucent, then add the chopped garlic and continue to sauté gently for 5 minutes, stirring oc-

casionally. Combine with the baked beans, Italiano Sauce and water in a casserole dish, cover tightly, and bake at 180°C/350°F/Gas Mark 4, for 45 minutes – 1 hour.

Beanburgers

Serves 4

440 g (15½ oz) can Whole Earth Baked Beans
3 slices wholewheat bread, crumbled
1 medium onion, peeled and chopped
¼ good size green pepper, chopped (optional)
½ tsp mixed herbs
wholewheat flour for coating

Mix all the ingredients except the flour thoroughly and leave to stand for 20–30 minutes. Carefully make into burger-shaped patties, dip in wholewheat flour, and sauté in a frying pan in a little oil, until both sides are slightly crispy and beginning to brown.

Serve garnished with lettuce, tomato slices, sautéed onion slices and alfalfa sprouts on a wholewheat hamburger bun or between slices of toasted Whole Earth bread.

Brown Rice Rissoles

Serves 4

1 can Whole Earth Brown Rice and Vegetables
50 g (2 oz) sunflower seeds, toasted
50 g (2 oz) bean sprouts, lightly chopped
25 g (1 oz) parsley, finely chopped
1 onion, peeled, chopped and sautéed
1 clove garlic, crushed
50 g (2 oz) wholewheat breadcrumbs
1 egg
oat bran
vegetable oil for frying

Combine all the ingredients except the bran and oil, using the egg to bind. Shape into patties, roll in oat bran and fry in hot oil until golden brown on both sides.

Brown Rice and Peanut Butter Loaf

Serves 4

250 g (10 oz) tofu
1 can Whole Earth Brown Rice and Vegetables
½ jar Whole Earth Crunchy Peanut Butter
1 onion, peeled, chopped and sautéed
4 mushrooms, sliced and sautéed
1 tbsp lemon juice
shoyu
freshly ground black pepper
2 tbsp Whole Earth Tomato Ketchup

Crumble the tofu into a mixing bowl and add the rest of the ingredients. Mix well. Oil a 450 g/1 lb bread tin or line it with foil, place the mixture in the tin and bake for 40–50 minutes at 180°C/350°F/Gas Mark 4.

Brown Rice and Baked Bean Bake

Serves 6

2 cans Whole Earth Brown Rice and Vegetables
1 can Whole Earth Campfire Style Baked Beans
1 large onion, peeled and chopped
4 mushrooms, sliced
150 g (5 oz) Cheddar cheese, grated
freshly ground black pepper
shoyu to taste

Topping
100 g (4 oz) rolled oats
50 ml (2 fl oz) vegetable oil
25 g (1 oz) fresh parsley, finely chopped

Sauté the chopped onion with the sliced mushrooms. Combine the brown rice, baked beans, cheese and vegetables in a mixing bowl and add shoyu and pepper to taste. Place in an oven-proof dish. Combine the topping ingredients and sprinkle evenly over the filling. Bake at 180°C/350°F/Gas Mark 4 until the topping is cooked and golden – about 20–25 minutes.

Italiano and Brown Rice Risotto

Serves 4

1 onion, peeled and chopped
1 stick celery, chopped
4 mushrooms, sliced
1 green pepper, de-seeded and chopped
1 clove garlic, sliced
vegetable oil for frying
1 can Whole Earth Brown Rice and Vegetables
3 tbsp Whole Earth Italiano Sauce
1 tsp root ginger, chopped
1 tsp oregano
cheese, grated (optional)

Sauté the onion, celery, mushrooms, green pepper and garlic until the vegetables are soft. Add the Brown Rice and Vegetables, Italiano Sauce, ginger and oregano and stir-fry together for 2 minutes, then place the mixture in a serving dish. This can be served sprinkled with grated cheese, or grated cheese can be melted on top.

Mushroom and Onion Stir-fry Brown Rice

Serves 4

1 onion, peeled and chopped
100 g (4 oz) mushrooms, thinly sliced
vegetable oil for frying
1 can Whole Earth Brown Rice and Vegetables
shoyu

Sauté the chopped onion and mushrooms in vegetable oil until tender. Add the Brown Rice and Vegetables and continue to stir-fry for a further 2 minutes. Add shoyu to taste.

Peanut Butter Rissoles or Loaf

Serves 3

1 cup dry wholemeal breadcrumbs
1 medium onion, peeled and diced
1 large carrot, scrubbed and grated
1 tsp dried parsley
2 tbsp Whole Earth Peanut Butter
½ tsp sea salt

1 egg, beaten (optional)
wholemeal flour (for coating)
vegetable oil for frying

Mix all the ingredients except the flour together and form into small patties 5 cm/2″ in diameter. Flip into the flour and fry in shallow oil till browned. If the egg is omitted the patties will be a little more crumbly.

The mixture can be baked as a loaf in a greased loaf tin at 180°C/350°F/Gas Mark 4 for 45 minutes.

Riz Provençale

Serves 2

225 g (8 oz) organically grown long grain brown rice
cold water in proportion 2 cups water to 1 cup rice
1 jar Whole Earth Italiano Sauce

Wash the rice, bring it to the boil in the water, cover and simmer for 40 minutes. Add the Whole Earth Italiano Sauce and simmer for another 10 minutes, or bake it by combining the ingredients, boiling for 5 minutes, pouring into a casserole and baking at 190°C/375°F/Gas Mark 5 for 25 minutes.

Vegetarian Chilli

Serves 4

440 g (15½ oz) can Whole Earth Baked Beans
100 ml (4 fl oz) water
125 g (4½ fl oz) vegetarian burger mix (I recommend Vegeburger mix)

Combine all the ingredients and cook gently for 15 minutes.

For a richer-flavoured chilli, substitute tomato juice for the water, sauté ½ a chopped onion and ½ a chopped green pepper in a little oil and add to the ingredients with 2–3 teaspoons of chilli seasoning (not ground hot chillies, unless you like it very hot!).

Yoghurt and Italiano Casserole

2 onions, peeled and chopped
2 sticks celery, chopped
1 green pepper, de-seeded and chopped (optional)
vegetable oil for frying

2 cans Whole Earth Brown Rice and Vegetables
shoyu
1 tsp marjoram
2 tbsp Whole Earth Tomato Ketchup
6 tbsp natural yoghurt
½ jar Whole Earth Italiano Sauce
100 g (4 oz) Cheddar cheese, grated (optional)
paprika

Sauté the vegetables in the oil, stir in the brown rice and season with shoyu, marjoram and tomato ketchup. Place a layer of the rice mixture in the bottom of a casserole dish, and fill with alternate layers of yoghurt, Italiano Sauce and rice, finishing with rice. Sprinkle with grated cheese and paprika and bake for 30–35 minutes at 200°C/400°F/Gas Mark 6.

ZWICKY (MILLOTTO)

Millotto Cheese Savoury

Serves 4–6

225 g (8 oz) Zwicky Millotto (savoury millet)
725 ml (1¼ pints) cold water
175 g (6 oz) grated Cheddar or Leicester cheese
2 eggs
150 ml (5 fl oz) milk
½ tsp salt
freshly ground black pepper
polyunsaturated margarine
parsley sprigs to garnish

Place the Millotto in a saucepan with the cold water. Bring to the boil, cover and simmer for 7 minutes. Stir, remove from the heat and leave covered for 5 minutes. Grease a 1.7 litre/3 pint oven-proof dish with margarine. Place a third of the Millotto in the bottom of the dish and cover with a third of the grated cheese. Repeat these two layers twice more, ending with a topping of grated cheese, having used all the Millotto and cheese. Beat the eggs with the milk, salt and pepper. Strain, and pour over the Millotto mixture. Dot with pieces of margarine. Bake in the oven at 180°C/350°F/Gas Mark 4 for about 40 minutes. Garnish with parsley and serve immediately with vegetables or salad.

6
BREADS and YEASTED DOUGHS

Of course it is better for your health to eat bread made from 100% organically grown whole grains which contain the germ and the fibre necessary for the body to function efficiently. But if your diet includes some wholegrain bread, plenty of fresh vegetables and fruit, pulses, and nuts and seeds, which all have a high fibre content, then a little deviation from the complete wholegrain loaf will not cause problems to your digestive system. In the following recipes I have included unbleached white flour, brown flour (81% wheatmeal and 85% wheatmeal) as well as 100% wholemeal flour and other grains to add a variety of taste and texture to your bread doughs. Most important is that none of the flours used is bleached or contains any additives, preservatives or colouring. I have chosen my favourite recipes supplied by manufacturers and added a few of my own best loved breads for you to try out. Baking bread and other yeasted doughs is really quite a simple process but it needs a bit of practice and patience to perfect. Here are a few hints which will save you a lot of disappointments.

1. Kneading dough well releases the gluten (protein) in the flour. Gluten has a stretchy, rubbery quality and forms tiny bubbles which are filled with carbon dioxide. The carbon dioxide is made when yeast feeding on natural sugars in the dough multiplies. A draught can flatten these bubbles and make the resulting bread too heavy and crumbly. Your dough is well kneaded if it does not retain the impression of a finger.
2. Too much heat kills the yeast but it needs warmth to live. A temperature of around 26°C/80°F is about right. For perfect yeasted doughs a warm kitchen, warm bowl and warm baking tins are essential.
3. Do not leave your dough to rise too long as this will weaken it and dry it out. The resulting bread will have a flat, cracked surface, a coarse texture and holes in it.
4. Although frozen dough will not result in the perfect loaf sometimes it is necessary to freeze some for an emergency. It will still taste better than most bought bread. The best time to freeze dough is when it has risen once, been knocked back and shaped and is in the tin ready to rise for the second time. Just place each tin in a good sized, oiled polythene bag, squeeze out the air, tie the opening 2.5 cm/1″ from the end and put it into the freezer. To defrost place the frozen tin still in its oiled polythene bag in a warm – not hot – place and leave to rise to double its size. It will then be ready for the oven.
5. You can store yeasted doughs in a refrigerator for up to 48 hours after the first kneading. Make sure the dough is placed in a good sized, oiled polythene bag from which the air has been squeezed out. Tie 2.5 cm/1″ from the opening and place in the fridge. When ready to bake just knock back the dough, shape into loaves, place in tins and leave to rise in a warm place until double in size. Then bake as instructed in the recipe.
6. One more very important tip which was given to me by George Marriage of Marriage's Flour Company is that 450 g/1 lb and 900 g/2 lb loaf tins vary enormously in size, so weigh your dough and make sure that the dough when placed in the tin reaches just over halfway up the tin, so that when the dough rises it will form a slight hump over the surface of the tin.

These tips are only guidelines. Remember, flours vary in texture depending on how finely the grains have been ground. The amount of liquid needed will vary according to the type of flour used, the fineness of the grain and the addition of any ingredient such as ground sesame seeds, soya flour or oatmeal that you might incorporate into the ingredients. Have a go at the manufacturers' suggestions when using their particular flour before experimenting. The recipes I have chosen here in this chapter have been tested not only by the manufacturers but also by myself and friends. They do work and have obviously been well tested by their creators. So good luck with these health-giving recipes.

ALLINSON

These recipes using Allinson products have been adapted by Lynda Girvan and are just a few of the many tasty and nutritious dishes created by her for Allinson's.

Cheese and Mushroom Plait

Serves 4

This is mouth watering and wholesome served with a side salad and choice of cheeses as a special lunchtime treat. Using the recipe for Allinson Wholewheat Bread on page 106, make a 450 g/1 lb loaf from one half of the dough and use the other half to make this recipe.

450 g (1 lb) Allinson Wholewheat Bread dough, risen (see recipe on page 106)
175 g (6 oz) button mushrooms, cooked and cooled (or use canned mushrooms)
100 g (4 oz) Cheddar cheese, grated
1 tsp mixed herbs
1 egg, beaten
freshly ground black pepper

Pre-heat the oven to 200°C/400°F/Gas Mark 6.
Without kneading the risen dough, place on a floured surface and roll to a rectangle about 30 cm × 15 cm/12″ × 6″. Place this on a greased, lined and warmed baking sheet and place the filling in the centre, allowing a border of 5 cm/2″ of dough.

Sprinkle on 25 g/1 oz of cheese, then a layer of mushrooms, dust with black pepper and herbs and finish with more cheese, reserving 25 g/1 oz of the cheese. Make even diagonal cuts every 8 mm/¾″ on both long sides of the rectangle. Fold in the ends of the dough and plait the diagonally-cut pieces over the top of the filling. Brush with beaten egg and sprinkle the remaining 25 g/1 oz of cheese down the centre of the plait. Bake in the pre-heated oven for 20 minutes until the plait is crisp and golden. Eat fresh – this is not suitable for freezing.

Danish Pastries

Makes 18

25 g (1 oz) vegetable fat
450 g (1 lb) Allinson Farmhouse Flour, plain
2 level tsp sea salt
1 sachet Allinson Easybake Yeast
250 ml (9 fl oz) water at 43°C/110°F
1 egg, beaten
175 g (6 oz) butter, straight from the refrigerator
a little beaten egg for brushing tops
icing sugar, flaked nuts, cherries and angelica to decorate

Fillings

1) Almond
50 g (2 oz) ground almonds
50 g (2 oz) soft brown sugar
few drops almond essence
a little egg white

(Mix all ingredients together in a bowl, using a small amount for each pastry.)

2) Apple and Sultana
100 g (4 oz) sweetened apple purée
1 level tsp cinnamon
25 g (1 oz) sultanas

(Mix all ingredients together and use a spoonful for each pastry.)

3) Almond and Apricot
50 g (2 oz) marzipan
50 g (2 oz) flaked almonds
50 g (2 oz) dried apricots, chopped

(Put a small amount of each in the centre of each pastry.)

Pastry

Rub the fat into the flour and stir in the salt and Easybake Yeast. Add the warm water and the egg and mix to a dough. Turn on to a work surface and knead the dough for about 5 minutes. Cover the dough loosely and leave to rest for about 5 minutes. Flour the work surface and rolling pin and roll out the dough to about 50 cm × 20 cm/20″ × 8″. Mark into thirds. Using a palette knife, dot the top third with half of the butter. Fold the bottom third up to the centre and the top third down over it. Using a rolling pin, seal the edges. Chill in the refrigerator for 30 minutes. Remove the dough from the refrigerator, roll out as before and dot the top third with the remaining butter. Having sealed the edges, quarter turn the dough, roll out again and fold as before. If the dough is still quite firm and cool, quarter turn and repeat rolling and folding once more. (If the dough has become warm, return it to the refrigerator for about 10 minutes before the last rolling.) When the final rolling and folding has been done the dough may be kept in the refrigerator for several hours or overnight if made up to be used later.

When you are ready to make the pastries, roll out the dough to 45 cm × 30 cm/18″ × 12″ and cut into 5 cm/2″ squares. To make star shapes, put about a teaspoonful of the chosen filling in the centre of each piece, make 3 cm/1½″ cuts into each corner of the squares, fold one side of each cut portion into the centre and press the points firmly into the filling. Brush with beaten egg. For envelope shapes, put about a teaspoonful of the chosen filling into the centre of each piece and fold each corner into the centre of the pastry. Brush with beaten egg.

Place the pastries, well spaced, on greased or parchment-lined baking sheets, cover loosely with polythene and 'prove' at room temperature until well risen (about 30 minutes). Pre-heat the oven to 220°C/425°F/Gas Mark 7 and bake for about 15 minutes until golden brown. Remove from the baking sheets on to a cooling rack. While still hot, brush the pastries with a thin glacé icing made from icing sugar and water and sprinkle with flaked nuts. Decorate with glacé cherries and angelica.

Farmhouse Croissants

Makes 12

These are a lovely light treat for Sunday breakfast and very good results are achieved using the Easybake Yeast.

25 g (1 oz) margarine
450 g (1 lb) Allinson Farmhouse Flour, plain or Brown Wheatmeal Flour, plain
2 level tsp sea salt
1 sachet Allinson Easybake Yeast
250 ml (9 fl oz) water at 43°C (110°F)
1 egg, beaten
175 g (6 oz) butter, straight from the refrigerator
a little beaten egg to brush tops

Rub the fat into the flour, then stir in the salt and the Easybake Yeast. Add the warm water and the egg and mix to a dough. Turn the dough on to a work surface and knead for 5 minutes. Cover the dough loosely and leave to 'relax' for 5 minutes. Flour the work surface and rolling pin and roll out the dough to 50 cm × cm/20″ ×8″. Mark into thirds. Using a palette knife, dot the top two thirds with half of the butter, fold the bottom third to the centre and the top third down over it. Using the rolling pin, seal the edges. Chill in the refrigerator for 30 minutes. Remove the dough from the refrigerator, roll out as before and repeat the procedure using the remaining butter. Seal the edges, then quarter turn the dough, roll out and fold as before. If the dough is still firm and cool, quarter turn and repeat. (If the dough has become warm, return to the refrigerator for 10 minutes before the last rolling.) When the final rolling and folding has been done the dough may be kept in the refrigerator for several hours or overnight if to be used later. Remove from the refrigerator, roll and fold again, then roll out to an oblong 45 cm × 30 cm/18″ × 12″. Cut into 6 squares. Divide each of these into 2 triangles and brush with beaten egg. Roll up the triangles from the long edge and shape to form a crescent. Place on warmed, greased baking sheets and prove, covered loosely with polythene, until they double in size – about 35 minutes. Pre-heat the oven and bake at 220°C/425°F/Gas Mark 7 for 20 minutes or until golden brown in colour. Cool on a wire rack.

—Pine Kernel Pizzas—

Makes 8 individual pizzas

225 g (8 oz) Allinson 100% Wholewheat Flour
15 g (½ oz) polyunsaturated margarine
pinch sea salt
2 tsp Allinson Easybake Yeast
150 ml (5 fl oz) tepid water

Sauce
1 small onion, peeled and finely chopped
1 clove garlic, crushed
1 tsp olive oil
425 g (15 oz) can or *450 g (1 lb) fresh tomatoes*
1 red pepper, de-seeded and chopped
1 tsp dried basil or *oregano*

Topping
50 g (2 oz) pine kernels
50 g (2 oz) mushrooms, sliced
1 green pepper, de-seeded and chopped
4 olives, halved and pitted
175 g (6 oz) Mozzarella or *Edam cheese, cut into
fine strips*

First make the tomato sauce. Sauté the onion and garlic together in the oil over a low heat for 2 minutes. Add the tomatoes (skinned if using fresh), chopped red pepper and the chosen herb. Bring to the boil, then cover, reduce the heat and simmer for 30 minutes.

Meanwhile, make the dough. Place the flour in a bowl and rub in the margarine. Stir in the salt and Easybake Yeast. Add the tepid water and mix to a dough. Turn out on a lightly floured surface and knead until smooth and soft. The dough will now be ready to use. Roll out to 5 mm/¼" thick. Cut into 7.5 cm/3" rounds and place them on lightly greased baking trays. Spoon the sauce on top and arrange the rest of the topping ingredients on this, finishing with cheese and half an olive on each pizza. Leave the pizzas in a warm place to rise (about 20 minutes). Pre-heat the oven to 220°C/425°F/Gas Mark 7. Bake the pizzas at the top of the pre-heated oven for 15–20 minutes. Serve hot.

—Pizza—

Serves 4–6

225 g (8 oz) Allinson Wholewheat Bread *dough,
risen (see page 00 for recipe)*
25 g (1 oz) butter
1 small onion, peeled and sliced
100 g (4 oz) mushrooms, sliced
225 g (8 oz) fresh tomatoes, sliced
1 tsp tomato purée
1 tsp mixed herbs
sea salt and freshly ground black pepper
100 g (4 oz) prawns, shelled
100 g (4 oz) Mozzarella cheese, cubed
6 thin slices red and green peppers
anchovies and black olives to garnish

Pre-heat the oven to 200°C/400°F/Gas Mark 6.

Do not knead the dough after it has risen; place it on a floured surface and roll out. With minimum handling, the dough will easily be rolled out to shape. Place on a well-greased and lined 20 cm/8" square baking tin, 2 cm/1" deep. Melt the butter and fry the onion. Add the mushrooms, half the tomatoes, the tomato purée and the herbs. Cook through gently for about 10 minutes to make a sauce consistency, then add salt and pepper to taste. Spread the mixture on the pizza dough base, sprinkle with the prawns, remaining sliced tomatoes and the cheese. Garnish with the slices of pepper, anchovies and olives. Bake in the pre-heated oven for 15 minutes, until the base is cooked through and the cheese golden brown. The pizza dough can be rolled to a square or rectangle to make a good shape to be cut into portions for serving at parties or for picnics.

Allinson Wholewheat Bread

Makes 2 450 g/1 lb loaves

600 g (1 lb 15 oz) Allinson Original 100%
  Wholewheat Flour
1 level dsrtsp salt
1 level dsrtsp sugar
15 g (½ oz) sunflower oil
1 sachet Allinson Easybake Yeast *and approx.*
  425 ml (15 fl oz) water at 43°C/110°F or 3 level
  teaspoons Allinson Dried Active Baking Yeast
  reconstituted as the packet instructions with
  275 ml (10 fl oz) of warm water, a crushed 50 mg
  vitamin C tablet and 1 teaspoon of the sugar from
  recipe

Put the flour, salt, sugar and oil in a warm bowl. If
using Allison Dried Yeast add the yeast liquid and
the remaining 150 ml/5 fl oz water. If using Easybake
Yeast, stir it in then add the water. Quickly mix, by
hand, to a soft dough. Knead on a floured surface,
stretching and folding the dough for approximately
10 minutes (this can be done more quickly in a food
mixer – follow the maker's instructions). When
mixed, cover the dough loosely with a piece of
polythene to prevent cooling or drying out. Leave to
'rest' like this for 5 minutes. Grease two 450 g/1 lb
loaf tins and put to warm. Halve the dough and
shape to fit the tins. Cover loosely with polythene
and leave to prove in a warm place for about 30
minutes or until the dough has risen about 2 cm/1″
above the tops of the tins. Pre-heat the oven to
240°C/475°F/Gas Mark 9 (or maximum temperature). When proved, place the loaves in the oven, on
the centre shelf, then turn the temperature down by
15°C/25°F or 1 Gas Mark to bake for 15 minutes.
Check the loaves – if they are over-baking turn down
the temperature a little more and bake for a further
15–20 minutes. Remove from the tins and cool on a
wire tray.

APPLEFORD'S LTD

Rye Bread with Orange and Caraway

To make a truly delicious chewy and not too heavy
bread you have to use a combination of wheat and
rye flours. You can use dark or light rye flour in this
recipe. The darker variety has much more flavour
but it does not rise easily and so the bread will be
heavier. The rising time is long because of the
smaller amount of gluten in rye flour.

15 g (½ oz) dried yeast or 25 g (1 oz) fresh yeast
250 ml (19 fl oz) warm water
1 level tbsp Appleford's Black Strap Molasses
175 g (6 oz) rye flour
225 g (8 oz) wholemeal flour
1 level tsp sea salt
1 tbsp sunflower oil
grated rind of 1 orange
1 level tsp caraway seeds
a little milk to brush top of loaf
a few caraway seeds to sprinkle on top

Sprinkle the yeast on the water, stir in ½ tsp of the
molasses and leave in a warm place for about 10
minutes. Mix the flours and sea salt in a large bowl.
When the yeast liquid is frothy, stir in the rest of the
molasses, the oil, orange rind and caraway seeds.
Make a well in the centre of the flour and pour in the
yeast liquid. Mix into a dough, knead for 10
minutes, then put into a greased polythene bag and
leave to rise in a warm place for 1½–2 hours. Knock
back and knead for 2 minutes more. With floured
hands, form the dough into an oval shape, place on
a greased baking tray and prick the top all over with
a fork. Slide the loaf on its tray into a greased
polythene bag and leave to rise for a further 1½
hours until doubled in size. Pre-heat the oven to
220°C/425°F/Gas Mark 7 20 minutes before you are
ready to bake the bread. Brush the top of the loaf
with milk and a sprinkling of caraway seeds. Bake
in the centre of the oven for 15 minutes then lower
the heat to 190°C/375F°/Gas Mark 5, and continue to
bake for a further 35 minutes. The loaf will be baked
when it sounds hollow when tapped underneath.
Cool on a wire rack.

DIETADE

Throughout the book you will find recipes using Dietade fruit sugar (fructose). I use it for recipes such as cheesecake where honey and dark sugars can change the flavour of a much loved dish. Here are two easy and delicious recipes using fruit sugar in yeasted bakes. According to the manufacturers this sugar can be used in moderation by diabetics but before doing so a doctor must be consulted.

Savarin

This rich French yeast dessert is quite delicious for those special entertaining evenings. Traditionally rum is used, but I sometimes use brandy and fresh orange juice mixed with 2 teaspoons of orange zest.

25 g (1 oz) fresh yeast
6 tbsp warm milk (43°C/110°F)
225 g (8 oz) strong wholemeal or *brown wheatmeal*
 flour, plain
100 g (4 oz) butter or *polyunsaturated margarine*
good pinch sea salt
25 g (1 oz) Dietade Fruit Sugar
4 eggs, lightly beaten

Syrup and Filling
3 level tbsps Dietade Fruit Sugar
200 ml (7 fl oz) water
2 tbsp rum mixed with juice of 1 orange or *lemon,*
 or 2 tbsp brandy mixed with juice of 1 large
 orange and 2 tsp orange rind, grated
fresh fruit to fill the centre and decorate the edge
 (I use grapes – halved and de-seeded – sliced
 fresh peaches and orange segments)

Place the yeast, milk and 50 g/2 oz of the measured flour in a bowl and beat well together with a wooden spoon until smooth. Leave in a warm place for 15–20 minutes, until frothy. Melt the butter or margarine in a saucepan over a pan of hot water. Sift the remaining flour and the salt into the frothy yeast liquid and stir in the sugar, eggs and melted butter or margarine. Beat well with a wooden spoon for 3–4 minutes, then pour the mixture into a well greased 23–25 cm/9–10″ savarin mould. (Place this on a baking sheet for easier handling.) Cover with a lightly oiled polythene bag and leave to rise to the top of the mould (about 25 minutes). Pre-heat the oven to 200°C/400°F/Gas Mark 6. Bake the savarin in the centre of the pre-heated oven for 18–20 minutes, until golden brown.

To make the syrup, heat the fruit sugar with the water in a saucepan. Boil for 30 seconds, then take off the heat, cool for 5 minutes and stir in the rum and orange liquid, or brandy, orange juice and rind.

When the savarin is cooked, leave it in the tin for a few minutes before turning it out on to a plate. While still hot prick it gently all over with a thin, pointed skewer or fine knitting needle, then pour over the warm syrup (reserve 2 tablespoons of the syrup to sprinkle over the fresh fruit). Leave to cool. Finally, fill the centre and decorate the edge with the fruit and sprinkle on the remaining syrup.

Rum Babas

Makes 16

Recipe ingredients as Savarin above.

Syrup
4 tbsp Dietade Fruit Sugar or *honey*
4 tbsp water
2–3 tbsp rum

275 ml (½ pt) whipped cream

Follow instructions for making the savarin dough and half fill 16 well-greased baba tins with this mixture. Cover loosely with oiled polythene bags, and leave to rise in a warm place until the dough has risen to about two thirds up the sides of the moulds. Pre-heat oven to 200°C/400°F/Gas Mark 6 and bake for 15–20 minutes until golden brown.

Heat the fruit sugar or honey in a small pan over a low heat, stir in the rum and let cool slightly. Cool the baked babas in their moulds for a few minutes before turning on to individual serving dishes. Prick the babas with a thin skewer or fine knitting needle and while still hot pour the warm syrup over them. When cool, fill the centres with whipped cream.

Easter Bread

Makes a 675 g (1½ lb) loaf

15 g (½ oz) yeast
150 ml (5 fl oz), less 1 dessertspoon, warm milk
225 g (8 oz) brown wheatmeal flour, plain†
3 egg yolks
75 g (3 oz) Dietade Fruit Sugar
25 g (1 oz) melted butter
60 g (2¼ oz) mixed fruit

†100% strong plain wholemeal flour can be used
  but in that case add 2 tablespoons more of warm
  water

Dissolve the yeast in the warm milk, mix in half of the flour and leave to rise. Beat the egg yolks and sugar together and mix into the risen dough with the melted butter. Add the remaining flour and the mixed fruit. Shape into a loaf, place on a baking tray and prove for 20–30 minutes. Pre-heat the oven and bake at 230°C/450°F/Gas Mark 8 for 30–40 minutes or until risen and brown.

Hot Cross Buns

Makes 12 buns

450 g (1 lb) brown wheatmeal flour, plain†
25 g (1 oz) fresh yeast or 1 level tbsp dried
1 level teaspoon Dietade Fruit Sugar
150 ml (5 fl oz), less 1 dessertspoon, milk
150 ml (5 fl oz), less 4 tablespoons, water
100 g (4 oz) currants
1 level tsp salt
½ level tsp mixed spices
½ level tsp cinnamon
½ level tsp nutmeg
50 g (2 oz) butter, melted and cooled
1 egg, beaten

Glaze
2 tbsp milk
2 tbsp water
40 g (1½ oz) Dietade Fruit Sugar

†100% wholemeal flour can be used but about 2
  tablespoons more water will then be necessary

Place 100 g/4 oz of the flour in a mixing bowl and add the yeast and fruit sugar. Mix the milk and water, warm to blood heat and add to the flour. Mix well and leave to froth (30 minutes for dried yeast, 20 minutes for fresh yeast). Sieve the remaining flour with the spices, stir the butter and beaten egg into the frothy yeast mixture, add the spiced flour and fruit and mix well. Knead until smooth (5–10 minutes). Leave to rise in a warm place until doubled in size (about 30–45 minutes). Shape into 12 buns and place on a floured baking tray. Leave to prove for 10–15 minutes. Pre-heat the oven and bake at 190°C/375°F/Gas Mark 5, on the centre shelf, for 20–30 minutes. Brush with glaze while still hot and sprinkle freely with fruit sugar.

DOVES FARM

The following recipes have been created by a wonderful caring cook, Clare Marriage of Doves Farm. All the recipes are unique to Clare and are tried and tested family favourites. You will find other recipes by Clare throughout this book; they are quite delicious and well worth your efforts in the kitchen.

Black Rye Bread

Makes 2 450 g/1 lb loaves

1 tsp honey
275 ml (10 fl oz) warm water
50 g (2 oz) fresh yeast or 25 g (1 oz) dried yeast
275 ml (10 fl oz) milk
1 level tbsp black treacle
500 g (1.1 lb) Doves Farm Rye Flour
500 g (1.1 lb) Doves Farm Brown Wheatmeal Flour
1 rounded tsp sea salt
1 rounded tsp caraway seeds

Dissolve the honey in the warm water, add the yeast and mix well. Leave for 15 minutes until frothy. Gently warm the milk and treacle until dissolved. Place the mixed flours, salt and caraway seeds in a bowl. Add both liquids, mix to a dough and knead. Cover and set aside in a warm place. Oil the loaf tins and flour the working surface in preparation for the next stage. Pre-heat the oven to 220°C/425°F/Gas Mark 7. After 1 hour remove the dough from the bowl and knead well. Cut the dough in half. Shape and pop it into the prepared tins. Bake in the pre-heated oven for 40 minutes.

Golden Wheatmeal Bread

Makes 5 450 g/1 lb loaves

850 ml (1½ pints) warm water
50 g (2 oz) fresh or 25 g (1 oz) dried yeast
1.5 kg (3.3 lb) Doves Farm Brown Wheatmeal Flour
1 level tbsp salt
1½ tbsp sunflower or corn oil

Put the warm water into a large bowl. Crumble in the yeast (or stir in dried yeast), stir well and immediately add two thirds of the flour. Mix to a batter, cover and leave to rise for 1 hour. Mix in the salt and add the remaining flour in small batches along with the oil, and mix well by hand. Remove the dough to a floured surface and knead for 5 minutes, adding more flour if it becomes sticky. Work briskly, without tearing the dough. Cut and shape the dough, place it in oiled tins and brush the top of the dough with water. Leave in a warm place for 30 minutes or until risen. Pre-heat the oven to 230°C/450°F/Gas Mark 8 and place a bowl of water on the oven floor. Bake the loaves for 30–40 minutes depending on size. The bread is cooked if, when removed from the tin, the bottom of the loaf sounds hollow when tapped.

Granary Garlic French Loaf

Makes 2 loaves

25 g (1 oz) fresh yeast
1 level tsp Barbados sugar
425 ml (15 fl oz) warm water
450 g (1 lb) Doves Farm Malthouse Flour
225 g (8 oz) Doves Farm Unbleached White Flour
1 generous tsp sea salt
1 egg yolk
1 tbsp sunflower oil
3 good size juicy cloves garlic, crushed
few sesame seeds or cracked wheat for top

Cream the yeast and sugar together and pour in 150 ml/5 fl oz of the warm water. Leave to stand, covered with a cloth, in a warm place until frothy – about 7–10 minutes. Mix the flours with the salt. Beat the egg yolk with the oil and the crushed garlic. When the yeast liquid is frothy make a well in the flour mixture and pour this in with the egg and garlic mixture and some of the warm water. Mix to a soft dough, adding the remaining water as you do this, but do not make the dough sticky. When making any bread recipe it is always best to add the liquid gradually. Knead for 7 minutes, then place in an oiled plastic bag and leave to rise in a warm place until doubled in size. (About 1 hour, less if the room is very warm.) When well risen knead for 2 minutes. Divide into two equal parts and roll out each piece to a thick oval 30 cm/12″ long and 20 cm/8″ wide. Roll the dough over like a swiss roll, pressing it gently together – this will lighten the dough. Shape each piece of rolled-up dough into a French loaf shape 35 cm/14″ long. Place the loaves on a greased baking sheet, leaving room for them to spread out. Slide the baking sheet into a large, greased plastic bag and leave the loaves to rise in a warm place until double in size (about 30 minutes). Pre-heat the oven to 220°C/425°F/Gas Mark 7. When well risen make six slanting indents in each loaf with the back of a knife, brush with lukewarm water and sprinkle on cracked wheat or sesame seeds. Bake on a shelf just above the centre of the oven for 15 minutes, turning the tray around after 10 minutes. Turn the loaves upside down and finish the baking for 3 more minutes. Cool on a wire rack.

Malthouse Bread

Makes 5 450 g/1 lb loaves

just under 850 ml (1½ pints) warm water
1.5 kg (3 lb) Doves Farm Malthouse Flour
25 g (1 oz) dried yeast or 50 g (2 oz) fresh yeast
1 level tbsp salt
2 tbsp sunflower or corn oil

Put 500 ml/just under 1 pint of the warm water into a large mixing bowl, add 2 tablespoons of the Malthouse Flour and the yeast, mix well and leave for 15 minutes. Add the remaining flour (keeping back a tablespoonful), the salt and the oil, and mix well. Add 300 ml/11 fl oz of the warm water and mix well to form a dough. Knead for 5 minutes, adding a dash of water if the dough becomes too stiff. Cover and leave in a warm place for 30–40 minutes. Knead the dough again, using the remaining flour for dusting. Cut to size, shape and place in oiled tins. Brush with water, cover and leave to rise for 20–30 minutes in a warm place. Pre-heat the oven to 220°C/425°F/Gas Mark 7 and bake for 30–35 minutes. Cool on a wire rack.

Organic 100% Wholemeal Bread

Makes 5 450 g/1 lb loaves

1.5 kg (3 lb) Doves Farm
Organic 100% wholemeal flour
25 g (1 oz) dried yeast
1 tsp salt
850 ml (1½ pints) warm water

Put half the flour, the yeast and salt into a bowl and mix thoroughly. Add the water at 35°C/95°F, mix well, cover and leave for 6–12 hours at room temperature. Add the remaining flour (keeping back a tablespoonful for dusting), mix thoroughly and knead well. Leave in a warm place for 15 minutes, then knead again using the dusting flour, mould into loaves and place in oiled tins. Leave the loaves to rise in a warm place for 15–20 minutes. Pre-heat the oven to 240°C/475°F/Gas Mark 8. Bake the loaves for 15 minutes, then turn down the heat to 190°C/375°F/Gas Mark 5 and continue to bake for a further 20 minutes. Remove from the tins and cool the loaves on a wire rack.

Savoury Enpanada

Serves 4

500 g (1 lb 2 oz) bread dough made with Doves Farm Organic Wholemeal Flour *(see above)*
2 large onions, peeled and chopped
3 stalks celery, chopped
1 carrot, peeled and chopped
3 cloves garlic, crushed
1 tbsp sunflower oil
225 g (8 oz) red kidney beans, soaked and cooked for 30 minutes
1 tsp sea salt
2 tsp thyme

Make up the bread dough and set aside for 1 hour. In a large saucepan lightly fry the chopped onion, celery, carrot and garlic in the sunflower oil. Add the soaked and par-boiled kidney beans, with their juices, to the pan. Add the salt and thyme. Simmer very gently for about one hour until the beans are cooked. Roll out the dough to form a large rectangle and place on a greased baking tray. Put the cooked beans in the middle parallel to the longer side. Brush all the edges with water and draw the dough up over the beans. Prick the top to allow the steam to escape. Leave to rise for 15 minutes. Pre-heat the oven to 220°/425°F/Gas Mark 7 and bake the enpanada for 30–35 minutes or until golden brown.

Serve covered with freshly grated cheese and accompanied by plenty of spicy tomato sauce.

Traditional Wholemeal Bread

Makes 5 450 g/1 lb loaves

850 ml (1½ pints) warm water
1 tsp honey
2 level tbsp dried yeast
1.5 kg (3.3 lb) Doves Farm Strong Wholemeal Flour
1 level tbsp salt
2 tbsp sunflower oil

Pour 275 ml/10 fl oz of the warm water into a bowl. Dissolve the honey in it and then stir in the yeast. Leave for 10 minutes until frothy. Put the flour into a large basin (reserving a little). Mix in the salt and oil; add the yeast mixture and most of the remaining water and mix for 5 minutes, gradually adding the last of the water. Knead well. Cover and leave in a warm place for 45 minutes. Oil the bread tins. Turn out the dough on to a lightly floured surface and knead for about 5 minutes, then cut into pieces. Mould the dough into loaves and place in the prepared tins. Leave to rise in a warm place for about 30 minutes. Pre-heat the oven to 220°C/425°F/Gas Mark 7. When the dough has risen put the loaves into the pre-heated oven and bake for about 30 minutes. Remove from the tins when cooked and cool on a wire rack.

Unleavened Bread (Chappatis)

Makes 6 portions

This is the oldest and simplest, most basic form of bread.

200 g (7 oz) Doves Farm Organic 100% Wholemeal Flour
½ tsp salt
150 ml (5 fl oz) warm water

Mix together the flour and salt, add the water and mix to a dough. Knead well, cover and leave for 30 minutes. Cut off a piece of dough the size of a large walnut and, using plenty of flour, roll into a 20 cm/ 8″ disc. Thoroughly heat a large, slightly oiled frying pan and cook the bread until brown, then turn it over and cook the other side. Keep the bread warm until ready to serve.

Unyeasted Barley Bread

Makes 1 large loaf

This has a delicious nutty, malt flavour. Barley flour is great in most bread recipes – all you do is substitute 1 teacup of barley flour for the basic flour you are using in any bread recipe. For example, if you are making French loaves with brown wheatmeal or unbleached white flour, incorporating barley flour will add flavour and more nutrients.

1 tbsp corn or sunflower oil
225 g (8 oz) Doves Farm Barley Flour
450 g (1 lb) Doves Farm 100% Stoneground Wholemeal Flour, plain
75 g (3 oz) sesame seeds, lightly toasted (toast in the oven)
2 tsp sea salt
4 tbsp cold pressed sunflower or sesame seed oil
500 ml (18 fl oz) boiling water

Heat the tablespoon of corn or sunflower oil in a large, deep, heavy-based pan, and toast the barley flour over medium heat, stirring with a wooden spoon until very slightly darkened (do not burn). Place in a large mixing bowl. Mix the flours, sesame seeds and sea salt together and rub in the 4 tablespoons of cold pressed oil. Now pour in the

boiling water and mix with a wooden spoon until the dough is stiff. If still too hot to touch then cool the hands in cold water, shake off excess water and form the mixture into a dough. Knead on a well-floured board until putty-like in texture, shape into a loaf and place snugly into a well-oiled 900 g/2 lb loaf tin. Slide the tin into a lightly oiled polythene bag and leave to prove overnight, or for at least 5 hours, in a warm place. Pre-heat the oven to 220°C/ 425°F/Gas Mark 7 and bake on the middle shelf for 15 minutes, then turn down to 190°C/375°F/Gas Mark 5 for a further 50 minutes.

Wholemeal Banana and Orange Bread

Makes 1 900 g/2 lb loaf

100 g (4 oz) butter
100 g (4 oz) brown sugar
1 egg
pinch of sea salt
225 g (8 oz) Doves Farm 100% Wholemeal Flour, self-raising
2 large or 3 small bananas
grated rind of 1 orange
2 tbsp natural yoghurt

Cream together the butter and sugar and beat in the egg. Beat in a pinch of salt and the flour. Mash together the bananas, orange rind and yoghurt and combine with the mixture. Pre-heat the oven to 180°C/350°F/Gas Mark 4 and bake the loaf in a well-greased 900 g/2 lb tin for about 1 hour. The cake will be cooked when it leaves the sides of the tin. When cooked leave the cake in the tin for 15 minutes before removing to a cooling rack.

GRANNY ANN

I love to use malt extract in bread making as it adds a mild sweetness without the use of sugar. The following three traditional recipes were carefully prepared by Joanna Hill and all are full of flavour.

Pumpernickel Rye Bread

Makes 2 450 g/1 lb loaves

1 tbsp Granny Ann Cookiemalt
150 ml (5 fl oz) water, finger-hot
15 g (¹/₂ oz) dried yeast
150 ml (5 fl oz) warm milk
50 g (2 oz) vegetable margarine
4 tbsp molasses
1 egg, beaten
675 g (1¹/₂ lb) rye flour
1 tsp salt
2 tbsp caraway seeds

Dissolve the Cookiemalt in the finger-hot water, in a small bowl. Sprinkle the yeast over the liquid and whisk well with a fork, then leave in a warm place for 10–15 minutes until frothy. Heat the milk and melt the margarine in it. Allow to cool, then stir in the molasses with the beaten egg.

In a large bowl place 100 g/4 oz of the flour, with the salt and caraway seeds. Stir in the yeast and the milk mixture. Mix well and leave to rise in a warm place for 30 minutes. Stir in another 100 g (4 oz) of the flour, cover with a damp cloth and leave to rise for another 30 minutes. Stir in the remaining flour and knead well for 10 minutes. If the dough is sticky, use more flour. Shape into two loaves and place them in greased loaf tins. Leave to rise in a warm place for 1 hour, covering with a cloth. Pre-heat the oven to 200°C/400°F/Gas Mark 6. Bake the loaves for 40 minutes, then remove from the tins and cool on a wire rack.

Rosemary Herb Bread

Makes 2 450 g/1 lb loaves

1 tbsp Granny Ann Cookiemalt
1 tsp honey
400 ml (14 fl oz) water, finger-hot
¹/₂ vitamin C tablet, crushed

15 g (¹/₂ oz) dried yeast
275 g (10 oz) strong brown flour
275 g (10 oz) wholewheat flour
100 g (4 oz) fine oatmeal
1 dsrtsp salt
50 g (2 oz) sunflower seeds
1 dsrtsp dried rosemary or 1 tbsp fresh
1 tsp vegetable oil

Dissolve the Cookiemalt and the honey in 150 ml/5 fl oz of the finger-hot water. Sprinkle the crushed vitamin C tablet and the yeast over the liquid and whisk well with a fork. Leave in a warm place for 10–15 minutes, until frothy. Grease two loaf tins.

In a large bowl combine the two flours, the oatmeal, salt, sunflower seeds and rosemary. Add the oil to the yeast mixture, then pour it into the dry ingredients. Mix to a manageable dough with the remaining warm water. Knead the dough for 10 minutes, until smooth and elastic. Divide into two, shape and place in the tins. Cover with a damp cloth and leave to rise, until the dough has doubled in size.

Pre-heat the oven to 190°C/375°F/Gas Mark 5 and bake the loaves for 10 minutes, then reduce the temperature to 160°C/325°F/Gas Mark 3 for a further 25–30 minutes. The loaves should sound hollow when tapped on the base with the fingertips. Remove from the tins and cool on a wire rack.

Wholemeal Bread

Makes 4 450 g/1 lb loaves

1 tbsp (15 ml) Granny Ann Cookiemalt
1 tbsp raw sugar
850 ml (1¹/₂ pts) water, finger-hot
25 g (1 oz) dried yeast
1 vitamin C tablet, crushed
675 g (1¹/₂ lb) strong wholemeal flour
675 g (1¹/₂ lb) wholewheat flour
1 tbsp salt
25 g (1 oz) polyunsaturated margarine

In a small bowl dissolve the Cookiemalt and 1 teaspoon of the sugar in 275 ml/10 fl oz of the finger-hot water. Sprinkle the yeast and the crushed vitamin C tablet into the bowl, whisk with a fork, then leave in a warm place for 10–15 minutes until frothy. Grease loaf tins or baking sheets.

Opposite: **Realeat** *Boboti (above) page 89, Vegeburger (below) page 90*

Overleaf: **Western Isles** *Hiziki with Rice and Almonds (above) page 98, Nori Tempura (below) page 98*

Weigh out the flours, mix together and put one cupful aside. Combine the flour, salt and sugar in a large, warm bowl. Rub in the shortening, add the yeast mixture and the remaining water and stir well. Sprinkle some flour from the reserved cupful on to a clean worktop. Rub the hands with flour, and knead the dough for 10 minutes until smooth and elastic. Divide the dough into four, then shape into loaves or rolls.

For tin loaves, flatten one piece of dough into a rectangle as wide as the tin, fold into three and place in the tin with the fold at the bottom. Alternatively, shape into rolls or loaves and place on the baking sheets. (Try rolling out small sausages of dough and tie each single strip into a knot, or use three to make a plait, and sprinkle with poppy seeds or sesame seeds.) Cover the tins or shaped loaves with a damp cloth and leave in a warm place to rise until the dough has doubled in size – this will take about 30 minutes. Pre-heat the oven to 190°C/375°F/Gas Mark 5 and bake for 10 minutes, then reduce the heat to 170°C/325°F/Gas Mark 3 for a further 25–35 minutes. When cooked the bread should sound hollow when tapped with the fingers. If the bread does not sound hollow after 45 minutes' overall cooking time, remove from the tins and cook for a further 5–10 minutes.

HÖFELS

The following recipes are exclusive to Höfels.

Flaked Barley Bread

Makes 2 450 g/1 lb loaves

85 g (3¼ oz) Höfels Barley Flakes
225 ml (8 fl oz) boiling water
40 g (1½ oz) fresh or 20 g (¾ oz) dried yeast
1 tsp sugar
225 ml (8 fl oz) warm water
1 level dstsp Höfels Sea Salt
30 g (1 oz) Barbados sugar
225 ml (8 fl oz) warm milk
725 g (1 lb 9 oz) Höfels 100% Wholemeal Norfolk
   Flour

Previous page: **Allinson** *Pizza (above) page 105, Cheese and Mushroom Plait (below) page 103*

Opposite: **Höfels** *Rye Bread Rolls (above left) page 114, Savoury Kibbled Wheat Scones (above right) page 114, Flaked Barley Bread (below) page 113*

Cook the barley flakes very gently in the boiling water for about 5 minutes, then put into a large mixing bowl. Meanwhile put the yeast and the teaspoon of sugar into another bowl, add the warm water and leave for about 10 minutes until frothy. Add the salt, brown sugar, warm milk and yeast mixture to the cooked barley flakes, then gradually stir in the flour. Turn on to a floured board and knead for about 10 minutes; shape the dough into a ball, place in a well-buttered bowl and turn to coat the surface. Leave, covered with a damp cloth, in a warm place for about 1½ hours or until doubled in bulk. Turn the dough on to a floured board and knead for 5 minutes. Shape into two loaves, place in well-greased tins and leave, covered, in a warm place until doubled in bulk (about 1 hour). Pre-heat the oven to 190°C/375°F/Gas Mark 5 and bake for about 50 minutes or until the loaf sounds hollow when tapped underneath.

Flaked Rye Bread

Make as Flaked Barley Bread, substituting rye for the flaked barley.

Kibbled Wheat Bread

Makes 2 450 g/1 lb loaves

250 g (9 oz) kibbled or cracked wheat
575 ml (1 pint) boiling water
2 level tbsp honey
1 tsp molasses (optional)
25 g (1 oz) fresh or 15 g (½ oz) dried yeast
275 ml (10 fl oz) lukewarm water
1 tsp sugar
850 g (1 lb 14 oz) Höfels 100% Wholemeal Norfolk
   Flour
1 dstsp salt

Put the kibbled wheat in a large mixing bowl and pour in the boiling water. Stir in the honey and molasses if required) and leave the mixture until it cools (about 20 minutes). In another bowl crumble the yeast and add the lukewarm water and sugar. The yeast mixture will be ready in about 10 minutes, when it is frothy. Meanwhile sift together the wholemeal flour and salt and add them to the grain mixture. Stir in the yeast and mix well, then knead. Grease two loaf tins and divide the dough between them. Cover the tins with a damp cloth and stand them in a warm place to allow the dough to rise until double in bulk (about 40 minutes). Pre-heat the oven to 200°C/400°F/Gas Mark 6 and bake the loaves for 45 minutes–1 hour.

Quick Tea Time Bread

Makes 1 450 g/1 lb loaf

This is very quick and easy to make and is a useful recipe when you find you need some bread in a hurry.

450 g (1 lb) Höfels 100% Wholemeal Norfolk Flour
1 dsp Barbados sugar
4 level tsps baking powder
1 tsp Höfels Sea Salt
150 g (5 oz) carton natural yoghurt
approx. 150 ml (5 fl oz) water

Pre-heat the oven to 220°C/425°F/Gas Mark 7. Mix all the dry ingredients together in a bowl, then add the yoghurt and enough of the water to make a dough. Knead, then put into a warm, greased 450 g/1 lb loaf tin. Bake for about 50 minutes or until golden brown.

Rye Bread

Makes 1 450 g/1 lb loaf

This is an easy bread to make and very tasty. It is left for 16–18 hours to prove and can therefore be made in the evening and left until after breakfast the next day to bake.

15 g (½ oz) dried or 25 g (1 oz) fresh yeast
pinch of Höfels Sea Salt
just over 285 ml (10 fl oz) warm water
375 g (13 oz) Höfels Rye Flour

Mix the yeast, salt and water in a bowl and gradually mix in the flour, using a wooden spoon – the resulting dough will be rather heavy. Turn on to a floured board and knead well; place the dough in a well-buttered bowl and turn to coat the surface, then put the bowl into a polythene bag and seal. Place the bowl in a fairly warm place for 16–18 hours – the dough will rise only slightly during this time. Remove from the bowl, turn on to a lightly floured board and knead for 2–3 minutes, then place the dough in a greased loaf tin and leave in a warm place for 1½ hours. Pre-heat the oven to 190°C/375°F/Gas Mark 5 and bake for about 1 hour.

Savoury Kibbled Wheat Scones

75 g (3 oz) kibbled wheat
150 ml (5 fl oz) milk
1 egg, lightly beaten
approx. 1 rounded tbsp grated onion
100 g (4 oz) grated cheese
200 g (7 oz) Höfels 100% Wholemeal Norfolk Flour
1 level tsp salt
1 level tbsp baking powder

Boil the milk with the kibbled wheat in a saucepan for 2 minutes, then allow to cool before beating in the egg, onion and cheese. Sift together the flour, salt and baking powder and add to the mixture. Mix well to make a soft dough, adding more milk if necessary. Shape into scones, place on a greased baking tray and bake in a pre-heated oven at 220°C/425°F/Gas Mark 7 for 10–15 minutes. Delicious served hot with butter.

Vitamin C Bread

Makes 2 loaves

2 level tsp Barbados sugar
25 mg tablet vitamin C
15 g (½ oz) dried or 25 g (1 oz) fresh yeast
approx. 425 ml (15 fl oz) water (warmed to 40°C/110°F)
675 g (1½ lb) Höfels 100% Wholemeal Norfolk Flour
2 level tsp Höfels Sea Salt
1 tbsp sunflower or corn oil

Put one teaspoon of the sugar, the vitamin C tablet, yeast and 150 ml/5 fl oz of the warm water into a bowl and leave for about 10 minutes until frothy. Mix the oil and the remaining 275 ml/10 fl oz of warm water and add with all the other ingredients to the flour. Mix well to form a firm dough. Knead on a floured surface for about 10 minutes, then divide the dough in two and place in warmed, greased tins and put inside a greased polythene bag. Leave in a warm place until the dough has risen just to the top of the tins. The dough will be ready when it will not retain the impression of a finger. Pre-heat the oven to 230°C/450°F/Gas Mark 8 and bake the loaves for 30–40 minutes or until they have shrunk slightly from the sides of the tins.

HOLLAND & BARRETT

Rich Sweet Yeast Dough

1 level tbsp dried yeast
1 level tsp Muscovado sugar
275 ml (10 fl oz) warm water
2 tbsp skimmed milk powder
1 level tbsp Holland & Barrett Honey
1 egg
450 g (1 lb) wheatmeal flour, plain
1 level tsp sea salt
50 g (2 oz) polyunsaturated margarine or butter

Sprinkle the dried yeast and sugar into 150 ml/5 fl oz of the measured warm water. Whisk and leave to froth in a warm place for 7–10 minutes. Stir the milk powder into the remaining warm water and add the honey. Beat the egg and stir into the milk and honey liquid.

Put the flour and salt into a large mixing bowl and rub in the margarine or butter. Make a well in the centre of the flour and pour in the yeast and milk liquids. Form into a soft dough, then knead for 10 minutes until it becomes smooth and elastic. Place in an oiled polythene bag and leave to rise in a warm place for 30 minutes. The dough will then be ready to use in the following recipes.

English Muffins

Makes 8–10

Follow the recipe above for Rich Sweet Yeast Dough.

After the first rising punch down the dough and let it rest in the bag for 10 minutes. Roll out to about 1 cm/½″ thick, cut into 7.5 cm/3″ rounds or triangles and dust with either corn meal or flour. Cover with the opened-up polythene bag and leave to rise in a warm place, on oiled trays, until doubled in size. Heat a pan or griddle to hot, reduce the heat to moderate and cook the muffins, browning them slowly for 5–6 minutes on each side.

Delicious hot with butter and Holland & Barrett honey.

Fig and Aniseed Ring

Prepare the dough as for the Swedish Tea Ring (see page 116) but use the following filling.

175 g (6 oz) Holland & Barrett Dried Figs, soaked in water overnight (cut the stalks off)
1 tsp Holland & Barrett Honey
1 tsp aniseed
a little beaten egg white sweetened with honey to glaze

Cook the figs with the honey and aniseed in a little of the soaking water until pulp-like. Mash well with a potato masher and spread over the rolled-out dough. Proceed as for the Swedish Tea Ring. When baked, brush with a little beaten egg white to which you have added a touch of honey.

Lemon Plait

Ingredients as Rich Sweet Yeast Dough
1 level tsp nutmeg, freshly ground
1 tbsp lemon rind, finely chopped
75 g (3 oz) Holland & Barrett Raisins
beaten egg to glaze

Mix the additional ingredients with the flour just before adding the liquids. Knead well and leave to rise in an oiled polythene bag in a warm place until doubled in size, about 40 minutes. Punch down and then let the dough rise again to double its size. (This process will result in a really light bread.)

Divide the dough into four strands and plait them together. Place the plaited dough on an oiled baking sheet. Slide the baking sheet into a large, oiled polythene bag and leave to rise in a warm place for about 25 minutes. Pre-heat the oven to 220°C/425°F/Gas Mark 7. Brush the dough with beaten egg and bake in the pre-heated oven for 15 minutes, then reduce the heat to 190°C/375°F/Gas Mark 5, and continue to bake for 15 minutes more.

Pecan Nut Ring

Prepare the dough as for the Swedish Tea Ring (see below) but use the following filling.

*100 g (4 oz) Holland & Barrett Dried Apricots,
    soaked in apple juice overnight*
*½ tsp ground cardamom seeds (pod them first and
    grind the seeds in a pestle and mortar)*
1 generous dessertspoon Holland & Barrett Honey
*40 g (1½ oz) Holland & Barrett Pecan Nuts,
    chopped*
*a little honey and a few pecan nut halves to
    decorate*

Cook the apricots, ground cardamom seeds and honey together for 5 minutes only. Liquidize with some of the apricot soaking liquid to make a smooth, jam-like consistency (not runny). Spread this over the rolled-out dough, sprinkle on the chopped pecan nuts and proceed as for the Swedish Tea Ring, below. When the ring is baked, brush with a little warm honey and dot with pecan nut halves.

Swedish Tea Ring

*1 recipe quantity Rich Sweet Yeast Dough (see
    recipe on page 115)*

Filling
175 g (6 oz) Holland & Barrett Dried Dates
½ tsp mixed spice
1 tsp lemon juice
few drops vanilla esence
pinch sea salt
50 g (2 oz) Holland & Barrett Flaked Almonds

While the dough is rising, steam the dates until soft and mushy. Place in a bowl and blend in the mixed spice, lemon juice, vanilla essence and sea salt until the mixture is a smooth, soft paste consistency. Roll out the dough to a rectangle about 35 cm × 25 cm/14″ × 10″. Spread the date mixture on top, leaving a 1 cm/½″ edge of dough free of filling on 3 sides and 2.5 cm/1″ of dough free along one long side. Sprinkle on the flaked almonds (save a few for decoration). Roll up as you would a swiss roll, place on an oiled baking sheet and shape into a ring. Dampen the edges and press gently to seal. Cut 2.5 cm/1″ slits in the top with kitchen scissors, cover with a large, lightly oiled polythene bag and leave to rise in a warm place until doubled in size (about 40 minutes). Pre-heat the oven to 220°C/425°F/Gas Mark 7. Brush with egg and bake for 15 minutes in the centre of the oven then reduce heat to 190°C/375°F/Gas Mark 5 for a further 20 minutes. Cool on a rack for 2 minutes, then brush with a mixture of beaten egg white and honey and sprinkle with the reserved flaked almonds. (You can lightly toast the almonds under a low grill before using them in the recipe if liked.)

KRETSCHMER

Apricot Nut Bread

Makes 2 450 g/1 lb loaves

215 g (7½ oz) unbleached white flour, plain
3 level tsp baking powder
½ tsp bicarbonate of soda
½ tsp sea salt
75 g (3 oz) sugar
50 g (2 oz) polyunsaturated margarine
450 g (16 oz) carton natural yoghurt
2 tbsp dried milk powder
1 egg
100 g (4 oz) finely snipped dried apricots
50 g (2 oz) Kretschmer Wheat Germ, Plain
50 g (2 oz) flaked almonds

Combine the flour, baking powder, bicarbonate of soda and salt. Stir well to blend. Cream the sugar and margarine thoroughly and beat in the yoghurt, milk powder and egg. Blend the dry ingredients into the creamed mixture and mix well. Stir in the apricots, wheatgerm and almonds, blending well. Spread the batter into greased loaf tins (or 20 cm/8″ sandwich tins). Bake at 180°C/350°F/Gas Mark 4 for 45–50 minutes or until a wooden toothpick inserted in the centre of the loaves comes out clean. Cool in the tins for 5–10 minutes, then remove from the tins and cool on a wire rack. Once cold, wrap in foil or plastic wrap and store overnight for easier slicing.

Cottage Bread and Rolls

Makes 2 450 g/1 lb loaves and 12 rolls

425–575 g (15–20 oz) brown wheatmeal flour
25 g (1 oz) dried yeast
40 g (1½ oz) brown sugar
1 tsp salt
1½ tsp dill
225 g (8 oz) soured cream
225 g (8 oz) cottage cheese
150 ml (5 fl oz) hot water
2 eggs, beaten
100 g (3¾ oz) Kretschmer Wheat Germ, Plain
little sunflower oil
1 egg, well beaten
1 tablespoon Kretschmer Wheat Germ, Regular, for
  tops of loaves and rolls

Combine a third of the flour, the yeast, sugar, salt and dill in a large bowl and stir well to blend. Heat the soured cream and cottage cheese together until lukewarm and add to the ingredients in the bowl. Add the hot water and beat with an electric mixer at medium speed for 2 minutes. Scrape the bowl occasionally. Add the eggs and a third more flour. Beat at high speed for 1 minute or until thick and elastic. Stir in the wheat germ with a wooden spoon, then gradually stir in just enough of the remaining flour to make a soft dough which leaves the sides of the bowl. Turn out on to a floured board and knead for 5–8 minutes or until the dough is smooth and elastic. Place the dough in a large greased bowl, turning to coat all sides, cover and leave to rise in a warm, draught-free place for about 1 hour or until doubled in size. Punch down, divide the dough in half and shape into rolls and loaves.

To make the rolls, divide half the dough into 12 pieces and roll each piece into a 20 cm/8″ rope. Tie into a knot and place in a well-greased bun tin or on a well-greased baking tray.

To make the loaves, divide the remaining dough in half, cut off a quarter of each piece, shape each piece into 3 pencil-thin ropes and plait together. Shape the large pieces into loaves, place the plaits on top of the loaves, and put the loaves into 2 well-greased tins. Brush the dough lightly with oil and cover loosely with plastic wrap. Allow to rise for 30–40 minutes for rolls and about 1 hour for loaves. Brush with beaten egg and sprinkle with 1 tablespoon wheat germ. Bake at 180°C/350°F/Gas Mark 4 for 20–25 minutes for rolls and 25–30 minutes for loaves, until golden. Cover the tops with foil for the last 5–10 minutes if the plaits brown too quickly. Remove from the tins immediately and cool on a wire rack.

Country Wheatmeal Bread

Makes 2 medium-sized loaves

Use 2 22 × 12 × 6.5 cm/8½″ × 4½″ × 2½″ loaf tins

360 g (12¾ oz) unbleached white flour, plain
25 g (1 oz) brown sugar
25 g (1 oz) dried yeast
2 tsp sea salt
350 ml (12 fl oz) milk
150 ml (5 fl oz) water
25 g (1 oz) butter or polyunsaturated margarine
1 egg
65 g (2½ oz) Kretschmer Wheat Germ, Plain
240–360 g (9–12 oz) stoneground wholemeal flour
sunflower oil for brushing tops of loaves (optional)

Combine two thirds of the unbleached flour, the sugar, yeast and salt in a large bowl. Stir well to mix. Heat the milk, water and butter in a medium saucepan until lukewarm and add to the ingredients in the bowl. Beat with an electric mixer at medium speed for 2 minutes. Scrape the bowl occasionally. Add the egg and remaining unbleached white flour and beat at high speed for 1 minute. Stir in the wheat germ with a wooden spoon, then gradually stir in just enough wholemeal flour to make a soft dough which leaves the sides of the bowl. Turn out on to a lightly floured board and knead for 5–10 minutes or until the dough is smooth and elastic.

Place the dough in a greased bowl, turning to coat all the sides. Cover with plastic wrap, then a towel. Leave to rise in a warm, draught-free place for about 1 hour or until doubled in size. Punch down, divide the dough in half and shape into loaves by rolling each piece into a 30 cm × 20 cm/12″ × 8″ rectangle. Roll up tightly beginning with the 20 cm/8″ side. Seal the lengthwise edge and the ends well. Put the dough into 2 greased 450 g/1 lb loaf tins (the correct tin size is important for best results). Brush the dough lightly with oil, cover the tins loosely with plastic wrap and allow to rise in a warm place for 1 hour or until doubled in size. Pre-heat the oven to 190°C/375°F/Gas Mark 5 and bake for 30–40 minutes until done. Use a lower oven shelf for best results. Cover loosely with foil for the last 5–10 minutes if the crust browns too quickly. Remove from the tin immediately. Brush the top crust with sunflower oil if desired and cool on a wire rack.

Wheat Germ Cheese Bread

Prepare as directed for Wheatmeal Bread, except to stir in 225 g/8 oz grated Cheddar cheese with the wheat germ.

Granary Beer Bread

Makes 1 loaf

A hearty bread to team with cheese and soup.

25 g (1 oz) dried yeast
150 ml (5 fl oz) warm water
150 ml (5 fl oz) light or brown ale at room temperature (no foam)
1 egg, slightly beaten
40 g (1½ oz) Barbados sugar
25 g (1 oz) polyunsaturated margarine, melted
1 tsp sea salt
225 g (8 oz) stoneground wholemeal flour
65 g (2½ oz) Kretschmer Wheat Germ, Plain
170 g (6 oz) unbleached white flour, plain
sunflower oil
1 egg beaten with 1 tbsp water

Dissolve the yeast in the warm water in a large bowl. Add the beer, beaten egg, sugar, margarine and salt to the yeast mixture and stir well to blend. Stir in the wholemeal flour and wheat germ with a wooden spoon and gradually stir in just enough of the unbleached white flour to make a soft dough which leaves the sides of the bowl. Turn out on to a floured board and knead for 5–10 minutes or until

the dough is smooth and elastic. Place the dough in a large, greased bowl, turning to coat all sides, cover and leave to rise in a warm, draught-free place for 1½–2 hours or until doubled in size. Punch down, divide the dough into 3 equal pieces and shape each piece into a 40 cm/16″ rope. Plait the ropes together, shape into a ring and seal the ends. Place in a greased 23 cm/9″ loose-bottomed cake tin. Brush the dough lightly with oil, cover the tin loosely with plastic wrap and leave to rise for 1–1½ hours or until doubled in size. Pre-heat the oven to 180°C/350°F/Gas Mark 4. Brush the loaf with the egg and water mixture and bake for 40–45 minutes. Cover loosely with foil for the last 5–10 minutes, if the crust browns too quickly. Remove from the tin immediately and cool on a wire rack.

Herb Plait

Makes 2 450 g/1 lb loaves

725–850 g (1 lb 10 oz–1 lb 14 oz) brown wheatmeal flour
40 g (1½ oz) sugar
25 g (1 oz) dried yeast
1 tsp thyme, crushed
1 tsp marjoram, crushed
1 level tsp sea salt
450 ml (16 fl oz) milk
100 g (4 oz) polyunsaturated margarine
3 eggs
90 g (3½ oz) Kretschmer Wheat Germ, Plain
vegetable oil for brushing baking tins
1 dsrtsp Kretschmer Wheat Germ, Plain
1 dsrtsp sesame seeds

Combine one third of the flour, the sugar, yeast, thyme, marjoram and salt in a large bowl and stir well to blend. Heat the milk and margarine together until warm to the touch (not scalding). The margarine does not have to melt completely. Add the warm liquid to the ingredients in the bowl and beat with an electric mixer at medium speed for 2 minutes. Scrape the bowl occasionally. Add 2 eggs plus the yolk of the third, and ⅓ more of the flour. Beat at high speed for 1 minute or until thick and elastic. Stir in the wheat germ with a wooden spoon, then gradually stir in just enough of the remaining flour to make a soft dough which leaves the sides of the bowl. Turn out on to a floured board and knead for 5–10 minutes or until the dough is smooth and elastic. Place the dough in a large, oiled bowl, turning to coat all sides, and allow to rise in a warm, draught-free place for 1 hour or until doubled in size. Punch down and divide in half. Roll each half into a 46 cm × 23 cm/18″ × 9″ rectangle and cut each into thirds lengthwise. Shape each strip into a rope and plait three ropes together for each loaf. Seal the ends and tuck under. Place on greased baking sheets, brush lightly with oil and cover loosely with plastic wrap. Leave to rise for about 30 minutes, until light. Pre-heat the oven to 200°C/400°F/Gas Mark 6. Brush the loaves with beaten egg white and sprinkle lightly with a dessertspoon each of wheat germ and sesame seeds. Bake in the pre-heated oven for 20–25 minutes. Cover with foil for the last 5–10 minutes if the crust browns too quickly. Remove from the baking trays immediately and cool on a wire rack.

Onion Buns

Makes 16

600–700 g (1 lb 5 oz–1 lb 9 oz) brown wheatmeal flour
15 g (½ oz) dried yeast
1 tbsp sugar
2 tsp sea salt
½ tsp freshly ground black pepper
450 ml (16 fl oz) milk
2 rounded tbsp minced onion
35 g (1¼ oz) butter or polyunsaturated margarine
2 level tsp mustard powder
1 egg
100 g (4 oz) Kretschmer Wheat Germ, Plain
sunflower oil for brushing tops of loaves
1 egg, well beaten

Combine half the flour with the yeast, sugar, salt and pepper in a large bowl and stir well. Heat together the milk, half the onion, the butter and mustard until warm to the touch (not scalding) and add the warm liquid to the ingredients in the bowl. Beat with an electric mixer at medium speed for 2 minutes. Scrape the bowl occasionally. Add the egg and half the remaining flour. Beat at high speed for 1 minute or until thick and elastic. Stir in the wheat germ with a wooden spoon, then gradually stir in just enough of the remaining flour to make a soft dough which leaves the sides of the bowl. Turn out on to a floured board and knead for 5–10 minutes or until the dough is elastic. Place the dough in a large, greased bowl, turning to coat all sides. Cover and leave to rise in a warm, draught-free place for about 1½ hours or until doubled in size. Punch down and divide the dough into 16 equal pieces,

shape them into smooth balls and place on greased baking sheets. Flatten to make buns about 9 cm/3½″ in diameter and brush them lightly with oil. Cover the baking sheets loosely with plastic wrap and leave to rise for about 45 minutes or until doubled in size. Pre-heat the oven to 190°C/375°F/Gas Mark 5. Soak the remaining tablespoon of onion in water for about 5 minutes. Drain. Brush the buns with beaten egg and sprinkle with onion. Bake in the pre-heated oven for 20–25 minutes until done, then remove from the baking sheet immediately. Cool on a wire rack.

Delicious with hamburgers. To make hot dog buns, shape the dough into 16 25 cm/6″ long buns by rolling on a lightly floured board. Taper the ends by rolling gently between the hands. Place on greased baking sheets and complete as directed above except to bake for 15–20 minutes only.

Wheat Germ Croissants

Makes 24

These are a real treat but because of their high fat content and low level of fibre they are very fattening, so eat and enjoy them very occasionally only! You can use wheatmeal flour instead of unbleached white and substitute polyunsaturated margarine for butter with only a very slightly heavier result.

275 g (10 oz) unbleached white flour
275 g (10 oz) softened butter
25 g (1 oz) dried yeast (2 tbsp)
225 g (8 fl oz) warm water
50 g (2 oz) Kretschmer Wheat Germ, Plain
1 egg
40 g (1½ oz) fruit sugar
1 level tsp salt
1 egg
1 dsrtsp water

Beat 25 g/1 oz of flour and the butter together until well-blended. Spread into a 30 cm × 15 cm/12″ × 6″ rectangle on waxed paper or foil and refrigerate until firm (about 30 minutes). Dissolve the yeast in the warm water in a large bowl. Add 225 g/8 oz of the flour, the wheat germ, egg, sugar and salt to the dissolved yeast and beat with an electric mixer at medium speed for 1 minute. Gradually stir in just enough of the remaining flour with a wooden spoon to make a soft dough which leaves the sides of the bowl. Turn out on to a floured board and knead for

5–8 minutes until dough is smooth and elastic. Roll the dough into a 36 cm/14″ square. Place the refrigerated butter mixture on one side of rectangle, fold the dough over the butter and pinch the edges to seal. Roll into a 51 cm × 36 cm/20″ × 14″ rectangle. Fold the dough in thirds and place on a baking sheet. Refrigerate the dough for 10 minutes to firm butter, then repeat the rolling, folding and refrigerating three more times. If the butter begins to break through, sprinkle with flour to seal. Wrap and refrigerate the dough for 2–3 hours after the last folding.

Cut the dough into thirds. Work with one third at a time and refrigerate the remaining pieces until ready to use. Roll one third of the dough into a 51 cm × 36 cm/20″ × 14″ rectangle then cut crosswise into 4 equal pieces. Cut each piece diagonally to form 2 triangles, roll up each triangle loosely, starting at the longest side and rolling towards the point. Place on ungreased baking sheets and curve to form crescents. Cover loosely with plastic wrap and leave to rise in warm, draught-free place for 30–45 minutes until light. Pre-heat the oven to 180°C/350°F/Gas Mark 4. Brush the dough with 1 egg beaten with 1 dessertspoon water and bake in the pre-heated oven for 18–22 minutes until golden.

—Wholewheat Pocket— Bread

Makes 10 rounds

25 g (1 oz) dried yeast (2 tbsp)
275 ml (10 fl oz) warm water (40°–45°C/
*   105°–115°F)*
1 dsrtsp sugar
35 g (1¼ oz) Kretschmer Wheat Germ, Plain
1½ tsp sea salt
1½ tsp sunflower oil
190 g (6½ oz) stoneground wholemeal flour
65–110 g (2½–4¼ oz) unbleached white flour,
*   plain*
1 dsrtsp sesame seeds
extra Kretschmer Wheat Germ, Plain for topping
*   (optional)*

Combine the yeast and warm water in a large bowl and stir to dissolve the yeast. Stir in the sugar and leave to stand for 5 minutes. Add the wheat germ, salt and oil to the yeast mixture and stir well to blend. Stir in the wholemeal flour with a wooden spoon and beat in just enough plain white flour to make a soft dough which leaves the sides of the bowl. Turn out on to a lightly floured board and knead for 10 minutes until the dough is smooth and elastic. Place dough in a greased polythene bag and leave to rise in a warm, draught-free place for about 1 hour, until doubled in size. Punch the dough down and divide into 10 equal pieces. Shape each piece into a ball and leave to stand, covered, for 5 minutes. Sprinkle each ball with sesame seeds and additional wheatgerm before rolling if desired. Roll into 15 cm/6″ rounds, place on greased baking sheets and leave to let rise, covered, for about 20 minutes. Pre-heat the oven to 230°C/450°F/Gas Mark 8 and bake for 5–7 minutes until browned. Remove from the baking sheet immediately and cool on a wire rack. To serve, cut in half and fill with desired fillings.

LOSELEY

—Naan Bread—

Makes 12 breads

This recipe using Loseley yoghurt is from India and is versatile and simple to make.

675 g (1½ lb) brown wheatmeal or unbleached
*   white flour, self-raising*
425 g (15 fl oz) Loseley Natural Yoghurt
½ tsp dried yeast, dissolved in a little warm water
large pinch of salt

Mix all the ingredients together and knead lightly. Cover with a wet cloth and leave for 24 hours. Divide into 12 equal portions and roll out each piece into an oval shape just under 5 mm/¼″ thick. Place on a greased baking tray, brush with melted margarine and grill each side for 2 minutes until brown. Serve warm.

These breads are delicious topped with salad vegetables, covered in grated cheese, then grilled until the cheese is light golden brown. The vegetables remain crisp and retain all their goodness under the cheese.

NATURE'S BOUNTY

Bran 'N' Fig High Fibre Loaf

Makes 5 450g/1 lb loaves

*kg (3 lb) organically grown 100% wholemeal flour,
plain or brown wheatmeal, plain
25 g (1 oz) dried yeast
1 litre (1¾ pints) warm water
100 g (4 oz)* Nature's Bounty Bran 'N' Fig
1 tsp sea salt

Make a batter by mixing half the flour, the yeast and 2 tablespoons of the Bran 'N' Fig together in a bowl. Pour in the warm water and mix well. Cover and leave to stand for 8–12 hours at room temperature. Now add the remaining flour, the salt and the remaining Bran 'N' Fig to the yeast mixture, stir thoroughly and knead for 5 minutes. Place in an oiled plastic bag and leave to rise in a warm place for about 20 minutes. Pre-heat the oven to 240°C/475°F/Gas Mark 8. Knead the risen dough for 2 minutes, divide into five equal pieces and mould into loaf shapes, place in oiled tins and bake in the pre-heated oven for 15 minutes. Turn down to 190°C/375°F/Gas Mark 5 and bake for another 20 minutes. Cool on a wire rack.

LOTUS

Pumpernickel

Makes 4 450g/1 lb loaves

This Pumpernickel is a flavoursome, chewy and delicious bread, with Lotus soya grits to add more protein. The soya grits are already cooked and can be added to many recipes such as cakes, biscuits and soups.

*1 litre (1¾ pints) warm water
100 g (4 oz) kibbled wheat or cracked wheat
1 tbsp blackstrap molasses
2 tsp Muscovado sugar
25 g (1 oz) dried yeast
675 g (1½ lb) strong wholemeal flour, plain*

*1 level tbsp sea salt (optional)
350 g (12 oz) dark rye flour
50 g (2 oz) buckwheat flour
50 g (2 oz) cornmeal
100 g (4 oz)* Lotus Soya Grits

From the measured water take out 275 ml/10 fl oz. Bring to the boil and pour over the kibbled wheat. Stir in the molasses and leave to soak for 1 hour before making your bread. Put the remaining warm water in a large mixing bowl, whisk in the sugar and yeast and leave to froth in a warm place for 10 minutes. Stir in the wholemeal flour with a wooden spoon and beat until the dough is smooth and stretchy (it will have a texture a bit like gluey mud!) Add the kibbled wheat and molasses mixture and all the other ingredients. Form into a dough with your hands, turn out on to a floured surface and knead for 7 minutes. If too sticky just knead in a little more wholemeal flour. Place in an oiled polythene bag and leave to rise in a warm place until nearly double in size (about 1 hour). Pre-heat the oven to 190°C/375°F/Gas Mark 5. Knock back and knead for 2 minutes more. Shape into 4 loaves and fit each snugly into the prepared tins. Bake in the pre-heated oven for 35 minutes. Ease out of the tins, turn upside down and bake for a further 5–7 minutes. Cool on a wire rack.

Evelyn's Sourdough Bread

Makes 2 1 kg/2.2 lb loaves

Sourdough bread is one of the simplest to make. I have achieved the best results using strong wholemeal flour but you can use home-grown English wholewheat flour with very good results. Sourdough bread requires a starter. Micro-organisms grow in the starter which cause the bread to rise.

Starter
*1 level tbsp dried yeast
575 ml (1 pint) warm water
2 level tsp honey or Barbados sugar
275 g (10 fl oz)* Marriage's Strong 100% Wholemeal Flour, *plain*

Combine the ingredients to form a spongy, muddy texture, place in a large bowl and leave it to ferment for 5 days. Stir each day. The starter will keep indefinitely in the refrigerator but it is best to use it once weekly. Make sure that the container is double in volume to the starter because it sometimes rises during storage. Just stir it when this happens.

This starter will need replenishing each time you make a batch of bread. The instructions for this are in the recipe for my Sourdough Bread below.

The dough for this is slightly stickier than for full yeasted bread. The batter in Stage 1 has to be made about 12 hours before you are going to bake your bread, so if you wish to bake in the evening start in the morning with Stage 1, and vice versa.

Stage 1

550 g (1¼ lb) Marriage's Strong 100% Wholemeal
 Flour, *plain*
225 g (8 oz) starter as above (stir before taking out)
850 ml (1½ pints) lukewarm water

Place the flour in a large mixing bowl. Make a well in the middle and add the starter. Now mix while adding the water a cupful at a time until you have the consistency of a thick batter. Beat the mixture well. Cover with a cloth and leave in a reasonably warm room overnight (if baking the following morning), or all day if baking the following evening.

Stage 2

Take out 225 g/8 oz from the mixture and add this to replenish it. (It is important to do this before adding any other ingredients.)

3 tbsp sunflower or *corn oil*
1 dsrtsp sea salt
775 g (1¾ lb) Marriage's Strong 100% Wholemeal
 Flour, *plain*

Fold in the oil, sea salt and flour very gradually with a wooden spoon. Use your hands towards the end of adding the flour, and mould well together. The dough will come easily away from the bowl but is softer and a little stickier than a full yeasted dough. Flour a work surface well (not wood or the dough will stick to it unless it is well sealed) and knead the dough for 5 minutes only. Divide into two equal parts and mould each to fit snugly into oiled bread tins. Slide each filled tin into a good sized polythene bag and leave to rise in a warm (not hot) place for 1½–2 hours. Pre-heat the oven to 220°C/425°F/Gas Mark 7. Brush the tops of the loaves with lukewarm water. Bake in the pre-heated oven for 20 minutes, then lower the heat to 190°C/375°F/Gas Mark 5 and continue to bake for 1 hour more.

Evelyn's Sourdough Rye Bread

Follow the previous recipe exactly until you reach Stage 2. Take out 225 g/8 oz and add it to the starter mixture in the refrigerator to replenish it, then instead of adding 350 g/12 oz of strong wholemeal flour add 450 g/1 lb rye flour. Proceed and bake in the same way as the Sourdough Bread.

You can add 2 teaspoons of caraway seeds or sesame seeds, or indeed any other flavoursome herbs and seeds to add variety to this loaf, just as you can with yeasted loaves.

Malted Wheatmeal Loaf

Makes 5 450 g/1 lb loaves

This is a fairly dry dough, with less liquid used than with other doughs. The ingredients of this flour give a moist loaf with good keeping properties.

1.5 kg (3 lb) Marriage's Country Fayre Brown
 Wheatmeal Flour
25 (1 oz) salt
40 g (1½ oz) fresh or *4 tsp dried yeast*
1 level tsp sugar
725 ml (1¼ pints) warm water
3 tbsp corn oil

Grease the bread tins. Place flour and salt to warm in a large mixing bowl. Cream the yeast and 4 tablespoons of the warm water together. (If using dried yeast, stir it into 275 ml/10 fl oz of the warm water with the sugar. Leave in a warm place until frothy – about 10–15 minutes.)

Make a well in the dry ingredients, pour in yeast mixture, oil and sufficient warm water to make a firm dough, mix together and knead for 2 minutes. Place the dough in a large mixing bowl and cover with a piece of oiled polythene. Leave in a warm place until doubled in size – about 40 minutes–1½ hours depending on room temperature. Knock back the dough, turn on to a lightly floured surface, weigh off 450 g/1 lb pieces of dough, lightly knead each piece and shape to fit the tins. Place the dough in prepared tins and cover with oiled polythene. Leave in a warm place to rise (about 30 minutes–1 hour). Pre-heat the oven to 230°C/450°F/Gas Mark 8 and bake for 20 minutes then reduce the heat to 200°C/400°F/Gas Mark 6 for a further 10 minutes. Remove from the tins immediately and cool on a wire rack.

This recipe can be made up as two 900 g/2 lb loaves, plus one 450 g/1 lb loaf. Allow an extra 10 minutes cooking time for the 900 g/2 lb loaves at the lower temperature.

Wholemeal Bread

Makes 3 450 g/1 lb loaves

850 g (1 lb 14 oz) Marriage's 100% Wholemeal Flour
15 g (½ oz) salt
20 g (¾ oz) granulated sugar (optional)
15 g (½ oz) polyunsaturated margarine
50 g (2 oz) fresh or 2 level tbsp dried yeast
approx 475–575 ml (17–20 fl oz) lukewarm water

Sift the flour, salt and sugar into a bowl and rub in the margarine or vegetable fat. Mix the yeast into the lukewarm water. (If using dried yeast sprinkle the yeast and sugar into the water and leave in a warm place for 10 minutes until mixture is frothy.) Add sufficient liquid to the dry ingredients to mix into a firm dough which leaves the bowl clean. A little more flour or water may be needed to give the required consistency.

Turn the dough on to a lightly floured work surface and knead until the dough is firm and elastic and no longer sticky (about 10 minutes). Roll the dough into a ball, place in a lightly greased polythene bag and tie the top loosely, allowing enough room for the dough to double in size. Leave in a warm room for 1 hour. Divide the dough into 3 equal pieces and roll out until the same length as the baking tins and approximately 2.5 cm/1″ thick. Try not to tear the dough – use a floured rolling pin to avoid this. Roll the dough up tightly like a swiss roll, push the ends under slightly and place in the lightly greased baking tins. Put each tin inside a greased polythene bag, again tying the top loosely, and leave in a warm room for 45 minutes or until the dough has doubled in size. Pre-heat the oven to 230°C/450°F/Gas Mark 8. Bake the loaves on the middle shelf of the pre-heated oven for 30–40 minutes or until the loaves shrink slightly from the sides of the tin and the crusts are golden brown. Remove from the tins and cool on a wire rack.

PAUL'S TOFU

Tofu Pizza

Makes 2 30 cm/12″ pizzas

I love pizza with dairy cheese such as a thinly sliced Mozzarella or, for children, grated farmhouse Cheddar cheese. I also like using tofu as an alternative and for those on a low fat diet it is a must. You can use any bread dough as a base for pizza (preferably wholemeal). For one 30 cm/12″ pizza base, when making bread cut off a 400 g/14 oz piece of the dough, roll it out in bran after the first rising, place on a pizza tray and freeze at this stage if you wish to make the pizza at a later date. It will only take 2 hours to defrost on the tray in a warm place. It is then ready to pre-bake if you wish and fill with the sauce of your choice. You can pre-bake pizza dough as directed in the following recipe but it is not essential, however, it does firm the base and avoid any sogginess.

2 tsps dried yeast
275 ml (10 fl oz) warm water
½ tsp Barbados sugar
2 tbsp olive oil
1 tsp malt extract
450 g (1 lb) wholemeal flour
2 tbsp sesame seeds
just under 1 level tsp sea salt
bran for rolling out the dough

Sauce
2 tbsp olive oil
1 large onion (about 225 g/8 oz) when peeled and chopped)
2 large cloves of garlic, crushed
794 g (1 lb 12 oz) can tomatoes (drain off 225 ml/ 8 fl oz of juice, reserving it for stock or soups), chopped
2 generous tbsp tomato purée
1 tsp basil
1 tsp oregano
2 bay leaves
1 level tsp herb salt or sea salt
freshly ground black pepper to taste
2 tbsp olive oil
1 large green pepper or ½ red and ½ green, de-seeded and chopped
100 g (4 oz) button mushrooms, sliced
2 medium courgettes, cut into thin 2.5 cm (1″) sticks
good pinch herb salt or sea salt
1 tbsp lemon juice

Topping
450 g (1 lb) Paul's Firm Tofu, cut into thin slices
50 g (2 oz) pumpkin seeds
black olives, stoned, to decorate
a little oregano
pinch herb salt

Dissolve the yeast in the warm water and stir in the sugar. Leave it to froth in a warm place for about 7 minutes. Warm the olive oil by pouring it into a hot cup and stir in the malt extract. Mix the flour, sesame seeds and salt together. When the yeast liquid is ready, make a well in the flour and pour this into the centre with the olive oil and malt. Form into a dough and knead with floured hands for 7 minutes. Place in an oiled polythene bag and leave to rise until it has doubled in size: approximately 40 minutes–1 hour.

Heat the oil in a heavy-based saucepan and sauté the onion and garlic for 6 minutes, until tender. Add the chopped tomatoes, tomato purée, basil, oregano, bay leaves, teaspoon of herb salt or sea salt and freshly ground black pepper. Bring to the boil and simmer for 30 minutes with the lid slightly off so that the mixture evaporates a little while cooking. Meanwhile, sauté the green pepper (or mixed red and green), the mushrooms and courgettes in the oil plus a good pinch of herb salt or sea salt and a little black pepper if you wish, for 4 minutes only. Stir in the lemon juice. Leave to one side. Pre-heat the oven to 200°C/400°F/Gas Mark 6.

When the dough has risen, knock back and knead for 2 minutes. Divide into two pieces and make a ball of each. Sprinkle the work surface with bran and roll each ball out to fit two 30 cm/12″ well-oiled pizza trays. Pinch up a lip around the edge to contain the sauce then brush the dough with beaten egg. Bake in the centre of the oven for 7 minutes, then take out and set aside to cool slightly. Ladle equal amounts of the tomato mixture on to the pizza crusts then spoon on the sautéed peppers, mushrooms and courgettes and spread equal amounts of the tofu slices on top with equal portions of pumpkin seeds, olives, a little oregano and a pinch of herb salt. Bake the pizzas on two shelves for 15 minutes, changing the trays around after 8 minutes. If a browner top is required then put under a hot grill for a few minutes. Leave to stand for at least 5 minutes before cutting. Serve with a fresh salad.

If you wish to freeze one of the pizzas then bake it with the sauce and topping for 10 minutes only. Let it get cold and then freeze. Defrost for 1½ hours. Bake it for 10 minutes once defrosted.

PREWETT'S

Burger Baps

Makes 12

You can use Prewett's 100% Wholemeal Organic Flour for this recipe but I prefer the Millstone Brown Wheatmeal plus some ground sesame or sunflower seeds to achieve a lighter, bun-like texture. Using dried yeast plus a vitamin C tablet gives quicker rising.

450 g (1 lb) Prewett's Millstone Brown Wheatmeal Flour, plain, less 2 level tablespoons
2 level tbsp finely ground sesame or sunflower seeds
1 rounded tsp sea salt
50 g (2 oz) Prewett's Safflower or Sunflower Margarine
25 mg vitamin C tablet
1 rounded tsp Prewett's Muscavado Sugar
350 ml (12 fl oz) mixed hot water and cold milk in equal proportions
15 g (½ oz) dried yeast
little milk for brushing
few whole sesame seeds for tops of baps

Put the flour, ground seeds and salt into a warm bowl and rub in the margarine. Crush the vitamin C tablet and place in a jug with the sugar and 150 ml/5 fl oz of the warm milk-and-water liquid. Sprinkle on the dried yeast, stir well and leave to froth for 7–10 minutes. Make a well in the centre of the flour mixture and pour on the yeast liquid and remaining milk-and-water. Form into a soft dough and knead on a work surface for 10 minutes (only flour the hands if necessary, do not flour the work surface). Place the dough in a lightly oiled polythene bag, press out the air, tie the opening and let it stand in a warm place for 10 minutes only. Knock back and knead for 1 minute more. Divide into 12 equal pieces and keep in the plastic bag while you roll each piece separately into a ball. Place the balls of dough on warmed, oiled and floured baking sheets. Press each lightly with the palm of the hand to flatten slightly into approximately 7 cm/3″ rounds. Slide the baking sheets into large, oiled polythene bags leaving enough room for the baps to rise. Leave to stand in a warm place (not hot) for about 45 minutes, until double in size. Pre-heat the oven to 220°C/425°F/Gas Mark 7. Brush the tops of the baps with milk and sprinkle on the whole sesame seeds. Bake in the pre-heated oven on two shelves, one slightly above centre and the other slightly below, for 10 minutes. Change the sheets round and continue to bake for another 7 minutes until golden brown. Cool on a wire rack. To keep the crusts of the baps soft just cover them with a clean cloth while they cool.

Crunchy Bread Sticks

Makes about 25

These are a very tasty nibble and simple to make.

100 g (4 oz) Prewett's 100% Wholemeal Flour, *plain*
100 g (4 oz) Prewett's Strong White Unbleached Flour, *plain*
50 g (2 oz) Prewett's Oatbran and Oatgerm or Wheatgerm and Wheatbran, *mixed*
1 level tsp herb salt
2 tbsp olive oil
2 tsps dried yeast
1 tsp Prewett's Muscovado Sugar
200 ml (7 fl oz) warm water
a little beaten egg and water for brushing

Mix the flours, oatbran and oatgerm (or wheatbran and wheatgerm), herb salt and olive oil well together. Sprinkle the yeast and sugar into the warm water, whisk well and leave to froth in a warm place for 7–10 minutes. When ready, pour the yeast liquid into the flour mixture and form into a soft dough. Knead the dough for 5 minutes. Place the dough in an oiled plastic bag and leave to rise in a warm place until doubled in size – about 30–40 minutes. Punch down and knead for just 1 minute more. Cut the dough into about 25 pieces. Roll each into a ball and then into thin sticks about 30 cm/12″ long. Place on warmed and oiled baking sheets, brush with the egg mixture and cover loosely with an oiled polythene bag. Leave to stand for 20 minutes in a warm place. Pre-heat the oven to 170°C/325°F/Gas Mark 3. Bake two trays at a time, changing the trays round after 15 minutes and continue to bake for a further 15–20 minutes. The sticks will be crisp and dark golden brown.

Crusty French Loaf

Makes 2

25 g (1 oz) fresh yeast
1 level tsp Prewett's Muscovado Sugar
425 ml (15 fl oz) warm water
575 g (1 lb 4 oz) Prewett's Millstone Brown Wheatmeal Flour, *plain*
110 g (4 oz) Prewett's Soya Flour
1 generous tsp sea salt
1 egg yolk
1 tbsp sunflower oil
few sesame seeds for top (optional)

Cream the yeast and sugar and add approximately one third of the warm water. Allow to stand, covered with a cloth in a warm place until it becomes frothy (about 7–10 minutes). Mix the flours with the salt. Beat the egg yolk with the oil. When the yeast liquid is frothy pour this into the flour and add the egg mixture and remaining water gradually until a soft dough is formed. The dough should not be sticky. Knead for 7 minutes. Place in an oiled plastic bag and leave to rise in a warm place until the dough is doubled in size – this usually takes about 45 minutes–1 hour. When the dough is well risen knead again for 2 minutes.

Divide the dough into two equal parts, rolling out each piece into a French-loaf shape about 35 cm/ 14″ long. Place the two loaves on a greased baking sheet, leaving enough room to allow them to spread. Put into an oiled plastic bag and again leave to rise in a warm place until doubled in size – about 30 minutes. Pre-heat the oven to 220°C/425°F/Gas Mark 7. When risen, make slanting indents in each loaf with the back of a knife, brush with lukewarm water and sprinkle on the sesame seeds if used. Bake in the pre-heated oven for about 15 minutes, turning the tray round after 10 minutes. Then turn the loaves upside down to finish baking for 3 more minutes. Cool on wire rack.

Fruit, Nut and Seed Loaf

Makes 2 450 g/1 lb loaves

A very fruity and nourishing tea bread.

225 g (8 oz) Prewett's 100% Wholemeal Flour, *plain*
225 g (8 oz) Prewett's Strong Unbleached White Flour, *plain*
good pinch sea salt
½ tsp freshly ground nutmeg
½ tsp ground cinnamon or *mixed spice*
¼ level tsp ground clove powder
grated rinds of ½ orange and ½ lemon
1 tsp Prewett's Muscovado Sugar
15 g (½ oz) (approx 1 level tbsp) dried yeast
225 ml (8 fl oz) warm water
1 tbsp blackstrap molasses or *malt*
50 g (2 oz) Prewett's Sunflower Margarine
350 g (12 oz) finely mixed dried fruit including raisins, chopped apricots, figs, dates and dried apple
50 g (2 oz) chopped almonds
50 g (2 oz) chopped sunflower or *pumpkin seeds*
a little honey and water to glaze

Mix the flours with the salt, spices and lemon and orange rinds. Sprinkle the sugar and dried yeast into the warm water. Whisk and leave to froth in a warm place for 7–10 minutes. Melt the molasses or malt and the margarine together in a small saucepan over a pan of warm water. Make a well in the centre of the flour mixture and pour in the yeast liquid and the melted molasses and margarine. Form into a soft dough and knead for about 5–7 minutes. Place the dough in an oiled plastic bag and leave to rise in a warm place until doubled in size. Return the dough to the mixing bowl and work in the fruit, nuts and seeds (reserve a little of the fruit, nut and seed mixture to decorate the cooked bread). Divide the mixture into two, shape into loaves and place in greased and lined loaf tins. Slide the tins into good sized, oiled polythene bags and leave in a warm place until well risen into a slight dome shape above the level of the tins. Pre-heat the oven to 200°C/400°F/Gas Mark 6 and bake the loaves in the centre of the oven for 30 minutes. Put to cool on a wire rack. While still hot brush the tops with the honey and water mixture and sprinkle on a little fruit, nuts and seeds. Lovely hot or cold, sliced and spread with butter or polyunsaturated margarine.

Malt Loaf

Makes 2 450 g/1 lb loaves

These are delicious and moist, and the recipe is enough for two – one will definitely not be enough when friends come to tea!

200 ml (7 fl oz) tepid water
1 heaped tbsp blackstrap molasses
3 rounded tsp dried yeast
450 g (1 lb) Prewett's 100% Organic Wholemeal Flour, *plain*
1 level tsp sea salt
150 g (5 oz) malt extract
50 g (2 oz) Prewett's Sunflower Margarine
175 g (6 oz) sultanas (golden are delicious)
a little flour for kneading and rolling out
1 tsp honey mixed with 1 tsp hot water to glaze

Oil and flour two 450 g/1 lb loaf tins.

Pour the tepid water in a jug, stir in just half a teaspoon of the molasses, sprinkle on the dried yeast, stir, and leave to froth for about 7–10 minutes in a warm place. Mix the flour with the sea salt. Melt together the malt, remaining molasses and the margarine in a saucepan (not on direct heat – place the saucepan in a pan of hot water which is over a low heat). When just melted stir in the sultanas, then pour the yeast liquid and malt mixture into the flour and mix with the hands to form a sticky dough. Rub the hands with a *little* flour and knead the dough on a work surface for 2–3 minutes, rubbing your hands with more flour as needed. (Do not use too much flour or the dough will get dry and heavy.) Break the dough into two equal pieces, shape each into an oblong the length of the prepared tins, roll out then curl up as you would a Swiss roll. Place in the tins, slide the tins into oiled polythene bags, leaving enough room for dough to rise, and leave to prove in a warm place for about 1½ hours. The dough should just reach the top of the tin when ready for baking. Bake in the centre of a pre-heated oven at 200°C/400°F/Gas Mark 6 for 40 minutes. While still hot brush with the honey and water mixture. Cool on a wire rack. Serve hot or cold spread with butter or polyunsaturated margarine.

Quick Pizza

Makes 1 30 cm/12" pizza

Follow the Yoghurt Scone recipe (see page 00) but omit the margarine and add 4 tablespoons olive oil and 2 tablespoons sesame seeds. Rub the oil into the flour as you would margarine. Roll out the dough to fit a 30 cm/12" pizza tray, brush surface with olive oil and sprinkle on some more sesame seeds.

Filling
1 large onion, peeled and cut in thin rings
1 clove garic, crushed
2 tbsp olive oil
2 small courgettes, thinly sliced
75 g (3 oz) button mushrooms thinly sliced
4 medium tomatoes, thinly sliced
1 tbsp tomato purée
1 tsp marjoram or sweet basil
175 g (6 oz) sliced Mozzarella or grated Cheddar cheese
a few stoned olives or anchovy fillets or pumpkin seeds for topping, plus a little more marjoram or basil

Pre-heat the oven to 180°C/350°F/Gas Mark 4.
  Sauté the onion and garlic in the olive oil until soft – about 5 minutes. Add the courgettes and mushrooms and continue to fry for 3 minutes more. Stir in the tomato purée and the marjoram or basil and spoon on to the pizza base. Arrange the sliced tomatoes on top. Place the slices of Mozzarella over the tomatoes or sprinkle on the grated cheese. Arrange the olives or anchovies on top of the cheese, or for children, sprinkle on a few pumpkin seeds – these give a milder flavour and are much liked. Finally, sprinkle on a little of the herb of your choice and bake for 25 minutes in the centre of the pre-heated oven.

Yoghurt Scones

Makes 12–14

This recipe will also make two 23 cm/9" thin pastry bases for Lentil Quiche, (see page 000), or use for any savoury pie.

175 g (6 oz) Prewett's 100% Wholemeal Flour, self-raising
175 g (6 oz) Prewett's Strong Unbleached White Flour, self-raising
good pinch sea salt
75 g (3 oz) Prewett's Sunflower Margarine
1 level tbsp malt extract
275 ml (10 fl oz) natural yoghurt or milk and yoghurt mixed
a little milk and bran for topping

Pre-heat the oven to 220°C/425°F/Gas Mark 7.
  Put both the flours in a mixing bowl with the sea salt and rub in the margarine. Melt the malt in a small saucepan over a pan of boiling water then stir it into the yoghurt and pour the liquid into the flour mixture. Form into a soft dough as quickly and lightly as possible and roll out on a floured surface to just over 1 cm/½" thick. Cut into rounds with scone cutter and place on greased baking trays. Brush with milk and sprinkle on a little bran. Place in the pre-heated oven: one tray just above centre, one just below, for 8 minutes. Change the trays around quickly and continue to bake for 6 minutes more until golden brown.

Cheese and Tarragon Scones

Simply leave out the malt from the previous recipe and add 175 g/6 oz grated Cheddar cheese, 1 heaped teaspoon dried tarragon and 1 level teaspoon dry mustard powder after rubbing in the margarine.

VECON

Vecon Savoury Scones

Makes 8

200 g (7 oz) 100% wholemeal flour
2½ tsp baking powder
50 g (2 oz) Vecon, chilled
100 ml (4 fl oz) milk

Pre-heat the oven to 200°C/400°F/Gas Mark 6.

Place the flour and baking powder in a bowl, add the Vecon in small pieces and rub into the flour. Add sufficient milk to bind the ingredients together to form a soft dough. Leave for 2 minutes, then knead lightly on a floured surface. Press the dough into an 18 cm/7″ circle and place on a greased baking sheet. Mark into 8 pieces with a knife. Brush the scone with milk and bake for 10–12 minutes in the pre-heated oven until well risen and golden brown. Serve warm or cold. These are best eaten the same day they are baked.

WHOLE EARTH

Bread Italiano Pizzas

You can make delicious pizzas in an instant using Whole Earth Italiano Sauce and Whole Earth bread. Slice the bread and lightly toast the slices, then put a tablespoon of Whole Earth Italiano Sauce on each slice, sprinkle the top with grated cheese and grill until lightly browned.

Bread Lasagne

This recipe is ideal when made with Whole Earth bread but you can use any bought bread, or even better your own home baked, wholewheat bread.

3 slices Whole Earth Wholewheat Bread
1 can Whole Earth Baked Beans
1 jar Whole Earth Italiano Sauce
50 ml (2 fl oz) water
3 spring onions
100 g (4 oz) grated cheese

In a small casserole with a lid make three layers, each with a base of a slice of bread covered with a third of the baked beans, 1 tablespoon Italiano Sauce, and 1 chopped spring onion. On top of the last layer put the remaining ½ jar of Italiano Sauce and pour the water over it all. Cover and bake for 30 minutes at 180°C/350°F/Gas Mark 4. Remove from the oven, sprinkle with the grated cheese and place under a hot grill for a few minutes until the cheese melts and begins to brown.

Opposite: **Kretschmer** *Wholewheat Pocket Bread (above) page 120, Onion Buns (below) page 119*

7
PASTRY

The recipes which follow include 100% wholemeal flour and other grains to make a variety of pastry dishes without the use of bleached white flour. You will find that the methods and water content for these familiar recipes sometimes differ from those used in white-flour pastry making; however the results are not only more flavoursome but also highly nutritious.

There are, however, some pastry recipes such as choux, flaky and puff pastry which give more successful results if lighter flours are used, so for these I suggest a choice, for example brown wheatmeal or unbleached white flour.

You will see in some of my own recipes that I use a creaming and light kneading method when making pastry because I have found that this results in a light, melt-in-the-mouth crust for pies and flans. Adding the flour gradually to the creamed water and margarine and kneading for 2 minutes after forming the dough helps to release the gluten (protein) (see notes on gluten on page 232) and lightens the dough considerably. But when using a particular manufacturer's recipe do stick to their method and ingredients, because all flours differ in their ability to absorb moisture. As the manufacturers have tried and tested their own recipes it is advisable to try their method until you get used to individual brands.

The section begins with two basic recipes, both my own, for savoury wholemeal shortcrust pastry and sweet wheatmeal pastry.

Opposite: **Marriage's** *Ratatouille Pie (above) page 141, Pierogi (below) page 140*

PREWETT'S

—Evelyn's Wholemeal— Savoury Shortcrust Pastry

This recipe seems to work using any brand of wholewheat flour, even local flours from small mills or home-ground wheat which sometimes have a coarser texture than the finer wholewheat flour which large commercial millers produce.

The following recipe will make sufficient pastry for a 25.5 cm/10″ quiche or flan dish.

100 g (4 oz) Prewett's Sunflower or Safflower
  Margarine
pinch sea salt
3 tbsp cold water
225 g (8 oz) Prewett's 100% Organic Wholemeal
  Flour, *plain*

Place the margarine, salt and water in a mixing bowl with 2 tablespoons of the measured flour and cream them together with a wooden spoon until well blended. Gradually add the remaining flour using your hands to mould the mixture lightly into a dough. Knead the dough with floured hands for 2 minutes. Place in a polythene bag and chill in the refrigerator for 30 minutes. Mould gently for a few seconds then roll out on a lightly floured surface. For beginners, place an opened polythene bag over the dough and roll the pastry out. This way you avoid using too much flour, which will spoil the texture of the pastry.

Using a palette knife ease the pastry from the work surface and lift one edge on to the rolling pin. Roll a little more pastry on to the pin and lift on to a lightly oiled flan dish or on top of the filling for a pie. Trim the edges and if making a flan or quiche prick the base and bake blind for 10 minutes in a pre-heated oven at 190°C/375°F/Gas Mark 5. If using as a topping for a vegetable or meat pie then trim the edges, prick in several places with a fork, brush a little egg and milk mixture on top and bake as the recipe suggests. (Make sure that fillings for pies are cooled before topping with pastry, otherwise the pastry will become soggy.)

For a variation in texture, taste and added goodness I sometimes add either 2 level tablespoons of sesame seeds or 2 tablespoons of grated Cheddar cheese to the mixture after creaming the margarine, salt, water and a little flour together. Blend in well and then add the remaining flour.

Evelyn's Sweet Wheatmeal Shortcrust Pastry

Use the same creaming and kneading method as in the previous recipe but use half and half 100% wholewheat and unbleached white flour plus 1 level tablespoon of soft brown or fruit sugar and only 2 tablespoons of cold water whisked with 1 egg yolk for the liquid. Cream the margarine with the egg yolk mixture, sugar, salt and 2 tablespoons of the measured flour and then gradually add the remaining flour. Chill and use as directed in the Savoury Shortcrust recipe.

Savoury Pastry Dishes

ALLINSON

The recipes that follow are a few cocktail savouries using a rich wholewheat cheese pastry as the base. With this pastry you can either make cheese straws or little savoury tartlets with a variety of fillings as suggested below.

Rich Wholewheat Cheese Pastry

225 g (8 oz) Allinson's Original 100% Wholewheat
  Flour
¼ level tsp sea salt
¼ level tsp dry mustard powder
good pinch cayenne pepper
100 g (4 oz) polyunsaturated margarine
75 g (3 oz) Parmesan or mature Cheddar cheese,
  freshly grated
2 egg yolks
1 tbsp cold water

Sieve the dry ingredients, rub in the margarine until the mixture resembles fine breadcrumbs and stir in the grated cheese. Whisk the egg yolks with the water and pour into the other ingredients. Form into a dough (add a little more water if it is too stiff) and use as the recipes suggest.

Cheese Straws

Pre-heat the oven to 200°C/400°F/Gas Mark 6.

Roll out 1 recipe quantity of Rich Wholewheat Cheese Pastry on a lightly-floured surface to about 8 mm/⅓" thick. Cut the pastry into thin fingers about 7.5 cm/3" in length and place carefully on a well-oiled baking sheet. Brush with a little egg white and bake near the top of the oven for just under 10 minutes. Cool on the baking sheet.

Aubergine and Mushroom Tartlets

This is a rich filling for tartlet cases, quite delicious and simple to prepare. (If soured cream is not available use natural yoghurt mixed with 2 tablespoons of double cream.)

1 recipe quantity Allinson Rich Wholewheat Cheese
  Pastry made into 30–35 tartlets (see above)

Filling
3 medium sized aubergines (approx. 225 g/8 oz
  each in weight)
1 medium sized onion, peeled and chopped
100 g (4 oz) small button mushrooms
2 tbsp olive oil
150 g (5 oz) carton sour cream
sea salt
freshly ground black pepper

Oil the aubergines and bake in the oven at 190°C/ 375°F/Gas Mark 5 for 45 minutes. Cut open and scoop out the pulp. Leave to cool. Sauté the onion in the oil for 5 minutes, add the mushrooms and fry for 3 minutes. In a blender or food processor purée the aubergine pulp with the onions and mushrooms until smooth. Scoop out and place in a mixing bowl, stir in the sour cream and season with sea salt and pepper to taste. When ready to serve spoon into the cooked and cooled pastry cases.

These tartlet cases can be filled with a variety of purées and pâtés.

—Guacamole Tartlets—

1 recipe quantity Allinson *Rich Wholewheat Cheese Pastry (see page 130)*

Filling
2 good-size ripe avocado pears
1 small green pepper, de-seeded and roughly chopped
½ small onion, peeled and roughly chopped
1 large clove garlic, crushed
1 tbsp lemon juice
¼ tsp sea salt
¼ tsp freshly ground black pepper
good pinch cayenne pepper
1 small carton soured cream
few drops Tabasco sauce

Pre-heat the oven to 200°C/400°F/Gas Mark 6.

Roll out the pastry thinly and using a small serrated cutter cut out 30–35 rounds to fit cocktail tartlet tins, or 20 slightly larger rounds to fit bun tins. Prick the bases of the tartlets and brush with egg white. Bake in the pre-heated oven for 10 minutes. (Use the shelf just above centre.) Leave to cool and fill only just before serving or the pastry will become soggy.

With a sharp knife make shallow cuts in the avocados from the base to the stalk end as if you were going to cut them into quarters. The skins will peel off easily if the avocados are ripe. Now cut right through to the centre and each quarter will fall away

from the stone quite easily. Chop roughly. Put all the ingredients except the Tabasco sauce and sour cream into a food processor or blender. Blend for 10 seconds only. Scoop out and stir in the sour cream. Taste. Add more seasoning if you wish. Add a few drops of Tabasco sauce and chill for 30 minutes. When ready to serve spoon the guacamole into the cooked and cooled pastry cases.

BROADLAND

—Pissaladière—

Serves 3

225 g (8 oz) 100% wholemeal flour, self raising
75 g (3 oz) Broadland Vegetable Suet
cold water to mix

Filling
1 large onion, peeled and finely chopped
1 clove garlic, crushed
vegetable oil for frying
450 g (1 lb) tomatoes, skinned and seeds removed, chopped
sea salt
freshly ground black pepper
1 tsp fresh basil, finely chopped
100 g (4 oz) courgettes, sliced and blanched
50 g (2 oz) Gruyère cheese, grated
50 g (2 oz) anchovies
25 g (1 oz) black olives, stoned and halved

Fry the onion and garlic in the minimum amount of oil. Add the tomatoes, salt, pepper and basil. Cool the mixture. Mix the pastry ingredients to form a dough, roll into 25 cm/10″ round and place on a greased baking tray. Place the vegetables on top of the pastry, arrange the courgette slices around the edge, sprinkle with the cheese and arrange anchovies and olives in a lattice pattern on top. Bake for 30 minutes at 190°C/375°F/Gas Mark 5.

Supreme of Chicken en Croûte

Serves 2–4

225 g (8 oz) 100% wholemeal flour, self raising
200 g (4 oz) Broadland Vegetable Suet
sea salt
1 small egg
cold water to mix

Filling
2 boned breasts of chicken
sea salt
freshly ground black pepper
vegetable oil for frying
50 g (2 oz) onion, peeled and finely chopped
100 g (4 oz) mushrooms, finely chopped
chopped parsley and rosemary
25 g (1 oz) white breadcrumbs
egg wash (mixture of egg and milk)

Season the chicken and fry gently in a little oil, 3 minutes each side. Leave to cool. Gently fry the onions, add the mushrooms, herbs, salt, pepper and breadcrumbs and cook a further few minutes then leave to cool. Mix the pastry ingredients to form a dough and roll out into two chevron shapes, each as long as a chicken breast and twice as wide.

Spread half the vegetable mixture in the centre of each piece of pastry and lay the chicken on top. Slash the pastry into diagonals 1.5 cm/½″ apart. Egg-wash the strips and press into place alternately over the chicken to completely cover it. Place on a baking tray and bake at 190°C/375°F/Gas Mark 5 for 30 minutes, glazing frequently with egg wash as they cook.

DOVES FARM

Here is Clare Marriage's recipe for pastry using Doves Farm organically grown 100% Fine Milled Wholemeal Flour plus two of my favourite fillings.

Asparagus and Tarragon Flan

Makes 1 23–25.5 cm/9–10″ flan

225 g (8 oz) Doves Farm Organic Fine Wholemeal Flour
100 g (4 oz) butter or margarine
pinch sea salt
50 ml (2 fl oz) water

Filling
175–225g (6 to 8 oz) asparagus, fresh or frozen
1 very small onion, peeled and finely chopped
150 g (5 oz) Cheddar cheese, grated
4 medium eggs
1 tbsp double cream (optional)
2 tbsps natural yoghurt
175 ml (6 fl oz) milk
½ tsp mace or nutmeg, freshly grated
freshly ground black pepper
½ tsp sea salt
1 level tsp dried tarragon

Rub the margarine into the flour and salt until the mixture resembles breadcrumbs. Add just enough water to form a dough. On a floured surface roll out the pastry to the desired thickness and transfer to an oiled flan dish. (Pastry is equally good pressed into place with the fingertips rather than rolled out.) Prick the base and chill for 10 minutes. Bake blind in a pre-heated oven for 10 minutes at 190°C/375°F/ Gas Mark 5. Leave to cool.

If using frozen asparagus steam for 10 minutes by placing the still-frozen spears in a colander which fits snugly on to the rim of a saucepan and cover. If fresh asparagus is used, cut off the woody ends and steam for 15–20 minutes until tender. When cooked cut off 5 cm/2″ long tips and set these aside to decorate the top later. Cut the remaining ends into small pieces. Spread these and the chopped onion in the cooked and cooled pastry base. Cover with most of the cheese, leaving a little for the top. Whisk the eggs with the cream, yoghurt, milk, mace or nutmeg, pepper and salt and pour the mixture over the cheese. Place the eight reserved asparagus spears around the top and sprinkle on the remaining cheese and the tarragon (the spears will float to the top when cooking and show a clear pattern when baked). Bake for 40–45 minutes in the centre of the pre-heated oven. Leave to stand for 5–10 minutes before serving. Delicious hot or cold.

Spring Onion Flan

Substitute 1 large bunch of spring onions for the asparagus and onion in the previous recipe. Chop the onions in thin rings using both the chive-like stems and the bulbs. Sauté in a little olive or sunflower oil for 1 minute only. Leave out the tarragon and mace and sprinkle a little freshly grated nutmeg on top.

Wholemeal Rough Puff Pastry

You can use Doves Farm unbleached white or brown wheatmeal flour but if using 100% wholemeal flour, as in this recipe, it is best to use fine milled pastry flour. A cool atmosphere is also advisable for making any flaky-type pastry.

175 g (6 oz) butter
225 g (8 oz) Doves Farm 100% Fine Milled
  Wholemeal Flour, plain
good pinch sea salt
1 tsp lemon juice
150 ml (¼ pt) iced water

The butter must be firm and cold but not hard. Cut it into small cubes about 2 cm/¾″ square. Sift the flour and sea salt into a mixing bowl and toss the butter cubes in this, coating them well. Pour in the lemon juice and iced water and mix all the ingredients with a small palette knife to form a soft, rubbery dough. Don't squash with the hands, just bring it gently together. Put the dough into a polythene bag and chill for 10 minutes.

Roll out the pastry on a well-floured surface into a rectangle about 30 cm/12″ long × 12.5 cm/5″ wide and 2 cm/¾″ thick. Fold the dough in three by folding the bottom third up and the top third over this. Turn the pastry round so that the fold is on your left. Seal the edges lightly with your fingertips and roll the pastry out to a slightly bigger rectangle making a thickness of 1 cm/½″. Fold as before and repeat the process a total of four times. Keep the

hands as cool as possible. Best results are achieved if the pastry is chilled in the refrigerator for 10 minutes between rollings. Finally chill for 20 minutes.

When needed, roll out to 0.5 cm/¼″ thickness for pie crusts, vegetable or meat pasties, sausage rolls, etc. and egg wash (a mixture of egg and milk) the top.

For recipes using Wholemeal Rough Puff Pastry see page 134 (Sausfry Sausage Rolls and Mock Chicken Vol-au-Vents).

GRANOSE

Granose do a marvellous range of vegetable protein foods which are quick to prepare and a good alternative for non-meat eaters living busy lives.

Mock Chicken and Sweetcorn Tarts

Makes 12

1 recipe quantity Wholemeal Savoury Shortcrust Pastry (see page 129)

Filling
100 g (4 oz) Granose Chicken-like Flavour Soyapro Slices
50 g (2 oz) frozen sweetcorn, cooked and drained
1 small onion, peeled and very finely chopped
50 g (2 oz) Cheddar cheese, grated
40 g (1½ oz) polyunsaturated margarine or butter
40 g (1½ oz) unbleached white flour
275 ml (10 fl oz) stock made with boiling water and ½ vegetable stock cube
1 tbsp fresh parsley, chopped
freshly ground black pepper

Roll out the pastry and cut into rounds to fill 12 small tartlet tins. Pre-heat the oven to 200°C/400°F/Gas Mark 6. Chop the Soyapro into small pieces and mix with the sweetcorn and onion. Melt the margarine in a saucepan, stir in the flour and cook for 1 minute, stirring constantly. Gradually stir in the hot stock and cook until the sauce thickens. Stir in the parsley, Soyapro, sweetcorn and onion. Spoon into the pastry cases. Sprinkle the cheese on top and bake in the pre-heated oven for 30 minutes until golden brown on top.

Protose and Lentil Pasties

Makes 6 good size pasties

These are very quick to prepare, tasty and nourishing.

*half the recipe quantity of Wholemeal Savoury
    Shortcrust Pastry (see page 129)*

Filling
*150 g (5 oz) Granose Protose
1 cup cooked lentils (cooked weight)
1 small onion, peeled and finely chopped
freshly ground black pepper
1 tbsp fresh parsley, chopped
egg-and-milk mixture to brush tops*

Mash the Protose and mix with all the other ingredients. Cut out 6 saucer-sized circles from the rolled-out pastry and spoon the Protose mixture into the centres of the pastry circles. Wet the edges with a little of the egg-and-milk mixture, join the edges into a pasty shape, seal and flute the edges. Brush with egg-and-milk, place on an oiled baking tray and bake in a pre-heated oven at 200°C/400°F/Gas Mark 6 for 25 minutes.

Sausfry Cornish Pasties

Makes 12

*double the recipe quantity Wholemeal Savoury
    Pastry (see page 129)*

Filling
*100 g (4 oz) Granose Sausfry
175 ml (6 fl oz) cold water
2 tbsp sunflower oil
225 g (8 oz) diced potato (leave skins on), cooked
100 g (4 oz) diced carrot, cooked
175 g (6 oz) onion, peeled and finely chopped
2 tbsp fresh parsley, finely chopped
freshly ground black pepper to taste
little egg and milk mixture to seal pasties and brush
    tops*

Mix the Sausfry with the cold water and leave to stand for 10 minutes. Form the mixture into small sausage shapes and fry gently in the oil until golden brown. When cooked, crumble the 'sausages' up and mix with all the other ingredients. (Use a fork to do this.) When the pastry is chilled, roll out and cut into 12 circles (saucer size). Divide the filling equally and place a portion in the centre of each circle. Wet the edges with the egg and milk mixture and join to form into a pasty shape. Place the pasties on an oiled baking sheet, brush with egg and milk mixture and bake in a pre-heated oven at 200°C/400°F/Gas Mark 6 for 25–30 minutes until golden brown.

Sausfry Rolls

Makes 18 rolls

I like to use a rough puff pastry (see page 133) for these rolls but you can use rich cheese pastry (see page 130) with a very tasty result. One recipe quantity of pastry ingredients will be sufficient for 225 g/8 oz of Sausfry.

*225 g (8 oz) Granose Sausfry
350 ml (12 fl oz) cold water
egg wash (egg-and-milk liquid)*

Prepare the pastry and chill. Mix the Sausfry with the cold water and leave to stand for 5 minutes. Roll out the pastry to a rectangle 45 cm × 15 cm/18″ × 6″ and cut into two strips each 7.5 cm/3″ wide. Divide the Sausfry in half and shape into two long rolls to fit the pastry strips. Place one in the centre of each strip. Brush the edges of the pastry with egg wash, fold over and seal the edges. Brush the tops with egg wash and cut each long roll into individual 5 cm/2″ pieces. Pressing gently with a sharp knife, make 2 diagonal slits on top of each small roll. Place on oiled baking trays (you will need two). Pre-heat the oven to 220°C/425°F/Gas Mark 7. Put one tray just above the centre and one in the centre of the oven and bake for 15 minutes. Change the trays around and bake for 10 minutes more until the rolls are puffed up and golden brown.

You can add a little finely chopped onion, garlic and herbs to the Sausfry mixture for a change in flavour. Simply mould into the reconstituted Sausfry and shape into a roll as directed.

HOLLAND & BARRETT

Aduki Bean and Pepper Quiche

Makes 1 18 cm/7" quiche

100 g (4 oz) 100% wholemeal flour
50 g (2 oz) soft vegetable margarine
cold water to mix

Filling
75 g (3 oz) Holland & Barrett Aduki Beans, *soaked overnight*
1 onion, peeled and finely chopped
1 clove garlic, crushed
1 tsp olive oil
1 green pepper, de-seeded and chopped
1 tomato, diced
¼ tsp dried or ½ tsp fresh rosemary
2 free range eggs
150 ml (5 fl oz) skimmed milk
freshly ground black pepper
25 g (1 oz) Red Leicester cheese, finely grated

Drain the aduki beans and place in a saucepan, with cold water to cover. Bring to the boil, reduce the heat and simmer for 45–50 minutes or until the beans are just soft. While the beans are cooking prepare the rest of the ingredients.

Sieve the flour into a mixing bowl and add the bran remaining in the sieve. Rub in the margarine until the mixture resembles fine breadcrumbs. Place the mixture in the refrigerator to rest until the beans are cooked. Sauté the onion and garlic in the oil over a low heat until soft, but do not allow to brown. Set aside. Add the chopped pepper and diced tomato to the onion mixture. Drain the beans when cooked and pre-heat the oven to 200°C/400°F/Gas Mark 6.

Add a little cold water to the rubbed in flour mixture – just enough to bind to a soft dough. Roll out on a lightly floured surface to a circle big enough to line an 18 cm/7" diameter flan ring or dish. Line the dish with the pastry and trim the edges. Place the beans in the pastry case and cover with the onion mixture. Beat the eggs with the milk, add the rosemary and pepper and pour into the flan dish. Sprinkle the cheese on top and bake in the centre of the oven for 30–35 minutes until well risen and golden brown in colour. Serve hot or cold.

Cheese and Sesame Straws

Makes 30

100 g (4 oz) 100% wholemeal flour
50 g (2 oz) soft vegetable margarine
½ tsp mustard powder
¼ tsp cayenne pepper
50 g (2 oz) Red Leicester cheese, finely grated
free range egg
milk to glaze
3 tbsp Holland & Barrett Sesame Seeds

Sieve the flour into a mixing bowl and add the bran from the sieve. Rub the margarine into the flour until the mixture resembles fine breadcrumbs. Stir in the mustard, cayenne pepper and cheese. Beat the egg and pour into the mixture. Bind together and knead lightly. Roll out on a lightly floured surface until 0.25 cm/⅛" thick and cut into strips 6.5 cm/2½" long by a generous 0.5 cm/¼" wide. Place on baking trays and glaze with milk. Sprinkle sesame seeds on top and bake in a pre-heated oven at 200°C/400°F/Gas Mark 6 on the top shelf for 10 minutes until golden brown. Transfer to wire cooling trays.

Christmas Chestnut Pie

Makes 1 15 cm/6" pie

Use a game pie mould for this pie, or a deep 15 cm/ 6" diameter cake tin. The cake tin will need to be lightly greased and lined with greaseproof paper to help ease the pie out.

225 g (8 oz) 100% wholemeal flour
100 g (4 oz) soft vegetable margarine
cold water to mix
beaten egg to glaze

Filling
275 g (10 oz) Holland & Barrett Dried Chestnuts,
    soaked overnight
450 g (1 lb) Brussels sprouts
2 sticks celery, finely chopped
175 g (6 oz) onion, peeled and finely chopped
2 cloves garlic, crushed
2 tbsp fresh parsley, chopped
2 tsp dried thyme
grated rind of a lemon
150 ml (5 fl oz) vegetable stock
freshly ground black pepper

Drain the chestnuts and cook until soft in a pan of water or in a pressure cooker at 7 kg/15 lb pressure for 20 minutes. While the chestnuts are cooking rub the margarine into the flour and place in the refrigerator to chill. Cook the Brussels sprouts until soft, then drain and mash. When the chestnuts are cooked finely chop them and place in a large mixing bowl. Mix the celery, onion and garlic with the chestnuts and add the chopped parsley, thyme and grated lemon rind. Season with pepper and knead the mixture with the hands. This helps to break down the chestnuts and give a smoother mixture. Now add the stock. Pre-heat the oven to 200°C/400°F/Gas Mark 6. Take the flour mixture out of the refrigerator and add just enough cold water to mix to a soft dough. Roll out two thirds of the pastry on a lightly floured surface to fit the chosen tin. Line with the pastry and place half of the chestnut mixture in the base, pressing down firmly. Now add the puréed sprouts and cover with the remaining chestnut mixture. Roll out the rest of the pastry, cover the pie and seal the edges. Decorate with pastry leaves and glaze well. Bake in the centre of the pre-heated oven for 20 minutes then lower the heat to finish cooking at 180°C/350°F/Gas Mark 4. Serve hot or cold. If serving cold leave in the tin to cool.

Lentil and Mushroom Pie

Makes 1 25 cm/10" pie

You can use aduki beans for this instead of lentils for a change.

225 g (8 oz) Holland & Barrett Red Split Lentils
425 ml (15 fl oz) water
1 vegetable stock cube
1 cinnamon stick
1 bay leaf
2 tbsp sunflower oil
1 large onion, peeled and chopped
175 g (6 oz) button mushrooms, sliced
3 large tomatoes, skinned and chopped
2 tbsp lemon juice
1 tsp coriander
1/2 tsp freshly ground black pepper
1 tbsp tomato purée
2 tbsp fresh parsley, chopped
1 egg, beaten
1 1/2 times recipe quantity Wholemeal Savoury
    Pastry (see page 129) using 350 g (12 oz flour plus
    75 g (3 oz) grated cheese added to the dough
a little beaten egg for glazing

Wash the lentils by placing in a sieve and letting cold water run over them for a minute. Remove any stones and grit. Place the lentils in a saucepan with the water, stock cube, cinnamon stick and bay leaf. Bring to boil and simmer with the lid on for 15–20 minutes by which time all the water should all be absorbed. If not, drain off the excess. Remove the cinnamon. Heat the oil in a saucepan and sauté the onion on moderate heat until golden. Add the mushrooms and continue to fry for 3 minutes. Stir in the tomatoes, lemon juice, coriander, black pepper and tomato purée. Cook for 2 minutes more then stir in the parsley. Let the mixture cool completely before adding the beaten egg. Pre-heat the oven to 200°C/400°F/Gas Mark 6.

Line a pie dish with half the pastry. Fill with the lentil mixture and cover with the other half of the pastry. Prick the top all over, crimp the edges and brush with a little beaten egg. Bake in the pre-heated oven for 40 minutes.

ITONA

—Wholemeal Pasties— with Ham and Soya Mince

Makes about 20

These pasties contain a mixture of minced bacon and Itona unflavoured natural soya mince. The 100 g/4 oz packet makes 350 g/12 oz when reconstituted and is equal to the amount of protein in the same quantity of meat. The flavour of the bacon is easily absorbed by the soya mince which is a great, inexpensive, cholesterol-free and nutritious filler.

350 g (12 oz) 100% wholemeal flour, plain, plus
*   350 g (12 oz) 100% wholemeal flour, self-raising*
or 700 g/24 oz wholemeal 100% plus one heaped
*   tsp baking powder*
75 g (3 oz) Cheddar cheese, grated
350 g (12 oz) polyunsaturated margarine
9 tbsp cold water
beaten egg to glaze

Filling
1 packet Itona TVP Unflavoured Mince,
*   reconstituted as directed on packet*
450 g (1 lb) minced bacon (as lean as possible)
225 g (8 oz) very finely chopped onion
450 g (1 lb) scrubbed potatoes cut into small cubes
*   (leave skins on)*
1 tbsp tomato purée
2 tbsp cooking apple, peeled, cored and finely
*   grated (optional but great)*
2 heaped tbsp fresh parsley, chopped
freshly ground black pepper to taste

Put the margarine, water and 4 tablespoons of the flour into a bowl and cream them well together for 1 minute. Add the cheese, mix together and gradually add the rest of the flour. Use a wooden spoon until mixture is too thick, then mix with your hands into a soft dough. Knead for 2 minutes. (This method is only necessary when using wholemeal flour. Creaming and kneading releases the gluten (protein) and lightens the pastry.) The pastry is just as good without the cheese but when introducing wholemeal for the first time the cheese gives a nice savoury taste. Put the dough into a plastic bag and chill for 30 minutes. Pre-heat the oven to 200°C/400°F/Gas Mark 6.

Mix all the filling ingredients together. Roll out the pastry. It makes it easy if you place a polythene bag over the pastry while rolling out. This way you can roll it out thinly without using too much flour, which dries out the pastry. Cut out saucer-size rounds. Place 1 heaped tablespoon of the filling in the centre of each round. Egg the edges and form into pasty shapes. Egg the tops. Put a sprinkling of bran on the greased baking sheets, place the pasties on top and bake in the pre-heated oven for 15 minutes, then turn down the heat to 180°C/350°F/Gas Mark 4 and continue to bake for 20 minutes more.

KRETSCHMER

Chicken and Broccoli Quiche

Makes 1 23–25.5 cm/9–10" quiche

This simple quiche is great at feeding six hungry people with just 225 g/8 oz left-over cooked chicken bits.

Oven temperature: 190°C/375°F/Gas Mark 5.

175 g (6 oz) brown wheatmeal flour
50 g (2 oz) Kretschmer Plain Wheat Germ
100 g (4 oz) polyunsaturated margarine
3 tbsp cold water
pinch sea salt

Filling
275 g (10 oz) fresh or frozen broccoli
225 g (8 oz) cooked chicken, chopped into small
*   pieces*
1 medium onion, peeled and cut into very thin rings
75 g (3 oz) Cheddar cheese, grated
275 ml (10 fl oz) milk
3 large eggs
sea salt and freshly ground black pepper to taste
1/4 tsp dry mustard
1 level tbsp Kretschmer Wheat Germ, Plain *plus 1*
*   level tablespoon grated Cheddar cheese for*
*   topping*
sprinkling of marjoram

Put the flour and wheat germ in a mixing bowl and rub in the margarine until the mixture resembles fine breadcrumbs. Add the salt to the water and pour into the flour mixture. Form into a soft dough and knead for 1 minute. Place the pastry in a polythene bag and chill for 30 minutes. Roll out and use to line an oiled flan dish. Prick the base and bake blind for 10 minutes in the oven pre-heated to 190°C/375°F/Gas Mark 5. Cool before filling.

Steam the broccoli for 10 minutes only, then chop into small pieces. Layer the chicken, broccoli, onion rings and cheese in the cooked and cooled pastry case. Whisk the milk with the eggs, sea salt, black pepper and mustard until well blended and pour on to the ingredients in the flan case. Mix the tbsp wheatgerm with the tbsp grated cheese and marjoram. Sprinkle the wheatgerm mixed with cheese over the filling and bake in the pre-heated oven for 45 minutes. Leave to stand for 5–10 minutes before serving.

Courgette Supper Pie

Makes 1 23–25.5 cm/9–10" quiche

1 recipe quantity of pastry for Chicken and Broccoli
*   Quiche (see above).*

Filling
2 tbsps olive or sunflower oil
1 medium onion, peeled and cut into thin rings
450 g (1 lb) courgettes, sliced
1 tsp marjoram
1/2 tsp tarragon
1/2 tsp sea salt
freshly ground black pepper
4 tbsp Kretschmer Wheat Germ, Plain
100 g (4 oz) Gruyère cheese, grated
50 g (2 oz) fresh Parmesan cheese, finely grated
2 eggs
75 ml (3 fl oz) milk
7 slices tomato

Bake the pastry case blind for 10 minutes in the oven, pre-heated to 160°C/325°F/Gas Mark 3. Leave to cool.

Heat the oil in a pan and sauté the onion and courgettes until just tender. Stir in the herbs, salt and pepper and spoon into the baked pastry case. Mix the wheat germ with the two cheeses and sprinkle all but 2 tablespoons of this mixture on to the sautéed vegetables. Whisk the eggs with the milk and pour the liquid into the centre of the vegetable mixture. Place the tomato slices on top and sprinkle on the remaining wheat germ and cheese mixture. Bake in the pre-heated oven for 40–45 minutes. Leave to stand for 5 minutes before serving.

LOSELEY

Broccoli, Cottage Cheese and Yoghurt Quiche

Makes 1 25 cm/10" quiche

1 recipe quantity Savoury Wholemeal Pastry (see page 129)

Filling
4 eggs, separated
225 g (8 oz) Loseley Cottage Cheese
225 g (8 oz) fresh or frozen broccoli, steamed for 10 minutes only, then cooled
50 mg (2 oz) Cheddar or fresh Parmesan cheese, grated
4 tbsp Loseley Natural Yoghurt
t tbsp cream (optional)
½ tsp sea salt
½ tsp mace or nutmeg, finely grated
1 clove garlic, peeled and crushed
freshly ground black pepper

Pre-heat the oven to 190°C/375°F/Gas Mark 5. Roll out the pastry and use to line a 25 cm/10" flan tin or dish. Bake blind for 10 minutes, then remove from the oven and leave to cool.

Whisk the egg whites for 1 minute. Add the yolks and whisk again. Stir in the cottage cheese. Chop the broccoli into small pieces (use the stems also). Add with all the other ingredients to the cottage cheese mixture, stirring gently so that you do not

mash the broccoli. Pour into the cooked and cooled pastry case. (You can sprinkle on a little more grated cheese if you wish.) Bake in the pre-heated oven for 40 minutes. If there is a little liquid remaining in the centre of the quiche when cooked just blot it gently with absorbent kitchen paper. Leave to set for 10 minutes before cutting. Delicious served with Orange, Onion and Tomato Salad.

Greek Style Spiced Onion Pie

Makes 1 23–25.5 cm/9–10" flan

1 recipe quantity Wholemeal Savoury Shortcrust Pastry (see page 129)

Filling
450 g (1 lb) shallots or onions, peeled and very thinly sliced
2 tbsp olive or sunflower oil
1 tsp caraway seeds
few drops Tabasco sauce or ¼ tsp cayenne pepper
maximum ½ level tsp sea salt
3 medium eggs
225 ml (8 fl oz) Loseley Natural Yoghurt
¼ tsp freshly ground black pepper
225 ml (8 fl oz) Loseley Soured Cream or 100 g (4 oz) cream cheese and 150 ml (5 fl oz) milk

Pre-heat the oven to 190°C/375°F/Gas Mark 5. Roll out the pastry and use to line a 23–25.5 cm/9–10" flan dish. Bake blind for 10 minutes, then remove from the oven.

Turn the oven temperature up to 220°C/425°F/Gas Mark 7. Sauté the shallots or onion in the oil until soft, about 7 minutes. Stir in the caraway seeds, Tabasco or cayenne, sea salt and black pepper. Take off the heat and leave to cool. Whisk the eggs with the yoghurt and sour cream or the cream cheese and milk mixture. Stir this into the onion mixture and pour into the baked pastry case. Bake for 5 minutes and then turn the oven temperature down to 180°C/350°F/Gas Mark 4, and bake for another 35 minutes maximum until set.

LOTUS

Soya and Mushroom Pie

225 g (8 oz) 100% wholemeal flour
pinch sea salt
100 g (4 oz) vegetable fat
water to mix

Filling
100 g (4 oz) Lotus Unflavoured TVP Chunks, soaked
   in water in which has been dissolved
2 tsp Lotus Brown Stock Paste
Lotus Brown Savoury Coater
225 g (8 oz) onions, peeled and sliced
100 g (4 oz) button mushrooms
pinch of powdered cloves
1 tsp fresh parsley, chopped
1 tsp Worcester Sauce or few drops Angostura
   Bitters
vegetable oil to fry
4 tbsp butter or polyunsaturated margarine
25 g (1 oz) wholewheat flour
1 bay leaf
pinch of powdered marjoram

Make the pastry using the rubbing-in method. Pre-heat the oven to 230°C/450°F/Gas Mark 7.

Soak the TVP chunks in the cold stock for 30 minutes until soft. Bring slowly to boiling point then drain, reserving the stock. Toss the TVP chunks in the coater and brown in a little hot oil. Lift out of the pan. Lightly cook the onion in the butter or margarine until golden. Add the mushrooms and cook for 3 minutes. Add flour and cook for 2 minutes. Add all ingredients to the stock (including any residue from the pan as that will add to the flavour) and put into a greased casserole dish. Top with pastry and decorate with any pieces left over.

Brush the top with milk, make two air vents in the lid and bake in the pre-heated oven for 10–15 minutes. Lower the heat to 180°C/350°F/Gas Mark 4, for a further 10–15 minutes, until golden brown. Serve with green vegetables and new potatoes.

MARRIAGE'S

Pierogi

Makes 30

These miniature pasties, originating from Poland, are made with a rich cheese pastry and have a mushroom filling. They make a lovely party dish and are delicious eaten hot or cold. This recipe is adapted from one devised by Anna Thomas for her book *Vegetarian Epicure*.

225 g (8 oz) polyunsaturated margarine
100 g (4 oz) cream cheese
1 egg, beaten
450 g (1 lb) Marriage's Brown Wheatmeal Flour,
   plain
1 level tsp sea salt
egg for glazing and sealing edges of pasties

Filling
1 large onion, very finely chopped (about 225 g/
   8 oz)
3 tbsp olive oil
450 g (1 lb) small button mushrooms, washed, well
   dried and finely chopped
1 tsp marjoram
3 slices wholemeal bread soaked in a little white
   wine
3 eggs, hard-boiled
2 tbsp sour cream or natural yoghurt
sea salt and plenty of freshly ground black pepper
   to taste

First make the pastry. Cream the margarine and cheese together, add the beaten egg with 1 table-spoon of the flour and cream it in. Sieve the remaining flour with the salt and gradually add to the creamed mixture. Form into a soft dough, place in a plastic bag and refrigerate overnight, or for at least 1 hour.

To make the filling, sauté the onion in the olive oil with the lid on the pan until soft. Add the mushrooms and marjoram and sauté for another 3 minutes. Remove from the heat and drain if there is too much liquid. Mash the soaked bread with a potato masher and stir into the mushroom mixture. Sieve in the hard-boiled eggs and add the sour cream or yoghurt, sea salt and black pepper. Allow to cool before filling the pasties. Pre-heat the oven to 190°C/375°F/Gas Mark 5.

Roll out the dough on a well-floured surface (place a plastic sheet over the dough as you roll –

this helps to stop it sticking and prevents the addition of too much flour which can dry out this delicious pastry). Roll out to 3 mm/⅛″ thick. Using a plain edge pastry cutter, 8 cm/3″ in diameter, cut out 30 circles. Place a heaped teaspoon of the filling in the centre of each circle, egg-brush the edges, fold up to the centre and press gently together. Brush the tops with egg and bake in the pre-heated oven for 15 minutes until golden brown.

Ratatouille Pie

Makes 1 25 cm/10″ pie

A lovely dish to eat hot or cold. It is topped with wholemeal breadcrumbs and grated cheese which gives a nice crisp layer to seal in the flavour. I have left out the aubergine which is a traditional ingredient in Ratatouille.

1 recipe quantity Wholemeal Shortcrust Pastry (see page 129) using Marriage's Strong Wholemeal Flour
1 large onion, peeled and chopped
2 medium courgettes, sliced
1 large green pepper or ½ red and ½ green, de-seeded and chopped
3 tbsp olive oil
2 cloves garlic
395 g (14 oz) can tomatoes, well drained and chopped
1 tbsp tomato purée
1 tsp basil
1 bay leaf
sea salt and freshly ground black pepper
3 eggs, beaten
100 g (4 oz) Cheddar cheese, grated
50 g (2 oz) wholemeal breadcrumbs

Bake a flan case as described on page 129 (Wholemeal Savoury Shortcrust Pastry). Heat the oil in a heavy based saucepan and sauté the onion and garlic for 10 minutes with the lid on. Add the courgettes and peppers and continue to cook for another 10 minutes with the lid on. Stir in the drained tomatoes, tomato purée, basil and bay leaf. Stir, taste and add sea salt and freshly ground black pepper to taste. Continue to simmer on a low heat for 5 minutes, then allow to cool. Stir in half the cheese and the beaten eggs. Check the seasoning again and add more if you wish. Pour the mixture into the baked pastry case. Mix the remaining cheese with the breadcrumbs and sprinkle on the top of the pie. Pre-heat the oven and bake at 200°C/400°F/Gas Mark 6 for 30 minutes or until the top is golden brown.

NATURE'S WAY

The next two recipes for Nature's Way products have been devised by Chrissy Howell and are both tasty and simple to prepare. She uses a variety of flours in her baking but Doves Farm self-raising brown wheatmeal seems to be her favourite for savoury and sweet pastry dishes. When using self-raising flour in making pastry or if you add baking powder you must not knead the dough as this will make the pastry tough.

Cashew Nut Quiche

Makes 1 19–20 cm/7½–8″ quiche

175 g (6 oz) brown wheatmeal flour, self-raising
75 g (3 oz) polyunsaturated margarine
2½ tbsp cold water

Filling
50 g (2 oz) butter or margarine
90 g (3½ oz) Nature's Way Cashew Nuts
1 medium onion, peeled and finely chopped
100 g (4 oz) cheese, grated
2 large eggs
275 ml (10 fl oz) milk
sea salt and freshly ground black pepper
1 medium tomato, cut into thin slices

Rub the margarine into the flour until the mixture resembles breadcrumbs. With the palm of your hand mix the water a little at a time into the mixture and form quickly into a dough. Place in a polythene bag and chill for 10 minutes. Pre-heat the oven to 180°C/350°F/Gas Mark 4.

Roll out the pastry and line a lightly oiled 19–20 cm/7½–8″ flan tin. Melt the butter or margarine and lightly fry the cashew nuts for a few minutes, then remove with a slotted spoon and put to one side. Sauté the onion in the remaining butter until transparent. Allow to cool, then place in the pastry case. Sprinkle the cheese on top. Beat the eggs, milk and seasoning and pour over the cheese. Sprinkle the toasted cashew nuts on top of the flan, arrange the sliced tomato around the edge and bake in the pre-heated oven for 40–45 minutes, until set and golden brown.

Millet, Cheese, Onion and Sweetcorn Pie

Makes 1 20 cm/8" pie

350 g (12 oz) brown wheatmeal flour, self-raising
175 g (6 oz) polyunsaturated margarine
4½ tbsp cold water

Filling
225 g (8 oz) cheese, grated
1 large onion
2 cobs sweetcorn or 175 g (6 oz) frozen sweetcorn,
*   cooked and drained*
175 g (6 oz) Nature's Way Millet
50 g (2 oz) vegetable margarine
575 ml (1 pint) water
1 egg

Make the pastry as described in the Cashew Nut Quiche recipe on page 00. Pre-heat the oven to 190°C/375°F/Gas Mark 5. Cook the sweetcorn until soft. Drain and leave to cool. Meanwhile, roll out the pastry and line a 20 cm/8" pie dish. Chop the onion and sauté in the margarine for 10 minutes. Add the millet and fry for a further 5 minutes. Add the water and cook for 15 minutes. Drain, and mix the millet and onion mixture with the cheese and place this in the pie dish. Cut the corn off the cob and sprinkle on top of the cheese mixture. Roll out the remaining pastry and cover. Brush with beaten egg or milk and bake in the pre-heated oven for 30 minutes.

a little sea salt to taste
freshly ground black pepper to taste
¼ tsp dry mustard powder
¼ tsp ground mace
1 level tsp tarragon, plus extra for sprinkling

Roll out the pastry and use to line a 23 cm/9" quiche tin. Bake blind in the oven pre-heated to 190°/375°F/Gas Mark 5.

Heat the oil in a saucepan and sauté the sliced leeks for 10 minutes with the lid on. Set aside to cool. Beat the eggs in a mixing bowl, add the yoghurt and whisk in. Crumble the tofu and whisk into the egg mixture. Season with salt and pepper and add the mustard, mace and tarragon. (A blender or food processor does this in seconds.) When the quiche case is cool, spread the base with the sautéed leeks, then pour in the tofu mixture. Sprinkle a little more tarragon on top and bake at 190°C/375°F/Gas Mark 5 for 35 minutes.

PAUL'S TOFU

Leek and Tofu Quiche

Makes 1 23 cm/9" quiche

1 recipe quantity Wholemeal Savoury Pastry (see
*   page 129)*

Filling
2 tbsp sunflower oil
225 g (8 oz) leeks (weight when washed and
*   trimmed), cut into thin rings*
4 eggs
150 ml (5 fl oz) natural yoghurt
225 g (8 oz) Paul's Firm Tofu

PREWETT'S

Basic Choux Pastry

This light, airy pastry is very versatile and can be used as the basis for many savoury and sweet delicacies. Use wheatmeal or unbleached white flour for best results. Most recipes use butter but I find polyunsaturated margarine equally successful.

65 g (2½ oz) Prewett's Brown Wheatmeal or
*   Unbleached White Flour, plain*
50 g (2 oz) Prewett's Sunflower Margarine
pinch sea salt
good pinch sugar
150 ml (5 fl oz) water
2 standard eggs
1 egg yolk

Sift the flour and salt on to a large piece of greaseproof paper. Heat the water, margarine and sugar in a saucepan over a low heat until the margarine melts. Bring to the boil then turn down to a very low heat, lift the sides of the greaseproof paper up and pour the flour into the hot water mixture. Beat briskly until the batter leaves the sides of the pan, then beat for one minute more. The mixture will form into a soft ball. Remove from the heat and cool for 5 minutes. Add the eggs one at a time, then the egg yolk, beating well for about 2 minutes after each addition. The dough will be smooth and shiny and ready for savoury or sweet recipes.

If you are not ready to use the dough immediately you can leave it for several hours, but make sure it is covered with a piece of greaseproof paper and the pan tightly lidded to keep the pastry soft and pliable.

Cheese Aigrettes

Serves 4

one recipe quantity Basic Choux Pastry
75 g (3 oz) Cheddar cheese, grated
a little cayenne pepper, optional
oil for deep frying

Make up the choux pastry as directed, adding the cayenne pepper with the flour. (Leave out the cayenne if these are intended for children.) Beat in the cheese after the eggs. Heat oil in a deep fryer (do not use a basket or the puffs will stick to it) until a cube of bread turns golden in 1 minute. Drop teaspoonfuls of the pastry into the hot oil, about five at a time, and fry for about 5 minutes until puffed and golden brown. Use a perforated spoon to take the puffs out. Drain on absorbent kitchen paper and serve immediately.

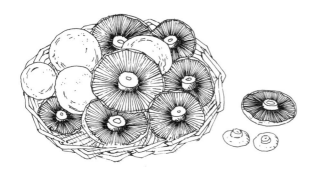

Gougère with Asparagus, Mushroom and White Wine Sauce

Serves 6

This is a rich, tasty recipe for a very special dinner party.

double recipe quantity Basic Choux Pastry (see above)
100 g (4 oz) Cheddar cheese, grated

Filling
450 g (1 lb) asparagus, frozen or fresh (not canned)
275 ml (10 fl oz) stock (use vegetable stock cube and hot water if no stock available)
275 ml (10 fl oz) dry white wine
2 tbsp olive or sunflower oil
50 g (2 oz) Prewett's Unbleached White Flour, plain
2 tbsp cream
1 egg yolk
1 scant tsp finely grated lemon peel
2 tbsp sunflower oil for frying
1 large onion (approx 225 g/8 oz when peeled and finely chopped)
1 small clove garlic, crushed
350 g (12 oz) small button mushrooms, sliced
sea salt
freshly ground black pepper

Pre-heat the oven to 200°C/400°F/Gas Mark 6. Oil and lightly flour a round pizza tray or ovenproof dish 28 cm/11″ in diameter. Beat in 75 g/3 oz of the cheese after the eggs. With the fingertips draw a circle on the floured tray 7.5 cm/3″ from the centre as a guide-line for placing your dough. Fit a large piping bag with a 2.5 cm/1″ nozzle and pipe the dough around your traced circle. Pipe another layer on top or alongside, using up all the dough. Brush the surface with egg and milk wash and sprinkle on the remaining 25 g/1 oz cheese. Bake in the centre of the pre-heated oven for 20 minutes, then turn down the heat to 180°C/350°F/Gas Mark 4 for 20 minutes more until puffed up and golden brown. When baked, slit with a sharp knife lengthwise through the centre and keep warm in a low oven until ready to fill.

If using fresh asparagus, cut off the hard, woody ends with a sharp knife, and just scrape the whites of the stems. Tie in a bunch and stand it upright in a saucepan. Pour in boiling, salted water to just below the green tips and boil for 12 minutes. If using frozen asparagus just steam it for 10 minutes. When cooked, cut off the tips, (about 4 cm/1½″) and put them carefully on a plate. Chop the stems and purée them with the cream. Leave to one side. Heat the stock and wine together. Pour into a jug. In a heavy-based saucepan heat the oil. Keep on a very low heat. When bubbly add the flour and let it cook for a few minutes, stirring all the time. Gradually pour in the hot stock and wine, stirring with a balloon whisk as you do this. After the sauce thickens continue to cook for 7 minutes more. Stir often to stop any sticking, then take off the heat. Cover the sauce with a piece of well-buttered greaseproof paper to stop a skin forming.

In a frying pan sauté the finely-chopped onion and the garlic on low heat for 10 minutes. Take care not to burn them. Keep a lid on the pan. Add the sliced mushrooms and cook for 3 minutes only, then add these to the white wine sauce and re-heat slowly. Now beat the egg yolk into the asparagus purée with the lemon peel. Take the sauce off the heat and stir in the purée. Season with freshly ground black pepper and a little sea salt if needed. Stir in the asparagus tips carefully with a fork, leaving a few to decorate the top. Take the Gougère out of the oven. Remove the top half and spoon on half the filling. Replace the top and spoon the remaining sauce into the centre hole. Decorate with the reserved asparagus tips and serve hot.

Gruyère Puff Pie

Makes 1 23 cm/9″ pie

double the recipe quantity of Basic Choux Pastry (see page 142)
100 g (4 oz) Gruyère cheese, grated
¼ tsp cayenne pepper

Pre-heat the oven to 200°C/400°F/Gas Mark 6.

Prepare the choux pastry as directed, adding the cayenne pepper to the flour. Beat in 75 g (3 oz) of the cheese after the eggs have been added. Spread the dough on to a lightly oiled and floured 23 cm/9″ pie dish and bake in the pre-heated oven for 20 minutes. Sprinkle on the remaining cheese, lower the heat to 160°C/325°F/Gas Mark 3, and continue to bake for 15 minutes more. Serve while still hot either alone or topped with sautéed vegetables. Ratatouille is a perfect accompaniment to this savoury delight.

PROTOVEG

Ham Style Pasties

Serves 5

450 g (1 lb) brown wholemeal flour, self-raising
225 g (8 oz) polyunsaturated margarine
6 tbsp water

Filling
115 g (4½ oz) Protoveg Ham Flavour TVP Chunks
2 small onions, peeled and finely chopped
450 g (1 lb) potatoes, peeled and grated
225 g (8 oz) cooking apples, peeled, cored and grated (cover with cold water to prevent discoloration)
freshly ground black pepper

Hydrate the Ham Chunks by the simmering method as described on the packet while the pastry is being made.

Make the pastry using the rubbing-in method and roll out to 3 mm (⅛ in) thickness. Cut into rounds about 15 cm/6 in in diameter. Drain the potatoes and apples and mix all the filling ingredients together, adding a little black pepper. Place a little of the filling on one half of each pastry circle, fold over the other half and seal the edges with a little milk or water. Make a small cut in the top of each pasty to let the steam out. Bake in a pre-heated oven at 190°C/375°F/Gas Mark 5 for about 45 minutes. Serve with peas and carrots.

Soya and Onion Pasties

Serves 6

450 g (1 lb) brown wheatmeal flour, self-raising
225 g (8 oz) polyunsaturated margarine
6 tbsp cold water

Filling
115 g (4½ oz) Protoveg Minced Soya and Onion Mix
100 g (4 oz) carrots
450 g (1 lb) potatoes
freshly ground black pepper

Hydrate the Soya and Onion following packet instructions. Peel and grate the carrots and potatoes. Drain the liquid from the Soya and Onion (reserve this for gravy). Add the potatoes, carrots and black pepper and mix thoroughly. Leave to cool. Make the shortcrust pastry using the rubbing-in method and roll out to 3 mm/⅛″ thickness. Cut into rounds about 10 cm/4″ diameter. Place the filling on one half of the pastry and fold over the other half. Seal with a little milk or water. Make a small cut in each pasty to allow steam to escape. Brush with milk and bake at 200°C/400°F/Gas Mark 6 for 20–25 minutes.

Serve with spinach or any other dark green vegetable.

VECON

—Borlotti Bean Vecon— Crumble Pie

Serves 4

I have included a savoury crumble mix in the pastry section because all that is missing is the water which would make it into pastry, and of course it's quick to prepare. You can use 75 g/3 oz margarine in the recipe and omit the cheese. A note here about beans: when a recipe calls for a small amount, dry weight, it is a good idea to soak and cook several times that weight. This cuts down the time needed to use the beans in other dishes. All you do is drain and freeze what is not required immediately.

Crumble Topping
175 g (6 oz) 100% wholemeal flour, plain
50 g (2 oz) polyunsaturated margarine
50 g (2 oz) Cheddar cheese, finely grated
1 rounded tsp Vecon, melted over low heat

Filling
100 g (4 oz), dry weight, borlotti beans
575 ml (1 pt) cold water for soaking
3 tbsp sunflower oil

1 large onion, peeled and chopped
1 large clove garlic, crushed
2 medium carrots, sliced into ovals
3 sticks celery, chopped (use green leafy ends also)
1 small green pepper, de-seeded and chopped
1 bay leaf
1 tbsp fresh chopped parsley
1 level tsp marjoram
1 level tbsp 100% wholewheat flour or barley flour
1 rounded tbsp tomato purée
2 tsp Vecon mixed with 575 ml (1 pt) hot water

Soak the beans overnight in the cold water. (Change the water two or three times if possible.) Drain the beans and add to 3 times their volume of cold water. Bring to the boil, boil vigorously for 7 minutes, then turn down to simmer, cover and cook for 40 minutes or until soft. (Pressure cook for 20 minutes only but soak and rinse as directed.)

To make the crumble topping, rub the margarine into the flour, stir in the cheese, and then the melted Vecon. The mixture should look like medium-fine breadcrumbs. Chill while you make the filling.

Pre-heat the oven to 190°/375°F/Gas Mark 5. Heat the oil in a saucepan and sauté the onion, garlic and carrots for 7 minutes with the lid on. Add the celery and cook for 3 minutes with the lid on. Add the green pepper, bay leaf, parsley and marjoram and continue to cook for 2 minutes more. Blend the flour and tomato purée well together and gradually pour the hot Vecon stock into this until well blended and smooth. Pour this liquid into the sautéed vegetables. Stir well in, then add the drained beans. Cook for just 3 minutes. Pour this mixture into an oiled pie dish 23 cm/9 in in diameter. Sprinkle on the chilled crumble topping and bake in the pre-heated oven for 30 minutes.

If you add 2½ tablespoons of cold water to the crumble mixture you will have pastry. Mix the ingredients quickly together. Form into a dough. Chill for 30 minutes and roll out on a lightly-floured surface. Make sure that the filling is cool before placing the pastry on top. Trim and flute edges, prick the top, brush with beaten egg and bake for 30 minutes at the same temperature as for the crumble.

Sweet Pastry Dishes

BROADLAND

—Fresh Fruit Shells—

Makes 12–16

225 g (8 oz) 100% wholemeal flour, self-raising
100 g (4 oz) Broadland Vegetable Suet
1 egg (size 5)
cold water to mix
sea salt
egg wash
a little fruit sugar

Filling
1 litre (1¼ pints) milk
few drops vanilla essence
4 egg yolks
100 g (4 oz) fruit sugar
75 g (3 oz) gram (chick pea) flour
fruit in season
apricot glaze (warmed and sieved apricot jam)

Mix the pastry ingredients (except the egg wash and sugar) together to form a dough. Roll out and line individual scallop shells or tartlet tins. Brush with egg wash, sprinkle with fruit sugar and bake at 190°C/375°F/Gas Mark 5, until crisp and brown. Cool on a wire rack.

Bring the milk and vanilla essence to the boil. Cream the egg yolks, sugar and gram flour together and whisk in the milk. Return the mixture to the pan and boil for 2 minutes, stirring constantly. Cool and use to fill the pastry shells. Decorate with fruit in season and apricot glaze.

DIETADE

—Apricot and Almond—
Pasties

Makes 12

These melt in your mouth and are simply delicious.

1 egg yolk
2 tbsp natural yoghurt
75 g (3 oz) polyunsaturated margarine
1 level tbsp Dietade Fruit Sugar
175 g (6 oz) 100% wholemeal fine pastry flour, plain
pinch sea salt
little egg and milk liquid to seal the edges of the
*   pasties*

Filling
675 g (1½ lb) ripe apricots or 225 g (8 oz) dried
*   (soaked overnight in apple juice and drained)*
100 g (4 oz) Dietade Fruit Sugar
1 egg white
1 tsp lemon juice
2 drops natural almond essence
100 g (4 oz) almonds, finely ground

Whisk the egg yolk with the yoghurt. Cream the margarine with the sugar for 2 minutes. Add the egg and yoghurt mixture plus 2 tablespoons of the flour and the sea salt, blending together with a fork. Gradually add the remaining flour, mixing well with your hands as the dough stiffens. Knead for 1 minute. Place in a polythene bag and chill for 30 minutes.

Meanwhile, cut the fresh apricots in half; stone and slice thinly. (If using dried, soaked apricots then drain well and slice thinly.) Whisk the sugar, egg white, lemon juice and essence together until well blended and gradually add the ground almonds until a paste is formed.

Pre-heat the oven to 200°C/400°F/Gas Mark 6. Cut the chilled pastry in 12 equal pieces, roll each into a ball and roll out on a lightly floured surface into circles about 10 cm/4″ in diameter. Divide the fruit and almond paste equally. Place apricot slices in the centre of each circle, dot the top with flattened bits of almond paste, egg-brush the edges of the pastry circles and fold over into a semi-circle, pressing the dampened edges together. Crimp the edges, fork the top in two places and egg-glaze the pastry. Place on an oiled baking sheet and bake in the pre-heated oven for 10 minutes, then turn down the heat to 180°C/350°F/Gas Mark 4 and continue to bake for a further 10–15 minutes until golden brown. While still hot sprinkle on a little fruit sugar. Serve hot or cold.

Bermuda Tart

Makes 1 23–25 cm/9–10" flan

*1 Recipe quantity Sweet Wheatmeal Shortcrust
 Pastry (see page 130), but use 1 tablespoon*
 Dietade Fruit Sugar *instead of the soft brown
 sugar*

Filling
75 g (3 oz) polyunsaturated margarine
40 g (1½ oz) Dietade Fruit Sugar
175 g (6 oz) desiccated coconut
*1 egg plus the white left over from the sweet pastry
 mixture*
Delicia *raspberry, strawberry* or *apricot jam*

Line a 23–25.5 cm/9–10" oiled flan dish with the pastry. Chill for 10 minutes, then spread with jam. Heat the margarine and fruit sugar until melted, then stir in the coconut and beaten egg. Spread the mixture evenly over the jam base. Pre-heat the oven to 190°C/375°F/Gas Mark 5 and bake near the top of the oven for 30–35 mins. Cover with foil or greaseproof paper if the coconut browns before it is set.

Ginger Cheesecake

Makes 1 23 cm/9" flan

1 recipe quantity Pâte Sucré (see below)
*350 g (12 oz) yoghurt cheese (to make this simply
 drip 725 ml/1¼ pints natural yoghurt through a
 muslin cloth overnight)*
225 g (8 oz) cream cheese
2 rounded tbsp Dietade Fruit Sugar
3 medium free range eggs
1 level tbsp ginger, freshly grated
1 generous tsp clear honey
*few pieces of crystallized ginger cut into small
 pieces, to decorate*

Pre-bake the pâte sucré for 10 minutes at 190°C/375°F/Gas Mark 5 and leave to cool. When the yoghurt has dripped, scrape off the yoghurt cheese (use the whey for soups or sauces), measure off 100 g/4 oz and place in the refrigerator for the topping. Blend the remaining 225 g/8 oz yoghurt cheese with the cream cheese, fruit sugar and eggs until really smooth. Stir in the fresh ginger and pour the mixture into the cooked and cooled pastry case. Bake in the pre-heated oven, which has been turned down to 180°C/350°F/Gas Mark 4, for 30 minutes. When cooked, blend the reserved 100 g/4 oz of yoghurt cheese with the honey and crystallized ginger and spread this over the still-hot cheese tart. Turn the oven off and return the garnished tart to the warm oven for a few minutes. Chill well before serving.

Pâte Sucré with Almond Filling

Makes 1 20 cm/8 in flan

Pâte sucré is a French sweet pastry which is thin, crisp and light in texture. It is a good basis for fillings such as cheesecake and fruit mixtures. You can mix the ingredients together using the traditional rubbing-in method of pastry-making, but the method described in this recipe allows more air to be incorporated into the pastry and lightens it considerably.

100 g (4 oz) brown wheatmeal flour, plain
pinch sea salt (optional)
2 level tbsp Dietade Fruit Sugar
2 egg yolks
50 g (2 oz) polyunsaturated margarine, softened

Filling
2 tbsp Delicia *raspberry* or *strawberry jam*
75 g (3 oz) polyunsaturated margarine
3 level tbsp Dietade Fruit Sugar
75 g (3 oz) almonds, finely ground
2 large eggs
25 g (1 oz) blanched split almonds (optional)

Sift the flour and sea salt (if used) into a large, shallow dish and make a well in the middle. Whisk the sugar and egg yolks together for 30 seconds then add the softened margarine and blend it in well. Pour this mixture into the flour. Flick the flour with fingertips into the liquid and very gently mix all together. Form quickly but lightly into a dough. Put the dough into a polythene bag and chill while you prepare the filling. Pre-heat the oven to 180°C/350°F/Gas Mark 4. Cream the margarine and fruit sugar for 2 minutes, gradually add the eggs until well incorporated, then stir in the ground almonds.

Roll out the chilled pastry very thinly on a lightly-floured surface. Ease it from the surface with a palette knife, lift on to the rolling pin and ease into an oiled 20 cm/8 in flan ring or tin. Trim the edges, reserving the trimmings. Spread a layer of jam in the pastry case, then spread the filling mixture over the jam. Roll out the trimmings and cut into thin strips. Place these in a lattice pattern on the top of the almond filling and sprinkle on the split almonds if liked. Bake in the centre of the pre-heated oven for 45 minutes, until golden brown.

Sweet Lemon Cheesecake

Makes 1 25 cm/10 in flan

Absolutely delicious and light as a feather.

1 recipe quantity Pâte Sucré (see page 147)
175 g (6 oz) cream cheese
2 eggs, separated
4 tbsp Dietade Fruit Sugar
2 level tbsp dried milk powder
200 ml (7 fl oz) thick natural yoghurt (Greek-style yoghurt is best)
2 level tsp lemon peel, finely grated or 1 tsp each lemon and orange peel, finely grated
4 drops pure vanilla or almond essence

Bake the pâte sucré blind for 10 minutes in the oven, pre-heated to 190°C/375°F/Gas Mark 5. Turn the oven down to 180°C/350°F/Gas Mark 4.

Cream together the cream cheese, egg yolks, fruit sugar, yoghurt and milk powder, citrus peel and chosen essence. Whisk the egg whites until stiff and fold lightly (do not whisk) into the cream cheese mixture. Scoop this into the partly baked pastry case and bake for a further 25 minutes.

KALIBU

The next two recipes use carob in place of chocolate.

Carob Bakewell Tart

Makes 1 20 cm/8" tart

¾ recipe quantity Sweet Wheatmeal Pastry (see page 130), using 175 g (6 oz) flour, etc. (you can use all wholemeal flour)

Filling
2 tbsp no-sugar apricot jam
1 level tbsp Kalibu Carob Powder
1 tbsp boiling water
75 g (3 oz) polyunsaturated margarine
50 g (2 oz) fruit sugar or Barbados sugar
2 small eggs, beaten
few drops vanilla essence

Use the pastry to line a lightly oiled 20 cm/8" loose-bottomed flan tin. Reserve the pastry trimmings. Pre-heat the oven to 170°C/325°F/Gas Mark 3. Spread the jam on the base and sides of the pastry case. Mix the carob powder with the water until smooth. Leave to cool. Cream the margarine and sugar for 3 minutes. Gradually add the beaten egg and gently fold in the flour, then finally stir in the carob and water mixture with the vanilla essence. (Once the flour is added do not beat the mixture too much – fold in as lightly as possible.) Pour the mixture into the pastry case. Roll out the pastry trimmings and use to make a lattice pattern on top of filling. Bake for 40–45 minutes in the pre-heated oven.

Carob Cream Buns

Makes 10

1 recipe quantity Basic Choux Pastry (see page 142)

Filling and Topping
150 ml (5 fl oz) double cream (more if you wish)
175 g (6 oz) Kalibu Carob Bar, plain

Pre-heat the oven to 200°C/400°F/Gas Mark 6.

Make up the choux pastry as directed. Allow to cool and spoon 10 level tablespoons on to a greased baking sheet, allowing plenty of space between each spoonful for the buns to expand.

Bake in the pre-heated oven for 20 minutes, then reduce the heat to 180°C/350°F/Gas Mark 4 and continue to bake for a further 15 minutes. Take the buns out, make a small slit in the side of each and return them to a very low heated oven (130°C/250°F/Gas Mark ½) to dry out for 5 minutes. (This last stage will ensure that the centres are not soft and doughy, which often happens.) Remove from the oven once again and leave to get completely cold on a wire rack.

To fill and top, whisk the cream until firm, cut the buns through the centres and spoon in the cream. Melt the carob bar by breaking it into small pieces and put them on a plate over a saucepan of hot water to melt. Spoon the melted carob carefully over the filled buns.

LOSELEY

—Mango Cheese Tart

Makes 1 25 cm/10 in tart

This sweet takes 24 hours to set so make it the day before it is needed. The cheese used is Ricotta which is traditionally made with sheep's milk, but you can use goat's or cow's curd cheese. You can also use fresh apricots or peaches instead of the mango.

25 g (1 oz) sesame seeds
½ tsp ground cinnamon
150 g (5 oz) 100% wholemeal flour
75 g (3 oz) unbleached white flour
100 g (4 oz) polyunsaturated margarine
25 g (1 oz) soft light brown or fruit sugar
2 tbsp cold water
1 egg yolk

Filling
225 g (8 oz) Ricotta or curd cheese
175 g (6 oz) Loseley Natural Yoghurt
3 level tbsp clear honey
3 drops natural vanilla essence
*finely grated rind of 1 lemon (approx. 1 rounded
     teaspoon)*
1 ripe mango or 2 large peaches or 8 ripe apricots
25 g (1 oz) flaked almonds, toasted

Mix the sesame seeds and cinnamon with the two flours. Put the margarine and sugar into a mixing bowl and with a wooden spoon cream for 1 minute. Whisk the water and egg yolk together until frothy and add to the margarine and sugar with 2 tablespoons of the flour and sesame seed mixture. Mix well together and gradually add the remaining dry ingredients, using your hands to form a dough as soon as the mixture stiffens. Knead for 1 minute. Place the dough in a polythene bag and chill for 30 minutes.

Pre-heat the oven to 190°C/375°F/Gas Mark 5. Roll out the dough on a lightly floured surface, lift on to the rolling pin and use to line a 25 cm/10 in oiled flan dish or tin. Prick the base and bake in the pre-heated oven for 20 minutes. Leave to get completely cold before filling.

If you have a food processor or blender just put the cheese, yoghurt, honey, vanilla essence and lemon rind into the bowl and process until smooth. If by hand, mix the same ingredients with a wooden spoon until smooth. Peel the mango and cut into small thin slivers. (If using peaches or apricots dip them in hot water for a few minutes and then peel.) Leave a few slices of fruit to decorate the top of the tart. Stir the mango pieces into the cheese mixture and pour this into the cold, cooked pastry case. Decorate the top with a few slices of the fruit and the lightly toasted almonds. Chill for 24 hours.

For a gourmet touch when entertaining marinate the mango slices in a little brandy and freshly grated ginger overnight, then stir the lot into the cheese mixture. These are also great made in individual bun-size pastry cases.

PAUL'S TOFU

Banana, Orange and Hazelnut Flan

Makes 1 23 cm/9″ flan

You can use a biscuit base (see the following recipe for Tangy Coffee Cheesecake) or the sweet shortcrust pastry which I give here. You can use all wholemeal flour instead of mixed wholemeal and white, and omit the egg yolk, substituting for it an extra tablespoon of cold water. However, the ingredients given here achieve a very light pastry.

1 level dsrtsp fruit sugar
75 g (3 oz) polyunsaturated margarine
1 egg yolk and 1 tbsp cold water or 2 tbsp cold water
100 g (4 oz) 100% wholemeal flour, plain
50 g (2 oz) unbleached white flour
pinch sea salt (optional)

Filling
3 good sized bananas, sliced
100 g (4 oz) fruit sugar or clear honey
grated rind of 1 orange
1 tbsp orange juice
1 tbsp lemon juice
2 drops pure vanilla essence
150 ml (4 fl oz) sunflower oil
½ tsp sea salt
350 g (12 oz) Paul's Firm Tofu
50 g (2 oz) roughly ground and toasted hazelnuts

Cream the sugar with the margarine until smooth, about 1 minute. Whisk the egg yolk with the cold water until it froths, then add to creamed mixture (or add the 2 tablespoons of cold water). Sieve the flours with the salt, if used, and add 2 tablespoons to the creamed mixture at the same time as adding the liquid. Blend well together and gradually add the rest of the flour. Form into a dough. Flour the hands and knead the dough for 2 minutes. Place in a polythene bag and refrigerate for 30 minutes. Pre-heat the oven to 190°C/375°F/Gas Mark 5. When well chilled roll the pastry out on a floured surface. Lift on to the rolling pin and place in a well-oiled 23 cm/9″ flan dish. Trim and crimp the edges, prick the base and bake blind for 15–20 minutes. Do not overcook. Cover with greaseproof paper if the edges get too brown. Remove from the oven and allow to get cold.

Purée all the ingredients except the tofu and hazelnuts in a blender or food processor. When smooth break up the tofu and gradually blend into the banana mixture. Pour into the cold cooked pastry case and chill for 3 hours. Toast the roughly ground hazelnuts in the oven for 15 minutes at 170°C/325°F/Gas Mark 3. Take care not to burn. When cold sprinkle on top of the chilled flan.

Tofu and Yoghurt Cheesecake

Makes 1 23–25.5 cm/9–10″ cheesecake

The original Swiss recipe for this cheesecake uses 350 g/12 oz cream cheese, but I have experimented and found that using 225 g/8 oz firm tofu and 225 g/8 oz yoghurt cheese the result is not only healthier, being lower in saturated fats, but also very tasty.

To make 225 g/8 oz of yoghurt cheese simply drip 450 g/1 lb of natural yoghurt overnight through a piece of muslin. (Save the whey and use in soups or stock.)

1 recipe quantity pastry as for Mango Cheese Tart (see page 149)

Filling
75 g (3 oz) dried apricots soaked in apple juice overnight
225 g (8 oz) Paul's Firm Tofu
225 g (8 oz) yoghurt cheese (see above)
75 g (3 oz) fruit sugar
4 eggs, separated
4 drops pure vanilla essence
juice of ½ lemon (1 tbsp)
rind of 1 lemon, very finely grated
50 g (2 oz) yoghurt cheese for topping
25 g (1 oz) each of roughly ground almonds and pumpkin seeds, lightly toasted, to decorate

Make the pastry and use to line a 23–25.5 cm/9–10″ flan tin. Bake blind for 10 minutes in a pre-heated oven at 190°C/375°F/Gas Mark 5. Remove from the oven and leave to cool.

Liquidize the soaked apricots in enough of their soaking juice to make a jam-like consistency. Cream the tofu, yoghurt cheese and fruit sugar together until well blended. Add the egg yolks one at a time. Stir in the vanilla, lemon juice and rind. Whisk the egg whites until stiff and standing in peaks, then fold them into the tofu mixture. Do not beat. Fold gently and allow air to circulate into the mixture. Pop bubbles carefully as you do this. This mixture should be light and fluffy. Spread the apricot purée over the base of the cooked and cooled pastry base and pour on the tofu mixture. Bake in a pre-heated oven at 170°C/325°F/Gas Mark 3 for 1 hour. Cover the cheesecake with a piece of foil or greaseproof paper if it browns too quickly. Leave in the oven to cool down after cooking. (This stops the centre from caving in.) Leave to get completely cold before spreading on the topping.

To finish, spread a thin layer of yoghurt cheese on top of the cheesecake and sprinkle on the roughly ground and toasted almonds and pumpkin seeds. Chill for a few hours before serving. You can decorate it with fresh fruit such as strawberries, raspberries or sliced fresh apricots or peaches if you prefer.

PREWETT'S

——— Mince Pies ———

Makes 12

These are not just for Christmas, as the filling is less rich than the usual festive mincemeat. Make the filling a minimum of a few days before needed, to allow a good flavour to develop. Jar and use when necessary.

You can use all wholemeal flour but I sometimes use three-quarters wholemeal and a quarter un-bleached white flour for an extra-light short pastry.

50 g (2 oz) sunflower seeds or almonds
50 g (2 oz) dates, steamed for 5 minutes only
50 g (2 oz) currants
50 g (2 oz) raisins
50 g (2 oz) sultanas
1 large cooking apple, cored and roughly chopped (leave skin on)
juice and grated rinds of ½ lemon and ½ orange
2 tbsp apple juice concentrate
½ tsp freshly ground nutmeg
pinch sea salt
50 g (2 oz) Prewett's Sunflower Margarine
4 tbsp brandy (optional)

Pastry
175 g (6 oz) Prewett's 100% Wholemeal Flour mixed with 50 g (2 oz) Prewett's Unbleached White Flour
1 dsrtsp fruit sugar
100 g (4 oz) Prewett's Sunflower Margarine
1 egg yolk
2 tbsp cold water

In a blender or food processor chop the sunflower seeds or almonds roughly. Add all the other ingredients and process until mushy. Jar for at least a few days before using.

When you are ready to make the pastry, cream the margarine and sugar for 1 minute. Whisk the egg yolk and water until frothy and add this to the margarine and sugar plus 2 tablespoons of the flour. Gradually add the remaining flour, using your hands when the dough stiffens. Knead for 2 minutes then place in a polythene bag and chill for 30 minutes. Pre-heat the oven to 190°C/375°F/Gas Mark 5.

Grease 12 individual bun tins and roll out the pastry thinly on a floured surface. To avoid using too much flour place a sheet of polythene over the pastry and roll over it. Use a medium and a small cutter. Place a medium-sized pastry round into each bun tin and spoon in the mincemeat. Egg-wash the edges of the small pastry rounds and pop them on top of the filling. They should just cover the edge of the lower pastry rounds. Fork the tops, brush with egg-wash and sprinkle on a little fruit sugar. Bake in the pre-heated oven for 20 minutes.

8
CAKES and BISCUITS

The recipes that follow will, I hope, encourage you to make those sweet tea-time treats with the finest ingredients available. If you experiment using healthy ingredients in your usual recipes you will find that your cakes and biscuits will be more flavoursome, just as light or crunchy and much more nutritious than those made with bleached white flour (the bleaching agent used is chlorine dioxide which is also used for cleaning drains), saturated fats and too much sugar.

Use 100% wholemeal or brown wheatmeal flour; and polyunsaturated margarine and unsaturated cold pressed oils such as sunflower or safflower – these are preferable to lard or the over-use of butter. I also advise using fruit sugar (fructose), Muscovado sugar, Barbados sugar or honey instead of 'pure' white sugar (sucrose). But all sweet concentrates should be used in moderation for the oc-casional treat rather than as a daily part of a healthy diet. In sweet baking, as well as 100% wholemeal flour, I try to incorporate other fibrous and nutritious foods such as nuts, seeds and dried or fresh fruit as much as possible. This is vitally important for those who have a sweet tooth because we need the fibre to help offset the adverse effects of certain foods – sugar, salt and saturated fats being top of the list. I am afraid there is no getting away from the fact that sugar is detrimental to our health – just be moderate and enjoy these indulgences very occasionally.

You will note that I use carob powder instead of cocoa. It comes in powdered and block form under the brand name Kalibu. This product is a healthy alternative to cocoa or chocolate and can be used in your favourite recipes in the same way.

Cakes

ALLINSON

Coconut, Orange and Lemon Cake

Makes 1 20 cm/8″ cake

225 g (8 oz) polyunsaturated margarine
150 g (5 oz) Muscovado or Barbados sugar
4 large eggs, separated
225 g (8 oz) Allinson 100% English Wholemeal
   Flour, *Self-raising*
175 g (6 oz) desiccated coconut
juice and grated rind of ¹/₂ an orange
juice and grated rind of ¹/₂ a lemon

Grease and line a 20 cm/8″ cake tin. Pre-heat the oven to 180°C/350°F/Gas Mark 4.

Cream the margarine and sugar for 3 minutes. Beat the egg whites for 1 minute and stir into the margarine mixture. Beat the yolks and add to the mixture. Mix the flour with the coconut and fold this in gradually. Finally stir in the orange and lemon rind and juice. Spoon the mixture into the prepared tin and bake in the centre of the pre-heated oven for 45–55 minutes.

Dundee Cake

Makes 1 17 cm/7" cake

150 g (6 oz) sunflower margarine or butter
150 g (6 oz) Muscovado sugar
50 g (2 oz) marzipan (see page 156 for recipe)
grated rind of 1 lemon
4 eggs (size 3 or 4), beaten
150 g (6 oz) sultanas
100 g (4 oz) raisins
100 g (4 oz) currants
50 g (2 oz) glacé cherries, washed, wiped and
  quartered
225 g (8 oz) Allinson 100% English Wholewheat
  Flour
1 tbsp sherry or milk
100 g (4 oz) almonds, blanched and split

Grease and line a 17 cm/7" cake tin and fasten thick brown paper around the outside of the tin. Pre-heat the oven to 170°C/325°F/Gas Mark 3.

Cream the butter or margarine, sugar and marzipan with the lemon rind until soft and creamy. Gradually beat in the eggs, beating well between each addition. Mix the fruit and flour together, then gently stir into the creamed mixture, adding the sherry or milk. Pour into the prepared tin and level the top, then cut a deep cross through the cake mixture side to side, or scoop a hollow in the centre to prevent it rising too high. Arrange the almonds on the top. Bake in the pre-heated oven for 2½–3 hours (check after 2 hours and turn down to 150°C/300°F/Gas Mark 2, if brown enough). Remove from the tin, cool on a cooling rack and store in an airtight container for 1–2 weeks before eating.

Whisked Fatless Sponge

Makes 1 17 cm/7" sandwich cake or
1 30 cm × 23 cm/12" × 9" sponge roll

3 eggs (size 3 or 4), separated
75 g (3 oz) fruit sugar
75 g (3 oz) Allinson 100% English Wholewheat
  Flour or Allinson Farmhouse Flour, plain

Filling
jam
150 ml (5 fl oz) whipped cream

Line and grease two 17 cm/7" sponge tins or one 30 ×23 cm/12" × 9" swiss roll tin. Pre-heat the oven to 220°C/425°F/Gas Mark 7.

In a large bowl, whisk the egg whites until stiff. Add the yolks and sugar and whisk until thick and creamy. Carefully fold in the flour until well incorporated, then pour the mixture into the prepared tins. Bake in the pre-heated oven for 7–8 minutes, until pale golden in colour and springy to the touch.

For sponge cakes, turn the cakes out of the tins, peel off the greased paper and place the cakes carefully on to a cooling tray. When cold, fill with cream and jam, sandwich the cakes together and dust the top with icing sugar.

For a sponge roll, turn the sponge out of the tin on to a sheet of caster-sugared greaseproof paper, and remove the greased lining paper. Use a large, sharp knife to trim the crust from each edge, turn the end of the greaseproof paper over one short end of the sponge and roll up together lightly. Leave to cool on a cooling tray. When cool, gently unroll the sponge and spread with jam and whipped cream or your chosen filling. Re-roll.

Orange Cream Roll

Makes 1 30 cm × 23 cm/12" × 9" sponge roll

1 recipe quantity Whisked Fatless Sponge (see
  above)
grated rind of ½ orange

Filling
150 ml (5 fl oz) double cream
1 tbsp Cointreau or concentrated pure orange juice
grated rind of ½ orange

extra cream and fresh or crystallized orange to
  decorate

Line and grease a 30 × 23 cm/12" × 9" swiss roll tin. Pre-heat the oven to 220°C/425°F/Gas Mark 7.

Follow the basic sponge recipe, incorporating the rind of ½ an orange with the egg yolks and sugar, and baking, turning out, trimming and rolling up as in the instructions for sponge roll.

To make the filling, whisk the cream until it forms soft peaks, then add the orange rind and liqueur or orange juice. Continue to whisk until stiff. Gently unroll the sponge, spread with the cream and re-roll. Refrigerate until ready to serve, then dust with icing sugar or sprinkle with extra liqueur or orange juice. Pipe with extra cream and decorate with fresh or crystallized orange.

Wholewheat Victoria Sandwich Cake

Makes 1 15 cm/6" layer cake

100 g (4 oz) Allinson 100% English Wholewheat
  Flour
1 level tsp baking powder
100 g (4 oz) sunflower margarine
100 g (4 oz) fruit sugar
2 eggs (size 2 or 3), separated
1 tbsp cold water

Grease and bottom-line two 15 cm/6" sandwich tins. Pre-heat the oven to 180°C/350°F/Gas Mark 4.

Cream together the margarine and sugar until light and fluffy. Beat in the two egg yolks and the cold water. In a separate bowl whisk the egg whites to a thick but not too stiff foam. Mix together the flour and the baking powder. Fold the flour thoroughly into the margarine mixture, then gently but thoroughly fold in the whisked egg whites. Divide the mixture between the two prepared tins, level with a palette knife and bake in the pre-heated oven for 20–25 minutes until risen and golden brown. Turn out on to a wire tray to cool, then sandwich together with the filling of your choice.

BILLINGTON'S

Apple and Ginger Squares

Makes 6 portions

450 g (1 lb) cooking apples, peeled, cored and
  chopped
175 g (6 oz) polyunsaturated margarine
150 g (5 oz) Billington's Light Muscovado Sugar
3 eggs
1 tbsp honey
225 g (8 oz) 100% wholemeal flour, self-raising
1½ tsp ground ginger
½ tsp cinnamon

Grease and line a 20 cm/8" square tin. Pre-heat the oven to 180°C/350°F/Gas Mark 4.

Cream the margarine and sugar until light. Add the eggs and then the honey. Sift the flour and spices into the mixture and mix well. Stir in the chopped apples, pour the mixture into the prepared tin and bake for 1½ hours in the pre-heated oven. Cut into six when cold.

Golden Banana Cake

Makes 1 20 cm/8" layer cake

2 ripe bananas, mashed
3 tbsp yoghurt
225 g (8 oz) Billington's Golden Granulated Sugar
100 g (4 oz) polyunsaturated margarine
2 eggs, beaten
350 g (12 oz) 100% wholemeal or brown
  wheatmeal flour, self-raising
¾ tsp bicarbonate of soda
½ tsp sea salt
a few drops of vanilla essence

Filling
150 ml (5 fl oz) double cream
2 ripe bananas, mashed
lemon juice

Grease and line two 20 cm/8" cake tins. Pre-heat the oven to 180°C/350°F/Gas Mark 4.

Mix the mashed bananas with the yoghurt. Cream the sugar and margarine until light. Add the eggs and mix well. Gradually add the sifted flour, bicarbonate of soda and salt. Combine with the mashed banana and yoghurt mixture and add the vanilla essence. Divide the mixture equally between the two cake tins. Bake for 35 minutes in the pre-heated oven until risen and golden. Turn out of the tins and allow to cool.

Make the filling by whisking the cream until thick. Mash the bananas and add a little lemon juice to prevent them discolouring. Beat the bananas into the cream and sandwich the mixture between the two cakes. If the cake is to be eaten immediately, decorate with a few slices of banana which have been dipped in lemon juice.

Raisin and Ginger Cake

Makes 1 20 cm/8" cake

150 g (5 oz) butter or polyunsaturated margarine
100 g (4 oz) Billington's Muscovado Sugar
2 eggs
225 g (8 oz) 100% wholemeal flour, self-raising
pinch sea salt
1 tsp ground ginger
100 g (4 oz) preserved ginger, chopped
50 g (2 oz) raisins
50 g (2 oz) mixed peel
25 g (1 oz) Billington's Golden Granulated Sugar *to decorate*

Line and grease a 20 cm/8" cake tin. Pre-heat the oven to 170°C/325°F/Gas Mark 3.

Cream the butter or margarine with the sugar, beat in the eggs and stir in the flour, salt, ground ginger, preserved ginger, raisins and peel. Pour the mixture into the prepared tin, sprinkle the golden granulated sugar over the top and bake for 1½ hours in the pre-heated oven. Turn out on to a cake rack to cool.

CAFÉ HAG

Tangy Coffee Cheesecake

Makes 1 20 cm/8" cheesecake

175 g (6 oz) digestive biscuits, crushed
50 g (2 oz) low fat soft margarine, melted
150 g (5 oz) fruit sugar
3 eggs
450 g (1 lb) low fat soft cheese
275 ml (½ pt) natural yoghurt
2 sachets gelatine
4 tbsp water
4 tsps Café Hag Decaffeinated Instant Coffee Granules *dissolved in 1 tbsp hot water*
fresh strawberries to decorate

Make the crumb base by mixing together the crushed digestive biscuits, the melted margarine and 50 g/2 oz of the sugar. Press the mixture into the base of a 20 cm/8" loose-bottomed cake tin. Chill in the refrigerator. Whisk the egg yolks and remaining sugar until pale and creamy and work in the soft cheese and yoghurt. Dissolve the gelatine in the water and add to the cheese mixture with the dissolved coffee. Whisk the egg whites until peaks form, fold into the mixture and pour on to the crumb base. Refrigerate until set, remove from the tin and decorate with fresh strawberries or any other fruit in season.

Banana Tea Cake

Makes 1 450 g/1 lb loaf

225 g (8 oz) 100% wholemeal flour
1 level tsp baking powder
½ tsp salt
175 g (6 oz) light Muscovado sugar
1 tbsp Café Hag Decaffeinated Instant Coffee Granules
150 ml (5 fl oz) skimmed milk
50 g (2 oz) low fat soft margarine
50 g (2 oz) Grape-nuts
2 bananas
1 egg, lightly beaten

Pre-heat the oven to 180°C/350°F/Gas Mark 4, and grease a 23 cm × 13 cm/9" × 5" loaf tin.

Mix together the flour, baking powder, salt, sugar and coffee granules. Bring the milk to boiling point and pour it over the margarine and Grape-nuts. Leave to stand for 5 minutes. Mash the bananas and mix with the flour, Grape-nuts mixture and the egg. Pour the mixture into the prepared tin and bake in the centre of the pre-heated oven for about 1 hour. Leave to cool in the tin for 10 minutes, then turn out on to a wire rack to cool.

Apple and Apricot Tea Cake

Instead of using 2 bananas use 1 medium cooking apple (peeled, cored and chopped) and 50 g/2 oz chopped dried apricots. Prepare as the Banana Tea Cake.

DIETADE

Dietade Chocolate Cake

Makes 1 21 cm × 10 cm/8½″ × 4″ cake

65 g (2½ oz) diabetic chocolate, plain
dash rum (optional)
50 g (2 oz) butter
40 g (1½ oz) Dietade Fruit Sugar
2 eggs, separated
65 g (2½ oz) walnuts, ground fairly finely
2 scant tbsp Dietade Diabetic Apricot Jam, warmed and sieved

Icing
100 g (4 oz) diabetic chocolate, plain
2 tbsp water
50 g (2 oz) Dietade Fruit Sugar
few drops sunflower oil

Oil and flour a cake tin 21 cm × 10 cm/8½″ × 4″. Pre-heat the oven to 180–190°C/350–375°F/Gas Mark 4–5.

Break the chocolate into small pieces, place in an oven-proof dish and add the rum if used. Put the chocolate into the oven to melt and retrieve as soon as it has melted. Cream the butter and fruit sugar together until light and fluffy, beat the egg yolks one by one and then beat in the melted but not hot chocolate. Whisk the egg whites until stiff and fold them into the mixture alternately with the ground walnuts. Bake for 35–40 minutes in the pre-heated oven. Leave the cake to cool in the tin, then turn out carefully upside-down on to a cooling rack. This is the way it should be iced too – straight side uppermost. When the cake is cold, spread the top and sides with warmed, sieved apricot jam. Leave to dry, then cover with chocolate icing. If possible leave overnight before cutting.

To make the icing, break the chocolate into small pieces. Put the pieces into an oven-proof dish and put in a warm oven for the chocolate to melt. Meanwhile, dissolve the fruit sugar in the water over a low heat. When dissolved, turn up the heat and cook the liquid until the 'small thread' stage has been reached. Remove the pan from the heat and leave to cool. When lukewarm, stir the sugar solution into the melted chocolate, then beat in the sunflower oil. Use immediately to ice the chocolate cake.

Dietade Doughnuts

Makes 8

The jam used here is Delicia, which is a full, fruity jam with no colouring or preservatives added.

100 g (4 oz) brown wheatmeal flour, plain
1 level tsp baking powder
pinch salt
20 g (¾ oz) Dietade Fruit Sugar
15 g (½ oz) skimmed milk powder
½ beaten egg
15 g (½ oz) melted butter or oil
Delicia *raspberry jam*

Blend all the ingredients, except the melted butter or oil and raspberry jam, to make a dough. Divide and roll into eight individual circles and place a teaspoon of jam on each. Mould the dough round the jam. Heat the butter or oil in a baking tin, place the doughnuts in it and bake at 190°C/375°F/Gas Mark 5 for 5–10 minutes until golden brown. Once cooked, roll the doughnuts in fruit sugar and leave to cool.

Marzipan

Makes 450 g/1 lb

175 g (6 oz) Dietade Fruit Sugar
225 g (8 oz) ground almonds
1 tsp lemon juice
few drops pure almond essence
1 egg, beaten

Stir the fruit sugar into the ground almonds, add the lemon juice and almond essence, then gradually stir in the beaten egg. Use the fingers to mould into a firm manageable dough. Knead for a few minutes and roll out as required.

Orange Cheesecake

Makes 1 13 cm/5″ cheesecake

225 g (8 oz) cottage cheese
150 g (5 oz) low fat natural yoghurt
1 orange
1 small lemon
25 g (1 oz) Dietade Fruit Sugar
1 egg white
1 digestive biscuit
15 g (1 oz) gelatine
8 g (¼ oz) butter or margarine
6 orange segments to decorate

Butter a 13 cm/5″ cake tin. Sieve the cottage cheese and blend with the yoghurt. Grate the rinds and squeeze the juice from the orange and lemon and add to the cheese mixture. Stir the gelatine into 3 tablespoons of hot water until dissolved and then pour through a strainer into the mixture. Mix in the fruit sugar, then fold in the stiffly whisked egg white. Turn the mixture into the prepared cake tin and leave in a cool place to set. When set, dip the tin into hand-hot water and turn out on to a plate. Crush the digestive biscuit with a rolling pin, coat the cheesecake with the crumbs and decorate with orange segments.

Simnel Cake

Makes 1 18 cm/7″ cake

This cake is traditionally served at Eastertime.

175 g (6 oz) butter or polyunsaturated margarine
175 g (6 oz) Dietade Fruit Sugar
3 eggs, beaten
225 g (8 oz) brown wheatmeal flour, plain
1 level tsp ground cinnamon
1 level tsp ground nutmeg
350 g (12 oz) currants
100 g (4 oz) sultanas
75 g (3 oz) mixed chopped candied peel
a little milk if necessary
450 g (1 lb) marzipan (see recipe on page 00)
Delicia apricot jam, warmed and sieved to use under marzipan icing

Grease and line one 18 cm/7″ cake tin. Pre-heat the oven to 170°C/325°F/Gas Mark 3.

Cream the butter or margarine and the sugar together, gradually add the beaten eggs, then fold in the flour, spices, mixed fruit and peel, adding a little milk to make a soft consistency. Place in the prepared cake tin. In the centre of the mixture place one third of the marzipan rolled into a round. Bake in the centre of the pre-heated oven for 1 hour, then lower the heat and bake for a further 3 hours at 150°C/300°F/Gas Mark 2. Cool on a wire tray.

After the cake has cooled roll another third of the marzipan into a circle and place on top of the cake which has been previously coated with the warmed apricot jam. The final third of the marzipan is divided into eleven equal parts, which are formed into balls and placed around the edge of the cake on top of the marzipan circle. The cake is then lightly grilled. Decorate with a model chicken and tiny Easter eggs for that festive touch.

DOVES FARM

Cherry and Almond Loaf Cake

Makes 1 900 g/2 lb loaf

100 g (4 oz) Doves Farm Brown Wheatmeal Flour, self-raising
100 g (4 oz) ground almonds
pinch of salt
100 g (4 oz) butter
100 g (4 oz) sugar
2 eggs
1 tsp almond essence
225 g (8 oz) glacé cherries

Well-grease a 900 g/2 lb loaf tin. Pre-heat the oven to 170°C/325°F/Gas Mark 3.

Mix together the flour, ground almonds and salt. Cream together the butter and sugar, and beat in the eggs and almond essence. Gradually add the dry ingredients and mix well, then fold in the cherries. Turn into the well-greased loaf tin and bake in the middle of the pre-heated oven for about 1 hour. When cooked, leave the cake in the tin for 10 minutes before removing to a rack for cooling.

Fruit Cake

Makes 1 23 cm/9" cake

225 g (8 oz) butter or polyunsaturated margarine
225 g (8 oz) brown sugar
3 eggs
275 g (10 oz) Doves Farm 100% Wholemeal Flour,
  self-raising
pinch of salt
1 tablespoon milk
175 g (6 oz) mixed dried fruits
50 g (2 oz) mixed peel, chopped
50 g (2 oz) glacé cherries, chopped (wash and pat
  dry before chopping)
50 g (2 oz) walnuts, chopped

Grease and line a 23 cm/9" deep cake tin. Pre-heat the oven to 150°C/300°F/Gas Mark 2.

Cream together the butter or margarine and the sugar, and beat in the eggs. Add the flour, salt and tablespoon of milk and mix well. Fold in all the fruit and nuts. Put the mixture into the prepared tin and bake in the centre of the pre-heated oven for 2–2½ hours. When cooked, a knife pushed into the centre of the cake should come out clean. Leave the cooked cake in its tin for 20 minutes before removing to a rack for cooling.

High Fibre Sticky Sultana Slice

Makes 1 450 g/1 lb loaf

2 tbsp malt extract
275 ml (10 fl oz) milk
50 g (2 oz) Doves Farm Bran
50 g (2 oz) brown sugar
175 g (6 oz) sultanas
1 egg
175 g (6 oz) Doves Farm 100% Wholemeal Flour,
  self-raising

Well-grease a 450 g/1 lb loaf tin. Pre-heat the oven to 180°C/350°F/Gas Mark 4.

Dissolve the malt extract in the milk. Add the bran, sugar and sultanas and leave for 1 hour. Stir in the beaten egg and mix in the flour. Pour into the well-greased loaf tin and bake in the pre-heated oven for 35–40 minutes. When cold, serve sliced on its own or with butter.

Pecan Nut and Carrot Cake

Makes 1 20 cm/8" cake

Simple and quick to prepare. You can use walnuts, but pecans have a milder flavour and taste delicious in this mixture. The filling is optional but great for special occasions. The cake without the filling will stay fresh for 8 days in a polythene bag in the refrigerator.

250 ml (9 fl oz) corn or sunflower oil
175 g (6 oz) Muscovado or Barbados sugar
1 scant tsp ground cloves
pinch sea salt
3 large eggs, separated
250 g (9 oz) Doves Farm Fine Milled 100%
  Wholemeal Flour, self-raising
75 g (3 oz) pecan nuts, roughly chopped
350 g (12 oz) juicy carrots, finely grated

Filling
275 g (10 oz) carton natural yoghurt dripped for a
  few hours through a muslin cloth
1 rounded tbsp instant dried milk powder
1 level tsp decaffeinated instant coffee granules
1 rounded tsp honey (or more if you wish)
2 drops vanilla essence
25 g (1 oz) pecan nuts, chopped

Grease and line a 20 cm/8" round cake tin. Pre-heat the oven to 170°C/325°F/Gas Mark 3.

Place the oil, sugar, ground clove and sea salt in a large mixing bowl and blend with a wooden spoon for 2 minutes. Stir in the egg yolks well in. Whisk the egg whites for 1 minute, then add to the oil mixture. Gradually fold in the flour as lightly as possible (do not beat). Finally stir in the nuts and carrots, again as lightly as possible (do not beat). Scoop the mixture into the prepared tin and bake in the pre-heated oven for 1¾ hours. Cool in the tin for 10 minutes, then transfer to a wire rack to become completely cold before filling.

To make the filling, scoop out the yoghurt cream from the muslin and place in a small mixing bowl. Stir in the dried milk powder. Mix the honey with the coffee powder and vanilla essence and stir into the yoghurt mixture. Add the nuts. It should be the consistency of thick whipped cream (the longer you drip the yoghurt the thicker the resulting cream or cheese will be).

When the cake is completely cold split in half as you would a gateau and spread on the filling.

FORCE

—Farmhouse Apple— Cake

Makes 1 20 cm/8" cake

275 g (10 oz) 100% wholewheat flour, self-raising
pinch sea salt
1 tsp mixed spice
175 g (6 oz) polyunsaturated margarine
50 g (2 oz) Force Whole Wheat Flakes
150 g (5 oz) fruit sugar
75 g (3 oz) sultanas
175 g (6 oz) cooking apples, thinly peeled, cored
*   and diced*
3 eggs, beaten
3 tbsp milk
decorate with thin slices eating apple and a little
*   warmed, sieved apricot jam (optional)*

Pre-heat the oven to 180°C/350°F/Gas Mark 4. Grease and line a deep 20 cm/8" cake tin.

Sieve the flour, salt and mixed spice into a large mixing bowl and rub in the margarine. Add the Force Whole Wheat Flakes, sugar, sultanas and diced apple and stir together. Gradually stir in the eggs and milk until the mixture has a consistency that will drop easily from a spoon. Place in the prepared tin and bake for 1½ hours in the pre-heated oven. To decorate, arrange the eating-apple slices on top of the cake and glaze with the apricot jam.

GRANNY ANN

—Honey and Almond— Scones

Makes approx. 16

450 g (1 lb) 100% wholemeal flour, self-raising
1 tsp salt
100 g (4 oz) butter or vegetable margarine
25 g (1 oz) light brown (raw) sugar
50 g (2 oz) almonds, finely chopped
1 tbsp Granny Ann Cookiemalt
2 tbsp honey
10 tbsp (150 ml) milk

Pre-heat the oven to 200°C/400°F/Gas Mark 7.

Place the flour and salt in a bowl and rub in the fat. Add the sugar and the almonds. Mix the Cookiemalt, honey and milk over a gentle heat and use this liquid to make a soft but not sticky dough with the dry ingredients. Turn on to a floured board, knead for a few minutes, then roll out to 2 cm/¾" thickness and cut into rounds. Place on a greased baking sheet and brush with beaten egg or milk. Bake in the pre-heated oven for 10 minutes. Cool on a wire rack.

For a different flavour, try replacing the milk with sour cream.

—Honey and Date— Squares

Makes about 20

1 tbsp Granny Ann Cookiemalt
5 tbsp honey
75 g (3 oz) polyunsaturated margarine
175 g (6 oz) 100% wholemeal flour, self-raising
½ tsp cinnamon
½ tsp salt
3 eggs, beaten
25 g (1 oz) raw sugar (optional)
175 g (6 oz) dates, chopped
100 g (4 oz) walnuts, chopped

Pre-heat the oven to 190°C/375°F/Gas Mark 5.

Blend the Cookiemalt, honey and margarine in a bowl until creamy. Combine the flour, cinnamon and salt in a separate bowl. Gradually beat the eggs and flour into the Cookiemalt mixture and mix well. Add the sugar, dates and walnuts and mix thoroughly. Spread the mixture into a shallow, greased baking tin and bake in the pre-heated oven for 30 minutes, until golden brown. Cut into squares whilst hot.

Iced Carob and Hazelnut Brownies

Makes about 20

175 g (6 oz) polyunsaturated margarine
175 g (6 oz) raw cane sugar
1 dsrtsp Granny Ann Cookiemalt
3 eggs, beaten
150 g (5 oz) 100% wholemeal flour, self-raising
75 g (3 oz) carob powder
3 tbsp boiling water

Icing
100 g (4 oz) block carob
2 dsrtsp water
2 dsrtsp vegetable oil
50 g (2 oz) roughly ground hazelnuts

Pre-heat the oven to 170°C/325°F/Gas Mark 3.

Cream together the margarine and sugar and stir in the Cookiemalt. Gradually combine the eggs and the flour, mixing well. Stir in the carob powder. Finally add the boiling water and mix well. Pour the mixture into a greased shallow baking tin and bake for 30 minutes in the pre-heated oven until rich and dark. Cool on a wire rack.

When the cake is completely cold, melt the carob by placing it in a small bowl over a saucepan of water and warming gently. When melted, add the water and oil and mix until smooth. Do not overheat. Spread the mixture over the top of the cake and sprinkle with the crushed hazelnuts. Cut into squares when the icing has set. Decorate with Smarties or other favourite sweets for an irresistible children's party treat.

Here are two more tasty recipes by Joanna Hill.

Malted Banana Bread

Makes 1 450 g/1 lb loaf

1 dsrtsp Granny Ann Cookiemalt
2 tbsp milk
100 g (4 oz) butter or vegetable margarine
100 g (4 oz) light brown (raw) sugar
2 eggs, beaten
150 g (5 oz) wholemeal flour, self-raising
3 ripe or over-ripe bananas
1 apple, sliced

Pre-heat the oven to 170°C/325°F/Gas Mark 4.

Mix together the milk and Cookiemalt over a gentle heat. Cream the margarine and sugar together in a bowl. Beat in the eggs, then fold in the flour. Mash the bananas and add to the mixture. Stir in the Cookiemalt liquid and mix well. Turn the mixture into a 450 g/1 lb greased loaf tin and make a hollow in the centre. Decorate the top with sliced apple and sprinkle with sugar and cinammon. Bake for 1 hour in the pre-heated oven.

Parkin

Makes about 20 portions

This recipe needs to stand overnight before baking.

4 tbsp Granny Ann Cookiemalt
4 tbsp molasses
100 ml (4 fl oz) vegetable oil
100 g (4 oz) 100% wholemeal self-raising flour
100 g (4 oz) Muscovado raw cane sugar
225 g (8 oz) medium oatmeal
½ tsp ground ginger
1 egg beaten in 150 ml (5 fl oz) milk

Combine the Cookiemalt, molasses and oil over a gentle heat, stirring well until mixed. Mix together all the dry ingredients, and add the Cookiemalt liquid and the milk. Mix well and allow the mixture to stand overnight. Pour the mixture into a well greased 25 cm × 15 cm/10″ × 6″ baking tin. Pre-heat the oven to 170°C/325°F/Gas Mark 3 and bake the parkin for 45 minutes. Cut into squares when cold.

HÖFELS

Bran and Fruit Cake

Makes 1 18 cm/7″ cake

275 g (10 oz) Höfels 100% Wholemeal Norfolk Flour
50 g (2 oz) Höfels Bran
3 level tsp baking powder
½ teaspoon Höfels Sea Salt
225 g (8 oz) polyunsaturated margarine
100 g (4 oz) Muscovado or Barbados sugar
100 g (4 oz) dried fruit
50 g (2 oz) chopped nuts
2 eggs
milk to mix

Opposite: **Itona** *Granny Ann Bread and Butter Pudding (above) page 190, Iced Carrot and Hazelnut Brownies (below) page 160*

Grease and line an 18 cm/7″ cake tin. Pre-heat the oven to 170°C/325°F/Gas Mark 3.

Mix the flour, bran, baking powder and sea salt. In another bowl cream the margarine with the sugar. Beat the eggs with 3 tablespoons of milk. Add the dried fruit and chopped nuts to the dry ingredients and add this to the creamed mixture a little at a time, alternating with a little of the beaten eggs and milk. The mixture should be fairly stiff, but a little more milk can be added if the mixture is too stiff to drop from a spoon. Put the mixture into the lined and greased cake tin and bake in the pre-heated oven for about 1½ hours. Leave for one day before cutting.

Fresh Fruit Cake

Makes 1 20 cm/8″ cake

225 g (8 oz) fresh fruit such as apples,
blackcurrants, gooseberries
225 g (8 oz) Höfels 100% Wholemeal Norfolk Flour
75 g (3 oz) polyunsaturated margarine
175 g (6 oz) Muscovado or Barbados sugar
2 eggs
2 tbsp milk
3 tsps baking powder

Grease a 20 cm/8″ cake tin. Pre-heat the oven to 180°C/350°F/Gas Mark 4.

Prepare the fruit (cutting up apples into small pieces) and then mix it with a small quantity of the flour. Cream the margarine and sugar, add the beaten eggs and milk, then stir in the flour and baking powder. Add the fruit. Mix really well and then place the mixture in the greased cake tin. Bake in the pre-heated oven for about 50 minutes.

Oat and Nut Cake

Makes 16 portions

350 g (12 oz) Höfels Breakfast Oatflakes
225 g (8 oz) polyunsaturated margarine
100 g (4 oz) brown sugar
100 g (4 oz) hazelnuts, ground

Pre-heat the oven to 190°C/375°F/Gas Mark 5.

Melt the margarine and add the sugar, oatflakes and hazelnuts, mixing well. Place the mixture in a well-greased, Swiss roll rin and bake in the pre-heated oven for 25 minutes. When cold, cut into squares.

Opposite: **Holland and Barrett** *Christmas Cake (above) page 162, Fig and Aniseed Ring (below) page 115*

Soya and Bran Cake

Makes 1 23 cm/9″ cake

175 g (6 oz) Höfels 100% Wholemeal Norfolk Flour
50 g (2 oz) soya flour
50 g (2 oz) Höfels Bran
225 g (8 oz) polyunsaturated margarine
75 g (3 oz) sugar
100 g (4 oz) dried fruit
2 eggs
2 tbsps honey or malt extract, slightly warmed

Grease and line a 23 cm/9″ cake tin. Pre-heat the oven to 170°C/325°F/Gas Mark 3.

Rub the margarine into the flour. Mix in the bran, soya flour, dried fruit and sugar. Beat the eggs and add to the dry mixture together with the slightly warmed honey or malt. Put the mixture in the greased and lined cake tin and cook for approximately 1¼ hours in the pre-heated oven.

Soya Flour Fruit Scones

200 g (7 oz) Höfels 100% Wholemeal Norfolk Flour
2 level tsp baking powder
75 g (3 oz) soya flour
50 g (2 oz) butter or margarine
25 g (1 oz) sugar
75 g (3 oz) currants
pinch Höfels Sea Salt
1 egg, beaten
approx 6 tbsp milk

Mix together the Norfolk flour, salt and baking powder. Rub in the butter or margarine then add the sugar, currants and soya flour and mix well. Add the beaten egg and enough of the milk to make a soft dough; roll out on a floured board to a thickness of 2–2.5 cm/¾–1″, cut into rounds and place on a greased baking sheet. Pre-heat the oven to 230°C/450°F/Gas Mark 8 and bake for about 10 minutes.

HOLLAND & BARRETT

Christmas Cake

Makes 1 17 cm/7 in square cake

225 g (8 oz) Holland & Barrett Currants
175 g (6 oz) Holland & Barrett Sultanas
100 g (4 oz) Holland & Barrett Raisins
75 g (3 oz) Holland & Barrett Dried Apricots
50 g (2 oz) Holland & Barrett Flaked Almonds
grated rind of 1 lemon
1 tbsp dry sherry (optional) or 1 tbsp fresh orange
 juice
2 tbsp molasses
175 g (6 oz) soft vegetable margarine
75 g (3 oz) Muscovado sugar
4 free-range eggs
200 g (7 oz) 100% wholemeal flour
50 g (2 oz) Holland & Barrett Ground Almonds
1 tsp mixed spice
1/2 tsp ground cinnamon
1/4 tsp ground nutmeg
1 tbsp skimmed milk

Grease and line a 17 cm/7 in square cake tin. Pre-heat the oven to 140°C/275°F/Gas Mark 1.

Mix the currants, sultanas and raisins in a bowl. Chop the apricots and almonds finely and add to the fruit. Stir in the lemon rind and sherry or orange juice, and cover. This helps to plump the fruit and let the flavour of the sherry or juice penetrate fully. Leave the fruit for several hours before using.

Put the molasses, margarine and sugar in a large mixing bowl and cream them together fully until the mixture is fluffy. Add the eggs one at a time, beating thoroughly between each addition. Sieve the flour, ground almonds and spices into the bowl, adding any bran remaining in the sieve. Add the milk and mix to a smooth dropping consistency. Spoon into the prepared tin and smooth top. Tie a double band of brown paper or newspaper around the outside of the tin as this will help to prevent the sides of the cake from becoming burnt. Bake in the centre of the pre-heated oven. Check the cake after 2½ hours, and then at half-hourly intervals. Test by inserting a skewer into the centre of the cake; if it emerges with no mixture adhering to it then the cake is cooked. (It should take no more than about 4 hours.) Remove from the oven and leave to cool in the tin until completely cold. Remove from tin and wrap in foil.

If you wish to decorate the cake here are some ideas. You may like to leave the cake fairly simple: a nice way of finishing off a cake that avoids adding extra sugar in the form of icing is to arrange a selection of shelled nuts around the cake: walnut halves, pecans, halved brazils, almonds, etc. Make a glaze by combining a tablespoon of Whole Earth (no sugar added) apricot jam with a tablespoon of Holland & Barrett clear honey and a teaspoonful of boiling water. This will make a smooth, shiny glaze. Brush this over the arrangement of nuts on the cake and tie a bright red ribbon around the sides.

If you prefer to finish the cake in a more traditional way, cover it with a thin layer of Prewett's raw cane sugar marzipan. Attach this to the cake by first brushing the cake all over with a fine coating of Holland & Barrett clear honey. Save some marzipan to make flowers or leaves to decorate the top of the cake. You could also arrange a few nuts on top and again finish with a bright ribbon.

Honey and Wheatgerm Buns

Makes 16

100 g (4 oz) polyunsaturated margarine
75 g (3 oz) Holland & Barrett Honey
2 eggs
150 g (5 oz) 100% wholemeal flour, self-raising and
25 g (1 oz) Holland & Barrett Wheatgerm
50 g (2 oz) Holland and Barrett Chopped Nuts
rind of 1 lemon, grated
a little milk

Pre-heat the oven to 200°C/400°F/Gas Mark 6.

Cream the margarine and honey and add the eggs. Mix in the flour and wheat germ carefully, then add the nuts, lemon rind and enough milk to make a soft, dropping consistency. Spoon the mixture into paper baking cases or greased bun tins and bake for 15–20 minutes in the pre-heated oven.

For a special occasion you can ice the buns with a mixture of 50 g/2 oz margarine, 50–75 g/2–3 oz brown sugar powdered in a coffee grinder, and add whatever flavouring you prefer – a little fruit juice or carob powder is nice. Just cream all the ingredients together and use to ice the buns.

These buns will freeze very well, with or without icing, for 3–4 months. Thaw for half an hour at room temperature.

Walnut and Honey Loaf

Makes 1 900 g/2 lb loaf

275 ml (10 fl oz) milk
225 g (8 oz) Holland & Barrett Clear Honey
1 vanilla pod
50 g (2 oz) polyunsaturated margarine
2 large eggs, beaten
340 g (12 oz) 100% wholemeal flour, plain
1 level tsp sea salt
3 tsp baking powder
75 g (3 oz) Holland & Barrett Walnuts, chopped

Pre-heat the oven to 160°C/325°F/Gas Mark 3.

Mix the milk with the honey, add the vanilla pod and stir over very low heat until well blended and just warm. Take off the heat. Take out the vanilla pod, rinse and dry to re-use. Combine the flour, salt and baking powder in a mixing bowl, rub in the margarine until the mixture resembles fine breadcrumbs, and stir in the walnuts. Now stir in the milk and honey mixture and the beaten eggs. Place the mixture in a well-oiled 900 g/2 lb bread tin and bake for 1 hour on the middle shelf of the pre-heated oven. Cool in the tin for 10–15 minutes, then turn out on to a wire rack.

KALIBU

The following tasty recipes are taken from *The Carob Cookbook* by Lorraine Whiteside, a very inventive cook.

Carob and Almond Layer Cake

Makes 1 20 cm/8 in 3-layer cake

4 eggs
75 g (3 oz) raw cane sugar
175 g (6 oz) 100% wholemeal flour
50 g (2 oz) Kalibu Carob Powder
2 level tsp baking powder
clear honey
175 g (6 oz) toasted flaked almonds

Grease and line a 30 cm × 20 cm/12 in × 8 in rectangular baking tin. Pre-heat the oven to 190°C/375°F/Gas Mark 5.

Place the eggs and sugar in a large mixing bowl and stand the bowl in a sink filled with hot water. Whisk the eggs and sugar together until thick and creamy – the whisk should leave a trail when you take it out of the mixture. Remove the mixing bowl from the hot water and fold in the flour, carob powder and baking powder. Pour the mixture into the prepared baking tin, spreading it evenly. Bake in the pre-heated oven for about 20 minutes. Cool on a wire rack. When the cake is cold, split into three equal rectangles. Spread honey on two of the rectangles and sprinkle with some of the flaked almonds. Sandwich the three layers together and spread honey over the top of the cake. Sprinkle with the remaining flaked almonds.

Carob Apple Cake

Makes 1 20 cm/8 in cake

100 g (4 oz) polyunsaturated margarine
100 g (4 oz) raw cane sugar
2 eggs, beaten
50 g (2 oz) chopped hazelnuts
100 g (4 oz) 100% wholemeal flour
1½ level tsp baking powder

Filling
450 g (1 lb) dessert apples
grated rind and juice of ½ lemon
2 tbsp raw cane sugar

Topping
50 g (2 oz) Kalibu Carob Bar, plain
little milk to mix

Grease and line a 20 cm/8″ cake tin. Pre-heat the oven to 180°C/350°F/Gas Mark 4.

Peel, core and slice the apples, and put into a saucepan with the water, sugar lemon juice and rind. Cook for about 20 minutes until soft, then leave to cool. Cream the margarine and sugar together until light and fluffy, gradually add the beaten eggs, then fold in the flour, baking powder and chopped hazelnuts. Pour the mixture into the prepared tin and bake for about 25–30 minutes in the pre-heated oven. Cool on a wire rack. When cold, cut the cake into 2 layers and fill with the apple mixture. For the topping, melt the carob bar in a bowl over hot water, adding a little milk to soften, then spread the melted carob over the top of the cake with a palette knife.

Carob Honey Squares

Makes about 10

175 g (6 oz) 100% wholemeal flour
50 g (2 oz) Kalibu Carob Powder
2 level tsp baking powder
50 g (2 oz) sultanas
3 tbsp safflower oil
2 tbsp clear honey
2 tbsp natural yoghurt
little milk to mix

Grease and line a 20 cm/8″ square tin. Pre-heat the oven to 180°C/350°F/Gas Mark 4.

Put the flour, carob powder, baking powder and sultanas into a large mixing bowl. Stir in the safflower oil, honey and yoghurt with enough milk to give a fairly runny consistency. Pour the mixture into the prepared tin and bake for about 30 minutes in the pre-heated oven, then cool on a wire rack. When cold, cut the cake into squares.

Carob Meringues

Makes about 8 complete meringues

4 egg whites
225 g (8 oz) raw cane sugar
100 g (4 oz) Kalibu Carob Powder
small carton fresh cream, whipped, for filling

Whisk the egg whites until very stiff. Add the carob powder and half the sugar and whisk again. Fold in the remaining sugar. Pipe small meringue swirls on to baking trays lined with waxed paper or greased greaseproof paper and bake in a cool oven, 130°C/250°F/Gas Mark ½ for several hours until crisp and dry. When cold, sandwich the meringue swirls together with whipped cream and serve as soon as possible, before the meringues lose their crispness.

Carob Owls

Makes approx. 12

100 g (4 oz) polyunsaturated margarine
75 g (3 oz) raw cane sugar
2 eggs, beaten
100 g (4 oz) 100% wholemeal flour
25 g (1 oz) Kalibu Carob Powder
1½ level tsp baking powder

Topping
3 tbsp clear honey
100 g (4 oz) desiccated coconut
50 g (2 oz) small seedless raisins
3 glacé cherries, cut into quarters

Pre-heat the oven to 190°C/375°F/Gas Mark 5.

Cream the margarine and sugar together until light and fluffy. Gradually add the beaten eggs a little at a time, then fold in the flour, carob powder and baking powder. Spoon the mixture into well-greased dariole moulds, allowing for the cakes to rise during baking. Place the moulds on a baking tray and bake for about 20 minutes in the pre-heated oven.

When the cakes have cooled, coat each one with honey and roll them in desiccated coconut. To make the owl's eyes, stick two raisins on to each cake with a little honey, and stick a quartered glacé cherry centrally slightly below the eyes to form the owl's beak.

Carob Rum Cake

Makes 1 23 cm/9 in cake

175 g (6 oz) polyunsaturated margarine
50 g (2 oz) raw cane sugar
2 tbsp clear honey
2 eggs, beaten
175 g (6 oz) 100% wholemeal flour
2 level tsp baking powder
50 g (2 oz) Kalibu Carob Powder
2 tbsp dark rum
2 tbsp natural yoghurt
little milk to mix
50 g (2 oz) Kalibu Carob Bar
1 tbsp milk
50 g (2 oz) chopped blanched almonds

Grease and line a 23 cm/9 in cake tin. Pre-heat the oven to 180°C/350°F/Gas Mark 4.

Cream the margarine, sugar and honey together until light and fluffy and gradually add the beaten eggs a little at a time. Carefully fold in the flour, baking powder and carob powder, then stir in the rum and yoghurt. If necessary add a little milk to produce a dropping consistency. Spoon the mixture into the prepared tin and bake in the pre-heated oven for about 30 minutes until the cake is firm to the touch. Cool on a wire rack.

While the cake is cooling, melt the carob bar in a bowl over hot water and stir in the milk to make a smooth coating. Spread the coating over the cake with a palette knife, allowing some of the coating to run down the sides of the cake. Sprinkle liberally with chopped blanched almonds.

Carob Strawberry Gateau

Makes 1 20 cm/8" 3-layer gateau

4 eggs
100 g (4 oz) raw cane sugar
175 g (6 oz) 100% wholemeal flour
50 g (2 oz) Kalibu Carob Powder
3 level tsp baking powder
1 tbsp hot water
a little fresh whipped cream for decoration

Filling
275 ml (10 fl oz) natural yoghurt
450 g (1 lb) fresh strawberries
1 tbsp raw cane sugar

Grease and line a 20 cm/8" cake tin. Pre-heat the oven to 180°C/350°F/Gas Mark 4.

Put the eggs and sugar into a large mixing bowl, stand it in a sink of hot water and whisk until thick and creamy. The whisk should leave a trail when you take it out of the mixture. Carefully fold in the flour, carob powder and baking powder. Add the hot water. Place the mixture into the prepared cake tin and bake for about 35–40 minutes until firm to the touch. Cool on a wire rack.

While the cake is in the oven, wash the strawberries and sprinkle with the raw cane sugar. Allow the sugar to soak in for about 10 minutes. Reserve about 12 strawberries for decoration. Slice the remaining strawberries into quarters and fold into the yoghurt.

When the cake is cold, cut into three layers. Sandwich the layers with the strawberry and yoghurt mixture. Cut the reserved strawberries in half and arrange on top of the gateau. Put the whipped cream into a piping bag with an 0.5 cm/¼" star nozzle and pipe around the strawberries.

KRETSCHMER

Banana Muffins

Makes 12

175 g (6 oz) unsifted all purpose flour
65 g (2½ oz) Kretschmer Wheat Germ, Plain
75 g (3 oz) Barbados sugar
3 tsp baking powder
½ tsp salt
2–3 medium, ripe bananas, mashed
100 ml (4 fl oz) milk
50 ml (2 fl oz) cooking oil
2 eggs

Combine the flour, wheat germ, sugar, baking powder and salt in a bowl. Stir well to blend. Combine the banana, milk, oil and eggs in a small bowl and beat slightly. Add the liquid ingredients to the blended dry ingredients and stir, just enough to moisten the dry ingredients. Fill paper-lined or greased individual bun tins about two-thirds full. Bake at 200°C/400°F/Gas Mark 6 for 20–25 minutes until done. Serve warm with butter.

Marbled Cheesecake Square

Makes 12 servings

115 g (4½ oz) brown wheatmeal flour, plain
50 g (2 oz) Kretschmer Wheat Germ, Plain
2 level tbsp fruit sugar or *Demerara*
100 g (4 oz) polyunsaturated margarine
350 g (12 oz) cream cheese (at room temperature)
75 g (3 oz) fruit sugar or *Demerara*
2 large eggs
4 drops pure vanilla essence
50 g (2 oz) carob bar or *cooking chocolate*
1 tbsp water
2 tbsp Kretschmer Wheat Germ, Plain

Topping
1 small carton soured cream
1 dsrtsp clear honey
few drops vanilla essence

Pre-heat the oven to 190°C/375°F/Gas Mark 5.

Combine the flour, the 50 g/2 oz of wheat germ and the 2 tablespoons of fruit sugar or Demarara in a bowl. Stir well to blend, then rub in the margarine and mix until crumbly. Take out just under 100 g/ 4 oz of this crumb mixture for topping the cake and spread this in a shallow baking tin. Press the remaining crumb mixture into an ungreased 23 cm/ 9 in square cake tin. Bake both tins in the pre-heated oven – 6 minutes for the topping and 9 minutes for the base – until lightly browned.

Cream the cheese with the 75 g/3 oz of fruit sugar or Demerara until fluffy, about 5 minutes. Beat in the eggs one at a time, then beat in 4 drops of pure vanilla essence. Melt the carob bar or cooking chocolate and the water together in a heavy pan over a very low heat. Remove from the heat and stir in 2 generous tablespoons of the cream cheese mixture, then the remaining 2 tablespoons of wheat germ. Pour the remaining cream cheese mixture on to the baked crumb mixture base. Then drop the carob or chocolate mixture by spoonfuls on to the filling. Swirl lightly with a fork to marble. Bake in the pre-heated oven for 25 minutes until set. Cool slightly for 5 minutes.

To top, simply combine the sour cream, honey and a few drops of vanilla essence together and spread over the still-warm cheesecake. Sprinkle with the topping crumb mixture and when cool refrigerate for at least 4 hours or overnight before serving.

Wheat Germ and Ginger Cake

Makes 1 20 cm/8" cake

75 g (3 oz) Kretschmer Wheat Germ, plain
225 g (8 oz) 100% wholemeal flour, self-raising
1 level tsp mixed spice
1 rounded tsp ground ginger
75 g (3 oz) stem ginger or *crystallized ginger, chopped*
175 g (6 oz) polyunsaturated margarine
225 g (8 oz) clear honey
3 large eggs, beaten

Grease and line a 20 cm/8" round cake tin. Pre-heat the oven to 170°C/325°F/Gas Mark 3.

Mix the wheat germ, flour, mixed spice and ground ginger together and stir in the stem (or crystallized) ginger. Melt the margarine and honey in a double saucepan or in a saucepan placed over a pan of hot water (only melt, do not boil). Pour this into the dry ingredients, then fold in the beaten eggs (do not beat). Spoon into the prepared tin and bake in the pre-heated oven for 1 hour. Test after 45 minutes by inserting a knitting needle or knife into the centre of the cake. If it comes out clean then your cake is cooked.

Wheat Germ Strawberry or Raspberry Shortcake

Serves 6–8

100 g (4 oz) brown wheatmeal flour, plain
50 g (2 oz) Kretschmer Wheat Germ, plain
2 slightly rounded tbsp. Demerara sugar
1½ level tsp baking powder
good pinch sea salt
¼ tsp powdered cinnamon
50 g (2 oz) white vegetable fat or *polyunsaturated margarine*
75 ml (3 fl oz) cold water
50 g (2 oz) butter, melted
2 tsp Kretschmer Wheat Germ, plain

Filling and Topping
fresh strawberries or *raspberries*
275 ml (10 fl oz) double cream, whipped and sweetened with a little honey or *575 ml (1 pint) natural yoghurt dripped through muslin overnight, then sweetened with a little honey*

Pre-heat the oven to 200°C/400°F/Gas Mark 6.

Combine the flour, wheat germ, sugar, baking powder, salt and cinnamon in a bowl and stir well to blend. Cut in the vegetable fat or margarine with a pastry blender until the mixture looks like coarse meal (you can use a knife). Add the water and melted butter and mix well. Divide the dough in half and spread each half into a 17 cm/7″ circle on a greased baking sheet. Sprinkle with the remaining 2 teaspoons of wheat germ. Bake in the pre-heated oven for 12–15 minutes, until lightly browned. Remove from the baking sheet and cool on a wire rack. When cold, sandwich the layers with strawberries or raspberries and the whipped cream or strained yoghurt. Sprinkle with additional wheat germ if desired.

Wheat Germ, Walnut and Banana Cake

Makes 1 25 cm/10″ cake

225 g (8 oz) sunflower or safflower margarine
175 g (6 oz) Muscovado sugar
4 large eggs, well beaten
450 g (1 lb) bananas, mashed
275 g (10 oz) 100% wholemeal flour, self-raising
75 g (3 oz) Kretschmer's Wheat Germ, Plain
100 g (4 oz) walnuts, cut into rough pieces

Grease and line a 25 cm/10″ round cake tin. Pre-heat the oven to 170°C/325°F/Gas Mark 3.

Cream the margarine and sugar for 3 minutes only, then add the beaten eggs a tablespoon at a time. Stir in the mashed bananas. Mix the flour and wheat germ together and fold lightly into the creamed mixture with the walnuts. Spoon the mixture into the prepared tin and bake for 1½ hours in the pre-heated oven. To test if completely cooked just insert a knitting needle or thin knife into the centre of the cake. If it comes out clean then the cake is cooked.

Wheaty Yoghurt Muffins

These are rather like bran muffins.

Makes 12

110 g (4½ oz) stoneground 100% wholemeal flour
50 g (2 oz) Kretschmer Wheat Germ, Plain
3 tbsp Muscovado sugar
½ tsp baking powder
½ tsp bicarbonate of soda
½ tsp salt
225 g (8 oz) natural yoghurt
6 tbsp polyunsaturated margarine, melted
1 egg, slightly beaten
75 g (3 oz) raisins

Combine the flour, wheat germ, sugar, baking powder, bicarbonate of soda and salt in a large bowl. Stir well to blend, then add the yoghurt, margarine, egg and raisins. Stir to just moisten the dry ingredients. Fill paper-lined or greased muffin pan cups or bun tins about two thirds full. Bake at 190°C/375°F/Gas Mark 5 for 20–25 minutes, until a wooden toothpick inserted in the centre comes out clean. Serve warm with butter or honey.

Wholewheat Cinnamon Raisin Muffins

Makes 14

110 g (4½ oz) brown wheatmeal flour
50 g (2 oz) stoneground 100% wholemeal flour
50 g (2 oz) Kretschmer Wheat Germ, Plain
50 g (2 oz) Muscovado sugar
3 level tsp baking powder
1 level tsp cinnamon
½ level tsp salt
100 g (4 oz) raisins
175 ml (6 fl oz) milk
75 g (3 oz) polyunsaturated margarine, melted
2 eggs, slightly beaten

Combine the flours, wheat germ, sugar, baking powder, cinnamon and salt in a bowl and stir well to blend. Stir in the raisins and add the milk, melted margarine and eggs to the dry ingredients. Stir to just moisten dry ingredients. Fill paper-lined or greased muffin pan cups or bun tins about three quarters full. Bake at 200°C/400°F/Gas Mark 6 for 15–18 minutes.

MARRIAGE'S

Wholemeal Queen Cakes

Makes 20

100 g (4 oz) polyunsaturated margarine
100 g (4 oz) soft brown sugar
2 eggs, beaten
175 g (6 oz) Marriage's 100% Wholemeal Flour,
*   self-raising*
pinch of salt
100 g (4 oz) currants

Pre-heat the oven to 200°C/400°F/Gas Mark 6.

Cream the margarine and sugar until fluffy, then gradually beat in the eggs. Sieve the flour and salt and shake the remaining bran into the flour. Gently fold the flour into the mixture with a metal spoon, then fold in the currants. Put spoonfuls into greased bun tins and bake in the pre-heated oven for 20 minutes.

NATURE'S BOUNTY

Bran 'N' Fig Carrot Cake

Makes 1 20 cm/8" cake

175 ml (6 fl oz) sunflower or corn oil
75 g (3 oz) Muscovado or Barbados sugar
1 level tsp clove powder
good pinch sea salt
2 large eggs
175 g (6 oz) 100% wholemeal flour, self-raising
50 g (2 oz) Nature's Bounty Bran 'N' Fig
50 g (2 oz) hazelnuts, medium to finely ground
225 g (8 oz) carrots, scrubbed and finely grated

Grease and line a 20 cm/8" round cake tin. Pre-heat the oven to 170°C/325°F/Gas Mark 3.

With a wooden spoon beat the oil, sugar, clove powder and sea salt well together for 2 minutes. Whisk the eggs and stir into the mixture. Stir in the flour, Bran 'N' Fig and hazelnuts and finally add the carrots. Spoon into the prepared tin and bake in the

pre-heated oven for 50 minutes. The cake is cooked when a knife inserted into the centre of it comes out clean.

NATURE'S WAY

Date and Oat Cake

Makes 1 18 cm/7" layer cake

50 g (2 oz) polyunsaturated margarine
100 g (4 oz) brown wheatmeal flour, self-raising
100 g (4 oz) oat flakes
50 g (2 oz) Nature's Way Desiccated Coconut
25 g (1 oz) Demerara sugar
2 apples, peeled, cored and chopped
50 g (2 oz) walnuts, chopped
1 tbsp clear honey
1 tbsp vegetable oil

Filling
100 g (4 oz) stoned dates, soaked for 30 minutes

Lightly grease two 18 cm/7" round cake tins. Pre-heat the oven to 190°C/375°F/Gas Mark 5.

Rub the margarine into the flour until the mixture resembles breadcrumbs. Add all the dry ingredients and mix well. Lastly add the honey and oil and work the mixture with the hands to form a soft dough. Divide the mixture in half, press firmly into the prepared tins and level the surface. Bake in the pre-heated oven for 40 minutes. Leave to cool before removing from the tins.

Strain the dates and remove any stones. Press the dates on to one half of the cake and place the other half on top.

Date, Walnut and Raisin Cake

Makes 1 18 cm/7" cake

225 g (8 oz) brown wheatmeal flour, self-raising
75 g (3 oz) Nature's Way Dates, stoned and chopped
75 g (3 oz) Nature's Way Walnuts, chopped
100 g (4 oz) Nature's Way Seedless Raisins
175 g (6 oz) polyunsaturated margarine
100 g (4 oz) Muscovado sugar
3 small eggs
approx. 150 ml (5 fl oz) milk
pinch ground nutmeg
Nature's Way Walnut Halves *for decoration*

Grease an 18 cm/7″ tin and line the base with greaseproof paper. Pre-heat the oven to 180°C/350°F/Gas Mark 4.

Mix the flour and nutmeg together, and rub in the margarine. Add the chopped dates and walnuts, the raisins and the sugar. Beat the egg and milk together and mix into the dry ingredients. Pour the mixture into the prepared tin, level the surface and place the halved walnuts on top. Bake in the pre-heated oven for 1¼–1½ hours.

Muesli Cake

Makes 1 18 cm/7″ cake

175 g (6 oz) Nature's Way Muesli
100 g (4 oz) Muscovado sugar
175 g (6 oz) mixed cake fruit
2 tbsp clear honey
225 ml (8 fl oz) apple juice
1 carrot, washed and grated
175 g (6 oz) brown wheatmeal flour, self-raising
2 tsp baking powder
2 tbsp crushed wheat flakes

Grease and line an 18 cm/7″ round cake tin.

Place the muesli, sugar, mixed cake fruit, honey and apple juice in a mixing bowl and leave to soak for 1 hour, or overnight.

Pre-heat the oven to 180°C/350°F/Gas Mark 4. Add the grated carrot, flour and baking powder to the muesli mixture and combine thoroughly. Pour into the prepared tin, smooth the top and sprinkle with the crushed wheat flakes.

Bake in the pre-heated oven for 1½–2 hours, or until a knife inserted into the centre comes out clean. Leave to cool for a few minutes before turning out on to a wire rack.

One-stage Cherry Cake

Makes 1 20 cm/8″ cake

225 g (8 oz) brown wheatmeal flour, self-raising
225 g (8 oz) Nature's Way Glacé Cherries, *washed, dried and halved*
175 g (6 oz) polyunsaturated margarine
175 g (6 oz) Muscovado sugar
3 eggs
50 g (2 oz) ground almonds
2 tsp baking powder

Grease and base line a 20 cm/8″ round cake tin. Pre-heat the oven to 170°C/325°F/Gas Mark 3.

Put all the ingredients into a bowl and beat for 3 minutes. Pour the mixture into the prepared tin and bake for 1½–1¾ hours.

Orange Cake

Makes 1 15 cm/6″ cake

225 g (8 oz) brown wheatmeal flour, plain
3 level tsp baking powder
4 eggs
175 g (6 oz) polyunsaturated margarine
175 g (6 oz) soft brown sugar
grated rind of 1 orange
100 g (4 oz) Nature's Way Seedless Raisins

Icing
100 g (4 oz) Muscovado sugar
juice of 1 orange
few drops of vanilla essence
Nature's Way Walnut Halves *for decoration*

Grease and line a 15 cm/6″ round cake tin. Pre-heat the oven to 180°C/350°F/Gas Mark 4.

Sift together the flour and baking powder. Beat the eggs in a basin and stand the basin in tepid water (or make sure the liquid is at room temperature). Beat the margarine until very soft, add the sugar, and cream well together until light and fluffy. Add the eggs and the orange rind gradually, beating well after each addition; if the mixture shows signs of curdling, add a little flour. Fold in the dry ingredients and the raisins slowly. Pour the mixture into the prepared tin, smooth the top and make a slight hollow in the centre.

Bake in the pre-heated oven for 30 minutes, then reduce the heat to 160°C/325°F/Gas Mark 3, and bake for a further 50 minutes, or until firm to the touch. Leave the cake on a cooling tray until completely cold, then ice with orange icing.

To make the icing, pass the sugar through a sieve, add the orange juice and vanilla essence and beat until smooth. Coat the top of the orange cake and decorate with the walnut halves.

OCEAN SPRAY

Cranberry Orange Ginger Cake

Makes 1 20 cm/8" cake

100 g (4 oz) soft polyunsaturated margarine
175 g (6 oz) soft brown sugar
1 egg
1 tbsp molasses
2 160 g (6½ oz) jars Ocean Spray Cranberry Orange Sauce
50 g (2 oz) crystallized ginger, chopped
225 g (8 oz) 100% fine milled wholemeal flour, plain
2 tsp ground ginger

Grease and line the base of a 20 cm/8" round cake tin. Pre-heat the oven to 180°C/350°F/Gas Mark 4.

Cream together the margarine and sugar, then add the egg, molasses, cranberry orange sauce and ginger pieces. Sift the flour and ground ginger together and stir into the mixture until well blended. Put into the prepared cake tin, level the top and bake in the pre-heated oven for 1¼–1½ hours until risen and browned and a skewer pierced into the centre comes out clean. Cool on a wire rack.

Cranberry Spice Cup Cakes

Makes 16

100 g (4 oz) soft polyunsaturated margarine
100 g (4 oz) soft light brown sugar
2 eggs
175 g (6 oz) brown wheatmeal flour, plain
1 tsp ground nutmeg
1 tsp ground cinnamon
½ tsp salt
1 level tsp baking powder
150 ml (5 fl oz) soured cream
100 g (4 oz) Ocean Spray Jellied Cranberry Sauce

Pre-heat the oven to 180°C/350°F/Gas Mark 4.

Cream together the margarine and sugar and beat in the eggs. Sift together the flour, spices, salt and baking powder and fold them into the mixture. Stir in the soured cream and cranberry jelly. Put paper baking cases into a bun tin tray (or well grease the bun tins) and half fill each case with the mixture.

Bake in the pre-heated oven for about 25 minutes, until lightly coloured and firm to the touch. Cool on a wire rack.

PAUL'S TOFU

The next two recipes are taken from Jane O'Brien's book *The Magic of Tofu*.

Pineapple and Tofu Cake

Makes 1 25 cm/10" cake

275 g (10 oz) Paul's Firm Tofu
225 g (8 oz) honey
4 tbsp vegetable oil
½ tsp sea salt
2 tsp baking powder
8 tbsp soya milk
1 tsp pure vanilla essence
225 g (8 oz) 100% wholemeal flour
1 medium can pineapple rings in own juice or fresh pineapple slices (reserve the juice)
2 tbsp honey
1 tbsp arrowroot

Pre-heat the oven to 190°C/375°F/Gas Mark 5.

Mix together the tofu, honey, oil, salt, baking powder, soya milk and vanilla. Add the flour and pour the mixture into a greased cake tin. Arrange circles of pineapple on top of the cake mixture. Mix the honey with a little pineapple juice and bring to the boil. Add the arrowroot, which has been stirred into a little pineapple juice until dissolved thoroughly, and simmer until the liquid becomes clear. Pour this sauce over the pineapple slices and bake the cake in the pre-heated oven for about 20 minutes.

Tofu and Carob Cake

Makes 1 25 cm/10" cake

225 g (8 oz) clear honey
200 ml (7 fl oz) vegetable oil
450 g (1 lb) Paul's Firm Tofu
1 tsp sea salt
1 tsp pure vanilla essence
275 g (10 oz) 100% wholemeal flour
175 (6 oz) carob powder

Pre-heat the oven to 180°C/350°F/Gas Mark 4.

Blend the honey, oil, tofu, salt and vanilla together. Add the flour and carob and mix well with a mixer or by hand. Bake in a greased tin in the pre-heated oven for about 30 minutes.

Light Fruit Cake

Makes 1 25 cm/10" cake

This recipe is taken from my book *Making Your Own Home Proteins.*

150 ml (5 fl oz) sunflower oil
350 g (12 oz) Paul's Firm Tofu
½ tsp sea salt
175 g (6 oz) clear honey
few drops pure vanilla essence
275 g (10 oz) 100% wholemeal flour, self-raising
1 level tsp fresh ground nutmeg
½ tsp ground cinnamon
50 g (2 oz) ground almonds
50 g (2 oz) sultanas
50 g (2 oz) raisins
50 g (2 oz) pre-soaked dried apricots, chopped and soaked in apple juice for 1 hour
25 g (1 oz) blanched almonds and a few glacé cherry halves to decorate

Grease and line a 25 cm/10" round cake tin. Pre-heat the oven to 150°C/300°F/Gas Mark 2.

Blend the oil, tofu, salt, honey and vanilla in a large mixing bowl. Sift the flour with the spices and gradually add to the tofu mixture, mixing well in. Stir in the ground almonds and the dried fruit, making sure the soaked apricots have all the surface moisture removed on absorbent kitchen paper before being added. Spoon into the prepared tin and bake for 40–45 minutes. Test the centre with a sharp knife: if the knife comes out clean then your cake is done.

PREWETT'S

Carob and Pecan Nut Festive Cake

Makes 1 23 cm/9" layer cake

175 g (6 oz) Prewett's Sunflower or Safflower Margarine
150 g (5 oz) Prewett's Light Muscovado Sugar
3 large eggs, beaten
175 g (6 oz) Prewett's 100% Wholemeal Flour, self-raising
3 drops vanilla essence
1 level tbsp carob powder
finely grated rind of 1 orange
50 g (2 oz) pecan nuts, chopped into small pieces

Filling
150 g (5 oz) double cream
225 g (8 oz) natural yoghurt
1 generous tsp honey
40 g (1½ oz) carob bar
1 dsrtsp Grand Marnier
Prewett's Raspberry Extra Jam

Topping
75 g (3 oz) carob bar
5 tsp milk
25 g (1 oz) pecan nut halves

Lightly oil two 23 cm/9" sandwich tins. Place the yoghurt in a piece of muslin and leave until as much of the whey has dripped through as possible (3 hours will be enough). Scrape the yoghurt cream off the muslin and refrigerate to use in the filling. Pre-heat the oven to 190°C/375°F/Gas Mark 5.

Cream the margarine and sugar until light and fluffy. Add the beaten eggs a dessertspoon at a time. Sift the flour and gradually fold into the egg mixture. Stir in the vanilla, carob powder, orange rind and chopped pecans. Divide the mixture between the two lightly oiled sandwich tins (weigh if necessary) and bake for 20–25 minutes near the centre of the pre-heated oven. (Change the tins around after 15 minutes.) Leave in the tins to cool for 5 minutes before turning out on to a wire rack.

To make the filling, whisk the double cream until thick. Stir in the dripped yoghurt and honey. Melt the carob bar in a bowl over a pan of hot water, stir in the Grand Marnier, then trickle this into the cream mixture. Refrigerate while the cake is cooling. When the cake is completely cold spread a thin coating of jam on both layers, then spread generously with the filling.

To make the topping, melt the carob bar as for the filling and stir in the milk to give a smooth coating consistency. Spread this on top of the cake using a palette knife. Decorate immediately with the pecan halves.

SUNWHEEL

Beetroot and Walnut Cake

Makes 1 18 cm/7" cake or 450 g/1 lb loaf

This recipe is taken from my book *Vegetarian Food Processor*. You will notice I have used sunflower oil instead of margarine, but it works very well. You might also be surprised to see beetroot as an ingredient in a cake but, combined with certain ingredients, it has a quite delicious flavour.

100 g (4 oz) (weight when peeled) raw beetroot, thinly peeled
100 g (4 oz) (weight when peeled) raw carrot, washed and scraped
50 g (2 oz) walnuts
175 ml (6 fl oz) Sunwheel Cold Pressed Sunflower Oil
75 g (3 oz) Barbados sugar
2 eggs, beaten
175 g (6 oz) 100% wholemeal flour
¼ tsp ground cloves
1 tsp cinnamon

Grease and line an 18 cm/7″ round cake tin or 450 g/ 1 lb loaf tin. Pre-heat the oven to 160°C/325°F/Gas Mark 3.

Set the steel blades in position on the food processor. Cut pieces of beetroot to fit the feed tube almost to the top, and push firmly down with the pusher. Repeat with the carrots and mix both together. Clean out the processor bowl. With steel blades in position chop the nuts roughly for a few seconds. Scoop out and leave aside. Still with the steel blades in position put the oil and sugar in the bowl and process for 15 seconds. Add the beaten egg gradually through the feed tube. Add the flour and spices a tablespoon at a time, using 'pulse' to merge each tablespoon in. Stop the machine. Take off the lid of the processor bowl, sprinkle the grated beets, carrots and nuts over the top of the mixture and replace the lid. Using 'pulse' incorporate the vegetables into the mixture. Scoop into the greased and lined tin and bake for 1 hour in the pre-heated oven. Test with a sharp knife. If it comes out clean then the cake is cooked.

Wheat and Corn Muffins

Makes 12

150 g (5 oz) 100% wholemeal flour, plain
75 g (3 oz) corn meal
½ tsp sea salt
1 large egg
3 tbsp Sunwheel Cold Pressed Sunflower Oil
75 ml (3 fl oz) clear honey
300 ml (just over 10 fl oz) milk

Pre-heat the oven to 200°C/400°F/Gas Mark 6.

Mix the dry ingredients together. Whisk the egg, oil, honey and milk well and fold the liquid into the dry ingredients as lightly as possible with a fork. (Do not mix too much, just until the flour is blended into the liquid.) Spoon into well-oiled muffin tins or bun tins and bake for 20 minutes in the centre of the pre-heated oven.

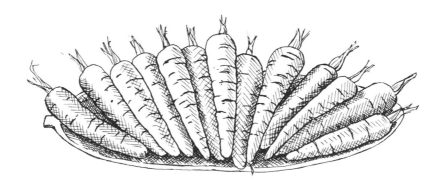

Biscuits

ALLINSON

Here is a selection of simple and tasty biscuit recipes taken from Allinson's *Wholewheat Cookery Book*.

Basic Creamed Biscuit Recipe

Makes 12–16 biscuits

This basic creamed biscuit recipe is easy to make and with different flavourings and ingredients can make a variety of biscuits.

75 g (3 oz) polyunsaturated margarine
75 g (3 oz) soft light brown sugar or *fruit sugar*
1 large egg
few drops of pure vanilla or *pure almond essence*
175 g (6 oz) Allinson 100% English Wholewheat or Farmhouse Flour, plain
pinch of salt
a little milk to mix

Pre-heat the oven to 180°C/350°F/Gas Mark 4.

Cream together the margarine and sugar. When light in colour, beat in the egg. Add the flavouring essence and then fold in the flour and salt. This should form a stiff paste. (If necessary add a little milk to bind the mixture.) Handle gently and place the dough on to a floured work surface. Roll out to about 5 mm/¼″ thickness and, using fancy cutters, cut into biscuits. Place on a greased baking sheet and bake in the pre-heated oven for 10–15 minutes until golden. Remove from the baking sheet and cool on a wire rack. These biscuits can be stored for several weeks in an airtight container.

Raisin and Hazelnut Biscuits

The variations are endless: you can add cinnamon or nutmeg, sesame or sunflower seeds, glacé cherries and chopped walnuts or coconut in the quantities given. Try this suggestion for raisin and hazelnut biscuits.

1 recipe quantity Basic Creamed Biscuit Recipe as above
75 g (3 oz) raisins
100 g (4 oz) hazelnuts, chopped

Pre-heat the oven to 180°C/350°F/Gas Mark 4.

Make up the basic biscuit recipe to the creaming stage. Then fold in 75 g/3 oz of the chopped hazelnuts and all the raisins. Fold in the flour and proceed as for the basic recipe. After placing the cut biscuits on to the baking sheet sprinkle the remaining 25 g/1 oz of chopped hazelnuts in the centre of each biscuit. Bake as for the basic recipe.

Bran Biscuits

Makes about 12 biscuits

A delicious high fibre biscuit, particularly good with cheese.

100 g (4 oz) Allinson 100% English Wholewheat Flour
1 level tsp baking powder
½ level tsp salt
25 g (1 oz) Allinson Broad Bran
25 g (1 oz) Allinson Bran Plus
100 g (4 oz) polyunsaturated margarine
50 g (2 oz) fruit sugar or *soft light brown sugar*
approx. 3 tbsp milk to mix
2–3 drops pure vanilla essence

Pre-heat the oven to 190°C/375°F/Gas Mark 5.

In a large bowl mix the flour, baking powder, salt and both brans. By hand, or with a fork, rub the margarine into the mixture. Stir in the sugar. Add the milk and form to a moist dough. Roll out on to a floured work surface to about 0.5 cm/¼″ thickness and cut into 5 cm/2″ rounds, or shape into two 17 cm/7″ circles and mark into wedges. Bake in the pre-heated oven for 15–20 minutes, until tinged a deeper brown and firm to the touch. They will firm up more when cooled on a wire rack.

Serve as a sweet biscuit, or they are delicious with cheese. They will store for several weeks in an airtight container. You can brush them with milk and sprinkle with extra bran or Demerara sugar before baking, for a more decorative biscuit.

BILLINGTON'S

Carob Biscuits

Makes about 48

225 g (8 oz) polyunsaturated margarine
75 g (3 oz) Billington's Muscovado Sugar
1 tsp vanilla essence
225 g (8 oz) 100% wholemeal flour, self-raising
50 g (2 oz) carob powder

Pre-heat the oven to 170°C/325°F/Gas Mark 3.

Cream the margarine, beat in the sugar and essence, then work in the carob powder and flour by degrees until the mixture is a paste consistency. Divide into pieces the size of a walnut, roll into balls and space at regular intervals on a greased tin. Flatten each one with a fork and bake in the pre-heated oven for approximately 12 minutes. Lift the biscuits carefully off the tin and on to a cooling rack.

Dutch Ginger Shortcake

Makes 20–24 biscuits

Very rich and only for those special occasions!

210 g (7½ oz) jar stem ginger in syrup
225 g (8 oz) unsalted butter
450 g (1 lb) 100% wholemeal flour, self-raising
225 g (8 oz) Billington's Light Muscovado Sugar
1 egg, beaten
100 g (4 oz) halved and blanched almonds

Grease and line a 32 cm × 23 cm/13″ × 9″ swiss roll tin with greased greaseproof paper. Pre-heat the oven to 180°C/350°F/Gas Mark 4.

Drain and chop the ginger, reserving the syrup. Rub the butter into the flour until the mixture resembles breadcrumbs, and then stir in the sugar. Mix in the beaten egg and ginger syrup and with floured hands knead together. Spread the mixture evenly into the prepared tin using the back of a floured wooden spoon, and press the chopped ginger and blanched almonds into the top of the cake. Bake in the centre of the pre-heated oven for 30–40 minutes, until lightly browned. Cool slightly then cut into fingers. When completely cold, remove from the tin and store in an airtight container.

Golden Peanut Biscuits

Makes about 48 biscuits

150 g (5 oz) smooth peanut butter
75 g (3 oz) polyunsaturated margarine
175 g (6 oz) Billington's Golden Granulated Sugar
1 egg
½ tsp vanilla essence
150 g (5 oz) 100% wholemeal flour, plain
½ tsp sea salt
½ tsp bicarbonate of soda

Pre-heat the oven to 190°C/375°F/Gas Mark 5.

Cream the peanut butter and margarine together, blending well. Beat in the sugar until the mixture is light and fluffy; then beat in the egg and vanilla essence. Sift the flour, salt and bicarbonate of soda and add to the creamed mixture in small portions, beating well each time until a dough forms. Roll the dough into 2.5 cm/1″ balls and place them 5 cm/2″ apart on an ungreased baking sheet. Flatten them by pressing with the back of a fork so that the prongs leave parallel furrows; turn the fork and press again, making furrows at right angles to the first ones. Bake the biscuits in the pre-heated oven for 10 minutes; the biscuits will still be soft when cooked. Leave to cool and crisp on the baking sheet, then store in an airtight tin.

Lemon Shortbread Fans

Makes 8 portions

100 g (4 oz) butter or *polyunsaturated margarine*
65 g (2½ oz) Billington's Golden Granulated Sugar
150 g (5 oz) brown wheatmeal flour, plain
3 tbsp brown rice flour
½ tsp salt
½ tsp baking powder

Topping
½ lemon
1 tbsp Billington's Golden Granulated Sugar

Grease a 18 cm/7″ fluted flan ring on a baking sheet, and dust with rice flour. Pre/heat the oven to 170°C/325°F/Gas Mark 3.

Cream the butter or margarine and the sugar until fluffy. Mix together the flour, rice flour, salt and baking powder, and work them into the creamed mixture. Press the blended mixture evenly into the flan ring. Shred the lemon rind on the coarse holes of a grater and sprinkle on top of the shortbread with the tablespoon of sugar. Bake in the pre-heated oven for 45 minutes. Cool slightly, then score into 8 segments and remove the flan ring. Cool completely before cutting apart. Store in an airtight tin.

CAFÉ HAG

Chewy Coffee Bars

Makes 16

175 g (6 oz) wholemeal flour
2 dessertspoons Café Hag Decaffeinated Instant Coffee Granules
½ tsp baking powder
pinch bicarbonate of soda
½ tsp salt
50 g (2 oz) low fat soft margarine
50 g (2 oz) walnut halves, roughly chopped
100 g (4 oz) Demerara sugar
2 tbsp clear honey
1 egg, lightly beaten
75 g (3 oz) dates, finely chopped

Pre-heat the oven to 180°C/350°F/Gas Mark 4. Grease a 28 cm × 18 cm/11″ × 7″ baking tin.

Mix together the flour, coffee granules, baking powder, bicarbonate of soda and salt. Rub in the soft margarine. Add all the other ingredients, mix well and pour into the prepared tin. Bake in the centre of the pre-heated oven for about 30 minutes. When cooked, mark into 16 slices and leave to cool in the tin for a few minutes, then carefully remove the slices and continue cooling on a wire rack.

DIETADE

Almond Petits Fours

Makes about 27

These melt in the mouth. You will need rice paper and a forcing bag fitted with a large rosette nozzle.

2 egg whites
100 g (4 oz) ground almonds
50 g (2 oz) Dietade Fruit Sugar
a few drops pure almond essence
a few glacé cherries, washed, patted dry and cut in half
a little angelica, cut in thin, small pieces

Pre-heat the oven to 180°C/350°F/Gas Mark 4.

Line the 3 baking trays with rice paper. Whisk the egg whites until stiff peaks form. Fold the ground almonds, sugar and almond essence into the stiff egg whites (do this lightly). Spoon the mixture into the forcing bag and pipe it on to the rice paper in rosettes. (You should get 9 on each tray.) Decorate the centre of each rosette with either a halved glacé cherry or a piece of angelica. Bake in the centre of the pre-heated oven for 20 minutes.

These are very delicate and must be baked in the centre of the oven, so you will need to bake them in 2 or 3 batches depending on the size of your trays.

Malted Sesame Biscuits

Makes 24

1 heaped tsp bicarbonate of soda
2 tbsp hot water
150 g (5 oz) polyunsaturated margarine
1 generous tbsp malt extract
75 g (3 oz) Dietade Fruit Sugar
a few drops natural vanilla essence
75 g (3 oz) sesame seeds
100 g (4 oz) 100% wholemeal flour, plain
75 g (3 oz) porridge oats

Pre-heat the oven to 150°C/300°F/Gas Mark 2.

Dissolve the bicarbonate of soda in the hot water. Melt the margarine and malt in a small saucepan over a pan of boiling water. Stir in the sugar and keep the mixture warm until the sugar has dissolved. Add a few drops of vanilla essence to the warm liquid. Put the sesame seeds, flour and oats into a mixing bowl and stir together. Pour the bicarbonate of soda mixture into the malt mixture, then add to the dry ingredients and mix all together. Roll into small balls and put on a well-oiled baking tray about 5 cm/2″ apart to allow for spreading. Bake for 20–25 minutes in the pre-heated oven. Leave to get cold on the baking tray.

Seed and Honey Snaps

Makes 24

1 tsp bicarbonate of soda
2 tsp hot water
2 tbsp clear honey
150 ml (5 fl oz) sunflower oil
50 g (2 oz) Dietade Fruit Sugar
40 g (1½ oz) sunflower seeds
40 g (1½ oz) pumpkin seeds
75 g (3 oz) medium oatmeal
100 g (4 oz) 100% wholemeal flour, plain
pinch sea salt (optional)
2 level tsp ground ginger

Pre-heat the oven to 150°C/300°F/Gas Mark 2.

Dissolve the soda in the hot water. Heat the honey, oil and fruit sugar in a small saucepan over a pan of boiling water until the sugar has dissolved. Grind the seeds until they are like small breadcrumbs (not powdered), in a food processor or blender. Put the seeds, oatmeal, flour, sea salt and ginger in a mixing bowl and stir together. Pour the honey and oil mixture plus the bicarbonate of soda mixture into the dry ingredients and mix well together. Roll into small balls and place on a well-oiled baking tray, 5 cm/2″ apart to allow for spreading. Bake in the pre-heated oven for 20–25 minutes. Cook on the baking tray until crisp.

Cashew and Cinnamon Snaps

Follow the recipe and instructions for Seed and Honey Snaps but replace the seeds and sugar with cashew nuts and ground cinnamon.

DOVES FARM

Buckaroons

Makes 12

50 g (2 oz) Doves Farm Maize Meal or Cornmeal
50 g (2 oz) Doves Farm Buckwheat Flour
50 g (2 oz) coconut, grated
100 g (4 oz) cooking apple, peeled, cored and
  grated
50 g (2 oz) Demerara sugar
2 tbsp water
1 large egg white, beaten
1 large apricot, cut into thin slices

Pre-heat the oven to 150°C/300°F/Gas Mark 2.

Mix together the maize meal, buckwheat flour, grated coconut, grated apple and sugar. Stir in the water and the beaten egg white. Form into little pyramids on rice paper or greased and floured tins. Press a thin sliver of apricot on top of each pyramid and bake in the pre-heated oven for 30 minutes.

Rye Ginger Biscuits

150 g (5 oz) Doves Farm Rye Flour
75 g (3 oz) porridge oats
2 tsp baking powder
2 tsp ground ginger
1 tsp brown sugar
½ tsp salt
50 g (2 oz) butter or *polyunsaturated margarine*
1 dsrtsp honey
1 dsrtsp golden syrup or *molasses*
2 dsrtsp lemon juice

Pre-heat the oven to 170°C/325°F/Gas Mark 3.

Place the rye flour, oats, baking powder, ginger, sugar and salt in a mixing bowl. In a saucepan melt the butter, honey, syrup and lemon juice, then add to the dry ingredients. Mix until the dough holds together. Break off walnut-sized pieces and flatten into biscuits with a fork on an oiled baking tray. Bake in the pre-heated oven for 20 minutes.

Traditional Shortbread

Makes 8 biscuits

150 g (5 oz) Doves Farm Brown Wheatmeal Flour, plain
pinch sea salt
25 g (1 oz) Doves Farm Brown Rice Flour
50 g (2 oz) fruit sugar
100 g (4 oz) butter, chilled and grated

Sift the flour, salt and rice flour into a mixing bowl and stir in the sugar and grated butter. With cool hands mix the ingredients together until like fine breadcrumbs. Press into a lightly greased 18 cm/7″ sandwich tin. Prick the top with a fork and cut into 8 equal portions (cut right through the mixture to the tin). Chill in the refrigerator for about 1 hour. Ten minutes before baking pre-heat the oven to 150°C/300°F/Gas Mark 2. Bake for 1 hour in the centre of the oven, then cool in the tin before placing on a wire rack. When firm and cold break into 8 wedges. Keep in an airtight tin.

FORCE

Carob Whole Wheat Flake Clusters

Makes 14–15

These are great for kids' parties.

225 g (8 oz) carob bar, plain
100 g (4 oz) Force Whole Wheat Flakes
50 g (2 oz) chopped hazelnuts
75 g (3 oz) raisins

Melt the carob in a bowl over a pan of hot water. Remove from heat and stir in the flakes, hazelnuts and raisins. Spoon the mixture into fluted paper bun cases, pressing the ingredients gently together. Leave to set in a cool place.

GRANNY ANN

Muesli Biscuits

Makes about 30

100 g (4 oz) polyunsaturated margarine
1 dsp Granny Ann Cookiemalt
1 dsp honey
100 g (4 oz) 100% wholewheat flour
2 tsp baking powder
75 g (3 oz) muesli
75 g (3 oz) raw cane sugar

Pre-heat the oven to 180°C/350°F/Gas Mark 4.

Melt the margarine over a low heat, then add the Cookiemalt and honey. Mix well. In a bowl combine the dry ingredients, and pour on the Cookiemalt liquid and mix well. To shape the biscuits, press small quantities of the mixture into a soup spoon. Place well apart on a greased baking tray and bake for 10 minutes in the pre-heated oven. Allow to cool on the baking tray for a few minutes, then transfer to a wire rack.

Coconut and Sesame Bars

Makes 30

1 tbsp Granny Ann Cookiemalt
100 g (4 oz) polyunsaturated margarine
100 g (4 oz) rolled oats
40 g (1½ oz) sesame seeds
75 g (3 oz) raw sugar
75 g (3 oz) desiccated coconut
1½ tsp sea salt

Grease a shallow baking tin, 25 cm/10″ square. Pre-heat the oven to 170°C/325°F/Gas Mark 3.

Melt the Cookiemalt with the margarine. Combine the dry ingredients in a mixing bowl, add the margarine and Cookiemalt and mix well. Press the mixture into the baking tin and bake for 15–20 minutes in the pre-heated oven. Cut into bars whilst still warm.

HÖFELS

Caraway Biscuits

Makes about 12 biscuits

100 g (4 oz) polyunsaturated margarine
50 g (2 oz) Demerara sugar
175 g (6 oz) Höfels 100% Wholemeal Norfolk Flour
1 level tsp baking powder
1 tsp caraway seeds

Pre-heat the oven to 230°C/450°F/Gas Mark 8.

Cream the margarine and sugar. Add the flour, baking powder and caraway seeds and mix to a firm dough. Knead well, then roll out on a floured board and cut into small rounds; bake on a lightly greased baking sheet for approximately 15 minutes in the pre-heated oven depending on thickness. The biscuits will be cooked when golden brown.

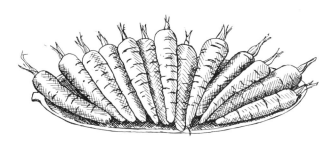

Carrot Biscuits

175 g (6 oz) Höfels 100% Wholemeal Norfolk Flour
1½ tbsp sunflower or corn oil
1 tbsp grated hazelnuts
175 g (6 oz) grated carrots
1 tbsp raisins
pinch Höfels Sea Salt
lemon rind, grated
a little cold water

Pre-heat the oven to 190°C/375°F/Gas Mark 5.

Put the flour in a bowl, make a hollow in the middle and pour in the oil. Begin to stir and add the hazelnuts, grated carrots, raisins, sea salt and grated lemon rind. Pour in water so as to obtain a mixture which sticks to the spatula. Place in spoonfuls on an oiled baking sheet and bake in the pre-heated oven for about 1 hour.

If you want a lighter biscuit, beat an egg white until stiff and add it to the mixture.

Digestive Biscuits

Makes about 24 biscuits

350 g (12 oz) Höfels 100% Wholemeal Norfolk Flour
150 g (5 oz) polyunsaturated margarine
50 g (2 oz) Demerara sugar
1 egg, beaten
approx. 4 tbsp of water
1 level tsp sea salt

Pre-heat the oven to 180°C/350°F/Gas Mark 4.

Mix the flour and salt, then rub in the margarine until the mixture resembles fine breadcrumbs. Add the sugar, beaten egg and enough of the water to make a soft dough; knead the dough on a floured board, then roll out to about 0.5 cm/¼″ thick and cut into rounds. Bake on a lightly greased baking sheet for 25–30 minutes, until golden brown. Do not overbake. These biscuits keep well in an airtight tin.

Oatmeal Biscuits

Makes 15

100 g (4 oz) Höfels Oatmeal
75 g (3 oz) Höfels 100% Wholemeal Norfolk Flour
1 tsp Höfels Sea Salt
65 g (2½ oz) white Flora or polyunsaturated margarine
½ tsp baking powder
cold water to mix

Pre-heat the oven to 200°C/400°F/Gas Mark 6.

Mix the dry ingredients well. Rub in the Flora or margarine, then mix with cold water to a stiff dough. Roll out on a floured board. Using a medium cutter, cut out about 15 biscuits. Bake on a greased tray for 15 minutes in the pre-heated oven.

If a sweeter biscuit is preferred add 25 g/1 oz of sugar with the dry ingredients.

Soya Flake Macaroons

Makes about 24

150 g (5 oz) Höfels 100% Wholemeal Norfolk Flour
3 level tsp of baking powder
pinch of Höfels Sea Salt
75 g (3 oz) polyunsaturated margarine
150 g (5 oz) Höfels Soya Flakes
75 g (3 oz) Demerara sugar
2 tbsp milk

Pre-heat the oven to 180°C/350°F/Gas Mark 4.

Mix together the flour, baking powder and salt. Rub in the margarine, add the soya flakes and sugar, mixing well in. Bind with the milk, then roll into walnut-sized balls and flatten slightly. Bake on a greased baking sheet for 20 minutes.

Soya and Millet Crunch

Makes about 16–20 portions

100 g (4 oz) polyunsaturated margarine
2 generous tbsp of honey
100 g (4 oz) Höfels Soya Flakes
100 g (4 oz) millet flakes
50 g (2 oz) Demerara sugar

Pre-heat the oven to 190°C/375°F/Gas Mark 5.

Put the margarine and honey in a pan and melt them gently, then add the soya flakes, millet flakes and sugar and stir well. Remove from the heat, press the mixture into a greased tin (a swiss roll tin would be suitable) and bake for 25 minutes in the pre-heated oven. Remove from the oven and mark into squares. Leave to cool in the tin.

HOLLAND & BARRETT

Honey Ginger Nuts

Makes 12 biscuits

75 g (3 oz) polyunsaturated margarine
*175 g (6 oz) 100% wholemeal flour, self-raising or
    plain with 1 tsp baking powder*
1 dsrtsp ground ginger
pinch sea salt
1 large egg, beaten
1–2 tbsp Holland & Barrett Honey

Pre-heat the oven to 180°C/350°F/Gas Mark 4.

Rub the margarine into the flour until you have a fine breadcrumb-like mixture. Add the ginger and salt then the beaten egg and honey. Mix well to form a soft but not too sticky dough. Chill in the refrigerator for 30 minutes. Roll out and cut into rounds. Place well spaced apart on a greased baking tray and flatten each biscuit slightly. Bake for 15–20 minutes in the pre-heated oven.

This biscuit dough can be frozen in a roll and when it is partly thawed, sliced up into rounds and baked. The dough will keep for 2 months in the freezer.

Honey Flapjacks

Makes 6–8 portions

50 g (2 oz) brown wheatmeal flour
100 g (4 oz) porridge oats
150 ml (15 fl oz) Holland & Barrett Honey
75 g (3 oz) polyunsaturated margarine

Pre-heat the oven to 180°C/350°F/Gas Mark 4.

Mix the flour and porridge oats in a bowl. Put the honey and the margarine together in a saucepan to melt. Add the melted liquid to the oats and flour and stir well. Pour the mixture into an oiled baking tray – a deep, square one or a round flan tin. The flapjacks should not be too thinly spread. Bake for 20–25 minutes in the pre-heated oven and cut into triangles or fingers while still hot. They are delicious hot or cold. These keep well in an airtight tin.

Mincemeat Flapjacks

Makes 8 portions

75 g (3 oz) polyunsaturated margarine
2 tbsp Holland & Barrett Clear Honey
3 tbsp mincemeat
175 g (6 oz) rolled oats

Pre-heat the oven to 170°C/325°F/Gas Mark 3.

Place the margarine with the honey and mince-meat in a saucepan and heat gently until the margarine has melted. Remove from the heat and stir in the oats. Lightly grease a 17 cm/7″ sandwich tin and press in the oat mixture. Bake in the centre of the pre-heated oven for 25 minutes until golden brown. Place the tin on a wire cooling tray and mark the flapjacks into 8 segments. Leave in the tin until quite cold. Store in an airtight container.

Sesame and Sunflower Seed Crunch Bars

Makes about 16

100 g (4 oz) sunflower margarine
50 g (2 oz) Muscovado sugar
1 tbsp Holland & Barrett Honey
175 g (6 oz) Holland & Barrett Jumbo Oats
50 g (2 oz) sunflower seeds
50 g (2 oz) sesame seeds

Grease a 30 cm × 23 cm/12″ × 9″ shallow oven tin, and line the base with greaseproof paper. Pre-heat the oven to 180°C/350°F/Gas Mark 4.

Toast the sunflower seeds and sesame seeds for 15 minutes in the oven. Melt the margarine, sugar and honey in a medium-sized saucepan over a pan of hot water. Remove from the heat, mix well together and stir in the other ingredients. Spread the mixture evenly into the prepared baking tray and bake for 15 minutes until golden brown. While still hot, with a sharp knife cut into finger slices, making sure that you cut right through to the tin. Leave to cool in the tin. When cold break off into individual bars.

HOLLY MILL

Crunchy Muesli Bars

Makes 16

100 g (4 oz) polyunsaturated margarine
100 g (4 oz) raw cane syrup
50 g (2 oz) dark brown sugar
1 tsp ground ginger
175 g (6 oz) Holly Mill Muesli
50 g (2 oz) stoned dates, chopped

Lightly grease a 28 cm × 18 cm/11″ × 7″ swiss roll tin. Pre-heat the oven to 180°C/350°F/Gas Mark 4.

Melt together the margarine, syrup and brown sugar. Stir in the ground ginger, muesli and dates and mix thoroughly. Pour into the prepared tin and spread evenly. Bake in the centre of the pre-heated oven for 30 minutes until golden brown. Whilst still warm cut into 16 bars and cool on a wire rack.

KALIBU

Carob Bourbons

Makes 6 complete biscuits

100 g (4 oz) polyunsaturated margarine
50 g (2 oz) raw cane sugar
1 dsrtsp natural yoghurt
150 g (5 oz) 100% wholemeal flour
25 g (1 oz) carob powder
75 g (3 oz) Kalibu Carob *Bar (for filling)*

Pre-heat the oven to 180°C/350°F/Gas Mark 4.

Cream the margarine and sugar together thoroughly and then add the yoghurt. Fold in the flour and carob powder – the mixture should be fairly stiff. Roll the mixture out fairly thinly and cut into 12 rectangles each measuring approximately 7.5 cm × 2.5 cm/3″ × 1″. Put on to a well-greased baking tray and prick each biscuit with a fork. Bake for about 10–12 minutes in the pre-heated oven. Lift the biscuits off the baking tray carefully with a spatula and leave to cool on a wire rack. Melt the carob in a bowl over a pan of hot water and use to sandwich the biscuits together.

Carob-coated Digestive Biscuits

Makes about 15–20

225 g (8 oz) 100% wholemeal flour
100 g (4 oz) polyunsaturated margarine
50 g (2 oz) raw cane sugar
1 egg, beaten
2 tbsp natural yoghurt
1 tbsp clear honey

Coating
100 g (4 oz) Kalibu Carob Bar, *plain*
1 dsrtsp milk

Pre-heat the oven to 180°C/350°F/Gas Mark 4.

Put the flour into a large mixing bowl and rub in the margarine until the mixture resembles fine breadcrumbs. Mix in the sugar, beaten egg, yoghurt and honey, blending all the ingredients together well. Roll out on a floured board and cut into 5 cm/ 2″ rounds with a plain cutter. Place on a well-greased baking tray and bake for about 25 minutes in the pre-heated oven. Cool on a wire rack.

While the biscuits are cooling, melt the block carob in a bowl over a pan of hot water. When melted, stir in the milk and blend well. Cover one side of each biscuit with the carob coating and leave to set.

Carob Macaroons

Makes about 10

1 egg white
50 g (2 oz) ground almonds
25 g (1 oz) Kalibu Carob Powder
25 g (1 oz) raw cane sugar
½ tsp almond essence
whole blanched almonds to decorate

Line a baking tray with rice paper or non-stick paper. Pre-heat the oven to 180°C/350°F/Gas Mark 4.

Whisk the egg white until stiff. Fold in the ground almonds, carob powder, sugar and almond essence. Put spoonsful of the mixture on to the prepared baking sheet, allowing room for the mixture to spread during cooking. Place a whole blanched almond in the centre of each macaroon and bake for about 20–25 minutes in the pre-heated oven until firm.

Carob Muesli Bites

Makes about 15–18

100 g (4 oz) Kalibu Carob Bar, *plain*
50 g (2 oz) polyunsaturated margarine
1 tbsp clear honey
175 g (6 oz) muesli
50 g (2 oz) almond nibs

Break the carob bar into pieces and melt in a pan with the margarine over a gentle heat. When melted, remove from the heat and stir in the honey. Lastly add the muesli and almond nibs, mixing well. Drop spoonsful of the mixture into small fluted paper cases and leave in the refrigerator to set.

Carob Rolled Oat Slices

Makes about 10

100 g (4 oz) Kalibu Carob Bar, *plain*
100 g (4 oz) polyunsaturated margarine
1 tbsp clear honey
225 g (8 oz) rolled oats
50 g (2 oz) desiccated coconut

Pre-heat the oven to 180°C/350°F/Gas Mark 4.

Break the carob bar into pieces and place in a saucepan. Add the margarine and honey and melt together over a gentle heat. Remove from the heat and add the rolled oats and coconut, mixing thoroughly. Spread the mixture evenly on to a greased shallow baking tin and bake for about 20– 25 minutes in the pre-heated oven. Leave to cool in the tin for a minute or two and, while still in the baking tin, cut into individual slices. Remove from the tin when completely cold.

KRETSCHMER

Chewy Apricot Bars

Makes 20 bars

75 g (3 oz) 100% wholemeal flour, plain
40 g (1½ oz) Kretschmer Wheat Germ, Plain
¼ tsp sea salt
3 eggs
100 g (4 oz) fruit sugar
150 g (5 oz) dried apricots, chopped
150 g (5 oz) walnuts, chopped
75 g (3 oz) desiccated coconut

Pre-heat the oven to 180°C/350°F/Gas Mark 4.

Mix together the flour, wheat germ and salt and stir well to blend. Beat the eggs until foamy. Add the sugar gradually, beating until the mixture is light-coloured and fluffy. Stir in the flour mixture and remaining ingredients and mix well. Spread evenly in a greased 23 cm/9″ square tin and bake in the pre-heated oven for 20–25 minutes until lightly browned. Cut into bars whilst slightly warm, then cool on a wire rack.

Fruit, Nut and Wheat Germ Roll

This is my own recipe using Kretschmer Wheat Germ. Naturally sweet and full of goodness!

225 g (8 oz) dates
100 g (4 oz) dried apricots, well washed
50 g (2 oz) Kretschmer Wheat Germ, Plain
225 g (8 oz) raisins
225 g (8 oz) mixed nuts and sunflower seeds
a few toasted sesame seeds for coating

Steam the dates and apricots for 20 minutes in a colander, putting the apricots at the bottom. When steamed, stir in the wheat germ. Put all the ingredients except the sesame seeds through a mincer, then knead the mixture well together for 1 minute. Roll into a sausage shape or cut into finger slices and coat with sesame seeds, pressing the seeds firmly into the mixture.

Old Fashioned Oatmeal Cookies

Makes 36

175 g (6 oz) porridge oats
50 g (2 oz) Kretschmer Wheat Germ, Plain
100 g (4 oz) fruit sugar or Demerara sugar
75 g (3 oz) raisins, chopped nuts, chopped prunes,
*   mixed dried fruit or flaked coconut*
½ tsp sea salt
1 tsp ground cinnamon
¼ tsp ground cloves
100 ml (4 fl oz) sunflower oil
2 eggs
flaked coconut, walnut or pecan halves for topping

Pre-heat the oven to 180°C/350°F/Gas Mark 4.

Mix together the oats, wheat germ, sugar, fruit or nuts, salt and spices until well blended. Beat the oil and eggs together in a large bowl, stir in the dry ingredients and mix well together. Drop the mixture in teaspoonsful on to greased baking sheets, decorate with flaked coconut, walnut or pecan halves and bake in the pre-heated oven for 10–12 minutes until lightly browned. When cooked, remove the cookies from the baking sheet immediately and cool on a wire rack. To store, put greaseproof paper between layers of biscuits in an airtight tin.

Refrigerator Rounds

Makes 36–40

175 g (6 oz) 100% wholemeal flour, plain
50 g (2 oz) Kretschmer Wheat Germ, Plain or Brown
*   Sugar and Honey*
50 g (2 oz) flaked almonds
225 g (8 oz) softened butter or polyunsaturated
*   margarine (see note below if using margarine)*
4 tbsp fruit sugar or Demerara sugar
1 tsp vanilla essence
1 tsp almond essence
1–2 tbsp Kretschmer Wheat Germ, Plain

Combine the flour, the 50 g/2 oz wheat germ and the almonds in a bowl and stir well. Cream the butter, sugar and flavouring essences thoroughly. Add the blended dry ingredients to the creamed mixture and mix well. Shape the dough into a 23 cm × 5 cm/9″ × 2″ roll, wrap in foil or plastic wrap and refrigerate for 1 hour or freeze for 30 minutes until firm (see note below). Pre-heat the oven to 180°C/350°F/Gas Mark 4. Cut the dough with a sharp knife into 0.5 cm/¼" slices. Dip one side of each slice into the extra wheat germ and place, wheat germ side up, on ungreased baking sheets and bake in the pre-heated oven for 12–15 minutes until lightly browned. Leave for 1 minute before removing from the baking sheet, then cool on a wire rack.

Note If you use margarine, refrigerate the dough for 4 hours or overnight before slicing.

Aniseed Refrigerator Rounds

Prepare as directed above but add 1 teaspoon crushed aniseed and omit the almonds and almond essence.

Lemon Refrigerator Rounds

Prepare as directed above but add 1 teaspoon grated lemon rind and omit the almonds and almond essence.

Wheat Germ Gingersnaps
Makes 36

200 g (7 oz) 100% wholemeal flour, plain
40 g (1½ oz) Kretschmer Wheat Germ, Plain
½ tsp bicarbonate of soda
¼ tsp salt
1½ tsp ground ginger
½ tsp cinnamon
¼ tsp ground cloves
100 g (4 oz) Demerara sugar
100 g (4 oz) polyunsaturated margarine
1 egg
2 tbsp blackstrap molasses
2 tbsp lemon juice
1 tsp grated lemon rind
extra wheat germ for topping

Combine the flour, wheat germ, bicarbonate of soda, salt and spices together. Stir well to blend. Cream the sugar and margarine thoroughly. Beat in the egg. Add the molasses, lemon juice and rind to the creamed mixture, beating well, then add the blended dry ingredients to the creamed mixture and mix well. Refrigerate the dough for 30 minutes. Pre-heat the oven to 180°C/350°F/Gas Mark 4. Shape the dough into 2.5 cm/1" balls. Dip the tops of the balls into the extra wheat germ and place, dipped side up, about 7.5 cm/3" apart on greased baking sheets. Bake in the pre-heated oven for 12–15 minutes until

lightly browned. Remove from the baking sheet and cool on a wire rack.

Wheat Germ Granola Bars
Makes 24 bars

225 g (8 oz) porridge oats
50 g (2 oz) desiccated coconut
100 g (4 oz) peanuts or other nuts, chopped
50 g (2 oz) polyunsaturated margarine
40 g (1½ oz) Barbados sugar
3 tbsp clear honey
1 tsp pure vanilla essence
1 level tsp grated lemon rind
40 g (1½ oz) Kretschmer Wheat Germ, Plain
75 g (3 oz) raisins or dried apricots, chopped

Pre-heat the oven to 150°C/300°F/Gas Mark 2.

Mix together the oats, coconut and chopped nuts in a greased 23 cm/9" square tin. Toss well and bake in the pre-heated oven for 20 minutes, tossing occasionally. Remove from the oven. Increase the oven temperature to 180°C/350°F/Gas Mark 4.

Put the margarine, sugar and honey into a medium saucepan, stir well to blend and cook over a medium heat until the margarine melts. Remove from the heat and stir in the vanilla and lemon rind. Trickle the butter mixture over the oat mixture, add the wheat germ and raisins or apricots and toss well. Press into the baking tin and bake for 10 minutes, until lightly browned. Cool in the tin. When cold, cut into bars. These can be wrapped individually in clingfilm or foil if desired.

MARRIAGE'S

Lemon Wholemeal Biscuits

Makes 28

100 g (4 oz) polyunsaturated margarine
100 g (4 oz) moist brown sugar
rind of 1 large or *2 small lemons, finely grated*
1 egg, beaten
150 g (6 oz) Marriage's 100% Wholemeal Flour, self-raising
pinch salt
75 g (3 oz) currants
40 g (1½ oz) bran

Pre-heat the oven to 190°C/375°F/Gas Mark 5.

Cream the margarine, sugar and finely grated lemon peel until light and fluffy. Mix in the beaten egg alternately with the flour and salt and add the currants. Roll teaspoonsful of the mixture into bran to form a ball, place on greased baking trays and flatten the balls of mixture to half their depth. Bake in the pre-heated oven for 15–20 minutes. Place on a wire rack to cool.

Mixed Fruit Slices

Makes 20 portions

Filling
275 ml (10 fl oz) boiling water
50 g (20 oz) raisins
50 g (2 oz) sultanas
50 g (2 oz) currants
1 large cooking apple, peeled, cored and chopped
juice and grated rind of 1 large lemon

Base
150 ml (5 fl oz) boiling water
75 g (3 oz) rolled oats
75 g (3 oz) Marriage's 100% Wholemeal Flour, self-raising
25 g (1 oz) desiccated coconut
75 ml (3 il oz) sunflower oil

Topping
3 eggs
50 g (2 oz) soft brown sugar
150 g (5 oz) Marriage's 100% Wholemeal Flour, self-raising

Lightly oil a swiss roll tin 31 cm × 23 cm/12″ × 9″. Pre-heat the oven to 180°C/350°F/Gas Mark 4.

Bring the filling ingredients to the boil and simmer for 10 minutes. Allow to cool. Meanwhile mix all base ingredients together and press into the lightly oiled swiss roll tin. Cover with the fruit mixture. Beat the eggs and sugar together until thick and creamy. Very carefully fold in the flour, spread over the fruit and bake in the pre-heated oven for 40–45 minutes. Mark into 20 squares and allow to cool in the tin for 5 minutes, then remove and leave to cool on a wire rack.

Spicy Lemon Shortbread

Makes 16 portions

175 g (6 oz) Marriage's 100% Wholemeal Flour, self-raising
1 tsp mixed spice
150 g (5 oz) polyunsaturated margarine
50 g (2 oz) soft brown sugar
grated rind of 1 large lemon

Pre-heat the oven to 150°C/300°F/Gas Mark 2.

Knead all the ingredients together well and divide in half. Press into two 18 cm/7″ sandwich tins and mark each into 8 segments. Bake in the pre-heated oven for 45 minutes. Score the segment divisions again and allow to cool in the tin for 10 minutes. Remove from the tin and leave to cool on a wire rack. When cold, break the shortbread along the scored lines.

NATURE'S BOUNTY

Bran 'N' Fig Biscuits

These are a tasty high-fibre biscuit.

100 g (4 oz) 100% wholemeal flour, plain
1 level tsp baking powder
50 g (2 oz) Nature's Bounty Bran 'N' Fig
100 g (4 oz) polyunsaturated margarine
good pinch sea salt
50 g (2 oz) fruit sugar or *Barbados sugar*
3 tbsp milk
few drops vanilla essence
1 tbsp Nature's Bounty Bran 'N' Fig to decorate

Pre-heat the oven to 160°C/325°F/Gas Mark 3.

Put the flour, baking powder and Bran 'N' Fig into a mixing bowl, rub in the margarine, then stir in the salt and sugar. Pour in the milk and form a softish dough. Roll out on a floured surface to approximately 5 mm/¼" thick and cut into biscuit shapes with a cutter. Place on oiled and lined baking trays, brush each with a little milk and sprinkle on the Bran 'N' Fig. Bake in the pre-heated oven for just under 20 minutes until a rich, warm brown. Cool on a wire rack where they will become firm. Store in an airtight container.

NATURE'S WAY

Walnut Bars

Makes about 28

100 g (4 oz) plus 2 teaspoons butter or
  polyunsaturated margarine
175 g (6 oz) Demerara sugar
1 egg
2 dsrtsp decaffeinated coffee granules
175 g (6 oz) brown wheatmeal flour, self-raising
225 g (8 oz) Nature's Way Walnuts, *coarsely*
  chopped
3 egg whites

With the 2 teaspoons of butter or margarine, grease an 18 cm × 28 cm/7″ × 11″ baking tin. Pre-heat the oven to 180°C/350°F/Gas Mark 4.

In a small mixing bowl cream the remaining butter with 50 g/2 oz of the sugar until the mixture is light and creamy. Beat in the egg, stir in the coffee granules, then add the flour a little at a time and beat well to blend. Turn the mixture into the prepared tin, spreading it out evenly. Bake in the oven for 15 minutes.

Meanwhile, in a saucepan combine the walnuts, the remaining sugar and the egg whites. Place the saucepan over a low heat, stirring constantly, and cook the mixture until the sugar has dissolved, then increase the heat to moderate and continue cooking, stirring frequently, for 10 minutes, or until the mixture leaves the sides of the pan. Remove the baking tin from the oven, spread the walnut mixture over the pastry with a table knife, return the tin to the oven and continue baking for another 15 minutes. Leave to cool before cutting into 8 cm × 2.5 cm/3″ × 1″ bars.

PLAMIL

Walnut Cookies

Makes about 12

For anyone not used to making their own biscuits, 'cookies' such as these are the simplest, as rolling out is not necessary.

150 g (5 oz) plain wholemeal flour
1 tsp soya flour
½ tsp bicarbonate of soda
¾ tsp cream of tartar
40 g (1½ oz) ground walnuts
50 g (2 oz) medium oatmeal
50 g (2 oz) vegetable fat
50 g (2 oz) Barbados sugar
diluted Plamil
3 or 4 roughly chopped walnuts

Pre-heat the oven to 190°C/375°F/Gas Mark 5.

Mix the raising ingredients with the flours and add the walnuts and oatmeal. Cream the fat and sugar, then mix in the dry ingredients, adding just enough diluted Plamil to bind (about 2 tablespoons). Knead, form into small balls and place on greased baking sheets, leaving plenty of space between them to allow them to spread. Press a few walnut chips into the top of each cookie and flatten slightly. Bake for 10–12 minutes in the pre-heated oven and allow to cool and become crisp before removing from the trays.

Hazelnuts can be used in place of walnuts, but if these are used 50 g/2 oz will be required as they contain less fat than walnuts.

PREWETT'S

Refrigerator Biscuits

Makes about 48

225 g (8 oz) Prewett's Millstone Brown Wheatmeal
   Flour, *plain*
1 level tsp baking powder
150 g (5 oz) Prewett's Sunflower Margarine, *chilled*
175 g (6 oz) Prewett's Light Muscovado Sugar
1 tsp vanilla essence
1 egg, beaten
grated rind of 1 orange (optional)
50 g (2 oz) bar carob or *plain chocolate*
50 g (2 oz) almonds or *hazelnuts, ground*
light Muscovado sugar to dust (optional)

Sift the flour and baking powder into a mixing bowl.
Cream the margarine and sugar together until light
and fluffy, then add the vanilla, beaten egg and
orange rind if used. Grate the carob or chocolate
bar. Gradually, with a light touch, incorporate the
flour, and finally stir in the grated carob or chocolate and the ground nuts, again with a light touch.
Form into a dough. Shape the dough into a 5 cm/2″
wide long sausage shape on a lightly floured
surface. Wrap in foil and chill in the refrigerator for
2–3 hours.
   When ready to bake, pre-heat the oven to 190°C/
375°F/Gas Mark 5. Cut thin rounds from the roll and
place (well spaced) on a lightly oiled baking sheet.
Sprinkle a little sugar (optional) on each and bake
for 10 minutes. Cool on a wire rack.

WHOLE EARTH

Marmalade Cookies

These cookies have a very light sweetness and
those with a sweeter tooth may want to add a few
teaspoons of honey to the recipe.

225 g (8 oz) oatmeal
100 g (4 oz) Whole Earth Orange Crunch Cereal
175 g (6 oz) butter, polyunsaturated margarine or
   sunflower oil
50 g (2 oz) chopped nuts or *sunflower seeds* or
   sesame seeds
100 g (4 oz) Whole Earth Orange Marmalade
40 g (1½ oz) desiccated coconut
1 egg
1 tsp vanilla essence

Pre-heat the oven to 180°C/350°F/Gas Mark 4.
   Combine the ingredients, place teaspoonsful on
an oiled tray about 2.5 cm/1″ apart and bake for 15
minutes in the pre-heated oven.

Peanut Butter Cookies

approx. 2 level tbsp Whole Earth Peanut Butter
100 g (4 oz) porridge oats
100 g (4 oz) wholemeal flour
50 g (2 oz) desiccated coconut (unsweetened)
1 egg
100 ml (4 fl oz) vegetable oil
4 tbsp honey

Thoroughly mix together the oil and honey, then stir
in the egg. Add all the other ingredients and stir
until well mixed. Drop teaspoon dollops on to a
baking tray and flatten to about 0.5 cm/¼″ with a
fork. Pre-heat the oven and bake for 10–12 minutes
at 180°C/350°F/Gas Mark 4.

9
HOT PUDDINGS

ALLINSON

The next two recipes are taken from Allinson's *Wholewheat Cookery Book*.

Farmhouse Apple Pudding

Serves 4

*450 g (1 lb) cooking apples, peeled, cored and
  sliced
juice and grated rind of 1 orange
25 g (1 oz) soft brown sugar
225 g (8 oz) Allinson Farmhouse Flour, self-raising
  or Allinson 100% English Wholewheat Flour plus
  3 level tsp baking powder
1 tbsp soft brown sugar
50 g (2 oz) polyunsaturated margarine
3–4 tbsp milk-and-water (1/2 and 1/2 mixed)
3 tbsp marmalade*

You will need a 1 litre/2 pint oven-proof dish about 20 cm/8" across. Pre-heat the oven to 190°C/375°F/ Gas Mark 5.

Prepare the apples and place in a saucepan with the orange rind and juice and the sugar. Cover the pan and simmer over a gentle heat until the apple is tender, but not broken up. Put into the oven-proof dish and allow to cool.

Measure the flour and sugar into a mixing bowl and rub in the margarine. Stir in the milk-and-water, bringing it together gently by hand into a soft dough. Cover the bowl and refrigerate for about 5 minutes.

Roll out the scone dough to a rectangle 25 cm × 20 cm/10" × 8". Spread the dough with the marmalade, then roll up from the long edge into a swiss roll shape. Cut the roll into 8–10 pieces and lay them, cut side uppermost, on top of the apple mixture. Bake in the pre-heated oven for about 15– 20 minutes, until the apple mixture is hot and the scone topping is risen and baked to a golden brown. Serve hot with custard, cream or ice- cream.

Spotted Dick

Serves 4

*100 g (4 oz) Allinson 100% English Wholewheat
  Flour or Farmhouse Flour, plain
1/4 level tsp salt
1 1/2 level tsp baking powder
100 g (4 oz) wholewheat breadcrumbs
75 g (3 oz) soft brown sugar
75 g (3 oz) shredded suet
1 egg (size 3–4), beaten
6–8 tbsp cold milk*

Grease a 1 litre/2 pint pudding basin.

Mix the flour, salt and baking powder in a bowl. Stir in the breadcrumbs, sugar and suet. Beat the egg with the milk, add to the dry ingredients and mix well. Put the mixture into the prepared basin, then cover with greaseproof paper and foil or a pudding cloth. Steam in a deep saucepan for 2 1/2–3 hours (or about 1 1/2 hours in a pressure cooker – see manufacturer's handbook for details).

When cooked, turn out on to a warm plate and serve with custard or a sweet sauce and sprinkle with Demerara sugar.

BILLINGTON'S

Figgy Pudding

Serves 4–6

225 g (8 oz) dried figs
100 g (4 oz) wholemeal breadcrumbs
50 g (2 oz) 100% wholemeal flour, plain
½ tsp bicarbonate of soda
1 tsp cream of tartar
½ tsp grated nutmeg
½ tsp ground allspice
pinch salt
50 g (2 oz) Billington's Golden Granulated Sugar
100 g (4 oz) shredded vegetarian suet
2 eggs
150 ml (5 fl oz) milk

Well grease a 1 litre/2 pint pudding basin.

Chop the figs coarsely; if possible use a food processor. Put them in a bowl and mix evenly with the breadcrumbs, flour, raising agents, spices, salt and sugar. Add the suet. Whisk the eggs with half the milk and use to bind the dry mixture. Add the remaining milk slowly, to obtain a stiff dropping consistency. Transfer the mixture to the prepared basin and seal securely with buttered greaseproof paper and foil. Place in a pan of simmering water which comes halfway up the basin's sides, and steam for 3 hours. When cooked, leave for 6–8 minutes in the basin to firm up, then turn out on to a warmed serving dish. Serve with freshly made hot custard flavoured with sweet sherry.

BROADLAND

Kiwi Fruit and Ginger Pudding

Makes 12 individual puddings

You can use yoghurt cheese instead of cream – it's delicious with ginger and fruit sugar.

450 g (1 lb) 100% wholemeal flour, self-raising
5 g (¼ oz) ground ginger
225 g (8 oz) Broadland Vegetable Suet
100 g (4 oz) fruit sugar

3 eggs (size 3) beaten with 275 ml (½ pt) milk
100 g (4 oz) crystallized ginger, diced
3 kiwi fruit, peeled and sliced
lightly whipped double cream flavoured with ginger and fruit sugar

Sieve the flour and ground ginger together, mix in the vegetable suet and fruit sugar and beat in the milk and eggs. Arrange the crystallized ginger in the base of 12 individual dariole moulds. Fill each mould ¾ full with mixture. Cover with greased greaseproof paper or aluminium foil and steam for 75 minutes. Unmould and surround with sliced kiwi fruit. Serve the flavoured cream separately.

DIETADE

Bananas in Caramel Sauce

Serves 3

1½ level tbsp Dietade Fruit Sugar
2 tbsp water
4 ripe bananas

Make a caramel by dissolving the fruit sugar in the water and heating until just a golden brown. Arrange the bananas in an ovenproof dish or on a plate over a saucepan of hot water. Pour the caramel sauce over them and cook slowly for about 10–15 minutes, basting them frequently with the caramel. Transfer the bananas to a dish and pour the remainder of the caramel over them; serve with ice-cream wafers or sprinkle with a few crushed cornflakes.

Lemon Cheese Soufflé

Serves 4

225 g (8 oz) cottage cheese
3 eggs, separated
juice of 1 lemon
grated rind of 2 lemons
25 g (1 oz) Dietade Fruit Sugar
8 g (¼ oz) polyunsaturated margarine

Pre-heat the oven to 200°C/400°F/Gas Mark 6.

Sieve the cottage cheese and mix with the egg yolks, lemon juice and grated rind. Mix in the fruit sugar. Whisk the egg whites stiffly and fold into mixture. Grease a soufflé dish with the margarine, tie greaseproof paper to 5 cm/2″ above the rim, fill with the mixture and stand the dish on a baking tray. Bake in the pre-heated oven for about 25 minutes until risen and set. Serve immediately.

DOVES FARM

—Baked Butterscotch— Pudding

50 g (2 oz) butter
100 g (4 oz) Doves Farm Wholewheat Semolina
75 g (3 oz) raw cane sugar
575 ml (1 pint) milk

Pre-heat the oven to 200°C/400°F/Gas Mark 6.

Melt the butter in a saucepan, stir in the semolina and brown sugar and cook for 1 minute. Continue stirring while adding the milk, and bring to the boil. Pour into a buttered oven-proof dish and bake in the pre-heated oven for 30 minutes.

—Chilled Butterscotch Dessert—

Follow the instructions for the baked pudding, but simmer very gently for 15–20 minutes, then pour into individual dishes and allow to cool. Then place in the refrigerator for about 1 hour. Decorate with a little cream before serving.

—Buckwheat, Apple— and Raisin Fritters

90 g (3½ oz) Doves Farm Buckwheat Flour
100 g (4 oz) Doves Farm Fine-Milled 100% Wholemeal Flour
a little sea salt (about ¼ tsp)
275 ml (10 fl oz) water
3 tbsp sunflower oil
1 large free range egg
2 heaped tbsp raisins, puréed in a blender

2 large cooking apples, peeled and cut into small pieces
¼ tsp clove powder
¼ tsp cinnamon
a little fruit sugar to serve (optional)

Sieve the flours into a bowl with the sea salt. Stir in the oil with half the water and the egg and blend using a fork until a smooth paste is formed. Gradually add the remaining water. Stir in the raisin purée, apples and spices. To cook, drop table-spoons of the mixture into about 1.5 cm/½″ of hot sunflower oil. Fry until a light golden brown and bubbly on one side. Flip over and cook the other side over moderate heat until it is also a light golden brown. Serve sprinkled with a little fruit sugar if desired.

—Fruit Fritters—

75 g (3 oz) Doves Farm Brown Wheatmeal Flour, plain
25 g (1 oz) Doves Farm Gram Flour (chick pea flour)
pinch sea salt
1 tbsp sunflower oil
150 ml (5 fl oz) water
1 egg white
choice of fruit from the following:
3 medium cooking apples (leave skins on) cored and thinly sliced
or
3 medium bananas, peeled, cut lengthwise and then cut into 3, making 18 pieces
or
1 small pineapple, skinned, cut into rings and hard centres removed with a small cutter
or
3 medium peaches, skinned by dropping in boiling water for ½ minute only, then cut in half, stones removed and fruit sliced into thin rings
soya oil for deep frying

Sieve the flours together, add the salt and make a well in the centre of the dry ingredients. Using a food processor or blender, or by hand, whisk the oil, water and egg white together, then gradually stir the mixture into the flour. Leave to stand for 1 hour before using. Dip your chosen fruit into the batter and fry in deep, hot oil until golden brown.

Little Maize Pancakes

Here is another family favourite from Clare Marriage using stoneground maize meal (whole corn meal). The pancakes can be made sweet or savoury. Maize meal is *gluten free* and ideal for those on a gluten-free and wheat-free diet.

100 g (4 oz) Doves Farm Maize Meal or Cornmeal
1 egg
150 ml (5 fl oz) milk
grated rind and juice of 1 orange
25 g (1 oz) chocolate or *carob chips*

Mix all the ingredients together in a pudding basin. Heat a well-oiled frying pan or griddle and when hot drop on spoonfuls of the mixture. Turn the pancakes over when brown and cook for another minute. Especially good eaten hot.

These little pancakes are equally delicious in their savoury form – add chopped onion or sliced olives instead of the chocolate chips or carob chips.

GRANNY ANN

Baked Cinnamon and Raisin Apples

Serves 4

4 small cooking apples
1 dsrtsp Granny Ann Cookiemalt
1 dsrtsp honey
2 tbsp mincemeat
75 g (3 oz) raw cane sugar
2 tbsp raisins
1 tsp cinnamon
100 ml (4 fl oz) cider
25 g (1 oz) butter or *polyunsaturated margarine*

Wash and core the apples and score a line around the middle of each. Place them in a shallow dish. Mix together the Cookiemalt, honey, mincemeat, sugar, raisins and cinnamon and use this to fill the centre of each apple. Pour the cider round the apples and top each with a knob of butter or margarine. Bake at 180°C/350°F/Gas Mark 4 for 45 minutes, basting frequently.

Granny Ann Bread and Butter Pudding

Serves 4

575 ml (1 pint) milk
vanilla pod or *a few drops vanilla essence*
8 slices wholemeal bread (approx 225 g/8 oz)
butter or *polyunsaturated margarine*
Granny Ann Cookiemalt
50 g (2 oz) sultanas
grated rind of 1 lemon
2 eggs
50 g (2 oz) sugar

Pre-heat the oven to 170°C/325°F/Gas Mark 3.

Warm the milk, add the vanilla pod and leave to infuse. Spread the slices of bread with the butter or margarine and then spread with the Cookiemalt. Cut the slices of bread into squares and arrange in layers, sprinkling sultanas and lemon rind on each layer. Beat the eggs and add them to the milk along with the sugar. Mix well. Remove the vanilla pod and pour the liquid over the bread. Sprinkle sugar over the top and bake for 30 minutes or until the custard is set and the top crunchy.

Malted Apple Pudding

Serves 4

50 g (2 oz) polyunsaturated margarine
1 tbsp Granny Ann Cookiemalt
150 g (5 oz) wholemeal breadcrumbs
50 g (2 oz) muesli
50 g (2 oz) raw cane sugar
grated rind and juice of half a lemon
½ tsp grated nutmeg
2 large cooking apples
150 ml (5 fl oz) boiling water

Pre-heat the oven to 180°C/350°F/Gas Mark 4.

Melt the margarine and Cookiemalt over a low heat. Add the breadcrumbs and muesli, and stir until evenly coated. In a bowl combine the sugar, lemon juice, lemon rind and nutmeg. Peel, core and slice the apples. Place a layer of apple in the bottom of a baking dish and cover with some of the lemon juice and sugar mixture. Build up layers of breadcrumbs, apple and sugar, finishing with a layer of crumbs. Pour in the boiling water and sprinkle a little sugar on top.

Bake for 45 minutes–1 hour in the pre-heated oven, until the apples are tender and the pudding brown and crisp on top. Serve hot with custard.

GRANOSE

Here are some recipes using soya milk.

Bread and Butter Pudding

Serves 4

2 eggs
½ tbsp fruit sugar
425 ml (15 fl oz) Granose Soya Milk
1 vanilla pod
1 tbsp ground almonds
5 small slices wholemeal bread
1 tbsp polyunsaturated margarine
20 g (¾ oz) sultanas

Pre-heat the oven to 190°C/375°F/Gas Mark 5.

Whisk the eggs, fruit sugar and a little of the soya milk together. Heat the remaining soya milk with the vanilla pod and stir in the ground almonds. Pour the hot milk on to the egg yolks and whisk lightly. Butter a pudding dish. Fry the slices of bread in the margarine until golden brown and line the dish with them, reserving one for the top. Sprinkle the sultanas over the bread, then pour in the egg mixture, removing the vanilla pod at the same time. Stand the dish in a tin containing 2.5 cm/1″ of cold water and bake for 25 minutes in the pre-heated oven.

You can make custard tart and egg custard using soya milk and fruit sugar, with delicious results.

The next two recipes are from Jane O'Brien's *The Magic of Tofu*.

Eggless Soya Milk Custard

Makes 450 ml/15 fl oz

425 ml (15 fl oz) Granose Soya Milk
2 tbsp honey
pinch sea salt
1 tsp pure vanilla essence
2 tbsp lemon juice, freshly squeezed
nutmeg to taste (optional)

Heat the soya milk, but do not allow it to boil. Add the honey and salt and stir until they are dissolved. Remove the pan from the heat and stir in the vanilla and lemon juice. Set the pan aside for about half an hour, then place it in the refrigerator for 1 hour, or overnight. Serve this poured over fruit or cakes as you would a custard sauce.

Rice Pudding

Serves 4

450 g (1 lb) cooked brown rice, weight when cooked
275 ml (10 fl oz) Granose Soya Milk
3–5 tbsp honey
1 tsp or a few drops pure vanilla essence
2 eggs (optional)
2 tsp lemon juice
1 tsp lemon rind, grated

Combine the ingredients, adding a little more soya milk if necessary. Place the mixture in a greased baking dish and bake at 170°C/325°F/Gas Mark 3, for 50 minutes.

Vienna Pudding

Serves 4

wholemeal sponge cake (about half a standard
    Victoria Sponge is sufficient)
2 tbsp sherry
75 g (3 oz) sultanas
75 g (3 oz) mixed peel, chopped
50 g (2 oz) fruit sugar
grated rind of 1 lemon
1 tbsp Demerara sugar
275 ml (10 fl oz) Granose Soya Milk
3 eggs

Well grease a 850 ml/1½ pint oven-proof glass dish. Pre heat the oven to 150°C/300°F/Gas Mark 2.

Cut the sponge cake into small pieces and place in a bowl (not in the ovenproof glass dish). Pour over the sherry and leave to soak for 15 minutes. Sprinkle over the sultanas, peel, lemon rind and fruit sugar and transfer this mixture into the well-greased ovenproof dish. Put the tablespoon of Demerara sugar into a small, heavy saucepan with about 3 teaspoons of water and dissolve the sugar very slowly over a low heat. Do not stir. Cook until a toffee consistency is achieved then carefully pour in the soya milk and heat gently until the toffee has dissolved. Take off the heat. Beat the eggs well in a bowl and pour in the warm milk. Mix well then strain the liquid over the sponge mixture. Make a tight-fitting cover with foil and bake in the pre-heated oven for 2 hours.

HOLLAND & BARRETT

Gingered Christmas Pudding

Makes 1 900 g/2 lb pudding

175 g (6 oz) Holland & Barrett Raisins
175 g (6 oz) Holland & Barrett Sultanas
100 g (4 oz) Holland & Barrett Currants
50 g (2 oz) Holland & Barrett Dried Apricots
75 g (3 oz) Holland & Barrett Flaked Almonds
40 g (1½ oz) stem ginger in honey
100 g (4 oz) carrots, peeled
grated rind of 1 lemon
50 g (2 oz) wholemeal breadcrumbs
25 g (1 oz) 100% wholemeal flour
75 g (3 oz) block vegetable margarine, chilled
2 free-range eggs
75 ml (3 fl oz) skimmed milk
2 tbsp brandy, rum or orange juice

Mix the raisins, sultanas and currants and place in a bowl. Finely chop the apricots and almonds and add to the fruit. Chop the ginger and grate the carrots. Add to the bowl with the lemon rind, breadcrumbs and flour. Stir thoroughly. Grate the margarine and add to the bowl. Beat the eggs with the milk and pour on to the dry ingredients with the brandy, rum or orange juice. Mix in thoroughly. Lightly grease a 900 g/2 lb pudding basin. Place the mixture in the bowl, pressing in firmly. Cover with a double layer of greaseproof paper and tie a cloth around the top, or use a piece of double-thickness foil. Steam the pudding for 4 hours or cook in a pressure cooker. (If using the latter, steam for 30 minutes, then add 15 lb weights and cook for a further 3 hours.) The puddings are best made a little while in advance. Put a fresh cloth or foil over the pudding if it is to be stored.

On Christmas Day, or when ready to serve, the pudding should be re-heated by steaming for 2 hours, or by pressure cooking at 15 lb pressure for 30 minutes. For more information on tying up and storing see Plum Pudding (page 196).

Steamed Almond Fruit Pudding

Makes 1 900 g/2 lb pudding

15 g (½ oz) sunflower margarine
1 tbsp Holland & Barrett Clear Honey
100 g (4 oz) sunflower margarine
65 g (2½ oz) fruit sugar
2 large eggs
100 g (4 oz) 100% wholemeal flour
50 g (3 oz) Holland & Barrett Ground Almonds
2 tbsp natural yoghurt
2 medium cooking apples
50 g (2 oz) sultanas
50 g (2 oz) Demerara or fruit sugar
1 level tsp ground cinnamon

Grease a 900 g/2 lb pudding basin well with the 15 g/½ oz margarine and trickle the tablespoon of honey inside the base of the bowl. Cream the margarine with the 65 g/2½ oz fruit sugar until it is fluffy, then gradually beat in the eggs. Mix the flour and almonds and add gradually to the creamed mixture. Stir in the yoghurt. Cut the apples into quarters, take out the cores and slice with the peel on. Mix the sliced apples with the sultanas, the 50 g/2 oz of Demerara or fruit sugar and the cinnamon.

Spoon a thin layer of the pudding mixture on top of the honey in the basin, then half the apple mixture, then another layer of pudding mixture and the rest of the apple mixture on top. Finally spoon the remaining pudding mixture over the top. Cover with a circle of greaseproof paper and make a lid with pleated foil which reaches below the lip of the basin. Tie with string to make a handle to lift the pudding out. Steam for 2 hours.

Opposite: **Dietade** *Savarin (above) page 107, Dietade Doughnuts (below) page 156*

KALIBU

Now four lovely recipes from Lorraine Whiteside's *The Carob Cookbook*.

Carob Almond Layer Pudding

Serves 6

100 g (4 oz) polyunsaturated margarine
50 g (2 oz) raw cane sugar
2 eggs, beaten
2 tbsp clear honey
100 g (4 oz) 100% wholemeal flour
50 g (2 oz) Kalibu Carob Powder
2 level tsp baking powder
1 tbsp natural yoghurt
225 g (8 oz) fluked almonds

Cream the margarine and sugar together until light and fluffy and gradually add the beaten eggs a little at a time. Stir in one tablespoonful of the honey and then fold in the flour, carob powder, baking powder and yoghurt. Grease a 850 ml/1½ pint pudding basin and spoon the remaining tablespoonful of honey into the bottom. Place a layer of flaked almonds on top of the honey, followed by a layer of the pudding mixture. Continue in this way, making alternate layers of flaked almonds and pudding mixture. Cover the basin with greaseproof paper or foil and secure, place in a steamer and steam for about 1½ hours. Serve with Honey Custard (see page 194 for the recipe) or natural yoghurt.

Carob Fig Pudding

Serves 6

175 g (6 oz) dried figs, soaked overnight
75 g (3 oz) polyunsaturated margarine
50 g (2 oz) raw cane sugar
grated rind of 1 lemon
50 g (2 oz) 100% wholemeal flour
50 g (2 oz) Kalibu Carob Powder

Opposite: **Whole Earth** *Black Cherry, Apple and Orange Crunch Crumble (above) page 198, Hedgerow Harvest Baked Pudding (below) page 198*

50 g (2 oz) fresh wholemeal breadcrumbs
25 g (1 oz) ground almonds
1½ level tsp baking powder
1 level tsp mixed spice
3 tbsp natural yoghurt
a little milk to mix

Drain the figs, remove the stalks and cut the fruit into small pieces. Cream the margarine, sugar and lemon rind together until light and fluffy. Fold in the flour, carob powder, breadcrumbs, almonds, figs, baking powder and mixed spice, then add the yoghurt and enough milk to produce a soft dropping consistency. Spoon the mixture into a well-greased 575–725 ml/1–1¼ pint pudding basin, cover with foil and secure. Steam for 2–3 hours. Serve with Honey Custard (see page 194 for the recipe) or natural yoghurt.

Carob Pineapple Upside-down Pudding

Serves 6

1 small fresh pineapple
2 tbsp clear honey
25 g (1 oz) glacé cherries
100 g (4 oz) polyunsaturated margarine
75 g (3 oz) raw cane sugar
2 eggs, beaten
100 g (4 oz) 100% wholemeal flour
50 g (2 oz) Kalibu Carob Powder
2 level tsps baking powder
2 tbsp natural yoghurt
a little milk to mix

Peel and slice the fresh pineapple into rings, cutting out the centre core. Well grease a 20 cm/8″ round cake tin and spread the clear honey inside the base. Arrange the pineapple slices on top of the layer of honey and place a glacé cherry in each centre core hole.

Cream the margarine and sugar together until light and fluffy and gradually add the beaten eggs. Fold in the flour, carob powder, baking powder and yoghurt. If necessary add a little milk to give a dropping consistency. Spread the mixture on top of the pineapple rings and bake at 180°C/350°F/Gas Mark 4 for about 40–45 minutes, until the top of the cake is firm to the touch. Carefully turn out the cake on to a round serving dish and serve hot with Honey Custard (see page 194).

Honey Custard

1 vanilla pod
275 ml (10 fl oz) milk
2 tbsp clear honey
2 egg yolks

Split the vanilla pod lengthways, place in a pan with the milk, and heat. Remove from the heat and leave to infuse for 10 minutes with a lid on the pan, then remove the vanilla pod and stir in the honey. Whisk the egg yolks in a large mixing bowl. Re-heat the milk to boiling point, then pour it over the egg yolks, stirring continuously. Return the mixture to the pan and stir continuously over a low heat until the custard thickens and becomes creamy. Serve immediately over hot puddings.

Steamed Carob Pudding

Serves 4

100 g (4 oz) polyunsaturated margarine
50 g (2 oz) raw cane sugar
2 eggs, beaten
100 g (4 oz) 100% wholemeal flour
50 g (2 oz) Kalibu Carob Powder
2 level tsps baking powder
1 tbsp clear honey
1 tbsp natural yoghurt

Cream the margarine and sugar together until light and fluffy and slowly add the beaten eggs. Fold in the flour, carob powder, baking powder, honey and yoghurt. Spoon the mixture into a well-greased 450 g/1 pint pudding basin, cover with greaseproof paper or foil and secure with string. Place in a steamer over a pan of hot water and steam for about 1½ hours.

Serve immediately with Honey Custard (see page 00 for the recipe) or natural yoghurt.

LOTUS

Apple Soya Crumble

Serves 4

450 g (1 lb) cooking apples, peeled, cored and thinly sliced
40 g (1½ oz) butter or polyunsaturated margarine
25 g (1 oz) Lotus Soya Grits
50 g (2 oz) 100% wholewheat flour
75 g (3 oz) brown sugar

Pre-heat the oven to 190°C/375°F/Gas Mark 5.

Rub the butter or margarine into the mixed soya grits and wholewheat flour until the mixture resembles breadcrumbs. Add 50 g/2 oz of the sugar. Place the sliced apples in a casserole dish and sprinkle over the remaining 15 g/1 oz of sugar. Sprinkle the crumble mixture on top and bake in the pre-heated oven for 35–40 minutes until golden brown.

MARRIAGE'S

Almond Crêpes

Makes 18

These thin and delicate pancakes are delicious spread with a little honey or stuffed with soaked, dried fruit. I sometimes add apricot brandy when entertaining – 1–2 tablespoons of liqueur added to the batter is sufficient.

75 g (3 oz) Marriage's Strong 100% Wholemeal Flour, plain
50 g (2 oz) almonds, very finely ground
good pinch sea salt
2 large eggs
1 tbsp fruit sugar
350 ml (12 fl oz) milk
2 tbsp sunflower oil
2 drops almond essence
little oil to brush pan

If you have a blender or food processor simply put the flour, almonds, eggs, fruit sugar, salt and half the milk into the jug or bowl and process until well blended. Gradually pour the remaining milk, oil and essence in and process until smooth. (If mixing by hand put the dry ingredients into a mixing bowl and make a well in the centre. Beat the eggs and place them with a quarter of the milk into the dry ingredients and mix with a fork, gradually adding the rest of the milk as you do so. Add the oil, the essence and blend well together.) Leave the batter to stand for 1–2 hours and stir before making the crêpes.

To fry the crêpes add 2 level tablespoons of batter to a lightly greased hot frying pan or crêpe pan. Cook quickly on one side until the edges are a light, golden brown and the centre is bubbling. Pop over and cook for a few seconds only on the other side.

—Apricot and Walnut— Upside-down Cake

Serves 8

75 g (3 oz) dried apricot halves
2 tbsp clear honey
50 g (2 oz) walnuts, coarsely chopped
100 g (4 oz) polyunsaturated margarine
100 g (4 oz) soft brown sugar
3 eggs
225 g (8 oz) Marriage's 100% Wholemeal Flour, *self-raising*
2 tbsp skimmed milk

Cover the apricots in boiling water and soak for 3 hours. Pre-heat the oven to 180°C/350°F/Gas Mark 4. Put the honey into the bottom of a greased fixed-based deep tin, either 18 cm/7″ square or 20 cm/8″ round. Drain the apricots and arrange them with the walnuts in the honey. Lightly cream the margarine and sugar, beat in the eggs, fold in the flour and add the milk. Spread the mixture over the fruit and smooth the top. Bake in the pre-heated oven for 45 minutes, until springy to the touch. Turn out and serve immediately.

MARTLET

The next two recipes are from my book *Vegetarian Food Processor*.

—Baked Apples with— Apricot and Walnut Stuffing

Serves 4

12 dried apricots, well washed or *175 g (6 oz) apricot pieces*
a little hot water
1 level tbsp clear honey
2 level tbsp Martlet Apple Juice Concentrate
½ tsp ground cinnamon
1 rounded tsp fresh ginger, grated (optional)
50 g (2 oz) walnuts, roughly chopped
4 large cooking apples, cored

Soak the apricots in the hot water, honey and apple juice concentrate for a few hours or overnight. Drain and reserve the liquid. Set the steel blades in position on a food processor and finely chop the apricots with 2 tablespoons of the soaking water, the cinnamon and ginger, if used. Stir in the walnuts. Place the apples on a greased oven-proof dish and stuff the centres with the apricot mixture. Make the soaking water up to 150 ml/5 fl oz with cold water and pour over the apples. Bake at 180°C/350°F/Gas Mark 4, for 45 minutes–1 hour. Baste the apples frequently during the cooking time.

—Baked Apples with— Fig and Aniseed

Serves 4

8 dried figs, trimmed
a little hot water
2 level tbsp Martlet Apple Juice Concentrate
juice and rind of 1 medium orange
½ tsp ground aniseed
4 large cooking apples, cored

Wash the figs and soak in a little hot water and apple juice concentrate for a few hours, then roughly chop. Drain and reserve the liquid. Set the steel blades in position on a food processor and finely chop the figs with the orange juice, rind and ground aniseed (not too mushy). Place the apples on a greased oven-proof dish and stuff the centres with the fig mixture. Make the soaking water up to 150 ml/5 fl oz with cold water and pour over the apples. Bake at 180°C/350°F/Gas Mark 4, for 45 minutes–1 hour. Baste the apples several times whilst cooking.

Crunchy Baked Apple Delight

Serves 4

675 g (1½ lb) cooking apples, cored, thinly peeled and sliced
150 ml (5 fl oz) water mixed with 4 tbsps Martlet Apple Juice Concentrate
¼ tsp clove powder
½ tsp ground cinnamon
175 g (6 oz) wholewheat flour
pinch sea salt
75 ml (3 fl oz) sunflower oil
1 tbsp Martlet Apple Juice Concentrate *mixed with 2 tbsp water*

Pre-heat the oven to 190°C/375°F/Gas Mark 5.

Put the thinly sliced apples in a pie dish 7.5 cm/3″ deep and 20 cm/8″ in diameter. Mix the 150 ml/5 fl oz of water and the apple juice concentrate with the spices and pour over the apples. Put the flour and sea salt in a mixing bowl and rub in the oil, then work in the 1 tablespoon apple juice concentrate and water mixture to form a crumbly mixture. Sprinkle over the apples. Leave to stand for 30 minutes, then bake in the pre-heated oven for about 35–40 minutes, until the apples, when pricked with a sharp knife, are soft and the top is beginning to brown.

PAUL'S TOFU

Carob Mint Pie

Serves 4

This recipe is taken from Jane O'Brien's book *The Magic of Tofu*.

100 g (4 oz) wholewheat breadcrumbs, lightly toasted
1 tsp cinnamon
2 tbsp vegetable oil
2 tbsp water
2½ tbsp honey

Filling
675 g (1½ lb) Paul's Firm Tofu
175 g (6 oz) honey
75 g (3 oz) carob powder
1 tbsp or a few drops pure vanilla essence (depending on type)
½ tsp cinnamon
pinch sea salt
½ tsp pure peppermint essence

Combine the breadcrumbs well with the other base ingredients and use the mixture to line a greased pie dish. Bake for 10 minutes at 180°C/350°F/Gas Mark 4, before adding the filling.

Blend all the filling ingredients in a liquidizer and pour the mixture on to the part-baked breadcrumb base. Bake at 220°C/425°F/Gas Mark 7 for about 45 minutes, or until the crust is brown.

PREWETT'S

Plum Pudding

Makes 4 450 g/1 lb puddings

3 level tsp mixed spice
1 level tsp ground ginger
1 level tsp ground cinnamon
175 g (6 oz) Prewett's 100% Wholemeal Flour, *plain*
175 g (6 oz) wholemeal breadcrumbs
¼ tsp sea salt
225 g (8 oz) Prewett's Sunflower Margarine
175 g (6 oz) large raisins, de-seeded

175 g (6 oz) sultanas
100 g (4 oz) currants
50 g (2 oz) mixed peel
50 g (2 oz) almonds, chopped
225 g (8 oz) Barbados sugar
4 large eggs, beaten
1 large cooking apple, with skin on, grated
1 large carrot, grated
juice and grated rind of 1 lemon
juice and grated rind of 1 small orange
½ tsp vanilla essence

Mix the spices with the flour, breadcrumbs and salt. Rub in the margarine and add the dried fruit, mixed peel, nuts and sugar. Stir in the beaten eggs, add the grated apple and carrot and finally mix in the juice and rind of the lemon and orange and the vanilla essence. Pack into four greased 450 g/1 lb pudding basins, and steam for 3 hours (see note below). Cover well and store until needed. Steam for 2–3 hours before serving.

Note The basins should be well greased and only three quarters full of mixture. Cut out a circle of greaseproof paper or foil larger than the top of the basin and press this under the rim. Place a square of cotton sheeting over the top. Tie some string under the rim, collect the two opposite corners of the cotton square up over the top and tie together, then tie the other two opposite corners of the square to make a handle. Make sure that you have clean paper or foil and a dry, clean cloth on your puddings when storing them.

Tutti Frutti Pudding

Serves 4–6

50 g (2 oz) large prunes, stoned and finely chopped
50 g (2 oz) dried apricots, washed and chopped
40 g (1½ oz) glacé cherries, chopped
25 g (1 oz) angelica, chopped
grated rind and juice of 1 orange
2 large eggs
75 g (3 oz) Prewett's 100% Wholemeal Flour, self-raising
100 g (4 oz) Prewett's Sunflower Margarine
75 g (3 oz) light Muscovado or fruit sugar
50 g (2 oz) wholemeal breadcrumbs
1 tbsp clear honey

Mix all the dried fruit together in a dish. Cream the margarine and sugar until light and fluffy. Whisk the eggs and gradually beat them into the margarine mixture. Mix the flour with the breadcrumbs and

fold into the creamed mixture. Stir in the orange rind and juice and finally lightly fold in the dried fruit. Trickle the honey into the base of a well-greased 850 ml/1½ pint basin and spoon in the pudding mixture. Cover with greased paper and a lid of pleated foil reaching over the lip of the basin. Tie with string to make a handle for lifting the pudding out. Steam for 2 hours.

WESTERN ISLES

Rice Pudding

2 eggs
240 ml (8 fl oz) milk
1 tsp vanilla extract
50 g (2 oz) honey, maple syrup, or Western Isles Apple Juice Concentrate
340 g (12 oz) cooked short grain brown rice (175 g/ 6 oz dry weight rice)
50 g (2 oz) walnuts, pecans or desiccated coconut
50 g (2 oz) raisins or chopped dates
½ tsp ground cinnamon
¾ tsp ground nutmeg
½ tsp lemon rind, grated
¼ tsp ground cloves

Beat the eggs, milk, vanilla and honey, maple syrup or apple juice together. Mix in the rice and other ingredients. Spread the mixture into a greased baking dish and bake for 30 minutes at 180°C/350°F/ Gas Mark 4. Stir once or twice during baking. Serve with a topping of chopped nuts or chopped fresh fruit as desired. Excellent hot or cold.

WHOLE EARTH

—Black Cherry, Apple— and Orange Crunch Crumble

4 medium cooking apples
¾ jar Whole Earth Black Cherry Jam
(approx. 225 g (8 oz) Whole Earth Orange Crunch
  cereal

Peel the apples and slice finely. Combine them with the jam and half the cereal. Place the apple and jam mixture in the bottom of a casserole dish and cover with the remaining cereal. Cover and bake for 30 minutes at 180°C/350°F/Gas Mark 4.

You can use drained peach slices in place of jam but be sure they are peaches tinned in apple juice, not in sugary syrup.

—Hedgerow Harvest— Baked Pudding

Serves 6

This recipe uses Whole Earth's Hedgerow Jam which combines beautifully with cooking apples.

450 g (1 lb) tart dessert apples such as Granny
  Smith, cored and very thinly sliced (leave skins
  on)
¼ tsp clove powder
½ tsp cinnamon
¾ jar Whole Earth Hedgerow Jam
75 g (3 oz) sunflower margarine
50 g (2 oz) Demerara sugar
1 large free range egg, beaten
115 g (4½ oz) 100% wholemeal flour
2 level tsp baking powder
2 tbsp natural yoghurt

Pre-heat the oven to 180°C/350°F/Gas Mark 4.

Place the very thinly sliced apple into a well-oiled 850 ml/1½ pint pie dish. Mix the ground cloves and the cinnamon with the jam and pour over the apples. Stir gently with a fork. Cream the margarine and sugar together until light and fluffy, then gradually add the beaten egg. Mix the flour with the baking powder and fold carefully into the creamed mixture, then stir in the yoghurt very gently. Spoon the mixture over the apples and jam, spreading it evenly with the back of a spoon. Bake in a pre-heated oven for about 45 minutes.

ZWICKY

——Almond Millet—— Pudding

Serves 4

575 ml (1 pint) milk
100 g (4 oz) Zwicky Millet Flakes
pinch of salt
15 g (½ oz) vegetable margarine
25 g (1 oz) Muscovado sugar
2 eggs, separated
75 g (3 oz) sultanas
25 g (1 oz) ground almonds
grated rind of 2 lemons
15 g (½ oz) almond flakes, browned

Pre-heat the oven to 170°C/325°F/Gas Mark 3.

Put the milk in a saucepan and add the millet flakes, salt and vegetable margarine. Bring to the boil, stir and simmer for 5 minutes. Allow to cool. Mix together the sugar, egg yolks, sultanas, ground almonds and half the lemon rind and stir into the millet flake mixture. Whisk the egg whites until stiff and then fold them gently into the millet mixture. Grease a 1.5 litre/2½ pint oven-proof dish with vegetable margarine and pour in the mixture. Bake in the pre-heated oven for about 40 minutes. Before serving sprinkle the browned almond flakes and remaining grated lemon rind over the top of the pudding.

10
COLD DESSERTS

CAFÉ HAG

Coffee and Ginger Ice Cream

Serves 4

3 dsrtsp Café Hag Decaffeinated Instant Coffee
   Granules
3 tbsp fruit sugar
2 tbsp hot water
575 ml (1 pint) double cream
100 g (4 oz) stem ginger, chopped
*whipped cream and slices of crystallized ginger to
   decorate*

Dissolve the coffee granules and sugar in the hot
water. Whisk the cream until soft peaks form. Add
the chopped ginger and coffee mixture to the cream
and stir until evenly distributed. Pour into a 450 g/
1 lb loaf tin and freeze for about 4 hours.

To serve, unmould and decorate with whipped
cream and slices of crystallized ginger.

Coffee Junket

Serves 8

1 litre (2 pints) milk
3 tsp fruit sugar
5 level tsp Café Hag Decaffeinated Instant Coffee
   Granules
2 tsp rennet

Warm the milk to blood heat. Add the sugar and
coffee granules, pour into a large serving dish and
add the rennet. Stir for a few minutes, then leave to
set at room temperature. Chill before serving.

Honeycomb Mould

Serves 4

2 large eggs, separated
65 g (2½ oz) fruit sugar
575 ml (1 pint) skimmed milk
4 tsp Café Hag Decaffeinated Instant Coffee
   Granules
1½ sachets gelatine
3 tbsp water
fruit to decorate

Whisk the egg yolks with the sugar until pale and
creamy. Bring the milk mixed with the coffee
granules to boiling point and pour over the egg
mixture. Return to the pan and, stirring continuously, allow the mixture to thicken. Do not boil.
Strain and leave to cool.

Dissolve the gelatine in the water and stir into the
cooled coffee custard. Whisk the egg whites until
really stiff and fold into the mixture. Turn into a
1 litre/2 pint ring mould and chill thoroughly until
set.

To serve, unmould the ring and decorate with
fresh or canned fruit, such as apricot halves.

CARRABAY

Carrageen and Apple Blancmange

Serves 6

1 litre (2 pints) skimmed milk
25 g (1 oz) Carrabay Carrageen
½ cup honey
juice of ½ lemon
2 large apples, peeled, cored and minced to a fine pulp

Pour the milk into the top of a double boiler. Put the carrageen, after washing, in a piece of cheesecloth about 20 cm/8″ square, tie the ends and suspend the bag in the milk. Simmer for 30 minutes. Press the bag against the side of the saucepan occasionally to release the gel. Stir continually. Remove from the heat, discard the bag, add the honey, lemon juice and apples and stir well. Pour the mixture into a lightly buttered 1 litre/2 pint mould, cover and refrigerate for 2 hours before serving.

Carrageen Blender Sweet

Serves 8

25 g (1 oz) Carrabay Carrageen
1 litre (2 pints) milk
225 g (8 oz) fresh strawberries, puréed
2 tbsp clear honey
pinch sea salt

Pour the milk into the top of a double boiler. Put the carrageen, after washing, in a piece of cheesecloth about 20 cm/8″ square, tie the ends, suspend the bag in the milk and simmer for 30 minutes. Press the bag against the side of the saucepan occasionally to release the gel. Stir continually. Remove from

the heat and discard the bag. Pour the milk mixture into a blender and add the puréed strawberries, honey and salt. Blend at high speed. Cover tightly and refrigerate for 2 hours before serving.

Carrageen Fresh Fruit Jelly

Serves 6–8

25 g (1 oz) Carrabay Carrageen
850 ml (1½ pints) water
225 g (8 oz) fresh raspberries, strawberries or mixed blackcurrants and redcurrants
100 g (4 oz) fruit sugar
pinch sea salt (optional)
banana slices sprinkled with lemon juice to stop browning

Add the carrageen to the water (after washing and picking over as directed on the packet). Bring to the boil and simmer for 15 minutes. Purée the fruit in a blender until smooth. Strain through a sieve on to the sugar, then strain boiling carrageen liquid over the mixture and stir well. Pop in the banana slices. Leave to cool, then refrigerate until set.

Carrageen Fluff

Serves 6–8

15 g (½ oz) Carrabay Carrageen
850 ml (1½ pints) milk
2 tbsp fruit sugar
3 tbsp carob powder
2 egg whites
50 g (2 oz) fruit sugar
1 tbsp Irish whiskey or whiskey liqueur
whipped cream or Irish cream liqueur to serve

Wash the carrageen and soak in cold water for 10 minutes. Drain, put into a saucepan with the milk and simmer gently for 20 minutes. Strain through a sieve, squeezing all the jelly through. Combine the 2 tablespoons of sugar with the carob powder and a little of the milk, return to the rinsed saucepan and simmer gently for 2–3 minutes until the carob loses its raw taste. Whisk the egg whites stiffly with the 50 g/2 oz of sugar. Fold the whiskey (or liqueur) into the carrageen mixture and then add the egg whites. Pour into individual dishes and leave overnight to set. Serve topped with a swirl of whipped cream or a spoonful of Irish cream liqueur.

For everyday occasions, omit the whiskey and add a ½ teaspoon of vanilla or ratafia essence.

DIETADE

Frothy Spiced Yoghurt

Serves 4

100 g (4 oz) natural yoghurt
2 eggs, separated
40 g (1½ oz) Dietade Fruit Sugar
½ tsp ground mixed spices
15 g (½ oz) diabetic chocolate

Warm the yoghurt in a basin placed in pan of hot (not boiling) water. Beat in the egg yolks and stir over the heat for 3 minutes. Remove from the heat, add the fruit sugar and spices and allow to cool. Whisk the egg whites stiffly and fold into the mixture when completely cold. Transfer to individual glasses and chill. Before serving dust with grated chocolate.

Lemon Flummery

Serves 4

4 eggs, separated
100 g (4 oz) Dietade Fruit Sugar
grated rind and juice of 2 lemons
8 g (¼ oz) powdered gelatine, dissolved in
 2 tablespoons water
175 ml (5 fl oz) double cream

Whisk together the egg yolks and fruit sugar until thick and creamy. Add the grated lemon rind and gradually add the lemon juice. Stir in the dissolved gelatine, fork in the whipped cream and finally the stiffly beaten egg whites. Place to chill in the refrigerator.

Melon and Ginger Ice Cream

Serves 6

I use Ogen melon for this recipe although honeydew melon will do. The Ogen is orange with fine green lines. It is smaller and rounder in shape than the honeydew and will stand firmly if you want to serve the ice cream in the shell. If using a honeydew then a small size is correct for this recipe. You will need a small ball scoop if you wish to decorate the ice cream with marinated melon balls.

Ice Cream
40 g (1½ oz) fresh ginger, grated
4 tbsp water
1 large Ogen or small honeydew melon
100 g (4 oz) Dietade Fruit Sugar
4 egg yolks
425 ml (15 fl oz) double cream
2 tbsp lemon juice

Marinade
1 tbsp Dietade Fruit Sugar
1 tsp fresh ginger, grated
2 tbsp brandy

First make the ice cream. Soak the grated ginger in the water for 10 minutes. Remove the ginger, squeezing out all the juice – you should have just under 150 ml/5 fl oz of ginger water. Cut the top off the melon and scoop out the seeds and fibres. (If you want to decorate the ice cream, using a small ball scoop take out 12 balls from the cut-off top of the melon. Set aside to marinate (see below) while the ice cream is chilling.) Spoon out the rest of the melon pulp into a small, thick saucepan, add the sugar and cook over low heat until you have a soft pulp. Mash with a potato masher, then take off the heat. Whisk the egg yolks until light and cream coloured. Put the saucepan back on a low heat. Stirring continuously, pour the egg yolks into the melon pulp and then whisk the lot until a creamy consistency is achieved. Let the mixture get cold in the refrigerator. Whip the cream until it thickens slightly. Stir the ginger juice and lemon juice into the cooled melon pulp, then fold in the cream. Transfer the mixture into a freezer container, cover with a lid and freeze for 2½ hours. Stir the mixture three times while it is freezing.

To marinate the melon balls, melt the fruit sugar in a small saucepan over a low heat. Add the grated ginger and stir, then add the brandy. Stir over a low heat. Put the melon balls into a small bowl and pour over the brandy and ginger sauce.

When the ice cream is well chilled, scoop it into the melon shell and decorate with the melon balls. Spoon the remaining sauce over individual servings.

GAYELORD HAUSER'S NATURAL SEASONINGS

—Delicious Hi-protein— Dessert

Serves 8

450 g (1 lb) cottage cheese
3 tbsp honey
½ tsp each of Vege-Sal, *vanilla extract, grated lemon rind and cinnamon*
¼ tsp grated nutmeg
5 egg yolks, lightly beaten

Pre-heat the oven to 180°C/350°F/Gas Mark 4.

Sieve the cheese (or put it in a blender) with the honey, lemon rind, cinnamon, vanilla, Vege-Sal and nutmeg, then blend it with the egg yolks. Pour the mixture into ramekins, filling them three quarters full. Set the cups in a shallow pan with 2.5 cm/1″ of hot water around them, place in the oven and bake for about 20 minutes. Test by piecing the centre with a knife blade, which should come out clean. Serve cold.

GELOZONE

The following recipes using Gelozone are the result of my own experiments using this vegetable gel and appear in my book *Vegetarian Food Processor*.

—Apricot and Ginger— Mousse

Serves 4–5

You can either use bottled stem ginger, which is soaked in syrup, or, as I prefer, freshly grated ginger root. Try to get unsulphured apricots which are dark in colour and have been dried naturally. (When making this mousse for children use 1 rounded teaspoon of cinnamon instead of the ginger.)

225 g (8 oz) dried apricot pieces, well washed
575 ml (1 pint) boiling water
4 cm (1½″) knob fresh ginger or 3 pieces stem ginger
2 tbsp Gelozone
4 rounded tbsp dried skimmed milk powder
50 g (2 oz) Barbados sugar
white of 1 large egg
toasted chopped hazelnuts to decorate

Pour the boiling water over the washed apricots and soak for a few hours or overnight. Drain the fruit, retaining the liquid and making it up to 575 ml/ 1 pint with cold water. Thinly peel and finely grate the ginger (or chop finely if stem ginger is used). Put the apricots, ginger and 285 ml/10 fl oz of the liquid into a heavy-bottomed saucepan and cook gently for 8 minutes, then blend until smooth. Mix the Gelozone, milk powder and sugar together and blend to a smooth paste with a little of the remaining liquid, then gradually add the rest. Bring slowly to the boil and cook for 2–3 minutes. Remove from the heat and stir into the apricot purée. Whisk the egg white until stiff, fold it into the apricot mixture and spoon the mixture into individual serving dishes. Sprinkle with toasted chopped hazelnuts and chill for at least 2 hours before serving.

—Carob and Orange— Mousse

Serves 4–5

A rich dessert for special occasions only.
1 tbsp carob powder
juice of 2 oranges plus water to make up 425 ml (15 fl oz) liquid
rind of 1 orange
2 eggs, separated
2 tbsp fruit sugar
2 tbsp Gelozone
150 ml (5 fl oz) double cream, lightly whipped
1 tbsp Grand Marnier (optional)

Blend the carob powder to a smooth paste with a little of the water and orange juice liquid, then gradually add the rest of the liquid and the orange rind. Stir in the Gelozone, bring to the boil slowly, stirring constantly, and simmer for 3 minutes. Cool the liquid until it is just warm. Set the steel blades in position on a food processor and blend the egg yolks with the fruit sugar until thick and creamy. Pour into a bowl, pour the warm carob liquid over the beaten yolks and fold together. Allow to cool and stiffen slightly. Clean and dry the processor bowl, set the egg white whisk in position and whisk the egg whites until stiff. Lightly whip the cream, stir in the Grand Marnier and add to the carob mixture. Finally fold in the stiffly beaten egg whites. Spoon into individual glasses and chill until set.

Mixed Dried Fruit Mousse

Serves 4–5

50 g (2 oz) each of dried prunes, figs, apricots and apple
575 ml (1 pint) boiling water
285 ml (10 oz) natural yoghurt
2 tbsp Gelozone
2 rounded tbsp Barbados sugar or 3 tbsp apple juice concentrate
2 tbsp double cream (optional)
few toasted almonds or walnuts, chopped, to decorate

Wash the dried fruit well and soak overnight or for a few hours in the boiling water. Cook the fruit gently for 10 minutes only. Drain and retain 285 ml/10 fl oz of the liquid plus 4 tablespoons. Take out the prune stones. Set the steel blades in position on a food processor and blend the fruit with 4 tablespoons of the liquid until it is a smooth purée. Leave to cool, then stir in the yoghurt and set aside. Mix the Gelozone and sugar with a little of the liquid until smooth, then gradually add the rest of the 285 ml/½ pint. Bring slowly to the boil, stirring constantly, and simmer for 2–3 minutes only. Leave to cool, then stir into the fruit purée. Whip the cream and fold into the mixture. Spoon into individual dishes and decorate with the chopped toasted almonds or walnuts.

Redcurrant Fool

You can use blackcurrants in this recipe but I prefer redcurrants as they are not so sharp. Fresh apricots are also delicious.

350 g (12 oz) redcurrants
2 rounded tbsp clear honey
juice of ½ lemon
275 ml (10 fl oz) water
2 tbsp Gelozone
275 ml (10 fl oz) thick natural yoghurt

Place the redcurrants, lemon juice, honey and half the water in a heavy-bottomed saucepan, bring to the boil and simmer gently for 3 minutes. Mix the Gelozone to a smooth paste with the remaining water, mix into the redcurrants and boil for 2 minutes, stirring constantly. Set the steel blades in position on a food processor and purée the cooked redcurrants until smooth. Leave to cool. Fold in the yoghurt, spoon into individual serving dishes and chill until set.

GRANOSE

Almond Custard

This recipe is taken from my book *Vegetarian Food Processor*. You can use cashew nuts instead of almonds, or add 1 tablespoon carob or cocoa powder to give a chocolate taste. You will need a double layer of muslin for straining the almond milk.

100 g (4 oz) almonds
850 ml (1½ pints) Granose Soya Milk
15 g (½ oz) polyunsaturated margarine
2 tbsp clear honey
3 tsp agar-agar
little grated nutmeg

Set the steel blades of a food processor in position. Grind the almonds as finely as possible, then gradually add 275 ml/10 fl oz of the soya milk through the feed tube while the machine is still running. Rub the margarine around the inside of a medium-sized saucepan, pour in the almond milk plus the remaining 575 ml/1 pint of soya milk, saving just a little to blend with the agar-agar, and gently simmer for 20 minutes over a low heat. Do not boil.

Drape the muslin over a colander which you have placed over a bowl. Strain the almond milk through this, squeezing well to extract all the milk (use rubber gloves because the liquid will be very hot). Sweeten with the honey. Blend the agar-agar with a little milk until smooth, then pour this into the almond milk, stirring constantly. Re-heat and simmer gently for 3 more minutes. Pour into individual serving dishes or 1 large serving bowl. Grate a little nutmeg over each serving and chill until set.

Serve with puréed fruit which you have sweetened slightly with apple juice concentrate.

HARMONY

—Sweet Rice Balls—

Makes 10

The rice used in this recipe is Harmony short grain organically grown rice. Quite delicious and easy to cook. Rice is rarely used in the West as a sweet except for white rice pudding, which is unfortunate because it makes a lovely light but satisfying dessert mixed with dried or fresh fruits. Here is my favourite, but experiment further and you will be surprised how delicious sweet rice balls can be. Cook the rice a day in advance or you can use leftovers. A food processor is useful for this recipe.

225 g (8 oz) Harmony Organic Short Grain Brown
  Rice
½ tsp sea salt
100 g (4 oz) raisins
2 tbsp lemon juice
grated rind of 1 lemon
2 pieces stem ginger, chopped into small bits
2 level tbsp apricot jam
50 g (2 oz) dried apricots
100 g (4 oz) almonds

Measure out the rice by cupfuls and wash well in a sieve. To each cup of rice add 2 cups of water. Bring the rice and water, plus the sea salt, to the boil then turn down to simmer, cover tightly and cook for 35 minutes on a low heat. Leave the lid on after cooking. This will soften the rice and make it more glutinous. Leave to stand for 10 minutes. Set the steel blades in position on the food processor, put the rice into the bowl and process briefly. This will break the rice grains up a little, which will help when making the rice balls. Take the rice out and leave overnight, covered, in the refrigerator. Soak the raisins with the lemon juice, rind, ginger and jam overnight. Soak the apricots in hot water overnight then drain. Chop the apricots and stir into the rice with the raisin mixture. Set the steel blades in position and chop the almonds until medium ground, but not powdery. Toast under a grill, using moderate heat, until lightly browned. Form the rice mixture into 10 balls and roll in the toasted almonds. Chill before serving.

—Variations—

Try toasted sesame seeds to coat and other soaked dried fruit such as chopped figs or dates, or add chopped nuts or sunflower seeds to the mixture to vary the flavour of this wholesome dessert.

KALIBU

The next four recipes are from *The Carob Cookbook* by Lorraine Whiteside.

—Carob Tropical— Fruit Pavlova

Serves 6–8

Absolutely delicious and definitely a dinner party special.

5 egg whites
150 g (5 oz) Kalibu Carob Powder
225 g (8 oz) raw cane sugar

Filling
2 tbsp clear honey
275 ml (10 fl oz) natural yoghurt
1 banana, peeled
1 fresh mango, peeled
50 g (2 oz) fresh strawberries
50 g (2 oz) black grapes, de-seeded
half a small fresh pineapple, peeled
1 small orange, peeled

Draw a 23 cm/9″ circle on a piece of greaseproof paper. Grease the circle thoroughly and place on a baking tray. Whisk the egg whites until very stiff. Whisk in the carob powder and half of the raw cane sugar. Fold in the remaining sugar. Spoon the meringue mixture on to the circle of greaseproof and spread evenly with a palette knife. Bake at 130°C/250°F/Gas Mark ½, for several hours until the meringue is crisp and dry.

Stir the honey into the yoghurt. Cut all the fresh fruit into small pieces and fold into this mixture. Pile the yoghurt and fruit mixture on to the meringue circle and serve immediately.

Carob Pots de Crême

Serves 6

425 ml (15 fl oz) milk
175 g (6 oz) Kalibu Carob Bar
25 g (3 oz) raw cane sugar
1 tbsp dark rum
4 egg yolks
whipped cream and Kalibu Carob Bar, *grated, to decorate*

Put the milk to warm in a pan over a gentle heat. Melt the carob in a bowl over a pan of hot water, remove from the heat when fully melted and stir in the sugar and the rum. Add the egg yolks to the mixture one at a time, mixing very thoroughly. Add the warmed milk, stirring continuously, and strain the liquid into the individual ramekin dishes. Place the dishes in a roasting tin in about 2.5 cm/1″ of cold water and bake for 30 minutes or so at 170°C/325°F/Gas Mark 3, until visibly set. After removing from the oven, leave to cool for a little while and then refrigerate for about 1 hour to chill. Before serving, decorate with piped whipped cream and sprinkle with grated carob bar.

Carob Ice Cream

Serves 6

575 ml (1 pint) milk
1 vanilla pod
4 egg yolks
75 g (3 oz) raw cane sugar
75 g (3 oz) Kalibu Carob Bar, *plain*
275 ml (10 fl oz) double cream, lightly whipped

Split the vanilla pod lengthways. Heat the milk and the vanilla pod together and leave to infuse for 15 minutes. Whisk the egg yolks and sugar together. Remove the vanilla pod and re-heat the milk. Add the hot milk to the whisked eggs and sugar, beating thoroughly. Melt the carob in a bowl over a pan of hot water. When melted, add to the milk mixture and allow to cool a little. Lastly fold in the double cream and pour into a container suitable for freezing. Freeze until it begins to set around the edges and then pour into a bowl, beat well and return to the freezing container. Freeze until solid. If you are serving the ice cream on its own, decorate with grated carob bar.

Carob Mousse

Serves 4

75 g (3 oz) Kalibu Carob Bar, *plain*
3 eggs, separated
grated Kalibu Carob Bar *for decoration*

Melt the carob in a bowl over a pan of hot water. Remove from the heat and stir in the egg yolks. Whisk the egg whites until stiff and fold into the carob mixture. Spoon into individual sundae glasses and leave to set in the refrigerator for about 2 hours. Just about serving, sprinkle with the grated carob bar.

LOSELEY

Rich Yoghurt and Fruit Ice Cream

Serves 6

This recipe is taken from my book *Making Your Own Home Proteins*. Strictly for special occasions. Puréed raspberries, strawberries, fresh apricots, peaches or nectarines are all equally good in this recipe. If using raspberries, then put them through a sieve after they have been puréed, to remove the seeds. To skin apricots, peaches or nectarines, just dip them in boiling water for a moment or two and peel.

The recipe involves making a rich custard sauce with yoghurt, cream and eggs. This has to be cooked slowly in a double boiler or pan over hot but not boiling water to prevent the yoghurt from curdling. See page 225 for notes about Loseley products.

575 ml (1 pint) Loseley Natural Yoghurt
150 ml (5 fl oz) Loseley Double Cream
3 tbsp clear honey
2 eggs and 2 egg yolks
few drops of vanilla essence
350 g (12 oz) fruit purée of your choice

Blend the yoghurt with the cream and honey. Whisk in the eggs and yolks and beat for 1 minute. When well blended, put into a double boiler or saucepan over a pan of hot, but not boiling, water and stir until the mixture thickens and coats the back of the spoon. Leave to cool. Stir the fruit and vanilla essence into the cooled custard and freeze in a lidded plastic container. Let the ice-cream soften in the fridge for about 30 minutes before serving.

You could try stirring a little Kirsch or other liqueur into the fruit before adding to the custard for that extra special dinner party.

Apple Mint and Carob Chip Fluff

Serves 4–5

This recipe is taken from my book *Vegetarian Food Processor*.

3 good size cooking apples, thinly peeled and cored
4 good size sprigs mint
3 level tbsp clear honey
2 tbsp water
200 ml (7 fl oz) Loseley Natural Yoghurt
2 egg whites
3 tbsp grated carob or chocolate bar

Cut the apples into chunks. Set the steel blades in position on a food processor and finely chop the apple. Clean and dry the bowl. Break off the tops of the sprigs of mint and set aside for decoration. Heat the honey and water in a heavy-bottomed saucepan. Add the mint sprigs and apple and cook gently for 5 minutes until soft and mushy. Take out the mint and set the apple mixture aside to cool. When cold, stir in the yoghurt. Set the egg whisk in position on the food processor and whisk the egg whites for 3 minutes, until stiff. Fold them into the apple mixture with the carob or chocolate chips, then spoon the mixture into individual serving dishes. Chill well and decorate with the reserved tops of the mint sprigs.

Chilled Yoghurt Pudding

Serves 6

150 g (5 oz) Loseley Double Jersey Cream
275 g (10 oz) Loseley Natural Yoghurt
75 g (3 oz) Muscovado sugar

Whip the cream carefully until fairly thick and gently blend in the yoghurt. Pour into a serving dish. Sprinkle on the sugar, covering the complete surface. Chill until required, allowing time for the sugar to melt on the surface.

Serve with a fresh fruit salad.

Fruit Brûlée

Serves 4–5

Another recipe from my book *Vegetarian Food Processor*. For this recipe you can use many different fruits. I prefer fresh apricots, plums or blackcurrants.

6 tbsp water
75 g (3 oz) fruit sugar
350 g (12 oz) fresh apricots, plums or blackcurrants
2 level tsp arrowroot plus 1 tbsp cold water
150 ml (5 oz) Loseley Soured Cream
1 rounded tsp soft brown sugar mixed with ½ tsp
  ground cinnamon for caramel topping

Put the water and sugar into a heavy-bottomed saucepan and heat until the sugar has dissolved. Add the fruit and cook until tender – no more than 5 minutes. Blend the arrowroot with the tablespoon of cold water until smooth and add to the fruit. Boil for 1 minute more. Set the steel blades in position on a food processor and blend the fruit until smooth. Spoon the fruit into individual flame-proof dishes, spread the tops with a thin layer of sour cream and sprinkle on the soft brown sugar and cinnamon. Set under a hot grill for a few seconds only until the sugar bubbles and caramelizes.

Fruit Cream

350 g (12 oz) fresh raspberries, blackberries or
  apricots
1 cup hot apple juice
2½ tsp arrowroot
275 g (10 oz) Loseley Soured Cream
3 tbsp brown sugar

If using berries, soak in the apple juice for 2 hours. If using apricots, blanch in hot water and peel off the skins. Take out the kernels and soak the apricots in the apple juice for 2 hours. Drain off the juice and reserve. Crush the fruit with a potato masher. Blend the arrowroot with a little of the apple juice. Heat the rest of the juice and stir it into the arrowroot paste, return to the pan and heat through, stirring constantly, until the sauce thickens and boils. Stir in the fruit. Pour the mixture into a shallow, oven-proof dish and cover with the sour cream. Sprinkle on the brown sugar and place under a hot grill until the top bubbles. Serve at once.

Yoghurt and Nectarine Ice Cream

Serves 8

This recipe (another from my book *Vegetarian Food Processor*) involves making a rich custard with yoghurt, sour cream and eggs. To prevent the yoghurt from curdling it is important to cook it slowly with the eggs in a pan over hot, not boiling, water, or preferably in a double boiler. You can use ripe peaches or apricots, instead of nectarines. Skin the fruit by dipping it in boiling water before peeling.

425 ml (15 fl oz) Loseley Natural Yoghurt
275 ml (10 fl oz) Loseley Soured Cream (2 small
  cartons)
2 eggs and 2 egg yolks
3 tbsp clear honey
450 g (1 lb) ripe nectarines
few drops pure vanilla essence
2 cardamom seeds (optional)

Set the steel blades in position on a food processor. Put the yoghurt, sour cream, eggs, egg yolks and honey in the processor bowl and blend for 1 minute. Clean and dry the bowl. Put this into a double boiler which contains hot, not boiling, water and stir until the mixture thickens and coats the back of the spoon. Leave to cool. Wash the fruit, slice in half, take out the stones and roughly chop. With the steel blades in position mash the fruit for 10 seconds. Split the cardamoms, if used, and crush the seeds as finely as possible using a pestle and mortar. Stir the seeds, a few drops of vanilla essence and the fruit into the cooled custard. Freeze in a suitable covered container. Place in the refrigerator for approximately 25 minutes before serving.

Yoghurt and Raspberry Ice Cream

Follow the method for Yoghurt and Nectarine Ice Cream but substitute raspberries for the nectarines. Purée the raspberries for 10 seconds, then sieve to remove the seeds. 350 g/12 oz of raspberries will be enough to give a full, fruity taste. Adding 1 tablespoon Kirsh to the fruit purée is delicious for special occasions. You can use strawberries in exactly the same way.

Yoghurt Syllabub

Serves 4

150 g (5 oz) Loseley Double Jersey Cream
grated rind and juice of 1 lemon
4 tbsp medium dry sherry
75 g (3 oz) fruit sugar
150 g (5 oz) Loseley Natural Yoghurt
50 g (2 oz) almonds, blanched, split and lightly
  toasted

Put all the ingredients except the yoghurt and almonds into a bowl and whisk well together, then whisk the yoghurt lightly into the mixture. Spoon into serving glasses and chill overnight. It will thicken in the refrigerator. When ready to serve, sprinkle on the toasted split almonds.

LOTUS

For those of you who like junket but who do not wish to use animal rennet, Lotus have produced a liquid vegetarian rennet not only for making junket but also for making soft and hard cheeses. A recipe leaflet about cheese-making is available from Lotus.

Vegetarian Vanilla Junket

Serves 4

575 ml (1 pint) milk, cow's or goat's
1 vanilla pod or a few drops vanilla essence
1 tbsp light Muscovado sugar
2 tsp Lotus Vegetarian Rennet
little grated nutmeg

Heat the milk and vanilla pod or essence in a saucepan to 55°C/110°F. Stir in the sugar, add the vegetarian rennet, stir and pour into individual serving dishes. Sprinkle a little freshly grated nutmeg on top, cool and serve.

Using individual dishes means that the junket will not fall apart as it would if served from a large dish.

Carob and Cinnamon Junket

Simply add 1 level tablespoon of carob powder to the ingredients above. Leave out the nutmeg and sprinkle on cinnamon instead. Make sure you mix the carob powder with a little cold milk first, then heat with the rest of the milk. You could also add 1 tablespoon Grand Marnier for a special-occasion sweet.

OCEAN SPRAY

Cranberry Soufflé

Serves 4–5

175 ml (6 oz) frozen orange juice concentrate,
  thawed
150 ml (5 fl oz) water
2 envelopes powdered gelatine
360 g (12½ oz) jar Ocean Spray Cranberry Sauce
275 ml (10 fl oz) can apple sauce
¼ tsp ground cloves
3 egg whites
whipped cream for decoration

Put the orange juice and water in a small pan, sprinkle over the gelatine and leave to soak for 5 minutes. Heat gently until all the gelatine has dissolved completely. Stir in the cranberry sauce, the apple sauce and ground cloves. Chill the mixture until beginning to thicken and set. Whisk the egg whites until stiff and fold gently into the fruit mixture. Pour into a 1 litre/2 pint soufflé dish and chill until set. Decorate with whipped cream and serve chilled.

PAUL'S TOFU

The following three recipes are taken from Jane O'Brien's informative book *The Magic of Tofu*.

Banana and Tofu Dessert

Serves 3–4

450 g (1 lb) Paul's Firm Tofu
1 or 2 ripe bananas
2 tbsp honey
1 tsp or a few drops of pure vanilla essence
pinch sea salt

Blend all the ingredients well and serve chilled.

Mocha Surprise Tofu Ice Cream

Serves 8

1½ tsps agar-agar powder
200 ml (7 fl oz) soya milk
100 g (4 oz) cashew nuts
575 ml (1 pint) water
100 g (4 oz) Paul's Tofu
225 g (8 oz) honey
2 tbsp carob powder
1 tbsp instant grain coffee, such as Swiss Cup or
    Barleycup
pinch sea salt
1½ tsp or a few drops pure vanilla essence
5 tbsp vegetable oil

Dissolve the agar-agar powder in the soya milk. Bring the milk to the boil, stirring constantly, and remove the pan from the heat immediately. Grind the nuts to a powder and add the water and soya milk. Place all the ingredients (except the oil) in a liquidizer and blend them until smooth. Taste for flavouring and sweetness, then continue to blend the mixture at high speed, adding the oil slowly. Place the mixture in an ice cream maker and follow the directions, or put into a container in the freezer. Remove the container and blend the mixture again before it freezes solid.

Whipped Cream Tofu

Serves 3–4

4 tbsp water
350 g (12 oz) Paul's Firm Tofu
½ tsp pure vanilla essence
½ tsp sea salt
2½ tbsp vegetable oil
100 g (4 oz) honey

Blend all the ingredients and adjust the flavouring to taste.

PLAMIL

Basic Vanilla Soya Ice Cream

This recipe is taken from my book *Making Your Own Home Proteins*.

100 g (4 oz) fruit sugar
725 ml (1¼ pints) Plamil Soya Milk
8 drops vanilla essence
4 tbsp cold pressed sunflower oil
pinch sea salt

Blend all the ingredients in a liquidizer or food processor. Place in either an ice cream maker or a plastic container with a tight-fitting lid. Place the container in the freezer, leave it until the ice cream begins to set, then beat it again and return to the freezer.

PREWETT'S

Pecan Nut and Wholewheat Flake Ice Crunch

Serves 4

This recipe is taken from my book *Vegetarian Food Processor*. Simple to prepare and voted an absolute winner by all who have tasted this crunchy cooler. You can use almonds or hazelnuts, which are a bit cheaper. The wholewheat flakes are more nutritious than cornflakes as they contain the whole grain, malt extract and a little raw cane sugar.

75 g (3 oz) pecan nuts
75 g (3 oz) Prewett's Wholewheat Flakes, crushed
75 g (3 oz) fruit sugar or Barbados sugar
3 egg whites
2 tbsp skimmed milk powder
275 ml (10 fl oz) natural yoghurt

Grind the nuts in a blender or food processor for 10 seconds only. They should be like breadcrumbs, not powdery. Put them on a baking sheet and toast under the grill for 1–2 minutes only. Take care that they do not burn. Leave to cool. Mix the crushed wheat flakes and sugar with the toasted nuts. Whisk the egg whites for 3 minutes until stiff. Stir the milk powder into the yoghurt. Fold the wheat flake mixture and the yoghurt into the egg whites. Put the mixture into a suitable container with a tight-fitting lid and freeze until quite firm. Remove from the freezer 25 minutes before serving to soften the mixture.

Delicious with a fresh or dried fruit salad.

WESTERN ISLES

Apple Juice Kanten Jelly

Serves 4

25 g/1 oz agar-agar flakes to 1.5 litres/2 pints liquid will give a good gel. Test by pouring a drop or two of warmed gel on to a cold plate. If too runny, add more flakes. If too thick, add a little more water.

1.5 litres (2 pints) water
4 tbsp pear and apple spread
240 ml (8 fl oz) Western Isles Concentrated Apple
  Juice
25 g (1 oz) agar-agar
1 pinch sea salt

Warm the water, pear and apple spread and apple juice concentrate together. When the liquid is smooth, add the agar-agar and salt. Boil until the agar-agar dissolves. Check the gel as above. Pour into a serving dish and leave to set in a cool place.

To vary, liquidize the gel and serve as a chilled mousse. For extra spicy sweetness add 75 g/3 oz washed raisins and enough cinnamon to taste when adding the agar-agar.

Toffee Apple Cream Custard

Serves 4

850 ml (1½ pints) water
120 ml (4 fl oz) Western Isles Apple Juice
  Concentrate or *other juice concentrate*
1 tbsp Western Isles Tahini
14 g (½ oz) agar-agar
pinch sea salt
2 tbsp barley malt (malt extract)
grated rind of 1 lemon

Mix half the water with half the apple juice concentrate and bring to the boil. Add the tahini and mix thoroughly. Soak the agar-agar in the remaining water and apple juice concentrate and boil until almost dissolved. Add the tahini mixture and a pinch of salt. In a separate pan, heat the barley malt. Add the lemon rind, then add to the agar-agar mixture.
Leave to cool.

Popcorn

Popcorn is a very versatile food that lends itself equally well to sweet and savoury recipes. For a wide variety of quick and easy snacks, experiment with different seasonings and sweeteners, such as barley malt, freshly ground black pepper, honey, peanut butter, Western Isles shoyu, sea salt, or just use the Western Isles no-salt seasoning. Be adventurous and try out any serving ideas that appeal to you!

For best results, heat 2 tablespoons of Western Isles cold pressed oil in a saucepan. Test the temperature by dropping in one or two corn kernels. When they pop, add enough corn (about 100 g/4 oz) to cover the bottom of the pan and quickly replace the lid. Shake until all the corn has popped.

For savoury or plain popcorn, add the contents of the seasoning sachet supplied with the corn and shake in. Empty the contents into a large bowl for serving.

Fruit and Nut Popcorn

100 g (4 oz) popping corn
50 g (2 oz) chopped nuts, toasted if wished
50 g (2 oz) dried fruit, washed
2 tbsp pumpkin, sesame or sunflower seeds

Simply add the ingredients to the popped corn and shake in to mix. Toss the mixture in melted butter or Western Isles corn oil.

Orange Honey Popcorn

100 g (4 oz) popping corn
50 g (2 oz) sunflower or pumpkin seeds or mixed nuts
3 tbsp Western Isles Corn Oil *or butter*
1/2 tbsp shredded orange peel
1/4 tsp grated nutmeg
3 tbsp honey or barley malt (malt extract)
juice of 1/2 lemon

Mix the seeds or nuts with the popped corn. Melt the honey or barley malt with the corn oil or butter and blend with the orange peel and nutmeg. Pour the mixture over the popped corn and seeds or nuts, add the lemon juice while the popcorn is still warm, and stir to mix well. Heat in a baking tin at 150°C/300°F/Gas Mark 4 for 15 minutes. Cool before serving.

Sweet-baked Popcorn

100 g (4 oz) popping corn
3 tbsp honey or barley malt (malt extract)
50 g (2 oz) raisins, washed
50 g (2 oz) almonds or hazelnuts, dry roasted in the oven for 15 minutes at 160°C/325°F/Gas Mark 3

Warm the raisins and nuts in the honey or barley malt. Mix well with the popped corn and pour into a baking tray. Bake at 160°C/325°F/Gas Mark 3 until lightly browned (about 10 minutes). Leave to cool, then cut into portions.

11
DIPS, PURÉES, PÂTÉS, SAUCES and PRESERVES

DIETADE

Green Tomato Chutney

Makes 8 450 g/1 lb jars

1 level tbsp sea salt
1.5 kg (3 lb) green tomatoes, skinned and chopped
2 large onions, peeled and chopped
1 large red pepper, de-seeded and chopped
approx. 550 ml/1 pint cider vinegar
350 g/12 oz Dietade Fruit Sugar
2 large cooking apples, peeled, cored and chopped
½ tsp ground cinnamon
1 tsp mustard seeds
2 fresh or 4 dried chillies, chopped
1 tsp allspice

Sprinkle the sea salt over the tomatoes, onions and chopped pepper and leave for 1 hour, then drain well in a colander. Put the cider vinegar and sugar into a thick saucepan, then add all the other ingredients. Bring to the boil and simmer gently with a lid on for 30–35 minutes, then jar in the usual way.

GAYELORD HAUSER'S NATURAL SEASONINGS

The following four recipes are from Gayelord Hauser's super collection.

Aubergine Caviar

1 large aubergine
100 ml/4 fl oz olive oil
1 small green pepper, de-seeded and diced
2 sticks celery, chopped
10 black, juicy ripe, olives, stoned and halved
¼ tsp Santay Pure Garlic Magic
1 medium onion, peeled and chopped
*3 large tomatoes, peeled and chopped or one 425 g
    (15 oz) can Italian tomatoes*
5 tbsps wine vinegar
2 tsps oregano
1 tsp basil
½ tsp Vege-sal

Place the unpeeled aubergine in a pre-heated oven at 180°C/350°F/Gas Mark 4, and bake about 1 hour until very soft. Allow to cool, then cut open. Remove the pulp and discard the skin. Heat the oil in a large pan, add the Santay Pure Garlic Magic, onion, green pepper and celery. Cook until the onion is golden. Stir in the aubergine and the remaining ingredients. Simmer, uncovered, for 20 minutes. Let cool, then chill. Serve cold on toast, crackers or pitta bread.

Dee-licious Low Sodium Dip

An excellent dip for salt-conscious individuals.

225 g (8 oz) low-fat yoghurt, quark or sour cream
1 tbsp Vegit

Mix the ingredients together.

Serve with raw vegetables, potato crisps or biscuits and other snacks. It tastes good even to people who are not salt-conscious.

Five Minute Tomato Sauce

2 tbsp vegetable oil (olive oil preferably)
4 medium size ripe, peeled and diced tomatoes or
  1 small can peeled tomatoes
½ tsp Santay Pure Garlic Magic
1 tsp Herbal Bouquet
Vege-Sal and Spike Seasoning to taste

Place all the ingredients in a heavy-based saucepan and bring to the boil, stirring occasionally. Cook for 5 minutes uncovered, and you'll have the tastiest tomato sauce. This must not be cooked for more than 5 minutes or it will turn sour.

Mexican Guacamole with Tofu

2 ripe avocados
225 g (8 oz) tofu
4 medium onion, chopped
1 large skinned tomato, mashed
Spike Seasoning to taste
a little lemon juice ⎫ *optional*
low salt soy sauce ⎭

Mash the avocados and tofu with a fork and mix in the mashed tomato, chopped onion and Spike seasoning. You may also like a few drops of lemon juice and a little shoyu. It tastes good with pitta bread or wholewheat crackers.

HOLLAND & BARRETT

Avocado Whip

Serve as a dip with crudités: fine strips of raw vegetables – choose from celery, carrot, cauliflower florets, red or green peppers, cucumber.

2 ripe avocados
25 g (1 oz) Holland & Barrett Ground Almonds
juice of half a lemon
225 g (8 oz) quark
freshly ground black pepper
sea salt

Cut the avocados in half and remove the stones. Scoop out the flesh and chop roughly. Place in the goblet of a blender and add the lemon juice, ground almonds and the quark. Blend together until smooth, season with black pepper and serve.

Chick Pea, Yoghurt and Sunflower Seed Dip

225 g (8 oz), dry weight, Holland & Barrett Chick Peas
75 g (3 oz) Holland & Barrett Sunflower Seeds
1 small carton natural yoghurt
juice of 1 lemon (approx. 2 tablespoons)
1 large clove garlic (more if you wish), crushed
1 tsp freshly ground coriander seeds
1 tbsp fresh mint, chopped
grated rind of ½ lemon
sea salt and freshly ground black pepper to taste

Soak the chick peas overnight, changing the water three times. Cook in fresh water until soft, about 1 hour. Drain. Toast the sunflower seeds in a dry pan, stirring constantly until lightly browned. Grind these with a little sea salt. Purée the peas in a blender or food processor with the yoghurt, lemon juice, garlic, coriander and mint. Stir the chick pea mixture into the ground sunflower seeds and blend in the grated lemon rind. Taste and season with sea salt and freshly ground black pepper if needed.

Flageolet and Avocado Purée

Flageolet beans are young kidney beans which have a delicate flavour and blend particularly well with avocados.

100 g (4 oz), dry weight, Holland & Barrett Flageolet
   Beans
2 good size ripe avocados
1 large clove garlic
2 tbsp lemon juice
3 tbsps cold pressed olive oil
¼ tsp cayenne pepper (optional)
2 tbsp yoghurt cheese (simply let 1 small carton
   yoghurt drip through muslin for several hours) or
   2 tbsp sour cream
sea salt and freshly ground black pepper to taste

Soak the beans overnight, changing the water at least twice. Rinse and boil in fresh water for 10 minutes. Simmer for a further 30 minutes or until soft. (Add a little sea salt about 5 minutes before the end of the cooking time.) Drain and leave to cool. Purée the beans in a blender or food processor.

Scoop out and purée the avocado flesh with the garlic, lemon juice, oil and cayenne (if used) until smooth, and stir into the bean purée. Finally stir in the yoghurt cheese or sour cream with a fork. Season with sea salt and freshly ground black pepper.

Delicious served on crisp Cos or Webb lettuce leaves as a starter.

Indian Lentil and Mushroom Pâté

A recipe is taken from my book *Vegetarian Food Processor*.

This pâté is rather like a very thick, firm dhal. In fact, adding more liquid to it would make it a perfect dhal to accompany a vegetable curry. You can use whole continental green lentils or the more common red split lentils.

225 g (8 oz) Holland & Barrett Continental Green or
   Red Split Lentils
850 ml (1½ pints) water
1 tsp sea salt
115 g (4 oz) small button mushrooms, sliced
3 tbsp peanut or sunflower oil

1 clove garlic
½ tsp ground cumin
½ tsp coriander seeds, crushed
½ tsp black mustard seeds, crushed
1 level tsp turmeric
1 dsrtsp fresh ginger root, grated
1 small green chilli, de-seeded and chopped
2 tbsp tomato purée
juice of 2 limes or *1 large lemon*
1 small cooking apple, thinly peeled, cored and
   chopped

Wash the lentils and pick over carefully for grit and small stones. Bring to the boil in the water and add the salt. Leave to simmer for 15 minutes if red split lentils; 20 minutes for the continental lentils (until soft but not too mushy). Drain and leave to stand in a colander until drained off, saving 2 tablespoons of the cooking liquid. Set the food processor slicing plate in position. Wash and wipe the mushrooms and slice. Sauté the mushrooms in 2 tablespoons of the oil until soft. Take out and put aside. Add the remaining 1 tablespoon of oil to the pan and fry the garlic, spices, ginger and chilli for 2 minutes (do not allow to burn). With the steel blades in position put the tomato purée, the fried spices, lime or lemon juice and chopped apple into the processor bowl. Blend until smooth. (You might have to add the 2 tablespoons of lentil cooking water if the mixture is not blending easily.) Scoop out into a serving bowl, stir in the mushrooms and mix with the cooked lentils.

This makes a beautiful stuffing for courgettes or marrow. Another idea is to spread it thickly on toast, sprinkle with a little grated cheese and put under the grill until lightly browned for a quick lunch or supper dish.

Middle Eastern Fig and Aniseed Jam

Makes 3 450 g/1 lb jars

Absolutely delicious and will keep for several months.

900 g (2 lb) Holland & Barrett Dried Figs
225 g (8 oz) fruit sugar (less if wished)
575 ml (1 pint) water
1 tbsp lemon juice
2 tsps aniseed, crushed
50 g (2 oz) lightly toasted Holland & Barrett Sesame
   Seeds
50 g (2 oz) Holland & Barrett Pine Kernels

Trim and cut the figs into small pieces. Dissolve the sugar in the water and bring to the boil. Add the lemon juice and figs and cook, stirring constantly, for 1 minute. Add the crushed aniseed and leave to cook gently until the fruit is pulp-like. Stir in the sesame seeds and pine kernels and jar as you would any preserve. Use as a spread or filling for puddings and pastries.

Nutty Pâté

Delicious in pitta bread, sandwiches or just as a dip.

100 g (4 oz) Holland & Barrett Almonds
75 g (3 oz) Holland & Barrett Hazelnuts
75 g (3 oz) Holland & Barrett Cashew Nuts
50 g (2 oz) Holland & Barrett Sesame Seeds
50 g (2 oz) Holland & Barrett Sunflower Seeds
6 tbsp cold pressed sunflower or safflower oil
6 tbsp natural yoghurt
1 tbsp shoyu
1 small onion, peeled and very finely chopped or
*   1 small bunch of spring onions, chopped (use all*
*   green parts)*
1 tsp mixed herbs
a little chopped red or green pepper
a little freshly ground black pepper

Toast the nuts and seeds in a thick, dry saucepan over medium heat, stirring constantly with a wooden spoon, for approximately 10 minutes. Grind the toasted mixture in a blender until powdery, then add to the remaining ingredients in a bowl and mix well together.

This pâté spread on hot pitta bread with salad makes a truly fabulous meal for lunch or supper.

Peach Chutney

Makes 7 jars (450 g/1 lb size)

This recipe is absolutely delicious with curry, in cheese sandwiches or with cold meat or bean salads.

500 g (1.1 lb) Holland & Barrett Dried Peaches
425 ml (15 fl oz) cider vinegar
350 g (12 oz) Demerara sugar
1 large green pepper, de-seeded and chopped
1 medium red pepper, de-seeded and chopped
3 large cooking apples, peeled and chopped
175 g (6 oz) Holland & Barrett Raisins
1 tbsp cayenne pepper
2 tbsp fresh ginger, grated

1 dessertspoon coriander
1/4 tsp clove powder
1 tbsp white or black mustard seeds
6 large cloves garlic, crushed

Wash and soak the peaches for 24 hours, then drain and chop. Put the cider vinegar and sugar into a large, thick saucepan and add all the other ingredients. Heat through for 3 minutes. Stir well, bring to the boil and simmer for 35 minutes with a lid on. Jar in the usual way if the family will let you get as far as the preserving pots!

The flavour is at its best after two weeks.

HUGLI

Sprouted Soya Bean Starter with Mango and Ginger Sauce

Serves 4

For how to sprout soya beans see page 00.

175 g (6 oz), dry weight, soya beans, sprouted
1 tsp Hugli Instant Vegetable Broth Mix (or to taste)
1 bunch radishes, trimmed and sliced
1/4 cucumber, diced
2 tbsp each, red and green pepper, finely chopped
1 bunch spring onions (about 6), finely chopped
*   (use green ends as well)*

Sauce
1 good size mango (or 2 medium peaches,
*   blanched, skinned and chopped)*
1 tsp fresh ginger, grated
1 tsp clear honey
1 dessertspoon shoyu
1 tbsp lemon juice

Cook the sprouted soya beans for 20 minutes in a pressure cooker or for 2 hours in a saucepan until soft. (Do not salt the water.)

Purée the cooked beans in a blender or food processor until smooth, adding Hugli vegetable broth granules to your taste. Mix with the chopped vegetables and spoon into four serving dishes. Combine all the sauce ingredients in a blender or food processor and spoon over the individual portions of bean purée. Stir in the sauce just before eating.

LOSELEY

Aubergine Purée with Mushrooms

This recipe is taken from my book *Vegetarian Food Processor;* it is a slightly richer starter, quite delicious and simple to prepare using a food processor or blender.

3 medium aubergines, each approx. 225 g (8 oz) in weight
a little vegetable oil for frying
1 medium onion, sliced
100 g (4 oz) small button mushrooms, washed and sliced
2 tbsp olive oil
150 g (5 fl oz) Loseley Soured Cream
sea salt and freshly ground black pepper

Rub a little oil over the skin of the aubergines and bake in the oven at 190°C/375°F/Gas Mark 5 for 45 minutes. Cut, scoop out the pulp and leave to cool.

Sauté the onion in the oil for 5 minutes. Add the mushrooms and fry for 3 minutes. Blend the aubergine pulp with the onions and mushrooms until smooth and transfer to a serving dish. Stir in the sour cream and season with sea salt and black pepper to taste. Chill before serving.

Carrot and Cucumber Chutney

This recipe is from my book *Wholefood Cookery Course.*

225 g (8 oz) carrots, scrubbed and very thinly sliced
225 g (8 oz) cucumber, chopped in small cubes
1 very small onion, peeled, finely chopped and crushed
1 dessertspoon fresh ginger, grated
1 tsp ground coriander
1/2 tsp cayenne pepper
3 tbsp lemon juice
1 small carton Loseley Natural Yoghurt
a little sea salt to taste

Mix all the ingredients together and serve as a side dish with curry.

Curry Dip with Crudités

150 ml (5 fl oz) Loseley Soured Cream or Natural Yoghurt
150 ml (5 fl oz) mayonnaise
1 tsp curry powder (medium hot)
1/2 level tsp paprika
1/2 level tsp fresh ginger, grated
1 level tsp methi (fenugreek leaf)

Mix all the ingredients together and serve with slices of raw vegetables (crudités) such as carrot, celery, cucumber, spring onions, cauliflower florets, chicory leaves and radishes.

Pecan Nut and Yoghurt Dip

10 pecan nut halves
1 large clove garlic, crushed
1 tbsp olive oil
275 ml (10 fl oz) Loseley Natural Yoghurt
1/2 small cucumber, finely diced
few drops lemon juice
a little sea salt and freshly ground black pepper

Mix all the ingredients together, saving a few pecan halves for decoration. Chill before serving.

LOTUS

Diane's Dhal

150 g (5 oz) Lotus Soya Grits
450 ml (16 fl oz) water
2 bay leaves
1 tsp mixed herbs
1 tsp Lotus Flavour-mix (brown stock)
1 medium onion, chopped
15 g (4 oz) butter or polyunsaturated margarine
1/2 tsp fennel or caraway or dill seeds, crushed
lemon juice
salt and pepper to taste

Soak the soya grits in the water, add the bay leaves and herbs and simmer gently for 15 minutes, then add the Flavour-mix. Cook the onion in the butter or margarine with the fennel or other seeds until tender. Add to the grits. Add lemon juice, salt and pepper to taste.

Serve with carrots, parsnips and green vegetables, or with baked artichokes and green olives. Can also be served with a green salad or as a filling in avocado pears.

Soya Hummous

This is a very quick method of making Hoummus as the soya grits only take a few minutes to soak and cook.

2 parts soaked, cooked Lotus Soya Grits to 1 part tahini
1 clove garlic, crushed
lemon juice to taste
salt to taste

See the previous recipe for the cooking method for soya grits.

Blend all the ingredients together. An electric blender helps to give it a smoother texture. Season with salt to taste and add more lemon and garlic if necessary. Serve garnished with chopped mint, chives and olives.

MERRYDOWN

Merrydown Horseradish Sauce

25 g (1 oz) freshly grated horseradish or 1 tbsp dried horseradish
4 tbsp boiling water (to soak)
1 tbsp Merrydown Cider Vinegar
1 tbsp Merrydown Honey Vinegar
110 g (4 oz) double cream, lightly whipped
a little salt and freshly ground black pepper

Note If using 25 g/1 oz horseradish the sauce will be hot; use 15 g/½ oz if you prefer a milder tasting sauce.

Put the grated horseradish in a bowl and pour on the boiling water. Leave for 30 minutes. Squeeze the excess moisture from the horseradish and put it in another bowl with both vinegars and the lightly whipped cream. Fold them gently together and season to taste with salt and pepper.

Serve with either beef or soya (TVP) burgers, wholemeal baps, lots of fresh crisp lettuce and tomato slices for a lunchtime snack.

OCEAN SPRAY

Cranberry Sauce

This sauce is absolutely delicious and can be served with many savoury dishes.

275 g (10 oz) Ocean Spray Cranberries
275 g (10 oz) cooking apples, thinly peeled, cored and chopped (weight when peeled)
150 ml (5 fl oz) apple juice concentrate
50 ml (2 fl oz) water
4 tbsp cherry brandy or brandy

Cook all the ingredients except the spirits gently in a saucepan for 20 minutes. Add the cherry brandy or brandy. Re-heat for 30 seconds. Jar and keep in the fridge when cool. The sauce will keep for 6 weeks even after opening.

PANTRY STOCK

Vegetarian Savouries with Mustard Dip

Makes about 30

185 g (6½ oz) packet Pantry Stock Savoury Rissole Mix
1 small onion, peeled and very finely chopped (a vegetable chopper is best to use)
1 tsp mixed herbs
½ tsp hot pepper sauce
75 ml (3 oz) natural bran
vegetable oil for frying

Dip
6 tbsp mayonnaise
1 tbsp made mustard
1 tbsp tomato purée
*1 tbsp mustard seeds, crushed (use a pestle and
    mortar or a rolling pin, putting the seeds between
    two sheets of kitchen paper)*
sea salt and freshly ground black pepper

Empty the rissole mix into a bowl and add 275 ml/
10 fl oz of cold water. Stir in the onion, mixed herbs
and hot pepper sauce. Roll teaspoons of the
mixture into small balls and coat with the natural
bran. Heat the oil and shallow fry the savouries for
5–10 minutes. Spear with cocktail sticks and serve
with the dip, made by mixing all the dip ingredients
together and pouring into a small dish.

PAUL'S TOFU

——Tofu Dip Delight——

This recipe is taken from my book *Making Your
Own Home Proteins*.

This is very good for a buffet party. Fresh herbs
are best, but in case they are not available I have
given the quantities for dried. However, I do not like
using dried parsley or mint in this recipe. In the
recipe I have recommended cold pressed sunflower
or safflower oil.

450 g (1 lb) Paul's Firm Tofu
4 tbsp cold pressed safflower or sunflower oil
*3 tbsp lemon juice or half and half wine vinegar
    and lemon juice*
1 tsp clear honey
2 tbsp fresh parsley, very finely chopped
1 tbsp fresh mint, very finely chopped

*1½ tbsp fresh marjoram, basil or oregano, or a little
    of all three, finely chopped (If using dried, then ½
    level tsp of each)*
1 medium onion, very finely chopped
1 medium red pepper, very finely chopped
16 cm (6") piece of cucumber, diced
1 tbsp capers
sea salt and freshly ground black pepper to taste

Combine the tofu, oil, lemon juice and honey in a
blender or food processor until smooth. Stir in all
the other ingredients, making sure that the vegetables are very finely chopped. Add the salt and
pepper last. You will end up with a lively, crunchy
dip. Chill before serving.

This is really good stuffed in pitta bread, in
sandwiches, or dolloped in crisp lettuce leaves on a
platter for a buffet party. Alternatively, just use it as a
dip scooped up with whole grain corn crisps (buy
these at a health store), or on finger croutons
(garlic-buttered, oven-toasted fingers of wholemeal
bread).

PROTOVEG

——Lentil and Smokey——
Snaps Pâté

This recipe is taken from *The Magic Bean* by Anna
Roberts.

225 g (8 oz) split red lentils
1 medium onion
575 ml (1 pint) water
1 dessertspoon shoyu
1 tsp dried mint
3 tbsp Protoveg Smokey Snaps Mince

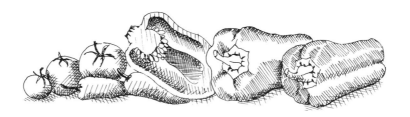

Wash and pick over the lentils, removing stones and grit. Chop the onion finely. Pour the water into a pan and add the lentils, onion, shoyu and mint. Cook until the liquid is absorbed. Remove from heat, mix in the Smokey Snaps and liquidize. Put the pâté into a serving dish, and place in a refrigerator for an hour or so before serving.

The pâté may be served on crackers or used as a sandwich spread.

REAL EAT

Vegefest pâté

This recipe was devised by Erica Kenyon for Vegeburger.

2 packs Real Eat Vegeburger Mix
1 small onion
2–3 cloves garlic
olive or *sunflower oil for shallow frying*
3 tbsp tomato ketchup
1 large tin chestnut purée (unsweetened)
1 tbsp honey
salt and pepper to taste
1 tsp lemon thyme ⎫
2 tsp parsley ⎬ *finely chopped*
2 tsp chives ⎭
4 small eggs
2 tbsp brandy or *sherry*
1 bay leaf

Make up the Vegeburger Mix following pack instructions and leave to stand. Meanwhile, finely chop the onion and garlic and fry until translucent. Fry the Vegeburger Mix in plenty of oil, either in burger shapes or as one slab, turning constantly for about 5 minutes. Allow to cool, then crumble and mix with the onion and garlic, then add the tomato ketchup, chestnut purée, honey, salt, peppar and all herbs except the bay leaf. Bind the mixture with the lightly beaten eggs and finally add the brandy.

Press the pâté firmly into a buttered terrine dish and place the bay leaf on top. Set the dish in a baking tray half full of water and bake at 190°/375°F/ Gas Mark 4 for approximately 1 hour. When cooled, cover with paper and place a heavy weight on top for a few hours. Serve cold, accompanied by hot buttered toast. The pâté is best if kept for several days before using.

SUNWHEEL

Chilled Haricot Bean Hors d'Oeuvres

This dish originates from the Middle East where it is usually eaten chilled, but it is equally delicious served hot. I prefer to use ripe fresh tomatoes but canned will do.

350 g (12 oz), dry weight, haricot beans
2 large cloves garlic
1 large onion (about 225 g/8 oz) when chopped)
1 good size carrot, diced
2 sticks celery (use green leaves as well), chopped
3 tbsp Sunwheel Cold Pressed Olive Oil or Sesame Oil
1 rounded tbsp fresh parsley, chopped
1 large bay leaf
1 rounded tsp basil or *marjoram*
1 tsp freshly ground coriander seeds
350 g (12 oz) ripe tomatoes, skinned and mashed
1 tbsp tomato purée
1 tbsp Sunwheel shoyu (if serving hot)
2 tbsp cider vinegar ⎫ *(if serving*
2 tbsp Sunwheel Cold Pressed Olive Oil ⎬ *cold)*
a few black olives, stoned and halved
1 tbsp fresh parsley, chopped

Soak the beans overnight, changing the water three times. Rinse and boil in 850 ml/1½ pints water for 10 minutes, turn down to simmer and continue to cook 20 minutes more. Meanwhile sauté the garlic, onion, carrot and celery in 3 tablespoons oil until soft, about 10 minutes. Stir in the parsley, bay leaf, basil or marjoram and coriander and continue to cook for just 1 minute, then add the tomatoes and tomato purée. Now stir this vegetable mixture into the cooking beans and continue to simmer for 1 hour more (or until the beans are soft). *If serving hot* stir in the shoyu just before serving. (You might need more shoyu depending on your taste.) *If serving cold,* chill the mixture, then stir in the vinegar and 2 tablespoons of olive oil. Dot the olive halves on top and sprinkle with chopped parsley.

Falafal (Ground Chick Pea Balls)

Makes 30–40

These ground chick pea balls are a traditional Middle Eastern delight. Serve on a bed of fresh lettuce with pitta bread and yoghurt. This recipe is a real treat and well worth the bother. It is taken from my book *Wholefood Cookery Course*.

500 g (1.1 lb) dry weight, chick peas
1 heaped tsp ground coriander
4 tbsp Sunwheel Cold Pressed Olive Oil
2 tbsp fresh parsley, finely chopped
3 large cloves garlic, crushed
2 tbsp Sunwheel Sesame Spread (tahini)
juice of 2 lemons (approx. 4 tbsps)
1/2 tsp freshly ground black pepper
sea salt to taste
1 level tsp cayenne pepper or *chilli powder*
    (optional but adds that extra umph!)
1 egg, beaten, to bind
wholemeal flour, plain, for coating
vegetable oil for deep frying

Soak the chick peas overnight, changing the water at least twice. Cook in fresh water for 1 hour. Drain, discarding the cooking water, and grate the chick peas through either a hand or electric cheese grater. Soft, powdery flakes will form. Do not add any water. Add the other ingredients, leaving the beaten egg until last. Form into walnut-size balls, making approximately 30–40. Roll each in wholemeal flour and deep fry for 3 minutes in hot oil. Drain on kitchen paper and keep warm in the oven.

Falafal are delicious served as an appetizer with a sauce made from a mixture of yoghurt, cucumber and fresh chopped mint.

Hummous

This recipe for Hummous comes from the Middle East. It includes tahini which, when combined with the chick peas, makes a highly nutritious complete protein food. I often serve Hummous stuffed into pitta bread with crisp lettuce leaves for a truly wholesome lunch.

225 g (8 oz) dry weight, chick peas
juice of 2 lemons
2 large cloves garlic
2 tbsp Sunwheel Sesame Spread (tahini)
2 tbsp Sunwheel Cold Pressed Olive Oil
sea salt and freshly ground black pepper
mint to garnish

Wash the chick peas well and pick over for stones. Soak them for at least 12 hours, changing the water three times. Rinse and cook in 1 litre/2 pints water for 1 hour or until soft. Add 1 tablespoon sea salt 10 minutes before the end of the cooking time. Put half the peas into a processor bowl with half of all the other ingredients and blend until smooth. (You might have to add a little cooking water, but only just enough to achieve a thick, creamy consistency.) Scoop out. Now put the other half of the ingredients into the processor bowl and blend as before until smooth, adding cooking water if necessary. Place in a serving bowl, add sea salt and freshly ground black pepper to taste and garnish with a sprig of mint.

Pistachio Dip with Crudités

100 g (4 oz) pistachio nuts
2 eggs yolks
175 ml (6 fl oz) Sunwheel Cold Pressed Olive or
    Sunflower Oil
1 tbsp lemon juice
1/2 tsp mustard powder
1/2 tsp sea salt
1/2 tsp freshly ground black pepper
1 clove garlic, crushed
1 tbsp fresh parsley, chopped

Crudités (raw vegetables)
1 bunch spring onions (use 7 cm/2 1/2" of the tops,
    saving the green parts to use chopped in salads
3 good size carrots, scraped and cut in half
    widthwise, then cut in thin sticks. Rub in lemon
    juice to prevent browning
3 inside tender sticks of celery cut into 7 cm (2 1/2")
    sticks
1/2 good size red pepper cut into thin strips from the
    centre to the base

In a blender grind the nuts to a powder and transfer to a mixing bowl. To make mayonnaise, put the egg yolks into the blender (no egg whites) with 2 tablespoons of the olive or sunflower oil, the lemon juice, mustard, salt, pepper and garlic. Blend at low speed until it is a smooth paste. Still on low speed, drop in the parsley and then pour in the remaining oil in a slow but steady stream. The machine will begin to make a gurgling sound when the mixture starts to thicken. When all the oil is poured in and well blended stop the machine. Put the mayonnaise into a bowl and beat in the ground pistachio nuts. Taste and season with more salt if you need it. You can also add a little more lemon juice if you like. Chill before serving with crudités.

Sunflower Seed and Aubergine Purée

Delicious as a dip which can be garnished with very thin rings of onion and stoned and halved black olives.

a little vegetable oil
2 medium aubergines
2 rounded tbsp Sunwheel Sunflower Spread
2 tbsp lemon juice
1 large juicy clove garlic, crushed
2 tbsp parsley, very finely chopped
1 level tsp freshly ground coriander seeds
sea salt and fresly ground black pepper to taste

Rub the aubergines with a little oil and bake in the oven at 180°C/350°F/Gas Mark 4 for about 1 hour until the flesh is cooked. Place under a cold tap to cool and then peel off the skins. Purée the aubergine flesh with the sunflower spread, lemon juice, garlic, parsley and coriander. When well blended add a little sea salt and freshly ground black pepper to taste.

WESTERN ISLES

Spiced Tomato Sauce

395 g (14 oz) can tomatoes
1 tbsp tomato purée
1 large clove garlic, crushed
1 green eating apple, peeled and roughly chopped
1/2 green and 1/2 red pepper, de-seeded and roughly chopped
2 tbsp celeriac, grated or 1 tsp celery seeds, crushed
1 tsp basil
1/2 tsp tarragon
1 tbsp lemon juice
1 tbsp Western Isles Shoyu
1 tsp Tabasco sauce or 1 level tsp cayenne pepper

Set the steel blades in position on a food processor. Put all the ingredients into the processor bowl and blend until smooth, then cook the mixture gently over a low heat until some of the liquid has evaporated and the sauce is thick. This will take about 20 minutes.

If you do not have a food processor, sauté the chopped apple and peppers until they are beginning to soften, add the rest of the ingredients and simmer for 20 minutes or so. Then sieve or blend in a liquidizer.

LIST OF COMPANIES

As well as the information from the following manufacturers, recipes have been provided for this book by *Holland & Barrett* and *Nature's Way*. These names are familiar to most readers as stockists and suppliers of an enormous variety of healthy foods, and I am grateful for their contributions.

Allinson

Dr T. R. Allinson was one of the pioneers of natural food. The introduction of the steel milling process in 1897 meant that wholewheat grain could be broken up and the fibre and wheatgerm eliminated from the flour. Dr Allinson was appalled and warned that without the valuable vitamins and bran (fibre) in the flour ill-health would be sure to follow. How right he was. He was so convinced that he established his own stone-grinding flour mill and later opened a bakery using his own flour to produce bread of the finest quality. His books on health and diet were published and mainly dealt with the importance of dietary fibre. He strongly believed that many digestive disorders were the result of eating processed, devitalized foods. We owe him the deepest respect and thanks for his hard work and dedication to a belief which was for our well-being and health. He would be delighted to know that today there is a growing awareness about food, that the name of Allinson is still alive and the flour in their mills at Castleford, Yorkshire, is tested daily in order to maintain a high-standard quality product which results in delicious bakes.

Stoneground flour and steel-milled flour do differ. In supermarkets you will find much cheaper steel-milled versions of 100% wholemeal or whole-wheat flour, but the more expensive stoneground flour is usually superior to steel-milled because the stone burrs, which grind the wheat, distribute the embryo oil (germ oil) at a slow speed and do not generate the high level of heat which the fast speed of steel plates achieves. Too much heat can destroy the germ oil, causing it to become rancid and thus rendering it nutritionally useless.

As well as manufacturing a range of flours *Allinson* produce two bran products, *Broad Bran* and *Bran Plus*, and a quick-acting yeast, *Easybake*. This is an excellent natural product in powder form which cuts down the time needed to make any yeast-risen recipe by eliminating the process of having to leave the yeast to froth. It also contains powdered vitamin C (asorbic acid), which has the effect of strengthening the gluten in the flour and helping the dough to rise.

Applefords Ltd

The *Applefords* products used in the recipes in this book are Cider Vinegar, Black Strap Molasses and Dietade Fruit Sugar. All are excellent products. Applefords also manufacture a new range of canned fruits which are packed in natural juices. These are delicious and far healthier than canned fruits which contain added sugar syrup. For more detailed information on diabetic foods write to: Applefords Limited, 14 Villiars Road, Kingston-upon-Thames, Surrey KT1 3AB.

Broadland

Shredded vegetable suet produced by *Broadland* is a new product and can be used in any recipe that requires animal suet. It is a healthier and tastier alternative, but gives a result indistinguishable in appearance from animal suet dishes. It is made from wheat flour and solid vegetable oil.

Café Hag

This manufacturer produces a range of decaffeinated coffees: Instant Spray Dried; Instant Freeze Dried (including 1-cup sachets); Instant Deluxe; Roast and Ground (suitable for percolators); and Filter Fine. Well worth trying if you drink a lot of coffee and want to cut down on caffeine – I serve the ground coffee to my most hardened coffee-drinking friends who find no difference in flavour between it and a good quality blend of freshly ground coffee.

Carrabay

This is one of the *Sunwheel* brand names to be found on a range of sea vegetables, such as carrageen and dulse. (*See Sunwheel*; also Carrageen and dulse (dillisk) in the List of Ingredients.)

Country Basket

Country Basket produce a range of wholewheat pasta which has a good flavour and texture.

Dietade (fruit sugar)

This product is manufactured by *Applefords Ltd*. It looks like caster sugar but is fructose, not sucrose. It is absorbed more slowly from the intestinal tract and does not cause blood sugar levels to rise as sharply as they do with cane or beet sugar. It can be used in place of ordinary sugar in any recipe, but it is slightly sweeter gram for gram, which means you use less and consume fewer calories to achieve an equivalent sweetness. The manufacturer suggests that fruit sugar can be used in moderation by diabetics after taking advice from a doctor.

Doves Farm

Doves Farm make a wide range of flours and meals, including some less common ones such as maize or cornmeal and rye flour. The best known of their flours is probably their stoneground wholemeal, which is made from a blend of fine English milling wheats and the best hard wheats from the American prairies. These are ground on millstones and the manufacturer says the stones are dressed by the miller using a rule of thumb based on long experience. He rubs the flour between thumb and forefinger to tell how the stones are grinding and if they need attention. This method of making flour is slower than modern methods, but it retains the essential B and E vitamins and does not shatter or sieve out the components of the whole grain.

Another popular flour is their organic flour, milled from grains grown on farms using only organic farming principles. Organic farmers use traditional methods such as crop rotation rather than artificial fertilizers and chemical sprays. Only the best bread-making wheats are selected for this flour.

Doves Farm brown wheatmeal flour is also stoneground, but some of the coarser bran is removed, leaving a delicious golden flour with a lighter texture than wholemeal. Rye flour is made from selected natural rye grain, ground by millstones. The delicious taste of rye complements any recipe using flour and adds variety on baking day. It is often used in breads and biscuits and blends particularly well with caraway, treacle, mixed spice, orange, olive and anchovy flavours.

Their Malthouse flour is a mixture of flours. The malted grains add a wholesome, crunchy texture and they contain a natural sugar, maltose, which is readily absorbed by the body, giving energy and strength. As the whole of the grain is used, this also provides useful dietary fibre.

Doves Farm 100% Wholemeal self-raising flour is milled especially fine, making its light, soft texture ideal for cakes and baking, yet it still retains all the nourishment of 100% wholemeal flour.

Euvita

Euvita do a wide range of wholegrain pastas which have a rich wholesome flavour yet are light in texture and are a far healthier alternative to pasta made with processed white flour.

Force

Force Whole Wheat Flakes contain whole wheat, sugar and malt. They contain the goodness of whole grain and are a better alternative to cornflakes.

Gayelord Hauser's Natural Seasonings

These seasonings were originally created by Gayelord Hauser, who has been described as the 'Dean of the natural food movement'. I, for one, have learned a great deal from his books over the years. Most of us who enjoy cookery would love to have a well-stocked herb garden because fresh herbs and spices are unbeatable and impart a full, yet delicate, flavour to fresh or cooked food. It is the same with freshly-picked organically-grown vegetables, but again not many of us have the luxury of a richly-stocked vegetable garden. Consequently we have to use what is available. Where herbs and spices are concerned there is a huge range of good quality dried varieties to choose from. As well as the seasonings, the delicious recipes given in this book are the creation of Gayelord Hauser and well worth trying.

Gelozone

Gelozone replaces animal gelatine and cornflour for thickening and gelling and can be used in both savoury and sweet dishes. It contains natural vegetable gums, namely guar and locust bean (carob), as well as carrageen which is extracted from the mineral-rich seaweed, Irish moss. It is also gluten-free, has a high fibre content of 80 per cent and is low in calories. It is suitable for slimmers and diabetics as well as vegetarians and vegans.

Granny Ann Cookiemalt

This product made by *Itona* is a very pleasantly flavoured pure malt extract. Home-baked produce will stay fresher for longer, the manufacturers say, because *Cookiemalt* attracts moisture. It browns at a fairly low temperature so your bread, cakes, biscuits and scones will have a rich golden colour.

Granose

Granose make a wide range of dried and canned foods which are quick to prepare as well as being wholesome and nourishing. Granose Savoury Cuts are made from the gluten (protein) in wheat flour. It has a meat-like flavour and its chewy, porous texture, which comes somewhere between beef steak and liver, easily absorbs flavours from stock, vegetables, herbs and spices. Unlike meat and soya protein it is not a complete protein (*see* TVP in the List of Ingredients). However, as you are unlikely to eat this food alone it is easy to complement it with other protein-rich foods which will balance the amino-acid content. Combined with pulses, (dried peas, beans and lentils) or fresh vegetables and dairy produce, you will achieve the correct balance. Granose Tender Bits is a wheat protein similar to Savoury Cuts and can be used in the same way. Granose Rissolnut is a savoury rissole mixture with onions, herbs and spices for making scotch eggs, savoury loaves and rissoles. Nuttolene Meatless Savoury Loaf is made from peanuts and salt. It is also gluten-free and high in protein. Granose Soya-pro Slices (rather like a meat loaf in texture) can be eaten hot or cold or cut into small chunks and used in casseroles or as an alternative to beef in such dishes as stroganoff. This high soya-based protein food comes in 'beef' flavour and 'chicken' flavour. Granose Sausfry is made from TVP and has a flavour and texture remarkably similar to meat-based sausages. You can use it as you would normal sausagemeat. When reconstituted its weight is doubled. To 100 g/4 oz dry sausfry you will need 175 ml/6 fl oz cold water. It is important to measure the water to achieve the right consistency.

Granose Soya Milk can be used in all recipes as an alternative to cow's milk. It is not however suitable for babies under 6 months.

Granose Soya Infant Formula is available in powdered form and is suitable for infants whenever mother's milk is not available. These are just a few of the vast range of Granose products. Your local health food shop will be able to advise you on their other products.

Höfels

Höfels' range includes flour, bran soya flakes, oatmeal, sea salt and other high quality products. Their flours are made from organically grown English grains and the flavour of their grains is deliciously natural. Their 100% wholemeal Norfolk Flour is made from soft wheat and has a medium-coarse texture and a rich, nutty flavour.

Hugli

Hugli make an instant vegetable broth mix (granulated as well as low-salt) and vegetable stock cubes. Both products are marvellous for making quick and tasty stock for soups and sauces, and they are quite delicious added to casseroles, stews, curries and grain or bean dishes. The produces are free from additives and have a subtle flavour. You will find many recipes throughout this book which use *Hugli* stock cubes and Instant Vegetable Broth Mix. They also make a range of soups, including Low Sodium Vegetable, Mushroom and Celery varieties. The soups can be used as thickeners or flavour extenders for casserole dishes or sauces, for example, their mushroom soup with extra milk or cream makes an ideal sauce for fish or fish pies.

Harmony

(*see* Western Isles)

Itona

Itona offers a range of TVP (*see* List of Ingredients) in 100 g/4 oz packs which reconstitute to the equiva-

Opposite: **Loseley** *Mango Cheese Tart (above) page 149, Yoghurt Syllabub (below left) page 208, Chilled Yoghurt Pudding (below right) page 206*

lent of 350 g/12 oz of prime, lean meat. No fat, no gristle, no waste. They cut the weekly meat bill dramatically with no loss of flavour or nutritional value. TVP has 50 per cent protein at 6 per cent moisture (roughly the equivalent of best beef) and 1 per cent fat, against an average of about 5 per cent for ordinary meat. Texture and 'biteability' is the same as meat. Itona TVP looks and tastes like meat, yet it's better for you than meat and costs a lot less! It is available as Beef Flavoured Mince and Beef Flavoured Chunks. *Itona* Natural Unflavoured TVP Mince will take on any flavour you want—used with chicken, for example, it will take on the flavour of the chicken, so making more of your meat. *Itona* TVP is also available in 675g/1½lb Budget Packs. *Itona* also manufacture *Granny Ann* products.

Kalibu

Sunwheel market block and powder carob (*see* List of Ingredients) under the brand name *Kalibu*. It is a healthier alternative to chocolate. In cooking, the powder can be used in any recipe where cocoa is called for, and the blocks of chocolate can be eaten as confectionery or melted for sauces and icings. Flavours of the bars include Hazelnut, Nut & Raisin and Mint & Orange, and carob-coated snacks include Cherry Yoghurt Bar, Ginger Fudge Bar and Carob Coated Muesli Bar. All have a delicious flavour.

Kretschmer

Kretschmer Wheat Germ is toasted and vacuum-packed and has a delicious nutty flavour. It contains all the nutrients of fresh, raw wheat germ. Wheat germ is a highly nutritious food and a valuable source of vitamin E and the B vitamins. It has a high protein content and is rich in fibre, low in calories, has no cholesterol, no salt and no preservatives. Being vaccuum-packed in a jar, with full instructions on how to store, this wheat germ stays fresh for longer and does not go rancid, which is a common problem with loose raw wheat germ if it is not carefully stored in airtight containers in cool surroundings. *Kretschmer* have devised delicious recipes, some of which I have used in this book, including some lovely yeast recipes.

Opposite: **Western Isles** *Apple Juice Kanten Jelly (above) page 210, Toffee Apple Cream Custard (below) page 210*

Lane's

Lane's Herb Salt is a delicious mixture of sea salt and herbs which enhances any savoury dish to which it is added.

London Herb & Spice Co.

This company makes a range of cook bags, mixtures of herbs and spices specially selected to complement individual dishes. They are bought in packs of twenty, like tea bags. They are very easy to use and impart a delicious flavour. The company also produces a range of unique herbal teas which all taste really good.

Loseley

Loseley natural yoghurt is made from low-fat separated Jersey milk and is 'set' in the carton. 'Live' means that the beneficial bacteria, *Lactobacillus bulgaricus* and *Streptococcus thermophilus,* which are used to make yoghurt, are still active.

Another product is *Lebnie*; a live natural yoghurt with a consistency similar to Greek Yoghurt. Loseley also make sour cream and double cream, both of which are pure and delicious products.

Loseley make their own 100% wholemeal flour from wheat organically grown on their farm. The flour is stoneground, none of the bran is removed and nothing is added to increase the keeping quality. They also sell frozen wholemeal shortcrust pastry which is available in 350 g packs and is equally delicious for sweet and savoury dishes.

Lotus

Lotus make a good range of TVP (*see* List of Ingredients): Brown Mince, Brown Chiplets, Natural Chiplets and Chunks. These are non-flavoured.

To complement these, their *Stock Flavours* include *New Brown Stock Paste.* This product, free of chemical flavours, has a good shelf life. One teaspoonful dissolved in 275 ml/10 fl oz of water gives a basic stock for use with TVP in soups, stews drinks and any savoury dish in place of beef stock. The *White Stock* is a good alternative to chicken stock cubes or broth.

Lotus Brown Savoury Coater is also free of chemicals – made from natural ingredients, it is ideal for use with TVP Chunks or Slices and gives them a tasty flavoured coating if browned in a little hot oil before adding to stews or casseroles.

For those who like junket but who do not wish to

use animal rennet, *Lotus* make a liquid vegetarian rennet, not only for making junket, but also for making soft and hard cheeses.

Marriage's

Marriage's wholemeal flour is stoneground, 100% whole wheat. It is ground on old-fashioned horizontal millstones from a blend of predominantly high protein (gluten) wheats and is, therefore, a strong wholemeal suitable for breadmaking and yeast cookery. Nothing is added and nothing is extracted during the manufacturing process, thus all the natural vitamins, wheat germ and bran are retained. Besides containing more protein than white flour, *Marriage's Finest Wholemeal* is rich in Vitamin B1 and iron, the vital nerve and blood foods. Their *Country Fayre* is a strong brown wheatmeal flour which is high in fibre and has added cracked malted grains and malt flour for extra flavour. The ingredients of this flour give a moist loaf with good keeping qualities, and less liquid is needed to mix the dough than with other wholemeal and wheatmeal flours.

Martlet

Apple juice concentrate made by *Martlet* is a very useful product to have in the store cupboard. It can be used to sweeten stewed fruit and fruit pies, stirred into natural yoghurt or poured over pancakes instead of sugar syrups. It can be used to make still or fizzy drinks, and kids love it at party time diluted with sparkling mineral water.

Martlet also make a mild-flavoured cider vinegar which is brewed using the whole apple. Like all cider vinegars it contains good amounts of calcium, phosophorus and potassium.

Nature's Bounty

Nature's Bounty Bran 'N' Fig, a product of *Dietary Specialities Ltd,* contains wheat bran, dried figs and raw cane sugar. It supplies extra fibre when added to porridge, muesli or granola, and in bread, cake and biscuit making.

Nature's Burger

Nature's Burger mix from *Fantastic Foods* is a carefully balanced blend of vegetables, wholegrains, legumes, nuts and seeds which is high in protein and fibre. The mix is easy to form into burgers and can either be eaten as you would meat burgers or be cut or crumbled and used in soufflés, omelettes, chilli con carne or stroganoff.

Pantry Stock

Pantry Stock savoury rissole mix is made from soya protein and contains no animal-derived products, chemicals, artificial flavourings or colours. This company also manufactures an excellent gravy mix, again totally vegetarian and chemical-free.

Paul's Tofu

Many recipes in this book use *Paul's* firm tofu (*see* List of Ingredients). *Paul's* tofu is firm and cuts easily into slices or cubes. If you want to make your own tofu *Paul's* supply nigari, which is the coagulant added to soya milk to make the tofu, and the wooden presses in which the finished tofu is formed. Both nigari and the presses are available by mail order from *Paul's Tofu*, The Old Brewery, Wheathampstead House, Wheathampstead, St Albans, Herts. Tel: 058 283 4241.

Plamil

Plamil soya milk is an alternative to cow's milk which contains no ingredients of animal origin. The major constituents of *Plamil* are soya protein isolate, sunflower oil and raw sugar, and it contains all the essential amino-acids required for human nutrition. Soya protein tends to lower plasma cholesterol, whereas animal proteins, including the casein in cow's milk, tend to increase plasma cholesterol. This could be useful in the prevention of atherosclerosis, where raised plasma cholesterol may be a factor. Soya protein has a low allergenic potential compared with cow's milk protein.

Prewett's

Prewett's are well-known for their wide range of fine quality flours and breakfast cereals. As well as their delicately flavoured sunflower and safflower margarines, great for cooking and spreading, they also manufacture an extensive range of traditional cheese made with vegetable rennet. Their quick-to-prepare *Main Course Vegetarian Meals* are produced in 'bacon', 'beef', 'chicken', and 'sausage and 'herb' flavours. These are simple to cook, nutritionally balanced, high in protein and dietary fibre yet low in cholesterol. They can be made into burgers or added to other ingredients to make tasty meals.

Prewett's also manufacture a range of low sodium sauces and salad dressings which are full of flavour and free of preservatives and animal derivatives.

Protoveg

A brand name of *Direct Foods Ltd*, *Protoveg* is made from soya beans. It is a protein food that can be used as the centrepiece of a meal, just as meat is used. It is quick to make, taking less than half the time it would take to prepare a meat meal; it is also free from animal fats and cholesterol, yet has adequate fibre and is low in calories.

Protoveg is sold in 130 g/4½ oz cartons, sufficient to give about 550 g/19 oz when hydrated. There are also economy packs – bigger cartons holding three separate 130 g/4½ oz sachets. When hydrated, it not only looks like meat but it can be used to replace meat in countless recipes – rissoles, pies, fritters, curries, stews or goulash.

Protoveg can be hydrated prior to use or, in certain recipes, it can hydrate during cooking. The 'mince' form is quicker to hydrate than the 'chunks'. A cupful of *Protoveg* mince plus 1½ cupfuls of water hydrates when it is simmered for three minutes. With the *Protoveg* chunks 2 cupfuls of water are needed and hydration takes 20–30 minutes. A tablespoon of vegetable oil may be added to the water while hydrating to enhance the flavour.

All the flavours are natural; the manufacturers use different extracts of yeast, seed-oils, spices and herbs. Flavours available are 'beef-like', 'ham-like', 'pork-like' and 'natural' (which is unflavoured). The latter is quite bland and needs flavouring with herbs, yeast extract, cheese, etc. Herbs are best added to the water before hydrating so that they are completely absorbed.

Protoveg also make a range called *Menus* – ready-made meals in a packet. They are traditional recipes except that *Protoveg* replaces meat; they include Curry, Stew, Goulash, Bolognese and Minced Soya with Onion (excellent in Shepherd's Pie).

Protoveg Sosmix is a meatless sausage mix which takes only five minutes to prepare. Add the right amount of water, within five minutes you can shape it and then fry or grill . . . or you can shape it like a burger and have an egg on top for breakfast. *Burgamix* is a meatless burger mix and *Sissles* has all the advantages of Sosmix but with a smoky-bacon flavour.

Realeat Vegeburger

As the name *Realeat* suggests, the vegeburger was initially introduced by its creator, George Sams, as a healthier alternative to beefburgers. Made only with natural ingredients, the vegeburger contains more protein, half the fat, and fewer calories than its meat equivalent. But unlike meatburgers, the vegeburger does not shrink on cooking and contains as much fibre as cooked brown rice. Unlike most other alternatives it is not soya-based – the ingredients list shows a mixture of sesame seeds, oats, soya flour, wheat protein, vegetables and herbs which complement each other to form a complete protein mix.

Vegeburger mix makes a great burger on its own, but you can add your own touches too since it holds together incredibly well. For example, you can add as much as 100 g/4 oz (a heaped teacup) of cooked rice to your mix and it will still shape easily into beautiful burgers. Try adding freshly chopped parsley, chopped olives, diced onion, sautéed mushrooms, or whatever else you might fancy – the vegeburger can take it. You can also turn vegeburgers into cheeseburgers by popping them under the grill with a slice of cheese on the top after they are cooked. And don't worry if you haven't got burger buns or rolls available – your vegeburger will be just as delicious between two slices of wholewheat bread with the usual trimmings. Vegeburger mix can also be used as a stuffing. Following the basic principles of the superb stuffed pepper recipe given on the back of the packet, you can also stuff courgettes, tomatoes, cabbage leaves, and more. (Cabbage leaves should first be soaked in boiling water for 5 minutes to soften them, then rolled around the stuffing. Use either a toothpick or string to keep the leaf rolled during cooking.)

Record

Record manufacture a range of wholewheat pasta which has much more flavour and is nutritionally superior to pasta made with processed white flour.

Their new product is a pre-cooked lasagne. It comes in two varieties: *Wholewheat Lasagne* and *Lasagne Verdi*, made using wholewheat and spinach. These are well worth trying as they cut down the preparation time enormously.

Soup Break

Soup Break is a made-in-the-cup soup containing only 14 calories per serving. It is available in five flavours – beef, chicken, oxtail, tomato and beef, and minestrone.

Sunwheel

Sunwheel and its other brand-names, *Carrabay* and *Westbrae*, produce many different and healthy products, from a range of cold pressed oils and peanut butters to seaweeds and kuzu (*see* List of Ingredients). All are high quality products, many with an eastern flavour, such as miso, shoyu, and tamari (*see* List of Ingredients). Their peanut butter is available in a smooth or crunchy texture and they make a sunflower seed spread and sesame seed spread (tahini). All the spreads can be used in both sweet and savoury dishes and are absolutely delicious.

Vecon

This all-vegetable spread from *Modern Health Products* can be used to replace salt or stock cubes in recipes. It is a nutritious and natural product, high in protein, vitamins and iron, low in fat and calories. There is no added salt; the salt content is entirely natural, being derived from the purely vegetable ingredients. *Vecon* enhances soups, casseroles, gravies and savoury vegetable or meat pies, and savoury pastry. It can even be melted and used in breadmaking, and it's superb in savoury scones.

Western Isles (Harmony)

Western Isles (formerly *Harmony*) offer food products of great variety, from sea vegetables such as dulse (*see* List of Ingredients), grains (a new product is a quick brown rice, which takes much less time to cook than ordinary brown rice) to concentrated fruit juices with no added sugar. They also make an excellent mayonnaise with no additives, colouring or preservatives.

The range of fruit and vegetable concentrates are well worth experimenting with. Fruit flavours include apple, blackcurrant, cherry, exotic fruit, grape, orange, raspberry, strawberry, banana colada and pina colada. They are great on pancakes or in cakes to sweeten as an alternative to sugar. They make yummy ice lollies, milk shakes and jellies, and with fizzy water as a *pure* pop drink. I've also used them successfully in jam-making. The vegetable cocktail concentrate is made from eight vegetables: tomato, carrot, beetroot, celery, green pepper, onion, sauerkraut and cucumber – great in soups, sauces, drinks and aspics.

Whole Earth

Whole Earth share and appreciate our concern about the quality of the food we eat. Since 1966 they have been supplying foods that always conform to a high standard of ingredient quality. This means never using any preservatives, sugar or artificial ingredients, and the barest minimum of salt, if any. They believe that a diet based upon whole foods such as wholewheat bread, pasta, brown rice, vegetables and beans ensures that our nutritional needs are satisfied without overdependence on animal and dairy foods or excessive use of fats, sugar, salt and refined and artificial ingredients. All *Whole Earth* products support and complement such a natural diet. With every food they produce, flavour is the number one priority. Every ingredient used is checked to make absolutely sure that there are no hidden residues they do not want to see in the finished product.

Among their products are no-sugar, natural fruit jams containing no artificial sweeteners, colourings, flavourings or preservatives; Old Fashioned Peanut Butter—made in the traditional way of freshly roasted peanuts seasoned lightly with sea salt; Orange Crunch Cereal, which has a very low Orange Crunch Cereal, which has a very low sodium content compared to many breakfast cereals, and is naturally sweet from the whole grains and date, fig and apple juice used in its manufacture; and baked beans and brown rice – the latter combination of beans and cereal grain providing a range of amino-acids which complement each other in the diet. *Whole Earth* brown rice and vegetables is a complete and delicious meal just as it comes from the can. It can be stir-fried – simply heat a wok or frying pan with a little sesame oil or other vegetable oil, empty in the contents of the can and stir-fry for no more than one minute. To steam it, bring water in the base of a steamer to boiling, place the brown rice and vegetables in the steamer basket, cover and steam for 2–3 minutes. To microwave, place the contents of the can on a dish, place in the oven and cook at full power for 2 minutes. If you open both ends of the can, you can push the contents out without disturbing the tubular shape of the food. Then serve 'castles' with your favourite sauce.

Zwicky

Zwicky make *Soya Bean Flakes* from natural soya beans which can be used in rissoles, soups and crumbles as a highly nutritious protein booster. They also do quick-to-prepare millet flakes and *Millotto* which is a millet-based savoury mixture and can be made into delicious rissoles that cook in a few minutes.

List of Ingredients

This list not only includes ingredients used in the recipe section but also gives information about other items which I think are important foods to become familiar with. If you read through this glossary then health foods will no longer be a mystery but exciting products to experiment with. You will find most of these ingredients on the shelves of your local healthfood shops.

Agar-agar A setting agent which is 100% vegetable in origin. It is produced from strong-tasting red seaweeds, but ends up as neutral-tasting colourless flakes. The flakes are traditionally freeze-dried in snow. It is great for making aspics, jellies and many delicious desserts. The quantity to use varies, depending on how firm the finished product is to be, but a good guide is about 1 teaspoon of agar-agar to 285 ml/10 fl oz of liquid. It will not set in the presence of acetic or oxalic acid – such acids are found in wine and distilled vinegar, chocolate, spinach and tomatoes.

Alfalfa When sprouted the seeds of the alfalfa plant contain 40% protein, are rich in vitamins and minerals and have the same amount of carrotene as carrots. The tiny shoots are thin and curl around each other in a light bundle. They are excellent for sandwiches and delicious in salads. The flour from the seeds is regarded in America as a vitally important food supplement because of it's high nutritional value. Unfortunately, the flour is not easily available in this country.

Arame A sea vegetable or seaweed which is rich in vitamins, including B_{12}, minerals and trace elements. It has a mild, sweet, nutty flavour. To prepare, soak the dried twine-like weed in cold water for 15 minutes. Steam or sauté and add it to stir-fry vegetables, soups, salads or risotto.

Arrowroot Is the starch obtained from the root of the West Indian arrow plant. Although it is refined it is less devitalised than cornflour and a better alternative.

Bancha Tea Or Three-Year Tea, is cultivated in the mountains of Japan. The twigs and the leaves are roasted several times. It is low in acids and virtually caffeine-free. It is reputed to have a neutralizing effect on both alkaline and acid conditions.

Barley Most commonly used in this country is pearl barley, but it is best to buy pot barley which is the whole grain and contains the bran (fibre) and the germ. Pearl barley is polished and lacks most of the valuable nutrients. Barley is easily digested and therefore good for babies and those with digestive disorders. It contains 12% protein and, in its whole state, a good supplier of vitamins and minerals. Malt extract is derived from barley and is a delicious and nutritious sweetener in bread, cake and biscuit making. Barley flour is great combined with wholewheat flour in bread making. It adds a slightly sweet, malty taste to the finished loaf. Roasted barley is also used in combination with rye and chicory to make an instant coffee substitute called Barley Cup.

Beans (See **pulses**).

Bran Or fibre, is the structural part of plants. Although it has no nutritional value it plays a vital part in the elimination of waste matter from the body. It absorbs water, becomes sponge-like and grips onto the walls of the colon. The colon muscles can then work efficiently to expel the faeces from the the body. A lack of fibre in the diet causes constipation. If prolonged this condition leads to ruptures in the wall of the gut. The lining of the colon swells through these holes and causes little pouches (*diverticulae*) which often become inflamed and extremely painful. This disease which is called *diverticulitis*, can lead to abscesses and make elimination impossible and surgery inevitable. There is a strong connection between a low-fibre diet and cancer of the colon. Findings also suggest that if we consume just over 25 g (1 oz), which is almost an average teacupful, of dietry fibre daily we lessen the risk of coronary heart disease. Tests have also shown that fibre can alter bacteria in the bowel making it less prone to disease. But research has also revealed that too much bran can be harmful. Dietry fibre contains phytic acid which inhibits the absorption of iron, calcium and zinc in the body. Cooking and other heat processes apparently lessen the level of this acid, but as with most nutrients there is an optimum intake, which, if exceeded, causes vital foods to become harmful. Foods which contain dietry fibre are whole grains, dried peas and beans, nuts and seeds and fresh fruit and vegetables. There is no fibre in meat or dairy produce so it is advisable to accompany these foods with those rich in fibre.

Buckwheat
This is not botanically a grain, but it is used as one. It has a very distinctive flavour and is rich in the B vitamins and iron. It contains rutic acid, which is known to have a good effect on the circulatory system. It is best to buy ready-toasted buckwheat which takes only 15 minutes to cook. You can also buy buckwheat spaghetti which is very light in texture and has a rich, nutty flavour.

Buckwheat Flour
This flour makes delicious pancakes and is great when included in bread and biscuit making. You can also use one level tablespoon as a binding agent in rissoles and nut or bean roast instead of an egg.

Bulgur
A whole wheat product, highly nutritious and simple to prepare. It is also full of flavour – the structure of the seed is such that the wheat germ and bran (fibre) are retained even when the grain is steel-milled. It is usually sold par-boiled, which greatly cuts down preparation time. It is widely used in Middle Eastern countries and is the basis of a delicious salad called Tabbouleh (see page 32).

Carob
Available in blocks or as powder, this is a product prepared from the Mediterranean carob or locust tree (known as locust beans). It is similar in flavour to chocolate, but a much cheaper and healthier alternative. It is, unlike cocoa, caffeine-free and naturally sweet. Another reason for using this product is that cocoa beans contain oxalic acid which 'locks-in' calcium in the diet and makes it unavailable to the body. Carob is also higher in fibre and iron, and lower in crude fat and sodium, than cocoa. It makes a delicious bedtime drink and can be used in any recipe where cocoa is an ingredient. Carob beans are made in a variety of flavours and can be melted as you would chocolate bars when making sweet sauces or for use in baking.

Carrageen
Also known as Irish moss, it is a celebrated folk remedy for colds, bronchitis and whooping cough. It is a sea vegetable (seaweed) and is used in the preparation of delicious jellies, blancmanges, aspics and puddings and to thicken stews, jams and marmalades.

Cider Vinegar
Is rich in potassium and calcium and reputed to help maintain the balance between the acids and alkalis of the body, necessary in maintaining full health. Dr Jarvis of Vermont, USA, in his book *Folk Medicine* describes in

detail his treatment for those suffering from arthritis, obesity, skin complaints and stomach upsets. He advises a dose of approximately one tablespoon in one cup of water to be taken first thing on an empty stomach and then again at meal times. He also recommends a gargle made up of one teaspoon to one cup of water. Used regularly throughout the day this will help to cure a sore throat within 24 hours. It can be used in the same way as other vinegars, in salad dressings, chutneys, and sweet and sour sauces for example.

Cornmeal Also known as maize meal or polenta, cornmeal is gluten-free and rich in vitamins and minerals. It is important to obtain stoneground whole cornmeal which contains the bran (fibre) and the germ. Cornflour is processed from cornmeal and is lacking in the valuable nutrients (see **arrowroot**). Cornflour makes delicious tea bread and is great in savoury dishes such as Italian polenta. (See page 53 for the recipe.)

Couscous Is produced from semolina which is a variety of wheat. It is similar in texture to bulgur but unlike bulgur it is processed and does not contain all the bran (fibre) and germ. You can use bulgur to make the popular Middle-Eastern dish Couscous named after the grain (see page 63 for the recipe).

Cracked Wheat Or kibbled wheat, is simple wholewheat split under pressure, but still retaining the nutritional value of wholewheat.

Dandelion Root The roasted root is used to make a very tasty coffee substitute. Symmingtons do one which is delicious.

Dillisk Also known as **dulse**, this is a mineral-rich seaweed.

Dulse Dulse is perhaps the richest organic source of iron. It also contains calcium, iodine, potassium and magnesium in abundance. It contains 25% protein and valuable amounts of vitamins A, B complex, C and E. In the past, it has been used as a tonic to help strengthen the blood, adrenals, kidneys and muscles. It is also useful in the prevention of scurvy and in the treatment of herpes.

Eggs (Free-Range) These eggs are the product of healthy hens fed on natural foods and given adequate space to scratch about and exercise in the open air. Research has revealed that battery eggs often contain residues of antibiotics, hormones and other drugs, regularly fed to battery hens, and that these residues can have an adverse effect on humans. There is controversy as to whether eggs, because of their cholesterol content, together with other cholesterol foods such as butter, cheese and animal fats, contribute to heart attacks. Eggs contain lecithin which breaks fats up into tiny globules that disperse easily. This process helps the body to utilize cholesterol normally. The amount of lecithin in eggs is considered enough to protect against high levels of cholesterol in the body. Eating raw eggs is not advisable because the albumen protein of the raw white can pass into the blood stream undigested and causes allergies in some people.

Five spice powder A mixture of star anise, fennel, cinnamon, cloves and pepper which gives an authentic eastern taste to oriental recipes. It can be bought from Chinese grocers or healthfood shops.

Fromage Blanc This low fat soft cheese is becoming very popular and is often suggested in recipes as a substitute for cream. Traditionally it was made with either single cream of full-fat milk. It is a very simple cheese to make if you have difficulty in obtaining it. This recipe is similar to the commercially sold fromage blanc which uses skimmed milk.
Heat 1 litre (1¾ pints) of skimmed milk, either cows' or goats' to 110°F/ 50°C. Remove from heat and stir in 4–5 drops of vegetable rennet, allow to stand for about 24 hours at an average room temperature of 30°C/ 60°F. Line a colander with

cheesecloth, place over a deep bowl and pour in the set milk and rennet mixture (it will look like junket). Suspend and let drip for about 1 hour. Roll the soft curds into a container and chill for 30 minutes. This is delicious mixed with a little fruit sugar or honey and served with fresh fruit or added to savoury white sauces, with onion, parsley and other herbs. The curds will keep for 2 to 3 days in the fridge.

Fruit Sugar (See **List of Companies** for notes on Dietade.)

Gluten This is the protein left after the starch has been removed from wheat flour. It is mainly used in Japan and China. It is not a complete protein (see TVP) for information on complete protein), but as this food is not usually eaten alone it makes a complete protein when combined with other complementary protein rich ingredients such as beans, nuts and seeds and dairy produce. Granose (see **List of Companies**) do gluten-based Savoury Cuts, used in many delicious dishes. For information on how gluten helps bread to rise see the introduction to the Breads and Yeasted Doughs section.

Wheat products should not be given to a baby of under six months. A child of this age is more likely to developed a gluten allergy. For more detailed information on gluten-free diets write to G.F. Dietary Supplies Limited, Lowther Road, Stanmore, Middlesex.

Goats' Milk Goats' milk and cheeses are available in most health or wholefood shops under different brand-names often supplied by local farmers. Much publicity has been given to the nutritional value and curative powers of goats' milk. Scientific research shows that certain allergy-producing proteins present in cows' milk are not present in goats' mik. Goat's milk has smaller fat globules than cow's milk, making it more digestible, especially for babies. Goats are highly unlikely to contract tuberculosis, brucellosis or meleteuses. Cows not only do so but transmit the disease to humans. For this reason cow's milk has to be pasteurized, destroying valuable nutrients and enzymes. It is now advocated that goat's milk is preferable for weaning babies. Many babies weaned on cow's milk develop allergies to it. Research has also revealed that in many cases of eczema, asthma, migraine, stomach disorders and hay-fever, the symptoms have either been alleviated or the patient cured by using goats' instead of cows' milk products.

Gomasio Unfortunately, this product is no longer available, having too short a shelf-life. However, it is very simple to make. To 20 parts sesame seeds you will need one part sea salt. Toast the sesame seeds in a dry heavy based saucepan on moderate heat stirring constantly until a deep golden brown and popping. Grind in a liquidizer with the sea salt until powdery in texture. It is delicious sprinkled on your boiled egg or on rice and vegetable dishes. Other recipes for gomasio suggest adding more salt but the quantities given here give a sufficiently savoury taste. Put on the table instead of neat salt for those who cannot resist the salt cellar.

Grains Or cereals, abound on the shelves of our healthfood shops. In their whole state they contain, with the exception of triticale and oats, approximately 9% to 14% protein, and are not only high fibre foods but rich in minerals and vitamins. (Triticale contains approximately 19% protein, oats 17%.) All wholegrain ground cereals have a shorter shelf life than processed grains because they still contain the valuable germ oil. It is advisable to use all untreated flours within two months. Store in a cool place away from light in airtight containers. Whole berries or grains will keep for up to one year if stored in the same way. Millet, which has a

Gram flour
longer shelf life, will keep up to two years in these conditions (see **millet**).
(Chick pea flour.) A high-protein flour made from ground chick peas which is used extensively in Indian and Middle Eastern cuisine. Tempara or Pakora (see page 80) are batters made using this delicious product. It can be used to thicken sauces and soups, added to gravies and made into batter.

Herb salt
A mixture of sea salt and ground herbs; a good alternative to using neat salt. Wonderful in soups, stocks, salad dressings and on a boiled or poached egg. Vegetable bouillon powder and vegetable stock cubes are very similar. Look at the labels and watch for the sodium (salt) content.

Hiziki
A sea vegetable (seaweed) similar to arame but slightly stronger in flavour. This is one of my favourite sea vegetables and can be used in the same way as arame.

Honey
Contains fructose and because of this is considered better than sugar (sucrose), being more easily assimilated by the body. Tests have shown that honey is easier for the kidneys to process than any other sugars. It is rich in vitamin C and the B vitamins as well as being well supplied with minerals. It also contains several enzymes and is a natural antiseptic and antibiotic. Honey can replace sugar in most recipes but only use three quarters the amount of honey. But all sugar concentrates should be used in moderation whether fructose or sucrose as all, unfortunately, contribute to tooth decay and other sugar-related diseases if eaten in excess.

Kibbled Wheat
(see **cracked wheat**).

Kombu
A sea vegetable, rich in vitamins and minerals kombu also contains natural sodium (salt) glutamate (a flavour enhancer which is not, unlike monosodium glutamate, concentrated). It is used in Japan as the basis of dashi (basic stock) and soups. Kombu is also used as a softening agent when cooking beans.

Kuzu
A pure white starch water-extracted from the root of the kuzu mountain vine. Traditionally prized in the East for its strengthening and alkalizing properties in digestion, it is used to thicken soups and sauces and is a good alternative to cornflour, which is the starch from cornmeal and virtually devoid of nutrients.

Lebnie
Lebnie is a live natural concentrated yoghurt which has the whey removed by centrifugal force. Its consistency is similar to Greek yoghurt. It is virtually fat-free and an extremely versatile food. You can use it in cheesecakes, quiches, cake fillings and ice cream with delicious results.

Malt Extract
(See **barley**).

Margarine
Unfortunately, most margarines, even some of those labelled 'high in polyunsaturates' are not a lot healthier than butter. Most margarines are hydrogenated, chemically hardened, which is the process used to create a texture for spreading. This process of hydrogenation changes polyunsaturated fat into a saturated fat. Fats chemically altered in this way can make essential fatty acids (see **oils**) unavailable to the body. In defence of margarine I should add that at least it has none of the antibiotic residues often found in the milk used to make butter. At the time of writing there is only one margarine on the market which does not go through the process of hydrogenation and that is Vitaquell.

Millet
A cereal widely used in Africa, India and Asia. The Hunzas who live in the foothills of the Himalayas and who are famous for their good health and longevity count on this grain as an essential ingredient in their diet. It is well balanced in essential amino-acids, rich in iron, and its protein utilization is greatly increased when combined with vegetables. It is gluten-free and can be used in breads and cakes for those on a

gluten-free diet. It also has a longer shelf life than other grains and will keep for up to two years in an airtight container.

Miso
A soyabean paste produced by lactic fermentation. The process, during which a culture is added to cooked soya beans and usually cooked barley or rice, is lengthy. Salt is gradually added until the mixture achieves a paste-like consistency. It is a high complete protein food (see **soya beans/TVP**), is cholesterol free and an aid to digestion. It is also claimed to help develop a resistance to disease and the most incredible and yet substantiated claim of all is that it can remove radioactive substances from the body. There are various types of miso. Mugi miso, the lighter variety and less strong in taste, consists of fermented soya beans and barley or rice. Hatcho miso is produced from soya beans only and is stronger in flavour and has a higher protein content. Miso must not be cooked or you will destroy the culture. To add to soups or stews you simply blend it with a little of the hot stock liquid then stir in at the end of cooking time and heat through. You will need no salt, stock cubes or powder when using miso.

Molasses
Or Black Strap Molasses, is the residue left after the sugar cane has been processed to produce white sugar. Although it contains several more times the iron content of liver, more calcium than milk and is well supplied with the B vitamins, it still contributes to tooth decay and other sugar-related diseases so use in moderation.

Muesli
A mixture of rolled wholegrains, to which are added dried fruits, nuts and seeds. It is usually served as a breakfast cereal with either milk or yoghurt. The rolled grains can be oats, rye, barley, wheat and millet. This is a very nutritious high fibre mixture and does not require extra bran (see **bran**).

Mu-Tea
Is an exotic blend of herbs and spices and is naturally sweet. It is reputed to be strengthening and invigorating. Mu is Japanese for 'unique'. It's delicious and a far better alternative to ordinary tea which contains caffein and tannin, both detrimental to health.

Nigari
A coagulant used in the process of making tofu, which is also known as bean curd or soya cheese, (see **tofu**). Nigari is the residue left after the salt (sodium chloride) and water are removed from sea water. This mineral-rich residue is sun dried and bought as crystals (either golden brown or white). Some health food shops stock nigari but if you have any difficulty then write to Paul's Tofu (see page 226 for the address).

Nori
A sea vegetable which, gram for gram, contains more vitamin A than carrots, more protein than cheese, meat or soya beans and more calcium than milk. As if that were not enough, it is also rich in trace minerals essential to good health, and it helps to emulsify fats and otherwise aid digestion. It comes in paper thin sheets which can be used in a variety of ways, from wrapping sushi (the Japanese equivalent to our sandwich) and rice balls to garnishing grain and vegetable dishes. To use as a garnish toast in the oven on moderate heat until crisp (do not grill as it burns easily) then crumble and sprinkle on the finished dish just before serving.

Nuts
Are a high protein food, rich in the B vitamins and although they have quite a high fat content they are rich in linoleic acid which helps control the level of cholesterol in the blood. (See **oils** for more information). Used in combination with wholegrains, dried legumes or dairy produce nuts can provide a complete protein food. (See **TVP** for notes on complete protein). Avoid salted nuts as these are usually treated with preservatives, colouring and other inhibitors and are often roasted in saturated fats. Healthfood shops have a large variety of shelled nuts to

Oats
choose from, usually of a high quality and fresh taste. You will find many delicious recipes which include nuts throughout the book.

A highly nutritious high fibre grain containing 17% protein. They are rich in minerals, especially iron, and have more B vitamins than any other cereal. Tests have shown that regular consumption of oats helps lower blood sugar levels. Avoid quick-cooking oats or instant porridge as these have usually been pre-heated to a high degree, killing off most of the nutrients. Jumbo oats, larger than porridge oats, take longer to cook and are nutritionally superior. Oatmeal comes in three grades: fine, medium and coarse (pin head). Fine oatmeal is good in breadmaking using the ratio approximately 75 g (3 oz) to the 450 g (1 lb). Medium oatmeal makes lovely crunchy biscuits either savoury or sweet and coarse (pin head) is delicious soaked overnight and made into a porridge for breakfast. I make it with skimmed milk, with added 2 tbsp sesame seeds and 1 tbsp malt extract. It is very tasty and satisfying on those cold winter mornings.

Oils
The difference between saturated, unsaturated and polyunsaturated fats are as follows:

Saturated fatty acids are mostly found in animals fats. Unsaturated fatty acids are found in both animal and vegetable fats. They include mono-unsaturated acids (mono means one) and all the polyunsaturates, (poly means many). Findings have shown that if we eat large amounts of saturated fats we will produce too high a level of cholesterol in the blood and thus become more vulnerable to heart attacks, thrombosis and gallstones. On the other hand unsaturated fats, high in linoleic acid, tend to lower the level of cholesterol. But it is important to note that vitamins B and E are also needed to maintain a low level of cholesterol. Polyunsaturated fatty acids are abundant in liquid vegetable oils. One of the most important acids is linoleic. Safflower seed oil is highest in this acid, sunflower second and corn oil third. Another important ingredient is lecithin, a substance manufactured by the body and naturally occuring in some foods. Like linoleic acid, research has shown that lecithin also helps lower the level of cholesterol. The oil from the soya bean, wheatgerm, walnut together with sesame and other vegetable oils, contain a good supply of lecithin. Olive oil contains mono-unsaturated fatty acids and although it is low in linoleic acid it has been found to increase the absorption of vitamins A, D, E and K and is easily digestible. (Mono-unsaturated fatty acids do not seem to contribute to heart disease.) What is of vital importance to the quality and nutritional value of these oils is the method used to extract it from the seeds. The most widely consumed oils are refined which means that they are often detergent-extracted, in other words subjected to high temperatures to extract oil quickly and cheaply. This process destroys most of the nutrients. In many cases chemicals are then added. Other methods of refining are less intense and do not destroy all the vitamins and minerals.

Cold pressed oil is whole and complete. This method of extraction is mechanical; the oil is simply pressed slowly from the seed. It retains all its nutrients and has a delicate flavour and fresh smell. These oils are best for salads and stiry-frying vegetables. Sesame oil does not turn rancid which is why it is most popular in tropical countries. It contains an ingredient called Sesamol which analysis has shown is the natural stabilizing ingredient and prevents the oil from going off.

Okara
This is the soya bean pulp left after the liquid (milk) has been filtered off in making soya milk or tofu. It is a high fibre food with approximately 3–5% protein. It is delicious toasted

and sprinkled on muesli, fruit crumbles or mixed with beans, nuts and seeds in making burgers as an alternative to breadcrumbs.

Postum Is the original instant coffee substitute with a delicious aroma and full flavour. This is achieved by mixing molasses and bran which are then roasted to a high temperature. Red wheat is then added and all the ingredients very finely ground.

Pulses These are dried beans, peas and lentils. Throughout the book you will find many recipes using these cheap and versatile high protein foods. Their protein content ranges from 17% to 25% with the exception of the soya bean which has approximately 38% protein. Pulses are a good source of vitamins and minerals, namely iron, calcium and vitamin B_1 thiamine and niacin. Vitamin C is present only when the beans are sprouted. Only the soya bean contains all the essential amino acids which the body requires to build protein. Meat, fish and dairy produce also contain these essential acids and are, like the soya bean, what is termed 'complete protein', (see **TVP** for information on complete protein). Through research it has been found that pulses used in combination with foods which contain the missing proteins will produce a complete protein with all the amino acids in balance. The complementary foods are wholegrains, nuts, seeds and dairy produce. One very important point, especially for those on a vegan diet, where neither meat or dairy produce is eaten, is that Vitamin B_{12}, essential for the functioning of all body cells, is only rarely found in the plant world. Sources of B_{12} include meat and all dairy produce, eggs, sprouted soya beans and other sprouted seeds, tempeh (a fermented soya bean food), seaweed and comfrey (if it is grown on soil rich in this vitamin). A deficiency of B_{12} can cause anaemia and severe damage to the central nervous system, both

of which can be fatal. The proper soaking and cooking of pulses is essential as they contain adverse substances in their raw state which are harmful to the digestion. The recipes in the book using pulses will give you the correct cooking method which destroys these harmful inhibitors (See **soya bean** for more information).

Quark This cheese is similar to paveer (Indian fresh lemon cheese) and is more widely available than fromage blanc. If this is not available in your health food shop you can make it yourself. Bring 1 litre/2 pints of skimmed cow's or goat's milk to the boil. Remove the pan from the heat and stir in 4 tablespoons of fresh lemon juice. Leave to stand for 10 minutes, then bring the mixture to the boil again and take immediately off the heat. Line a large colander with muslin or cheesecloth and place this over a deep bowl. Pour in the curdled milk mixture and let most of the whey run through the muslin. Tie the top and let the whey drip out for about 1½ hours. Don't try to hasten the process as the flavour develops during the dripping. Scrape off the curds and chill before use.

Rennet (Vegetable) This is produced using a non-animal enzyme. Ordinary rennet is an enzyme which comes from the stomach lining of a suckling animal. Both types of rennet act as coagulants in cheese making. You can now buy a wide range of traditional cheeses made using vegetable rennet, in healthfood shops.

Rice Brown rice contains all the fibre (bran) and germ of the whole grain. Only the outer tough and indigestible husks are removed. It is a good source of protein, minerals and vitamins, particularly B vitamins. There are several varieties of brown rice to choose from. Surinam and Australian long grain rice are thin varieties, and take 25 minutes to cook. I use these to accompany curries. Italian short and long grain are chewy and take 35 minutes to cook. I like the short grain in sweet rice puddings and for making savoury and sweet rice balls. The long grain Italian is perfect for risottos and stuffing vegetables. White rice has the outer layers (bran) and germ removed by a process which takes away a large proportion of the protein, the B vitamins and most of the minerals.

Converted rice is rarely sold in this country but is mentioned in American cookbooks. The whole grain goes through a process whereby it is treated with steam under immense pressure. This forces the nutrients from the outer layers into the centre of the grain. The rice is then milled in the same way as white rice but does not lose too many of its valuable nutrients. It cooks more quickly and has a lighter texture than other sorts of rice.

Wild rice is very expensive and not widely available. It is not botanically related to other rice grains as it belongs to a different species. Its protein content is much higher than ordinary rice and it has several times more B vitamin. Wild rice takes about 30 to 35 minutes to cook and is absolutely delicious.

Brown Rice Flour can be used for making puddings, in bread and biscuit making, as a thickening in soups or in batter mixtures.

Rooibosch Or Red Bush Tea, is the tea which, I think, has the flavour nearest to ordinary tea. It tastes a bit like Earl Grey, is caffein-free and very low in tannin. The plant, which grows in South Africa, is acclaimed for its curative powers, is rich in vitamin C and has a high mineral content. A very good tea to start with if herb teas are new to you.

Rye Flour Has a distinctive flavour. It is lower in gluten than wheat flour and, on its own, does not rise well enough to make a light loaf. It is best mixed with strong wholewheat flour. There are two types of rye flour; dark and light. The darker variety has a higher fibre content and contains the valuable germ, so try to obtain this for your bread making.

Salt It is now accepted that a high sodium (salt) intake is damaging to our health. It can cause fluid retention which in turn can result in high blood pressure and excessive weight gain. Although sodium is a vital element in regulating fluid balance in the body, an excessive intake over a prolonged period forces the body to dilute the concentration by increasing the water in the blood stream. This not only increases the volume of blood in the blood vessels but the amount of water flowing into the body tissues. Salt is 40% sodium. We need less than 1 g daily (about ½ level tsp) but statistics show that we often consume ten times that amount. Sea salt has a slightly lower sodium content than ordinary land salt but the level if still pretty high. Not only do we add salt when cooking but most canned and packeted foods either contain nearly 1 g of sodium. There are several salt substitutes on the market which are very low in sodium and will help cut down sodium intake drastically if regularly used instead of ordinary salt.

Seeds These are higher in linoleic acid than nuts (see **oils** for information on linoleic acid) and are jam packed with vitamins and minerals. Pumpkin seeds contain approximately 20% protein. Tests have shown that these seeds seem to be a powerful healing aid in bladder disorders. Sesame seeds contain approximately 20% protein, are higher in linoleic acid and lecithin (see **oils** for more information on lecithin) and very rich in minerals, especially calcium. Sunflower seeds are not just for those little caged pets, they contain 25% protein, are rich in the B and E vitamins and their linoleic content is 47%.

Shoyu Naturally fermented soy sauce. This is made from soya beans brewed over a period of 18 months with roasted wheat and sea salt. The fermentation process produces a source of vitamin B_{12}, the one vitamin rare in the plant world. When added to foods such as whole grains, pulses, nuts and seeds, it increases the amount of protein that can be digested. Like miso, it should be added towards the end of cooking time, so that its properties are not destroyed. (See also **tamari**.) You will find brands of 'soy sauce' on the market which are synthetically compounded with additives. These are best avoided as they are vastly inferior to the natural product.

Soya Beans Are approximately 40% protein, equal to that of top quality beef steak but unlike meat they contain unsaturated fats (see **oils**) and are the cheapest source of 'complete protein' available today. (For more information on complete proteins and further information on soya beans see **TVP**.) However it is very important to note that proper soaking and cooking of the soya bean, indeed all pulses, is vital because they all contain adverse substances such as glycosides, saposides and alkaloids which are harmful to the digestion. This particularly applies to the soya bean, which contains a trypsin inhibitor that prevents the body assimilating the important amino acid methionine. Proper soaking and cooking renders these substances harmless. Soak the soya beans for at least 12 hours before cooking, changing the water 3 times. Bring the beans to the boil and let them boil for 10 minutes. Turn down to simmer and cook for approximately 3 hours or until soft. Pressure cook for 30 minutes but make sure you still soak in the way directed.

Soya grits It is a versatile version of the protein-rich soya bean, is quick to cook (3–5 minutes), and can be made into meat replacement dishes at a cost well below the price of the cheapest cuts of meat. Serve soya grits in savoury dishes, omelettes, sweets, cakes, as a replacement for nuts in biscuits, or as a topping on casseroles and puddings.

Soya Flour This flour is even higher in nutritional value than the beans and is approximately 50% protein. There are several varieties on the market, varying in degrees of fat content: full fat contains 20% fat, medium fat flour approximately 7% fat and no fat soya flour is also available. There is a cooked, highly nutritious, soya flour, which can be added to a health drink or used in cooking in the same way as uncooked soya flour. I add soya flour when making bread in the ratio of 55 g (2 oz) to 455 g (1 lb) of wholemeal flour for an extra protein boost. It is great for thickening soups and casseroles. It also blends well in white sauces using half and half soya flour and unbleached white flour.

Soya Milk Low in calories, low in saturated fats, soya milk is cholesterol and sodium (salt) free. It contains more iron and slightly more protein than cows' milk, with the same amount of the B vitamins. It is also easy to digest and has an alkaline reaction in the body. For those who have a lactose intolerance or allergy to cows' milk it is an invaluable alternative. There are medically approved infant soya milk formulae on the market if mother's milk is not available, which will give your child a healthy start. Making your own soya milk works out very cheap and is simple to produce. 450 g (1 lb) soya beans yields approx. 7 pints of soya milk, (see my book *Making Your Own Home Proteins*).

Tahini A sesame seed paste made from ground sesame seeds (see **seeds** for nutritional value). This spread is frequently used in Greek and Middle Eastern cooking. The lighter Tahini is produced from polished seeds where the outer layer has been removed. This skinning process can mean a loss in valuable nutrients near the surface.

Tamari (See **shoyu**.) Unlike shoyu, tamari is wheat-free; naturally brewed in the

Tamarind The bean pod-like fruit of the tamarind tree is very sharp-tasting, like citrus. Just soak the dried fruit in warm water for 1 hour and press the mixture through a sieve. You will have a thickish tangy liquid for adding to curries.

Tempeh This is a delicately flavoured complete protein food. (See **TVP**) for information on complete protein). It is made from partially-cooked and split soya beans mixed with a culture (similar to that used in yoghurt and cheesemaking) which ferments slowly over 24 to 30 hours. When fermented the beans are more digestible and contain more B vitamins with the addition of B_{12}. Tempeh is also low in fat, has no cholesterol and is very rich in iron. It has a chicken-like flavour and a smell similar to fresh-picked mushrooms and can be used in many savoury dishes instead of meat. (See my book *Making Your Own Home Proteins* on how to make and use tempeh.) The culture is only obtainable at present by mail order from: Micro-Audit Ltd, Wheathampstead House, St Albans, Herts AL4 8QY. Full instructions are given with the culture. In the near future tempeh will be available for you to use straight from the packet.

Tofu Or bean curd (soya cheese), is a complete protein (see **TVP**), rich in minerals and with a good supply of B and E vitamins. It is also cholesterol-free with a quarter the calories to be found in an equivalent portion of meat. Most protein foods have an acid reaction in the body whereas tofu has an alkaline effect. It is made from the soaked soya beans. These are then ground up with water, cooked, and then strained through a double thickness of cheesecloth. (The pulp left is okara.) At this stage you have soya milk. The milk is mixed with a coagulant (see **nigari**), which curdles it, the whey is drained off, and the solids set into what looks like a smooth wobbly cheese. These curds are pressed with a heavy weight until the desired texture is achieved. The longer you press the firmer the tofu becomes. Paul's Tofu company (see page 226), supply a simple tofu-making kit which is well worth buying if you want to experiment with this marvellous food.)

From just 340 g (12 oz) of soya beans you can make 50 g (just over 1 lb) of firm, sliceable tofu (see my book *Making Your Own Home Proteins* for step-by-step instructions on how to make perfect tofu).

Silken tofu is made in the same way as firm tofu but a thicker milk is used and the curds are not separated from the whey. This is good for salad dressings and light desserts.

Smoked Tofu is now available and it is absolutely delicious and worth experimenting with in dips, mousses and pâtés.

Triticale Is 'man made' as it is produced by crossing wheat (*Triticum*) with rye (*Secale*), hence its name. It is nutritionally superior to wheat as it contains 19% protein, is richer in minerals such as iron and phosphorous and has more of the essential amino acids. It is not very easily available but well worth asking for. It is delicious sprouted.

TVP TVP (Texturized Vegetable Protein) is a much maligned and misused modern miracle food. It is produced from the soya bean which is the vegetable protein equivalent to meat. The bean contains approximately 40 per cent complete protein which is equal to the protein content of top quality steak. A complete protein food is one that contains all the amino-acids which the body needs to build protein. There are approximately twenty known amino-acids making up human protein. The body produces fourteen and the other eight, which are known as essential amino-acids, must be obtained from the diet. Meat, fish, dairy produce and the soya bean have these essential acids in the necessary proportions. However, unlike meat and dairy produce, the soya bean contains unsaturated fats and is very high in lecithin, which is known to reduce the level of cholesterol in the blood, thus lessening the possibility of heart attacks. As it is also the most alkaline of foods it helps correct acidity in the system. One harvest of this worthy bean grown on one acre of land will provide enough protein for one person for approximately six years, but that very same harvest fed to animals will only yield enough protein for one human being for approximately eighty days, which makes it the cheapest source of minerals and complete protein on the market today. Just 150 g/5 oz TVP (a complete protein food) when reconstituted is equal in protein to that contained in approximately 450 g/1 lb of lean beef steak.

Umboshi Plums These salt pickled plums are one of the most special of Japanese foods. Highly prized for their health-giving properties, they are rich in enzymes and lactic acid and are considered to be a beneficial for the digestion.

Wakame Wakame is a long, feather-like dark green sea vegetable. It has thirteen times more calcium than milk, which makes it a mineral that is particularly important for growing children and pregnant women. It contains an abundance of trace minerals, notably iodine, and is one of the rare vegetable sources of vitamin B_{12}, often lacking in vegetarian diets. It has a mild flavour and thus, like arame and nori, is recommended for those who are not yet familiar with the distinctive taste of sea vegetables. The alginic acid in wakame helps to precipitate dangerous heavy metals. This action is much enhanced when wakame is used with fermented foods like miso or shoyu.

Wheatgerm (See Kretschmers in the **List of Companies**.)

Yoghurt Yoghurt must be live to be useful to our bodies. To be live means that beneficial bacteria, *lactobacillius bulguricus* and *streptucocus thermophilus*, two complementary cultures, are present and living. If stabilizers and sweeteners are listed on the label then the yoghurt is not live. Scientific research has shown that the bacteria in live yoghurt kills harmful bacterial in the large intestine, by turning milk sugar (lactose) into lactic acid and harmful bacterial cannot live in lactic acid. The bacteria in yoghurt can also manufacture B vitamins in the intestine. Those who are taking antibiotics, which are known to cause vitamin deficiency, would be well advised to eat yoghurt regularly. You can make yoghurt easily either using a dried starter culture (see **yoghurt culture**) or a small amount of natural live yoghurt. Cow's, goat's, sheep's or soya milk all make delicious yoghurt. Those very tasty greek yoghurts, one is made with cow's or sheep's milk contain the live cultures mentioned above, but the thick creamy consistency is achieved by draining off most of the whey from ordinary live yoghurt. I call this yoghurt cheese which I use as an alternative to double cream mixed with an optional touch of honey or fruit sugar.

Yoghurt Culture This is simply a mixture of dried live cultures, *lactobacillius bulgaricus* and *streptococus thermophilus*, both of which are needed to make natural live yoghurt.

INDEX